6134

10896

# THE BIRTH OF THE GOSPEL

*Der Vorchristliche Jesus*
*Ecce Deus*
*Mors Mortis*
*Etc.*

# The Birth
# of the Gospel

A STUDY OF THE ORIGIN AND PURPORT

OF THE

PRIMITIVE ALLEGORY OF THE JESUS

By William Benjamin Smith

**EDITED BY**
Addison Gulick

PHILOSOPHICAL LIBRARY, INC.
NEW YORK

# Table of Contents

CONTENTS OF APPENDIX

# Preface

## Presenting William Benjamin Smith.

It is somewhat out of the usual for a new book to come to print from the pen of a person born a century ago, who had an unspectacular academic career, terminating a number of decades in the past. When a scholar's work so persistently holds its value, an editor owes at least a brief answer to the questions who this man was, and where he lived.

William Benjamin Smith was born Oct. 26, 1850 in Stanford, Kentucky, but his family brought him four years later west to Missouri, and his chief childhood memories centered around a farm just outside of St. Joseph, on the far border of that state. In Kentucky his father had been a lawyer. In the new home he was a farmer with literary interests.

A precocious child, William Benjamin made his preparations for college by studies in a local academy, and he could have started college at the age of about 14, except for the violent death of his father at that date at the hands of Unionist soldiers. The next three years young Smith helped to put the family farm onto a paying basis, after which the devoted exertions of his mother and sisters made it possible for him to take a university education. He could not be admitted to Harvard or Yale for lack of Greek but he did enter, in 1868, the University of Kentucky, in Lexington, Ky. Starting nominally as a Freshman he kept far ahead of the calendar and graduated two years later, having taken principally Latin, Greek, Mathematics, and Physics. He then became Instructor in his "Alma Mater," in English and in Old Testament history. In 1871 he received the M.A. degree. In 1873-4 he was Adjunct Professor of Geology, Zoology, and Botany. By this time he had achieved by his own efforts a reading knowledge of Hebrew, French, German and Italian. Assyrian was a later accomplishment; in Greek and Latin his university had schooled him. Smith's teaching tasks brought him into contact with the critical Old Testament scholarship that was then taking shape, and through this and through contacts with natural science he arrived at intellectually skeptical conclusions that greatly perturbed the school's administration. It was felt at that time that these radical doubts disqualified him for any state university career. In consequence, for a while, he found himself "unemployable," till finally in 1875 St. John's College (Catholic) at Prairie du Chien, Wisconsin, accepted him to teach Mathematics and Latin.

From 1877 to 1879 he studied in Göttingen, Germany, winning prizes at the Mathematical-Physical Seminar—the first American who ever achieved such honors in Göttingen—and obtained his Ph.D. "summa cum Laude." Thus armed, he returned to America, and after some delay became Professor of Physics at Central College, Fayette, Missouri, in the autumn of 1881. While there, he married, 1882, Kathleen Merrill. She died seventeen years later. Of this, his only marriage, there were four children. In 1885 he removed to the chair of Physics at the University of Missouri, Columbia, Mo., but transferred after three years to the department of Mathematics, and then in 1893 removed to Tulane University, New Orleans, to teach Mathematics there. Then in 1907 he became Professor of Philosophy for that University. From his retirement, 1915, to his death Aug. 6, 1934, he lived in Columbia, Mo. In recognition of his studies in the New Testament he was recipient of the LL.D. degree, 1931, from the University of Missouri.

Smith's skepticism, rather than alienating him from the study of religion, posed its interpretation as a problem for him to try to master philosophically and historically. In particular he felt that the challenge to arrive at a sound historical account of the origin of Christianity was every bit as strong upon skeptical students as it could ever be upon the orthodox. Till we understand that event, he said, our whole comprehension of history is built on sand.

As a teacher of Philosophy Smith concerned himself much with the problems of the *one* and the *many;* also with the semblance of a cosmic mind-and-matter dualism. Sensing dualism as inacceptable, he answered it in terms of radical idealism, of the Berkeleyan stamp,—a view-point, that is, which resolves dualism by conceding full reality only to the mental world. The slight allusions that the reader will find in this book to matters of philosophy are interpretable in the terms of Berkleyanism.

In his Biblical studies Smith largely accepted the Old Testament findings of his predecessors—though he knew Hebrew, Aramaic, and not a little Assyrian—and he concentrated his own studies on the New Testament. He published in his lifetime two books and almost innumerable articles on this subject, and these comprised but a fraction of the studies he completed. In date these writings spread from the early '80's on until 1933. To avoid "embarrassing" his employers, as he put it, the earlier papers were signed with a *nom de plume*—"Conrad Maschol." These came out in Unitarian periodicals. Later he used his own name and to a considerable extent published through the *Monist* (Chicago), the *Open Court* (Chicago) and the *Hibbert Journal* (London). Smith's first book-sized publication on Biblical criticism, *Der vorchristliche Jesus* (1906), was an outgrowth and expansion of an article on the problem of the historicity of the place-name Nazareth. Not more than portions of that book have ever been printed in English, though in German it had a second edition. Interesting to relate, Paul Wilhelm Schmiedel, of Zurich, a theologian with whom Smith had already had a friendly controversy in the Hibbert Journal, was so impressed with the importance of the work, though he disagreed with its conclusion, that he willingly wrote a personal introduction of Smith, to be used as a foreword to the German book.

Smith is known to the American reading public more particularly through his *Ecce Deus* (in German 1911, English Edition 1912), his religious-philosophical article *Mors Mortis* (in *The Monist* Vol. 28, pp. 321–351, 1918, also reprinted separately), and through his homometric translation of Homer's Iliad (edited by Walter Miller, Macmillan, 1944).

In the field of biblical studies Smith was largely at home with the German critical literature, and quite accustomed to the blunt rough-and-tumble that is so generally characteristic of German intellectual controversy. But in his mind this method was something quite objective, and to be understood as fully compatible with high mutual esteem. Only when controversy seemed to stem out of self-interest instead of conviction, his patience quickly came to an end, and when disputes were supported by "Character-assassination" his ire was timeless and implacable. Even against such a theologian as Harnack, when he accredited an early church father's libel against an ancient "heretical" leader, Smith rose up in defense and refutation. Such things go naturally with rough words; yet outside of controversy Smith was a peculiarly gentle and sympathetic personality, one who though publicly known as a religious radical formed many of his closest friendships among the most conservative of traditional believers. He was loved by children, and could hold 'teen-agers fascinated with his conversation. Among adolescents who imagined they had outgrown "Alice in Wonderland," he could re-awaken appreciation by the intriguing discovery that Carroll was telling two stories with one set of words.

Smith's biblical studies were to him a duty and an enthusiasm, his personal contribution toward solving our century's need for religion that can face realities and be at home in a world of scientific perspectives. That he was deeply religious will be more than evident to any thoughful reader of his article *Mors Mortis*. Those who read this volume, however, must hold in mind that this is an objective study of history, and not a presentation of Smith's own personal religion.

The present work was completed in a sense—but only in a sense—in 1927, and at that date Smith tried to interest some publisher in it. As he was unsuccessful, the only account of this particular investigation that has been presented to the public thus far was Smith's author-abstract of the book, which he entitled "Milk or Meat?"* (*Hibbert Journal,* Vol. 31, p. 372–383, 1933), published the year before his death. Only recently, after various vicissitudes the unpublished book came back to the notice of a group of Smith's friends in Columbia, Missouri, and they arrived at the opinion that it should still be possible, after some editing, to present this invaluable study to its public.

The assignment of this labor of love to the present editor came about through circumstances almost accidental,—as much as anything, it would seem, because he had had many long conversations with Dr. Smith on the various aspects of Smith's almost endless biblical investigations. In accepting the task there is no pretense made of ability to appraise such matters as the philological controversies in which Smith's work has been entangled. But on that score undoubtedly William Benjamin Smith's already voluminous published studies leave him even posthumously his own most effective advocate. Considerable rearrangement of the parts of the book has been judged advisable, but while doing this the actual wording of Smith's argument has been preserved scrupulously his own.

Nineteenth and twentieth century literature is only scantily referred to in this work. The added footnotes do not undertake to provide coverage. Students of this aspect may well consult the references in the historicist work by Maurice Goguel, *Jesus the Nazarene, Myth or History?* 1926, and the publications of van den Bargh van Eysinga. For the latter see page xvii footnote.

The editor owes sincere thanks to Dean Emeritus W. C. Curtis, of the University of Missouri for counsel and effective cooperation. To Mr. Y. Kenley Smith, William Benjamin Smith's eldest surviving son, a most heart-felt appreciation is due for a very encouraging attitude and for cordial acquiescence in such reorganization of the text as seemed to be requisite.

ADDISON GULICK
3 Concord Avenue
Cambridge, Massachusetts

* We acknowledge the courtesy of the *Hibbert Journal* in acceding to the inclusion in this volume of material there published.

# An Orientation by the Editor

## I. THE TEMPORAL SEQUENCE.

*. . . Jesus said, Behold, Father,*
*A strife of ills upon earth*
*From thy breath wanders in.*
*(Man) strives to flee the bitter chaos*
*And knows not how he will fare therethrough.*
*On this account send me, Father;*
*Bearing seals, I shall descend;*
*Aeons whole shall make way through,*
*Mysteries all shall lay open,*
*And forms of Gods shall show,*
*And secrets of the Holy Way,*
*Having called it Gnosis, I shall deliver.*

\* \* \* \* \*

*This is the Christ, the Son of Man, portrayed from the unportrayable Logos.*

\* \* \* \* \*

*His voice we have heard, but his form we have not seen . . . for his shape, which descends from above from the Unportrayed One, what sort it is, nobody knows.*

These words, so tells us Bishop Hippolytus, are culled from the liturgies and teachings of the earliest school of Gnostics, the Naassenes,* who composed them long before the crucifixion could have occurred at Jerusalem, perhaps even before the time designated by Luke for the nativity. The being here celebrated was a heaven-dwelling but also spiritually immanent intermediary entity between God the Absolute and Man the Finite,—a sort of celestial Pattern-Man, reminding one of Plato's Man the Idea. According to Hippolytus the Naassenes called him by many names, Anthropos, Arsenothene,† Son-of-Man, Christ, and Jesus‡. This Jesus the Christ, Arsenothene, functioned as a voluntary redeeming messenger coming to earth by traversing the concentric spheres of the celestial "Aeons" from the outermost sphere inward to as far

* See Appendix, pp. 157 ff.

† By this is not meant Hermaphrodite, argues Smith, but rather the reverse, totally sexless, and equally prototype for either man or woman. *Editor*

‡ Namely, Savior. Compare Mt. 1:21 "Thou shalt call his name Jesus, for he shall save his people. . . ."

as earth. They described his work on earth as bringing "the kingdom of the heavens within us as a treasure, as leaven hid away in three measures of meal."* Redemption they expounded by the simile of the two births,† the second birth of redemption being that of "the water and the spirit,"‡ water being for these Naassenes symbolic of spirit. Also "unless ye drink my blood and eat my flesh, not at all may ye enter into the kingdom of the heavens."§ Before redemption, "tombs are ye, whited, but full within of bones of the dead, because there is not in you the living man";|| but at redemption "they shall spring forth" and be freed from carnality. The Naassene preaching message was, "Awake, thou that sleepest, and the Christ shall illumine thee."

These Naassenes had a cosmology which started with chaos and a "Monad" Creator. The Creator sowed broadcast the Logos¶ upon the chaos, and got in some places nothing, in other places thirty, sixty or a hundred fold, to spring up into the cosmos of factual existencies.

If this Naassene lore is indeed pre-Christian, with its almost innumerable passages strikingly parallel to New Testament counterparts, and with its concepts so suggestive of primitive Christianity yet so far from mature orthodoxy, a dozen new questions spring up at once. But the crucial chronological question, on which all else depends, can be solved only by way of technical scholarly comparisons for which this chapter has not the space. For the cumulative evidence our studious readers must turn to the Appendix at the end of this volume. Here and now it must suffice us to run over the leading conclusions that are there established by William Benjamin Smith:—

Hippolytus correctly records the developmental order of the early Gnostic "sects," namely,—The Naassenes preceded the Peratae, who developed out of them. The Sethians developed in their turn out of the Peratae. Likewise Simon of Samaria founded his elaborate and influential speculations on the thoughts of his predecessors the Sethians. Now Smith reminds us that Simon's long career was largely previous to the Apostle Peter, both by all church traditions and no less by the internal evidence from his doctrines, since his concepts of redemption were too primitive to be placed otherwise. *A fortiori* the Naassene school, coming at least three stages before Simon, was inescapably pre-Christian, though how long before is impossible to state in years. Internal evidence of their literature also proves this, for they knew nothing of a cross, or of a resurrection, or even a Savior visible upon earth; and similarly they had no earmarks of acquaintance with Simon.

* Compare with Matt. $13^{33}$.
† Compare with John $3^3$.
‡ Compare with John $3^5$.
§ Compare with John $6^{53-54}$.
|| Compare with Matt. $23^{27}$.
¶ Namely "idea" or "norm" in the Platonistic sense. For this parable compare Matt. $13^{3-8}$.

Moving on from the Naassenes to the whole assemblage of Gnostics that Hippolytus surveyed, Smith found a convincing temporal sequence in the growing concept of the Savior. Starting vague, celestial, abstract and invisible, step by step in the successive schools he begins to be visible, corporeal, tangible, and more and more human, taking on little by little the attributes given to Jesus in the New Testament.

As a broad religious movement, then, Gnosticism belied the characteristics of a Christian heresy. That would have necessitated that they be a block of schools which drifted away, through lapse of time and dimming memory, from following correctly a Master who had walked and taught in Galilee; history however says their relation to Christianity was the reverse, *not a divergence but a slow approximation.* By corollary, New Testament Christianity is more or less a sister movement to that of the Jewish Gnostics, indeed to the Naassenes and several other schools, even a younger sister.

## 2. THE PRE-CHRISTIAN JESUS.

The argument already covered makes us well acquainted with a pre-Christian Jesus-concept. Smith followed through on this thought in his book, *The Pre-Christian Jesus,* published in German as *Der vorchristliche Jesus* when it turned out not to be possible to find a publisher for it in English. In German it went through two editions, 1906 and 1911 respectively. The chief objective in this book was a survey of all internal evidences in the New Testament for the existence of this Jesus-lore previous to Christianity. In summary, Smith found:—

An intensive search of the post-apostolic writings demonstrated that until at the earliest A.D. 150, the *Epistle to the Romans* was entirely unknown among all church fathers, whether in Rome or elsewhere. As Smith had already published evidences that *Romans* was a strangely synthesized composite that had to be of late date, the whole effect was to render this epistle inelegible as witness about the Christ of history.

The book of *Acts,* he found, unintentionally lets slip the information that knowledge about "the Jesus," apparently a considerable mass of such lore, existed beforehand far and wide over the known world, and was carried by men who knew nothing of an actual Palestinian ministry of this Jesus. Christianity was not propagated by the slow missionary process, but burst forth almost simultaneously all over the area of the Jewish diaspora. This fact, Smith detects, was so embarrassing to the writer of *Acts* that that author invented as a covering explanation a period of early persecution and scattering of the Christians in Judaea, which the internal evidence of his own book refutes as non-existent. It appears indeed that the Apostles did not find cause to flee from Jerusalem. Couple this with the records of early Gnostic Jesus-doctrines and of collected sayings early ascribed to Jesus, and a picture comes together of a situation well calculated to make the pre-Christian Jesus-doctrine transmute with startling rapidity and almost spontaneously into the newly evolving Christian doctrine.* No early Judean persecution was in the least necessary to make the teaching spread.

A significant and very typical example of pre-Christian material used in the Gospels is the well-known parable of the Sower. We have already summarized the Gnostic version,† employed by them as a creation allegory. It appears beyond possible doubt to Smith that the Synoptist writers snatched up a cosmological allegory that was already in existence, but used it with less than cosmological meaning. Thanks to Hippolytus many further similar examples are recorded. How many additional unverified borrowings there may be from further cults of the Diaspora is impossible to know, because thus far our acquaintance with first century cults is too scant.

The appellation "of Nazareth" now comes under scrutiny in a chapter of *Der vorchristliche Jesus*. In the Greek it reads "the Nazorean," which Smith indicates conveys no meaning to a Greek reader. After he had joined for a while in the age-long search for the supposed town in Galilee, he concluded that no geographer, either Greek or Jewish, in the centuries just before and just after Christ knew of any such locality. The current identification is from the Middle Ages. But he argued there was no need for this town. It was merely invented by some Greek to explain an incomprehensible Aramaic word, and then this fictitious geography was accepted and incorporated into the narrative by the biographers of Jesus. The Jesus the Nazorean means simply "The Savior the Helper" or "The Savior who helpeth." The same Semitic root is used in other related languages in ascriptions directed to other gods.

The early Jesus-lore, as the earliest Gnostics had it, and as Apollos and other Alexandrians knew it before Paul, failed to include the concepts of the crucifixion and resurrection and ascension of the Redeemer. Resurrection is here the key concept;—whence came it? While this is hardly a crucial feature in Smith's argument, he suggests the probability that this thought comes primarily from a double meaning of the Greek word *anastasis*. All pious Jews looked for the triumph (*anastasis*) of the Messiah, but typically not for his victory by resurrection. But in the circles that became the first Christians, *anastasis* took on its other meaning, "resurrection." There can have been other

---

* The independently reached conclusion by Smith, that the Gospels were something else than history, has a number of scholarly antecedents and parallels. Of these the Dutch radical school is most important, for which see p. xvii f.n.; but note also: Bruno Bauer (1809–1882), Arthur Drews (1865–1935) both representing Germany, J. M. Robertson (1856–1933) Britain, Georg Brandes (1842–1927) Denmark, P.-L. Couchoud, France, author of Histoire de Jésus, 1944.

† P. xiv; see also p. 169.

influences, but the mode of use of this word strongly suggests that this verbalization had been a significant factor in building the Christian doctrine.

Thus in their sum-total the evidences that Smith brought together in *Der vorchristliche Jesus* make a strong case for the existence before the supposed time of Christ of a body of lore, known in the Book of Acts as "the things of the Jesus," which through some sort of process of allegory-building, came to be expanded into a narrative form, standing in no sort of relationship to any factual person.

### 3. Ecce Deus

William Benjamin Smith's three main treatises *"Der vorchristliche Jesus," "Ecce Deus,"* and the present book, are in some respects a consecutive trilogy. Yet it would be a serious mistake to try to regard them as co-ordinated members of a single exposition, which would be coherent from start to finish. They are much more like three successive exploratory expeditions, each of which extended the area of knowledge farther afield than what had been achieved before, while the final, farthest flung excursion of all, successfully brought in new data which both extended and revamped the previous partial conclusions.

It has been indicated that the chief accomplishment of what we may call "Book I,"—*"Der vorchristliche Jesus,"* was to make clear the existence of a movement antecedent, possibly by many decades, to the alleged date of the Gospel events, a movement that built up a non-terrestrial, subjective image of an immaterial and invisible Jesus. This book also upheld the conclusion that the Jesus of the Gospels was a non-factual materialization of this supraterrestrial being.

The task of *Ecce Deus*, Book II of Smith's series, was to bring to light the allegorical and esoteric nature of the four Gospels.* In it Smith assembled evi-

---

\* The main thesis of *Ecce Deus*, as also of *Der vorchristliche Jesus*, is almost exactly the same as was worked out, mostly at an earlier date, by the Netherlands school of radical New Testament criticism, prominent representatives of which are A. D. Loman (1823–1897), Allard Pierson (1831–1896), J. van Loon (1838–1907), H. U. Meyboom (1842–1933), G. J. P. J. Bolland (1854–1922), and G. A. van den Bergh van Eysinga (b. 1874, publishing since 1901). Like W. B. Smith they started with a critique of the witness to Jesus found in the Pauline epistles. But where Smith proceeded principally through reasoning from Hippolytus and Enoch, the Dutch group gave greater emphasis to the evidence from a scholarly examination of Philo Alexandrinus. Van den Bergh van Eysinga's book in German, *"Die holländische radikale Kritik des neuen Testaments"* (1912) mentions the gratification of the Dutch group at the publication of Smith's two books presenting arguments essentially the same as theirs, but with a different documentation, worked out independently and without knowledge of them. Smith's article in the *Hibbert Journal*, 1933, shows that he then knew and appreciated the writings of Bolland and van den Bergh van Eysinga. In recent years the Dutch radicals have been consolidating their position through extensive meticulous scholarship, but they apparently have not proceeded to Smith's new thesis of the present book and of 1933. A succinct recent summary of their position is found (in Dutch) in van den Bergh van Eysinga's article, "Bolland over het ontstaan van het Christendom," *Godsdienst-wetenschappelijke Studien* No. 4. (1948) pp. 29–42, esp. pp. 40–42.

dences that the entire story told by the Synoptics,—*a fortiori* that told in the
fourth Gospel,—was allegory to the last details. The leading motive in the
writing of these scriptures, he believed, was to reinforce monotheism. To that
end, he argued, the Savior ("the Jesus"), conceived purely as an *aspect* of the
indivisible and invisible Godhead, was made the allegorical actor in a narrative that was staged as though it had taken place on earth, in order to vivify
God's nature, and his attitude toward mankind. Smith argued that there are
only two alternatives, with no *"tertium quid"*:—(1) Jesus was a man living
visibly in this material world, exalted later toward divinity by his devoted
followers; or (2) He was God himself, invisible and supernal, presented symbolically. He brought forward many lines of evidence that the entire portrayal
was totally allegorical, leaving therefore no other possibility than that the
Christ was purely an esoterically symbolized divinity. Indeed the Gospel
authors repeatedly state the claim that the teaching was not to the multitude
but to the few, comprehensible only to those having "ears to hear." In the present work, in the chapter on "Symbolistic Warp and Woof," Smith goes over
much of this argument, but with a new orientation and a new *"tertium quid."*
The symbolism he finds ramifying down into the last details of Gospel, with
endless repeats and rehearsals, diversified only through innovations in the
methods of portrayal employed, as though the text were a veritable anthology
of the varied symbolic procedures for delineating the same few major topics.

There are a few further items, handled in *Ecce Deus,* that still need a brief
resumé here. Smith there points out that it is impossible to get down to any
sort of factual *residue* in the Gospels by eliminating the miraculous and looking for the personality behind this miraculosity—as so many modernists are
prone to attempt—because from first to last the supernatural is so completely
of the essence of the whole narrative that scratching it out leaves nothing of
significance to contemplate. Even the moral teachings, though far superior in
Smith's estimate to that of the Pagan contemporaries, differed, he points out,
in no wise from teaching that was entirely familiar and current in Judaism of
that date.

Smith shows that the nature of the Gospel message is clearly defined as "repentance," or literally "turning about," and that the biblical meaning of this
word is turning to monotheistic worship. In both Old Testament and Apocrypha, as well as in many citations from the Epistles he presents corroborations
of this. Any attentive study of the symbolism of miracle or narrative brings
the same result. Polytheism is vanquished symbolically in miracles of exorcism
and in cures of illness, blindness, and whoredom. In comparing John with
the Synoptics, Smith finds their parallel portrayals executed through such diverse symbols, that when they are woven each into narrative form, they give
the impression of being the biographies of two almost unrelated lives.

There are also some incidental items, all of which contribute to the total impression of a symbolic method. The word "Iscariot" Smith expounds as traceable etymologically to the Aramaic meaning "the Surrenderer." Thus Judas Iscariot signifies "The Jew Who Surrenders,"—once more a symbolic entity, as are also, e.g., the symbolically and parabolically presented individuals named Lazarus—in Aramaic "Lack Help."

All of Smith's arguments up to and including *Ecce Deus* give great weight to the seeming influence of early non-Palestinian Gnosticism as a fore-runner and pattern-maker for Christianity. In this he agreed with his contemporaries of the Dutch school of Gospel interpretation along mythical lines (Loman, Bolland *et al.*). The Gnostics, as Smith has brought out, assuredly produced very early a highly allegorical literature, established guiding patterns of symbolic representation, and created a liturgy that preceded and greatly influenced those of every branch of "orthodox" Christianity.* And yet, we shall see that later studies brought him to some quite fundamental considerations opposed to allowing that the influence of the Gnostics on the Gospels could be predominating. He found it to be rather an incidental modifier, more of the surface than of the essence of Christianity. More of this will be seen in the main body of this book.

*Ecce Deus,* as we have seen, gave an analysis by which every part of the Gospel story was seen as allegory; but the actual central figure, identified for the time being as the Supreme God Himself, was in a certain sense lifted above the vicissitudes of an allegorical entity. We shall see that in his later studies, comparing the various appellations of the Jesus—Son-of-Man, Son-of-God, the Elect, etc.,—with their original use in the older Scriptures, Smith uncovered clues which drew even this central figure himself completely into the symbolic fabric. Thus in the forthcoming chapters Smith presents a definite emendation of the thesis set up in *Ecce Deus,* throwing his favor to the new "*tertium quid*" that had not been perceived at the time he wrote his earlier books. In these chapters he argues that the Jesus of the Gospels, already shown by the Gnostic documents not to be a man transformed into a god, was also not god made into a man (as Smith had contended in the earlier books), but was an idealized Jewish national self-portrait done entirely in allegory. We shall also find how this major step forward in the deciphering of the great New Testament allegory brings with it many new interpretations of the key-concepts in the Christian propaganda—new group-meanings for the belief in the Transfiguration, Passion, Crucifixion, Death, Burial, Resurrection, Ascension, Final Advent,—every one of these undergoing a stupendous mutation of meaning

* Cf. also Wetter, *Altchristliche Liturgien* (1921, 1922).

when lifted out of a supposed individual life and relocated as part of a great race-allegory.

## 4. CRITERIA

Several of the norms of critical appraisal to which Smith held himself are listed below. We may say that these make the pattern of logic in Smith's biblical studies. Although they are presented for simplicity in the editor's wording, all are assembled from explicit declarations made by Smith, here and there in his writings.

1. The criteria of evidence are the same when applied to "sacred" documents as when applied to "secular." A statement which would be judged reliable (or unreliable) were it found in Homer or Xenophon or Julius Caesar, is neither made more nor less reliable if found instead in a text that has been canonized.

2. If the modern student would do valid work, the mental attitude which he brings to the documents must be dispassionate and objective. Even in reputedly liberal circles the full significance here is not always realized. It has been said that the only way to "understand" the Gospels is to approach them on bended knees. Yet the same person who says this would probably agree that in a legal proceeding the next of kin to the litigating parties should not be placed on the jury.

3. In the case of documents that may have been redacted, original narrative is relatively direct, simple, and self-consistent, while later editing, interpolating, and rewriting produce an accession of inconsistencies, involvedness, and bad syntax. On this score Smith makes free use of his own collossal familiarity with Greek linguistic usage, rather than depending on such methods as the statistical analysis of word frequencies, or the like.*

4. Discrepancies found between parallel narratives written by different authors may come from different techniques for transmitting the same thought. The more symbolic the literary form, the greater may be the seeming contradictions in the tangible statements, even while there may be underlying agreement.

5. Allegory is never fact, and fact is never allegory,—a consideration which the early church fathers grossly overlooked, and to which many modern expounders fail to give due weight. Any allegory incorporated into actual living violates the most elementary rules of pedagogy; and an action having allegorical signification can be at the moment of performance nothing better than pantomime. (cf. the discussion of Mary Magdalene, p. 64).

6. The studious reader should be alert to any self-revelation of the author's

---

* Not that Smith does not study word-frequencies, but that when he does so it is with other purposes, e.g., to uncover the leading preoccupations of the author being studied.

reasons for making a statement, e.g., whether to visualize a teaching, or to complete an allegory, or to provide a setting, or to fulfil an alleged prophecy. This applies particularly where a statement partakes of the incredible, or if it disagrees with statements of others.

7. Dispassionate biblical study leads to the maxim that in the Gospels any event that explicitly or implicitly constitutes a prophecy-fulfillment is always purely on the authority of the prophecy itself. Since this fulfillment of an ofttimes imaginary prophecy serves the evangelist himself as a completely sufficient basis for his statement, it follows that the reader is not called upon to presuppose the least vestige of fact in the incident so ear-marked. (Cf. here the expunged miracle of riding the two asses, Matt. ch. 21. and the treatment of the same infra, p. 59).

8. Any prophecy, circumstantially correct, of a "future" event which actually came to pass, is to be understood as written after the event and back-dated. This principle is nothing new. It has long been in use to determine which of the New Testament records antedated and which postdated the fall of Jerusalem, A.D. 70.

9. In trying to discover the truth about events that happened long ago, we cannot look for clear-cut syllogistic demonstrations, but must be willing to give attention to the many little granules of circumstantial evidence. Although no *absolute* certainty is established by this inductive method, yet in the cases where the pointers are numerous enough and consistent enough, they may set up a not less convincing *virtual* certainty. Smith uses this pattern effectively in many connections, the present work included, while sometimes apologising to the reader for the repetitive monotony of establishing a point by this mode of argument.

\* \* \* \* \*

We feel that the careful reader, mindful of the above principles, will find that Smith's evidence presented here in *The Birth of the Gospel* is astonishingly strong for the conclusion that the Gospel narrative took form from the start as an esoteric symbolic propaganda, totally and seriously allegoric.

ADDISON GULICK

*"The deepest can be said in symbols only"*
                              *Goethe*

# Chapter One

# *Author's Foreword*

## 1. AT THE CRADLE OF THE CULT.

"A mighty maze, but not without a plan."

When we attempt to trace the primitive Christian faith back to its birth, at least to its early infancy, we find that from the very start it was empire-wide. All round the Mediterranean its heralds shout the tidings simultaneously, from shore to shore, in every city where a synagogue is built, wherever the omnipresent Jew may gather his group to worship. When Paul visits Damascus on a tour of terrorization, he finds Ananias with other "disciples" all acquainted with his record. At Lydda and at Joppa such Disciples are found already established before Peter's arrival. At Antioch pioneers from Cyprus and Cyrene appear abruptly, as if sent down from heaven to convert the Greeks, and there the converts are first called Christians. When Paul comes to Ephesus he finds "certain disciples," for he had been preceded by the learned and eloquent Apollos of Alexandria, a missionary "instructed in the way of the Lord," "fervent in spirit" and accustomed to "teach accurately the (doctrine) about the Jesus," although knowing only the "Baptism of John." In Rome, according to the *Epistle,* there was already a well-established and world-famed church before Paul had left the Eastern Mediterranean: at Puteoli, in Italy, were "found brethren" when he landed there, and as they "came to Rome . . . the brethren, when they heard of us, came to meet us." Everywhere, then, the way is already paved for the Apostles, the faith already familiar and more or less accepted; they startle no one but proceed at once to argue the matter in the synagogue and to "expound the way of God more accurately."

So the New Faith is presented (unwillingly enough) in *Acts* as an empire-wide phenomenon practically simultaneous everywhere in its apparition, blazing out suddenly like summer lightning all round the Eastern shores of the Midland Sea.—And this, too, without any perceptible relation to any activity or history enacted in Judea, Galilee, Palestine, or elsewhere. We read of "the (doctrine) about the Jesus" as the burden of the zealous Alexandrian's

1

pleas, but no biographic career is suggested. Everywhere without exception the appeal seems to be made to a religious consciousness already present, which is swayed this way or that in the Synogogue by discussion of the Scriptures of the Old Testament, nowhere is there any recourse to alleged facts of a Palestinian Life, or to the authority of a Matchless Teacher, or to a peerless Personality that had but lately trod the stage of history in Jerusalem or the Holy Land. Thus, the Jews of Beroea showed themselves "more noble than those in Thesalonica"—not by summoning witnesses or cross-questioning Paul and Silas—but by "examining the scriptures daily, whether these things were so." It was, then, a matter of doctrine, to be tested solely by the Old Testament word.

Well, now, if such be the case, and it seems beyond denial, the question at once becomes urgent: How shall we render this state of fact understandable? How shall we conceive of a general historical situation such as shall make the proceedings already so briefly hinted not only comprehensible but thoroughly natural, if not necessary, on the part of the persons concerned? An obvious answer would be that we must discover some prevailing religious consciousness alike or nearly so throughout the region in question, some state of mind and feeling approximately the same in all quarters, a mental and emotional plight of which the wide-spread awakening may appear as the natural un-forced expression. It seems equally clear that no recent biographic fact in any country can cut much figure in the explanation sought. Had the movement turned about any such, we should surely have heard something about it, some one would surely have brought it conspicuously forward.

Yet more, however, even in this age of motion, which would well-nigh abolish distance, the distinction of here and there still prevails,—right powerfully. A local event, though it be of no great significance, seems one thing where it happened and altogether another 1000 miles away. The popular consciousness is very differently colored, even at a few leagues' remove. If, then, some recent biographic occurrence in this or that district had formed the focus of this endless and often passionate Jewish propaganda and discussion, we should certainly look to see it flaming out brightly in the nearer region but paling down sensibly as it spread abroad. Surely it must be at the centre and origin that the agitation is most lively. Also we might expect to find the debated facts in the front of the fight: the champions would affirm and reaffirm and would invoke their witnesses and confirmatory proofs; the opponents would deny in whole or in part, would impeach the witnesses and challenge the champions to produce unprejudiced and decisive testimony. Such seems the natural habitual conduct in such debates, and it is hard to imagine any other as likely.

Nevertheless we find all this inverted, turned topsy-turvy in the Christian Propaganda. It is not a unifocal but a multifocal agitation; it does not burst forth in Palestine and thence spread by degrees over all the empire; on the contrary, it is practically at once here, there and everywhere. Nor is it concerned with any biographic features: no local proofs are offered, no witnesses are summoned or challenged, no allusions are made to confirmatory facts, no contradictions are advanced by the gainsayers. From the start it figures solely as an affair of ideas, of Old Testament interpretation, of doctrinal discussion: the opposing forces are passages quoted from the Psalms, the Prophets, the Law and the History in the Old Testament; these and these alone are marshaled, deployed, maneuvered throughout this year-long century-long battle of conceptions.

Such is the outstanding all-embracing fact—so ineffectually disguised in the first chapters of *Acts*—that confronts us at the cradle of Christianity and imperiously demands explanation. As already stated, that explanation can be found only in some general condition of the religious consciousness prevailing all round the Midland Sea. That consciousness presents two widely diverse forms or phases: the Jewish-monotheistic and the Gentile-polytheistic. On the details of this latter it were needless to dwell; they have been made the subject of exhaustive research and are matters of common or at least accessible knowledge. It is well-known that the Pagan mind, particularly the oriental, had long been steeped in pessimism, that it yearned inexpressibly for relief, for deliverance from the woe of the world, that it was gravely dissatisfied with the current mythology in terms of which it was accustomed willy-nilly to conceive, that it sought comfort and even redemption in mysteries and cults, the common aim of which was to bring the worshipper in some wise into close relation, if not immediate touch, with God, to fuse and mingle the divine with the human, and so to pass over in a fashion the attributes of the one into the other.—All this must be borne constantly in mind, as explaining in some measure the success of the Propaganda from the nature of the material on which it had to work,—but not as by any means clearing up the nature of the Propaganda itself.

The *active* principle in this marvelous evangelization must rather be sought in the other, the monotheistic, phase of general consciousness. The Gentile was indeed discontent with his Legion of Demons and willing to be won over to the worship of One God, even though that might be the Roman State, as embodied in the Caesar-dynasty, and at any moment in the Emperor himself; but this dummy was of course unsatisfactory or even absurd, and the only teaching fit to supply every spiritual need was an importation, the strict Monotheism (along with the rigid morality) of Israel, at that time scattered like sand— several millions indeed—over the whole Empire of Rome. The Proselytism of Gentiles had long* been carried on zealously by the Jews, and every synogogue

* Since B.C. 139 at the latest, as documented in *Maccabees*.

was a centre of its radiation; but it was laden too heavily, if not with national pretentions, at least with racial peculiarities,—it could not hope to convert the world. The Law with its endless details of rites and requisitions stood inevitably in the way, and Circumcision seemed to bolt the gate with a bar of iron. The Cult of Israel did in truth appear to meet nearly all demands of the religious situation, but there was needed a thorough Transformation to adapt it to the times, to the temper of the Nations.

Now it is in the mutual interaction of these two phases of the General Consciousness, resulting in precisely this *Transfiguration,* that we seek for the genesis and the progress of the Early Propaganda. As so naturally conceived, the problem in hand might appear simple enough, even easy to grasp and handle by the average mind. Alas, however, it is involved at every turn in a mass of difficulties that reduce one almost to despair. The doctrines and prejudices of well-nigh 1800 years lie thick-set in rank undergrowth all about, and even were these prejudices all cleared away, there would remain the soil from which they sprang, a fertile mould sown with every seed and form of fancy, often exquisitely beautiful but not seldom misguiding.

It may prove a toilsome task to pierce through all these chaotic layers down to the spiritual Rock beneath, but there is no getting round it, the work must be done. Above all, it is necessary to season ourselves to the Israel-Mode of consciousness, the tribal reaction in which the Individual almost vanishes and leaves the Race sole-reigning and supreme. It is the duty of the writer to present such matters to the reader in adequate fullness and clearness, faithfully and without disguise; and to such an attempted presentation this book is devoted. Perhaps some readers may shy at such names as *Psalms of Solomon, Enoch, Assumption of Moses;* so be it; yet they may feel satisfaction in knowing that such material has not been neglected, but has been used in construction and now lies at command, whenever they may feel disposed to consult it.

Such, then, is the aim of this volume, to render the Genesis of the Christian Movement understandable as an historical process, natural and reasonable, though unique, throughout. Unique, because never, at any other moment in the annals of man, have such determining conditions combined themselves as at this epoch of the Christian Birth. As such it certainly deserves and demands the most careful and conscientious study, pursued with all rational reverence, equally removed from the scoff of the sceptic and the blind adoration of the priest.—Such a scrutiny may suffice to shape a thoroughly genetic and yet thoroughly satisfactory answer to Prof. Loofs' question: "Who was Jesus Christ?"—a query that this savant, at once so able and so honest, has proclaimed it impossible to answer, save in terms of Faith, for which no historical or logical reason can be given. Yet, strange to say, the answer found is in harmony with the First *Postulate* of the Halle historian: "Jesus of Nazareth has had a visible existence among Men"—not forsooth as a homeless tramp on the shores of "deep Galilee," but as Israel the Race, called "Son-of-Man" and "Son-of-God," *crucified* on the Cross of history but *transfigured* and glorified in the Religion of Man.

## 2. JEWISH NATIONAL CONSCIOUSNESS

Above all, if the reader would trace his way successfully through the arguments to come, he must for the nonce lay aside the fashion of western thought that is his own, and must don the garb of a hellenized Jew of nineteen centuries ago; he must season himself to a climate in which the Individual almost vanishes and leaves the Race sole-reigning and supreme. This *Jewish National Consciousness* appears as a well-nigh unique fact in human annals. Persistent in earlier and later history, throughout a span of several millennia, its expression in the first century A.D. rose to crisis intensity, as what the mathematician might call a "singular point" in the curve or surface of history. It is amazing to think and hard to conceive of a whole people possessed of this one (not evil) obsession of folk-unity not only on this occasion and that, but throughout the stretch of say thirty centuries of race experience! Yet in some quality and degree it was always present, moulding and coloring the individual life, as nowhere else recorded in all the annals of man.

The Apocalyptic visions of the Jews were born of this possession, as examples to be cited later will amply attest, and much the same may be said of the later Talmudic and Qabbalistic literature, a dense and dark forest, through which only carefully trained feet may safely wander. Our logical concern, however, is only with the earlier Scriptures hardly reaching below the first century of our era; the dreary tale of the following ages is significant only as attesting the abiding presence and controlling influence of the Consciousness in question.

In the Old Testament it is plain beyond any quibbling that the focus of interest is not the world at large, not any laws of nature or principles of universal action, not even the achievements of any remarkable individuals, but rather the Origin, Career and Destiny of the Chosen People of God. Of the Patriarchs we learn little more than their names till we come to Abraham conceived as the specific progenitor of the Race, and he is of importance only as such an "exalted Father" of the Folk and as fixing the standard by which his posterity might be judged through all time to come.—Something similar may be said of the other shining spots in this long-drawn canvas, as the eponymous Israel (Jacob) and the dynasty-founder David: they glow not in and for themselves, but rather "by way of example," whether for imitation or for warning, as representatives of the solely significant national life.

Nor does it hold merely for the narrative portions of Scripture; it is manifestly true for the legal parts as well. The Torah was given to Israel as a People, as a unit, it was not given to the world at large,—though of course it could be kept only by the individual's observance of its precepts. But how thoroughly even this latter was felt to be a national function, is strikingly shown in the fact that there was One Temple and One only and that all sacrifices were to be offered there. The possibility of such service passed away with the final ruin of Jerusalem, A.D. 135, but the restoration thereof has remained the cherished hope of Jacob for millennium on millennium and has been a burning question even in the discussions of Zionism today.

Not less dominant, as every one knows, is the Israel-Idea in the Prophets; the wished-for, hoped-for glory of Zion brightens their every page and is the keynote of their every cry. Most of them know nothing of any personal Messiah, while such as employ the notion at all employ it very rarely and then only as a personification or symbol of the triumphant Nation of the future. As conquering king, the Anointed, the Root of Jesse, the Son of David is merely the Agent, Surrogate, Embodiment of the People itself.—Even in the *Song of Songs,* it was felt that if the medley deserved place in the Canon, the passion it celebrated could be naught else than the mutual and exclusive devotion of Israel and its God—The books of *Proverbs, Job,* and *Qoheleth* (Preacher) present apparent—and in a measure only apparent—exceptions, which it were out of place to discuss here; only be it observed that whatever the original of the Man of Uz, the devout Jewish reader could hardly have failed to detect his resemblance in character and fate to the Israel-Folk, unshaken by calamity from its unique fidelity to God.

There remains the *Book of Psalms,* in which Christian commentary for many generations has found preeminently the Religion of the Individual, the cry of the personal soul to its God, unmindful of racial considerations, as fitting on the lips of a Pilgrim Father or Russian Serf as on those of David or an exile by the water of Babel. It has been assumed as self-evident that the "I," in any of the 100 Psalms that employ it, refers almost if not quite exclusively to the writer thereof, who pours forth his personal plea of complaint to his personal God, with rarely ever a thought of any other than himself. Now and then, at long intervals, some messianic form was supposed to flit across the Psalmist's field of view, which he would jot down in more or less unintelligible terms, but in the main it was a prayer for relief from his own unbearable bodily ills and the persistent persecutions and annoyances of his vexatious neighbors without number,—this it was that floated up to the throne of God from the pen of the querulous poet. He might, indeed, throw in an occasional postscript recommending Israel also to divine mercy—much as a minister of to-day may remember in supplication the President and Cabinet, or even perhaps the Governor of his State.

This inadequate conception of the Psalter has prevailed among Christians almost unchallenged even down to very recent times and is still cherished tenderly in many respectable quarters. As recently as 1912 Emil Balla of Kiel University published an able and interesting work on The *"I" of the Psalms (Das Ich der Psalmen)*, in which only niggardly concession is made to the doctrine of the "Collective I," namely, as to Ps. 129, and the other 99 such I-Psalms are all explained as individual in reference, as largely in the wise of the Assyrian-Babylonian prayers or thanks for recovery from rheumatism or other distempers!

The "Collective" interpretation was familiar enough to the Jews, being recognized by the Seventy in the superscription to their Greek translation of Ps. 56, as also in the Targums and Midrash. It was also acknowledged occasionally by the Fathers and in the Middle Ages. Later it seemed to escape almost entirely from the Christian consciousness (though retained by De Wette and Olshausen), until recalled in 1888 by Smend in his epoch-making memoir in the *Zeitschrift fur alttesteamentliche Wissenschaft (Journal of Old Testament Science).* "On the 'I' of the Psalms." Since then it has been accepted by such authorities as Reuss and Cheyne, in its last extreme by Engert, Matthes, Stade, Ehrlich, and to a great extent by a host of others, who would yet allow the presence of more or less individualism in some of the Psalms. Critics in much less number still hold aloof and insist on regarding the "I" as strictly personal,—among them such scholars as Baudissin, Bertholet, Budde, Duhm, Gunkel, Koenig, and Sellin.

It may well be granted that some Psalms and parts of Psalms were originally written as expressions of only personal experience, of hopes and fears, desires and sufferings, devotions and aspirations, of gratitude and exultation. But it seems likely that many or most of these were so modified and generalized as to reflect the national consciousness, before admission to the sacred company of the Holy Scriptures.* Hence it may be that so many are ascribed to David, who as founder of the royal Dynasty was felt to stand and speak not for himself but for all the People of God. Let the reader peruse these Psalms and note how the Psalmist is oppressed in superpersonal fashion and afflicted beyond all measure, how the *nations* surround him and mock him and rend him; how

---

* In the Jewish liturgy the *Prayer* proper (Tefillah), called also *'Amidah* and more commonly *Shemoneh 'Esreh* (from its originally *Eighteen* Benedictions, now nineteen),—composed under direction of the Nasi Gamaliel, in bitter anguish and intense desire, after the Fall of Jerusalem,— devotes seven of its petitions to the Messianic Hope, and "all the prayers for individual well-being, for material prosperity, for life, health, and wealth, are drowned in the pathetic, heart-rending national prayer for the restoration of exiled Israel to the land of its fathers." Other petitions abound in this great Prayer-Book, but they are all "permeated with the great, all-embracing hope, to which they are really subordinate," that Israel "be restored to its ancient inheritance, and the glory of the one, true God would fill the earth." *Greenstone, The Messiah Idea in Jewish History,* 285.

his "enemies" swarm in his diction (appearing over 100 times), with his "foes," and his "haters" and "whom he hates" (nearly 50 times); how the "ungodly," the "wicked," the "*heathen*" beset him at every turn; how the waves of calamity overwhelm him, and how he is buoyed up solely by the promises of God to *Israel,* with their frequent fulfilment in *Israel's* history. Strong in YHVH's word, which can not fail, the poet bears up under every outrage and defies even *death:* "Yea, I have a goodly heritage. . . . I have set YHVH always before me. With Him at my right hand I shall not be moved. Therefore my heart is glad, And my soul exults, And my flesh abides in safety. For Thou wilt not surrender my life unto Sheol, nor suffer Thy Beloved (or Holy or Pious) to look on the pit," Ps. 16$^{6\text{-}10}$ Who was the Holy, the Beloved of YHVH? There is but one answer: Israel and Israel alone. Nowhere is YHVH conceived as loving the Individual, but everywhere the People,—the National entity is His treasure, His love. Abraham is called "His friend,"* but only as embodying in himself the Chosen Race.

But it is no one passage nor two nor a dozen that can represent properly the case for the Racial Consciousness in the Psalms. One must read all or a goodly number of them to sense the atmosphere that pervades and enswathes them all, an atmosphere of communal feeling, of national experience, of racial pride and aspiration almost peculiar to the Israel-Folk and in general far removed from any personal ambition, hope or fear that could probably have swayed the mind of any "sweet Singer of Israel."

It has seemed due to the reader to give at least some faint glimpse of the true state of the case, especially in a matter where error abounds and is so firmly entrenched, but any close argument would be out of place and moreover superfluous, since the presence of the "collective I," at least in a large number of the Psalms is now generally conceded, though there are many diversities of judgment on details.

For the aims of our general argument, so much is even more than sufficient,

---

* Only in Is. 48$^{14}$ we read of Cyrus, "My friend shall wreak his pleasure on Babylon." The text is corrupt, and any conjecture would be rash. But Cyrus is also called "His Anointed (Messiah, Christ)," as ordained by YHVH to a special work of Salvation for Israel. Again, in Is. 38$^{17}$ we read: "Behold, it was for my peace, etc. But Thou hast in love to my soul delivered it from the pit of corruption. For Thou hast cast all my sins behind Thy back." This however, is not in the Hebrew, still less in the Septuagint Greek. The prayer is intelligible only as the cry of the king before a recovery. The text has suffered deeply, but Duhm translates the whole v. 17 thus: "And hold back my soul . . . From the pit of nothingness, . . . And cast behind Thy back . . . All sins of mine"—as is required by the metre as well as the sense. So vanishes the conceit of YHVH's love to Hezekiah's Soul.—It may be well to note that in the famous verse 16$^{10}$ quoted above, the security against death can be understood only of Israel the Race, and so understood it formed the essence of the nation's faith and hope. The uncompromising Balla would give it a personal reference by *inserting* the word "now" (jetzt), "Thou wilt not *now* surrender, etc.!" But this insertion is quite unwarranted and maims the whole thought of the whole passage (vv. 5–11), which is plainly full of the idea of permanence, of the abiding safety vouchsafed Israel by its God.

without such a minute study of the Psalms as might delay the movement of thought and perhaps tire the reader. Be it only observed in passing, that the gain in dignity, in elevation, in moral grandeur, in spiritual beauty, in religious significance is incalculable, when, instead of self-centered personal complaints and frettings about the vexations and disappointments of the individual life, we recognize in these Psalms the awe, the agony, the dismay—but never the despair—of the Bard, of the National Soul, at the fearful, the age-long, the unceasing, the incomprehensible afflictions of the People Israel, the Treasure of YHVH, His Elect, His Friend, His Only-Begotten, Well-Beloved Son. In this regard, and in this only, do they tower aloft in solitary sublimity as expressions of amazement, of grief and of pain, but even more of Faith, of Hope and of Love,—alone in the literature of mankind.

\* \* \* \* \*

The writer has not forgotten that on the borders of this subject there be many interesting and inviting questions, such as concern the relations of the New Faith to the old mythology, the astrologies and mysteries, particularly to the countless phases of the Gnosis, most of all to the Docetic,\* that seem to peep at us here and there through so many expressions of the Fathers and even the pages of the New Testament itself. The paths of the astralists are pleasant and skirt many a faery province, but they are beset with pitfalls even for the wariest feet; here and there they may offer some secure and cosy inn, but they are strewn with untimely wrecks and with signs that guide into ditches and swamps.

We may also be sure that the Gentile mind carried over into its Jewish school not a few mystic notions and rites derived from earlier associations, and it may well be worth while to track these down to their original heathen haunts; neither dare we forget that in the thought of Clement, the great Alexandrian, true Gnostic and true Christian were interchangeable, nor that at least two important Epistles (to *Colossians* and to *Ephesians*) are deeply dyed with Gnostic phrases and with Gnostic thoughts. But no such matters, however interesting, appear essential to the comprehension of the Primitive Propaganda as a coinage of Hebraic consciousness in Hellenic moulds, and any satisfactory treatment of such collaterals would not only be a wide digression, but would enlarge the present volume beyond any judicious size.

Now, then, the volume is committed to the uncovenanted mercies of the reader, not without hope that though it may dip it may yet not sink in the current of years, and it is in such resignation to the verdict of the future that the writer would cast it silently into everlasting time.

---

\* For Docetism, see Appendix, p. 206 ff; also in Chapt. V, Ignatius, p. 90 ff. *Editor.*

## Chapter Two

# The Title Son-of-Man as Used
# in Daniel and Enoch

### 1. In Daniel

The meaning of the title Son-of-Man, when used in the Gospels to designate the Christ, has been long and much contested, and it might now seem natural to present in the first place some outline of the various solutions hitherto attempted. But these are so many and so diverse that any attempt to sketch them at this point could not fail to bewilder more than enlighten, and accordingly it seems better to proceed first to the study of the previous sources for an interpretation.

The phrase *Son-of-Man* (*ben-adam*) is frequent in the Old Testament. The word *adam* (sometimes with the article, as in *kol-ha-adam*, all-the-man) is properly a collective noun or class-name for Man, human beings; so that *ben-adam* means simply "human individual," a member of the species *homo*. It is a favorite with Ezekiel, who so designates himself nearly a hundred times as a mortal man, in contradistinction from God. Often it is used as a poetical parallel for *man,* as in Job 25[6]—'How much less man, that is a worm! And the son-of-man, that is a worm!' In the passionate prayer, Ps. 80, for deliverance from captivity, the phrase unequivocally designates *Israel*—described as a *vine* brought out of Egypt, planted in Palestine, torn up by the boar (cp. Iliad ix, 539), cut down and burned with fire, and the *Psalmist representing the People* says (vv. 14–17): "Turn again, we beseech Thee, O God of hosts: Look down from heaven, and behold, and visit this Vine,[15] And the stock which Thy right hand planted. And *the son that Thou madest strong for Thyself* ...[17]Let Thy hand be upon the man of Thy right hand, Upon the *son-of-man whom Thou madest strong for Thyself.*" The italicized words, in fact, the whole of v. 17 should perhaps be omitted as a later insertion (so marked *dl* in Kittel's *Biblia Hebraica,* p. 973), but it matters not; the all-important point is that some Hebrew poet here identifies *son-of-man* with the *Vine Israel.* So used, the term is a title of the highest honor: "the boar," the heathen he regards not as men but as wild beasts, only Israel, as the only true God-worshipper, is truly Man.

This rather late conceit reappears conspicuously in Daniel 7, where instead of the Hebrew *ben-adam* we find the Aramaic *bar-enosh* "a son of man" which with its variant *bar-nasha,* "the son of man," was in early Christian days the regular term in Palestine for an *individual man.* The prophet sees four *beasts* emerge from the main—the four great monarchies from Assyrian to Greek—"and then" (v. 13), "I saw in the night-visions, and, behold, there came with the clouds of heaven one like-son-of-man, and he came even to the Ancient of Days, and they brought him near before Him.[14] And there was given him dominion, and glory, and a kingdom, that all the peoples, nations, and languages should serve him: his dominion is an everlasting dominion, which shall not pass away, and his kingdom that which shall not be destroyed." The interpretation of the Vision follows (v. 17): "These great beasts, which are four, are four kings, that shall arise out of the earth. [18]But the Saints of the Most High shall receive the kingdom, and possess the kingdom forever, even forever and ever. ... [21]I beheld and the same horn (Antiochos Epiphanes) made war with the Saints, and prevailed against them; [22]And the kingdom and the dominion, and the greatness of the kingdoms under the whole heaven, shall be given to the People of the Saints of the Most High: his kingdom is an everlasting kingdom, and all dominions shall serve and obey him."

Here, then (about 165 B.C.), the same is said of the Son-of-Man as of the "Saints of the Most High," who are of course *Israel.* Hence again the Equation *Son of Man = Israel,* which is the Key to the understanding of the New Testament and Protochristianity. Notice carefully the exchange and equivalence of the ideas of Person and Nation: In v. 17 the four beasts are "four kings,"* but in v. 23 "the fourth beast shall be a fourth kingdom." Over against these monstrous brutal polytheistic powers, the Saints, sole worshipers of the Sole God, are figured not as Beasts but as Human, "like-Son-of-Man" (v. 13). That such is the meaning here is perfectly plain and beyond any doubt; it is enough to quote Prof. R. H. Charles, who with a light touch and apparent reluctance declares, "In Daniel the phrase seems merely symbolical of Israel" (*The Book of Enoch,* 315).

This might appear like a sufficient glorification of Jacob, to denote him as Human and all other men as Beasts, but it was an easy step further to hint that He was superhuman, was in fact divine, at least angelic. Again and again in this same *Book of Daniel* we meet with heavenly beings in form of men. Thus "as the appearance of a man" ($8^{15}$), "the man Gabriel" ($9^{21}$), "a man clothed

---

* Knowing, as he surely knew, that these Beasts had ruled the earth for many centuries, and that there had been many individual kings and even dynasties, in writing "Four Kings" Daniel *must* have meant "Four Kingdoms"—a usage observed in all Apocalyptic.

in linen" etc. ($10^5$, cp. Mark. $14^{51}$, $16^5$), "Michael shall stand up, the great prince that stands for the children of thy people" ($12^1$), "the man clothed in linen, who was above the waters of the river" ($12^6$). Clearly the temptation was great to *translate* this Human Picture of Israel to the sky, where it would appear as the "Son-of-Man" "coming with the clouds of heaven" ($7^{13}$), and no one would look for severe logical consistency in such high-wrought fancies.

## 2. In *Enoch*

*The Exaltation of Symbolic Israel* into the heavens was completed in the literature of the last two centuries B.C. that has descended to us partially under the name of *Enoch*,* a literature of which, though it was lost in its original (Aramaic?) version, large blocks have come down to us in Ethiopic, and some in Greek, translations.† Written under the inspiration of *Daniel*, much of it consists of cosmological extravagances that possess no respectable interest for today but a considerable part, the 'Similitudes,'‡ is occupied with what might be called the Revelation of the Son-of-Man, or the Elect of God. Here this notion of the Son-of-Man, "undoubtedly derived from Daniel vii," as Prof. Charles observes,§ is developed and rounded out into that of a distinct personality (all the while imagining Israel), which is wholly a "supernatural being . . . not even conceived as being of human descent" (compare the High Priest Jesus in Heb. $7^3$, "fatherless, motherless, without genealogy, without beginning of days or end of life," a still more sublimated picture of Ideal Israel). He "sits on God's throne," (Enoch $51^3$), which is likewise His own throne, $62^{3, 5}$; $69^{27, 29}$; possesses universal dominion $62^6$, and "all judgment is committed unto Him, $41^9$; $69^{27}$" (Charles, l.c.).

Such, one may say, is nothing less than Deification, but it is at least implicit in various Psalms ($2^{7, 12}$, $110^{1-5}$) as well as in Daniel $7^{13}$, where "one like-Son-of-Man came with the clouds of heaven and came to the Ancient-of-Days"— and when we remember that YHVH, this Ancient-of-Days, himself is seated and rides upon the clouds as the throne of His glory,|| we see that the words of Enoch are merely more explicit: "And in those days the Elect One will sit on my throne"; "and the Lord-of-Spirits seated him (the Elect) on the throne of His glory"; "pain will seize them where they see the Son-of-Man sitting on the

---

* I.e., under the nominal authorship of the great grandfather of the patriarch Noah. *Editor*.

† Those portions of this literature that have reached us through Old Slavonic translations do not contain references to a Son of Man, nor use any kindred expressions. *Editor*.

‡ Chs. 37–71 of the Ethiopic version, usually dated about 70 B.C. *Editor*.

§ R. H. Charles, author of *The Book of Enoch* (1893), the major translation of the Ethiopic *Enoch* into English (with annotations). *Editor*.

|| Ps. $18^{9-14}$, "He rode upon a cherub and flew, yea, He swooped on the wings of wind,"— many similar.

throne of his glory."—"And the Son-of-Man was revealed unto them, and he sat on the throne of his glory, and the sum of judgment was committed unto him, the Son-of-Man"; "for the Son-of-Man has appeared, and sits on the throne of his glory."—Also the notion of "universal dominion" (En. 62[6]),—"And the kings and the mighty and all that possess the earth will glorify bless and extol him who rules over all, who was hidden"—seems taken directly from Dan. 7[14, 27] (already quoted) where the like is said of the Saints and the Son-of-Man, whose identity with each other and with the People Israel appears to be fixed beyond any doubt whatever.

Moreover the denotation "Elect One," so very frequent in Enoch and used above as synonymous with Son-of-Man, identifies this later with "Israel mine Elect" and "Jacob my Servant." ... "Jeshurun whom I have chosen" (Is. 45[4], 44[2]). Everywhere in *Enoch* (as in *Isaiah*) *Elect* refers to Israel only. Thus, 93[2], "And Enoch spoke: Concerning the *children of righteousness* and concerning the *Elect of the world* and the *plant of uprightness*—of these I will speak to you, etc." Here the three italicized phrases are manifestly equivalent; the last has already met us in En. 10[16]: "and the plant of righteousness and uprightness shall appear," and even Charles, so loth it would seem to recognize the National Consciousness in these Apocrypha, yet says in his note "i.e. Israel. Israel springs from a seed that is sown by God." The reference is to 62[8]: "And the congregation of the holy and Elect will be sown, and all the Elect will stand before Him (God, the 'Most High,' 'Lord of Spirits') on that day." Elsewhere (84[6]) Enoch prays the Lord to "establish the flesh of righteousness and uprightness as a plant of seed forever," which means of course enduring dominion of the People Israel. Again (93[5]) he thus refers to Abraham: "A man will be chosen as the plant of righteous judgment, and after him will come forever more the plant of righteousness." The allusion to the Race of Israel could hardly be more unmistakable, unless it be in 93[8], where he declares of the Captivity, "and the whole race of the Elect root will be dispersed." The glorification to follow (the 7th Week) is thus proclaimed (93[10]): "And at its close the elect of righteousness of the eternal plant of righteousness will be elected to receive sevenfold instruction concerning His whole creation." Remember that this "plant" is certainly and admittedly "Israel," and it becomes clear as noon that the conception of Israel as the *Elect,* the *Son-of-Man* reigns throughout the *Book of Enoch* absolutely.

It seems needless to multiply citations. It should be clear on its face that the term *Elect* implies a class from which the election is made. You can not *pick out* one, if there be only one in the first place. The *Elect One,* the *Son-of-Man,* must then be One of a certain class, chosen out from all unto altogether especial honor by the Supreme Being. That class is the Nations, Races, or Families of Mankind; that One is the People Israel, beyond any question. This shines out vividly in Enoch's indifferent use of singular and plural in speaking of the Elect, as for example in the foregoing quotations. The seer treats Israel as One or as Many, just as convenience may bid. So in Is. 64⁵, "thou didst take away *him* that joyfully worked righteousness, *those* that remembered Thee in Thy ways," where "him" and "those" mean quite the same. This choice of Israel is surely a notion that reigns in the Old Testament; thus, "For thou art a holy People unto YHVH thy God, and YHVH hath chosen thee to be His own treasure* out of all peoples that are upon the face of the earth" (Deut. 14²); and so, "For Yah hath chosn Jacob unto himself, Israel for his own possession" (Ps. 135⁴), and in the prophets, especially the Younger Isaiah, as in 45⁴, "Jacob my Servant and Israel mine Elect." Can such a guiding thought have been absent from the New Testament where we read "This is my Son the Elect," and "If this is the Christ of God, the Elect" (Luke 9³⁵, 23³⁵)? We must at least hold firmly to the identity of Israel with the Elect and the Son-of-Man.

So important a fact, however, will bear still further emphasis. In En. 69²⁷ "the sum of judgment was committed unto him, the *Son-of-Man*," while in Dan. 7²² it reads, "Until the Ancient-of-Days came, and judgment was given to the Saints of the Most High" (i.e., the Son-of-Man), so that *function* is the same in the two. Yet the most distinctive passage in *Enoch,* touching the Son-of-Man, is found in 48²⁻¹⁰: "And at that hour that Son-of-Man was *named* in the presence of the Lord of Spirits and his *name* before the Head-of-Days (the Ethiopic phrase for Daniel's Ancient-of-Days). ³And before the sun and the signs were created, before the stars of the heaven were made, his *name*† was

---

* In certain chants (Piyyutim) of the Jewish Prayer-Book, in the form of dialogues between God and His People, Israel is constantly addressed by God as "My Treasure"—as in the Piyyut *Segaluthi,* For the Fourth Sabbath after Passover.

† This *naming* is quite as prominent, if not quite so explicit, in *Isaiah:* thus (44⁵), "one shall say 'YHVH's am I,' and another shall call himself by the *name* of Jacob; and another shall write on his hand Unto YHVH, and with *name* of Israel sur*name* himself." Also "Everyone that is called by My *name*" (43⁷), "Mine Elect," "the People which I formed for myself" (43²¹), and "Hear ye this, O house of Jacob, who are called by the *name* of Israel" (48¹), and "YHVH hath called me from the womb . . . made mention of my *name*"—Israel (49¹), and "that they might be *called* terebinths of righteousness, the Planting of YHVH" (61³), "and thou shalt be called by a *new name*" (62²). Further examples of this unexampled racial-religious consciousness: "When he (Abraham) was but one I called him, and I blessed him, and made him many" (Is. 51²); "Thus saith thy Lord YHVH, and thy God that pleadeth the cause of His People" (51²²); "Thy seed shall possess the nations" (54³); "This (glorification) is the heritage of the servants of YHVH" (54¹⁷); "Behold I have given him for a witness to the peoples, a prince and commander to the peoples" (55⁴); "all the trees of the field shall clap their hands" (55¹²); "nations shall walk at thy light, and kings at the brightness of thy rising" (60³); "The branch of my planting, the work of my hands, Wherein I glory" (60²¹); "They are the seed that YHVH hath blessed" (61⁹); "Return for thy servants' sake, The tribes of thine inheritance" (63¹⁷); "For they are the seed blessed of YHVH" (65²³).—Repeatedly the *parallelism* shows that "Mine Elect" = "My People," as in Is. 65²².—The evidence is overwhelming that in the literature of Israel the National-Racial Consciousness is completely Master, the Individual consciousness sinks almost wholly out of sight.

*named* before the Lord of Spirits (hence Phil. 2⁹, 'God . . . gave him the *name* . . . above every name, etc.' Here then is found the core of the Pauline doctrine of the Christ, as Charles and the rest clearly perceive, but they forget to tell us that this *Preexistent* is Personified Israel, the Genius of Jacob!). ⁴He will be a staff to the righteous on which they will lean and not fall (a clear and penetrating insight: the National Consciousness, the Genius of the Race, is in every age the strength and stay of the Individual, without which he would go to the ground; the seer has builded better than he knew), and he will be the *light of the Gentiles* (this phrase from Isaiah 42⁶, 49⁶, where it denotes Israel sole and single, the 'Servant' of YHVH, 'My Salvation unto the end of the earth,' is *decisive;* all becomes quite clear as we dog the steps of the seers in their advancing Personification, in conceiving the Racial Spirit as an Individual) and the hope of those who are troubled in heart (so Israel has imagined his mission to the world). ⁵And all that dwell on earth will fall down and bow the knee before him (hence Phil. 2¹⁰, 'Wherefore God . . . gave unto him the *name* that is above every *name;* that in the *name* of Jesus every knee should bow . . .') and will bless and laud and celebrate with song the Lord of Spirits (hence in Rev. 5⁹, 'And they sing a new song, saying, etc.'; again 14³, 'And they sing as it were a new song before the throne, etc.,' and 15³, 'they sing . . . the song of the Lamb'). ⁶And for this reason has he been *chosen* (this word marks him as *not a special creation* but as *selected* from a class; and properly, as set forth above, p. 13) and hidden before Him before the creation of the world and forever more (the seer thinks of the Eternal Counsels of God and naturally regards the many long centuries of Israel's insignificance and humiliation as a *Hiding* by YHVH, and the Exaltation to follow as a *Revelation* of the *Son-of-Man*). . . . ⁹And I will give them over into the hands of Mine *Elect* ('Israel Mine *Elect*,' Is. 45⁴) : as straw in fire . . . they will burn before the face of the holy ('but the chaff will he burn up with unquenchable fire,' Matt. 3¹²) . . . ¹⁰for they have denied the Lord of Spirits and His Anointed."

This latter term, "Anointed" (Messiah, Christ), can certainly not introduce a new and dominant figure of which we have not heard hitherto and shall not read hereafter. "The Lord of Spirits and His Anointed" can be nothing else than the Lord and his Elect, the Son-of-Man, the People Israel, on whom the discourse has thus far centered. The designation "Anointed" (*mashiach*) may be and indeed is applied to any one appointed by God to a special religious task, as even to Cyrus (Is. 45¹),—there was many an Anointed or Messiah. In Is. 61¹ Charles thinks "anointed" refers to the "Servant of Jehovah," which Duhm regards as "a grave mistake" (*ein arger Missgriff*). A frequent reference is to the King as the Representative of Israel. After the fall of the Kingdom the idea in large measure lapsed, but the hope of the restoration of Israel still burned bright, and this was naturally associated with the thought of a reestablished kingship and hence of an Anointed Leader, though it is remarkable what an insignificant part such a Messiah appears to play. Of course, such a Ruler would be more or less idealized. Never in the Old Testament is the term Messiah used in the familiar technical sense of the Redeeming King, the Deliverer of his People, much less the Savior of the world. The present Enochian text is supposed to be the first example of such a use, but it is no such use at all. It is plain that (in its setting) naught else can be meant than the *Elect,* the *Son-of-Man,* the People Israel Personified. A second and similar use by Enoch is found in $52^4$, where an angel says to Enoch "All these things which thou hast seen serve the dominion of His Anointed that he may be potent and mighty on the earth." In the following verses 6 and 9 the same being is called the "*Elect One,*" and the plain reference is again to Israel Personified, to the Genius of Jacob.

A few decades later, after the surrender of Jerusalem to Pompey, we find two passing mentions of the "Anointed" in the *Psalms of Solomon* ($17^{36}$, $18^6$) too trivial for quotation, aside from critical questions involved. More important is the noteworthy predominance of the national idea from first to last in these Psalms, the writer is thinking solely of his People,—upon whom "chastisement has come as upon a first-born, an only son" ($18^4$),—and very little of any representative King, for "the Lord himself is our King forever and eternally" ($17^{46}$). Still later are three or four cursory notices in *Fourth Ezra,* which are without significance since they date from the reign of Domitian (A.D. 81–96) and are inspired by the destruction of Jerusalem (A.D. 70). Likewise in that strange mosaic the *Apocalypse of Baruch* we find half a dozen such notes as "then will the Messiah begin to reveal himself" ($29^3$ in the Syriac version), "then will the lordship of my Messiah reveal itself" ($39^7$), a "lordship" to endure till "the world devoted to destruction comes to an end" ($40^3$), "and all alike will be delivered into the hands of my Servant the Messiah" ($70^9$), "when the time of my Messiah shall come" ($72^2$)—there follows a scene resembling Matt. $25^{31-46}$. But this writer also is agonizing over the Fall of Jerusalem (A.D. 70), and his side-glances at the notion of the Messiah (even if *not every* allusion were to Israel) at so late a date mean little or nothing, being provoked by the general Jewish-Christian movement of the day. The atmosphere is indeed that of John's *Revelation.*

There is then in all this scanty Messianic phraseology nothing against the view herein set forth. Certainly the rehabilitation of political Israel, the Jewish State, would be connected with violent struggles in war, in which some one or more, like Judas Makkabi, were sure to be preeminent and to merit the name of Deliverer and perhaps the title of King, the Successor of David, the "Anointed," the Messiah. How far any such a one would be dressed out in fanciful description with extraordinary or even over-earthly attributes depended upon the mood and the imagination of the writer or patriot himself. Some were as wary as a scientist of today, expecting naught far out of the common; others dropt all the guide-reins of prudence and looked and called for direct inroads of Omnipotence from on High. A few may well have understood the Son-of-Man coming on the clouds of heaven not as a poetic fancy but as a "hard-boiled" fact. Such persons we have always with us, and in times of high ferment their influence may not be unimportant. None of this affects the position thus far maintained that the National-Racial Consciousness is controlling and well-nigh exclusive in the religious literature of Israel, and specifically that the terms *Elect* and *Son-of-Man* were appropriated to the People, to the Genius of the Race, and the term "Anointed" (Messiah or Christ) when applied to an Individual designated him as the Representative or Impersonation of that People of God.

*       *       *       *       *

To return, then, from this wearisome but necessary digression, in *Enoch* the "Anointed" is none other than the *Elect,* the Son-of-Man, the People Israel. Thus it appears that *Daniel* has been taken over by *Enoch,* and this latter by the Protochristian, each refining on his predecessor's Personalization of Israel. To summarize, the phrase "Son-of-Man" is found in *Enoch* only in the so-called *Similitudes* (chs. 37–71), dating not later than 64 B.C., and there only in the section $46^2$–$71^{17}$, about 15 times. In two other places Enoch himself is addressed from on High as "son-of-man." The first case ($60^{10}$) follows the example of Ezekiel, constantly so-called, and merely illustrates the familiar Aramaic-Syriac use of the phrase, in the sense of "man," "human," without special significance, as applicable to one person as to another. In the second case ($71^{14}$) Michael tells Enoch: "Thou art the son of man who art born unto righteousness, and righteousness abides over thee and the righteousness of the Head of Days forsakes thee not." This is of course mere foolishness, "a deliberate perversion of this phrase as it appears in the *Similitudes*" (Charles, p. 183).—We need not consider the contention of Drummond, Bousset and others, following in the wake of Hilgenfeld's polemic against Volkmar, that the fifteen uses of the phrase are Christian interpolations, since if they *were,* the whole case would be closed in favor of the thesis here maintained, since *such* an interpolator, least of all men could have thought of the Gospels as history.—In the fifteen technical uses, then, we find exclusive reference to Israel idealized and personalized; the *National Individuality* is meant, the *Spirit of the Race*. This result is so decisive for any rational view of Christian Origins that it may be well to mass and re-arrange the evidence.

It is admitted by Charles, the highest orthodox authority, that in Dan. $7^{13}$, its first historical appearance, the phrase Son-of-Man is "merely symbolical of

Israel," i.e., it means Israel and nothing else. The depreciatory "merely" is merely a sign of the great scholar's reluctance to admit the weightiest exegetical fact, which must control our interpretation of a large section of literary history, but about which he maintains a deep silence.

It is not denied but conceded that Enoch derived the term from Daniel and is conscious of the Danielic sense at every turn of his own frequent usage. So much is seen in his persistent employment of the term "Head-of-Days" as applied to God, an Ethiopic rendering of the phase "Ancient-of-Days," (joined with "Son-of-Man" in Dan. $7^{13}$) and denoting of course the Supreme Being.

The main function of the Son-of-Man in *Enoch* is judging, "the sum of judgment is committed unto him" ($69^{27}$), of judgment upon all the powers of earth. But we have just seen that this is a chief function ascribed in *Daniel* to the Son-of-Man, to "the Saints," to Israel ($7^{22, 26}$).

This judgment is followed by Ruling in *Daniel* ($7^{14, 22, 27}$, already quoted). So likewise in *Enoch*: "This Son-of-Man . . . will arouse the kings and the mighty from their couches and the strong from their thrones, and will loosen the reins of the strong and grind to powder the teeth of the sinners. And he will put down the kings from their thrones and kingdoms ($46^{4, 5}$). . . . All who dwell on earth will fall down and bow the knee before him ($48^5$) . . . pain will seize them when they see that Son-of-Man sitting on the throne of his glory. And the kings and the mighty and all that possess the earth will glorify and bless and extol him who rules over all, who was hidden. For the Son-of-Man was hidden ($62^{5-7}$). . . . And with that Son-of-Man will they eat and lie down and rise up forever and ever ($62^{14}$). . . . And so there will be length of days with that Son-of-Man, and the Righteous will have peace, and the Righteous his path of uprightness in the name of the Lord of Spirits forever and ever" ($71^{17}$).—Here "length of days" instead of "eternal life" marks the interpolator (Charles, p. 184).

The term Son-of-Man is in *Enoch* equivalent to *Elect* or *Elected;* it is applied exclusively to the same Being, and this epithet, My Elect, the Elected designates Israel and Israel only (of course, as Idealized, Personalized, and even in some measure spiritualized and universalized). It seems taken directly from Isaiah, where we read "Israel Mine Elect . . . Jacob My Servant, . . . Jeshurun whom I have chosen" ($45^4, 44^2$). Indeed, the conception of Israel as "the People," the Elect of God, may justly be said to form the core not only of the Bible but of all Hebrew History. The term is used in *Enoch* about 16 times; in one other case ($61^7$) the phrase is "that One," with perhaps the same reference, though probably the allusion is to God, the "Lord of Spirits." That this "Elect One" is identical with the "Son-of-Man" is superfluously evident. Thus "Elect One will in those days sit on My throne" (says God, $51^3$); "On that day Mine Elect One will sit on the throne of glory" ($45^3$); . . . "the Elect

One has appeared" ($51^5$, as the Son-of-Man, who was "hidden," appeared); "when the Elect One shall appear" ($52^9$); "Ye mighty kings ... shall have to behold Mine Elect, how he sits on the throne of glory and judges" ($55^4$); "And the Lord of Spirits placed the Elect One on the throne of glory" ($61^8$); "Open your eyes and lift up your horns, if ye are able to recognize the Elect One!" ($62^1$) "And the Lord of Spirits seated him (the Elect) on the throne of His glory and the spirit of righteousness was poured out upon him"* ($62^2$).—Now we have already seen that the Son-of-Man does all these things, in particular it is he that "appears" and "sits on the throne of glory" and judges,—and no one will contend that there were two such "supernatural" persons sitting on the same "throne of glory" and doing the same things. Nay, it is indubitable that only one such, ideal Israel and Israel alone, is in mind of the Seer, as appears clearly in $53^6$: "And after this the Righteous and Elect One will cause the house of his Congregation to appear." Charles himself declares "the houses, etc., are the synagogues." Now in Ps. $149^1$ we read of "His praise in the assembly of the Saints," apparently the original of Enoch's "the Congregation of the Saints ('holy') and elect will be sown" ($62^8$) and "When the congregation of the righteous shall appear and sinners are judged" ($38^1$)—and the uniform allusion to Israel is unmistakable.—Someone may object, "But the Elect One is here distinguished from the house of his Congregation, the People." Precisely; just as the necessity or convenience of rhetoric often leads us to speak of John Bull or Uncle Sam as distinct from the People of England or America.

The Ethiopic *Book of Enoch* (the Slavonic *Book of the Secrets of Enoch* does not count in this discussion)† abounds in the general, often plural, terms the *righteous,* the *elect,* the *holy* (Saints), which in the *Similitudes* occur respectively 43, 32, 17 times; and Charles himself observes "there is apparently no significance in the difference" (of singular and plural). Now there can be no shadow of doubt as to the reference in these Old Testament terms, all denoting Israel only (proselytes included). As just noted, "the Elect One" may be distinguished from "the elect ones," as in $40^5$: "And the second voice I heard blessing the Elect One and the elect ones who cleave to the Lord of Spirits," and $45^3$: "On that day Mine Elect One will sit on the throne of glory ... and their souls will grow strong within them when they see Mine elect ones, etc."

None of which need surprise us. As already observed, the singular and plural are often used indifferently. Why might not the Seer think and write of the People now as a Unit (the Elect One, the Son-of-Man, the Righteous, the

* Exactly so in Is. $44^3$; "I will pour my spirit upon thy seed," says YHVH to *Israel*.
† See footnote, p. 12. *Editor.*

Anointed), and again as a Collectivity (the elect, the righteous, the [holy] Saints)?† Nor strange indeed that the texts should vary, that in 45³, where Charles reads "Mine elect ones," Dillmann and Beer should follow many mss. in reading "Mine Elect One." Sometimes the one, sometimes the other would better fit the general context of expression. As already said, we do the like today, we speak alike of Britain and the British, France and the French, Turks, Turkey, and the Turk. In this impartial use of singular and plural Enoch treads in the footprints of Daniel, who says (7²⁷), "And the kingdom and the greatness of the kingdom under the whole heaven, shall be given to the *People of the Saints of the Most High: his* kingdom is an everlasting kingdom, and all dominions shall serve and obey *him*." This is decisive, if anything can be.—The Jewish Translation here puts *their* for *his* and *them* for *him,* but merely for sake of the sense.

In truth, it seems impossible to read these *Similitudes* and not perceive that the Seer is thinking and speaking all the while of his own People Israel, the Danielic Son-of-Man, the Elect, the Righteous (Servant), the Holy (Saints), that he is telling the tale of their (or *his*) tragic history, of the nigh-coming vengeance upon all his foes (whether pagans or apostate Jews), of his exaltation to "the throne of his glory," there to sit in judgment upon all mankind and to inaugurate the new and triumphal kingdom of "the people of the Saints of the Most High; their kingdom is an everlasting kingdom, and all dominions shall serve and obey them" (Dan. 7²⁷).—The idea is the same in the Maccabean Chasidic section of *Enoch* (chs. 89–99), only there the writer contents himself with a tamer view of history, with the notion of the People as *Sheep* assigned to faithless Shepherds (89⁵⁹–90²⁵); these are finally punished for their sins, and the "Lord of the Sheep" (YHVH) assumes direct control. But the whole of the section of *Similitudes* (chs. 37–71) seems to be little more than a rather tedious elaboration of the Danielic pronouncement.

Now, Prof. Charles,* in discussing the mysterious phrase Son-of-Man, does indeed avow "its supernatural import in *Enoch*"; "The Son of Man as portrayed in the *Similitudes* is a supernatural being and not a mere man. He is not even conceived as being of human descent, as the Messiah in En. 90³⁷" (where naught whatever is said of "Messiah" or "human descent," but only "a white bull was born, with large horns"!!). Yet while he admits "The title 'the Son of Man' in Enoch was undoubtedly derived from Dan. ch. 7," he adds immediately "but a whole world of thought lies between the suggestive words

---

† The like phenomenon presents itself often in our thinking. Thus in the "realized end, means and end is their unity." "In the organism the separate organs are the means of the life of the whole, while the end is simply the organized unity, the whole itself. The means and end are thus identical, the meaning being the organism viewed as plurality, the end the same thing viewed as unity." Stace, *The Philosophy of Hegel*, p. 277.

* *Op. cit.,* Appendix B, p. 315.

in *Daniel* and the definite rounded conception as it appears in *Enoch*." Here it is the orthodox apologist speaking, not the scholarly critic, and his statement must be rejected *in toto*. It is not true that "a whole world of thought" or even a narrow intermediate state lies between the two conceptions. On the contrary, they are as near alike as two peas, they are practically the same. It is astonishing, the paucity of proof that the critic is able to bring for his "whole world of thought." Here is all he has to offer: "In *Daniel* the phrase seems merely symbolical of Israel, but in *Enoch* it denotes a supernatural person."—This "but" is quite out of place. There is no opposition, rather perfect agreement, for in *Daniel* also "it denotes a supernatural person," namely, the People of Israel *personified*, exactly as in *Enoch*.—"In the former, moreover, the title is indefinite, 'like a Son of Man,' as in Rev. 1^13, 14^14, but in *Enoch* it is perfectly definite and distinctive, 'the Son of Man.' "

That is all! Two minute considerations only—the one practically a restatement of the other—and both quite misleading! True, in *Daniel* the Being indicated by the phrase "like-Son-of-Man" does *symbolize* Israel; but it is none the less for that a "supernatural person," which indeed he is emphatically and absolutely, as the two verses 7^13-14 set forth in "perfectly definite and distinctive" manner. This "supernatural person," who reigns as an eternal king before "the Ancient-of-Days," is described as "like-son-of-man," i.e., human-like, to mark him off from the lower orders of being, the *Beasts* that have gone before (7^2-12). In *Daniel* he is a Symbol, but also a person wholly supernatural, and what more can be claimed for Enoch's representation? Nothing. The *designations* are slightly different: "like-Son-of-Man" and "the Son-of-Man," but the two *beings designated* or symbolized are exactly one and the same, Israel,—as we have seen with all desirable clearness. Enoch has adopted the Danielic symbolism *in toto* and has done nothing further than to trick it out in a variety of more or less fanciful phrases; his "Son-of-Man" is certainly a symbol of Israel.

With this wholly unwarranted distinction between the notions of the two Seers, the great scholar dims out (though unintended) the central regulative fact that Enoch is speaking throughout of the People Israel (of course, idealized and personalized) under the titles "Son-of-Man" and "Mine Elect One." It is unfortunate that he has sprinkled his pages of commentary with "Messiah" and "Messianic"*—which nowhere appear in his text or translation, save at 62^2 in his own *wrongly* inserted parenthesis "(i.e. the Messiah)," where it should be (i.e. the Elect One), expanded in his discussion, p. 16—and yet nowhere does he hint at the patent fact that the Seer is sketching a thoroughly patriotic intensely nationalistic view of the tragedy of the People Israel, and

---

* It would have been truer to his quoted text (90^37, p. 258), had he written "white bull" and "white bullish."

especially delineating the Epilogue of its wondrous exaltation to everlasting dominion and enthronement as Judge and Ruler of the Universe.

That such is the Enochian notion is plain also in certain minor features: as in the two uses of the term Anointed (Messiah, Christ). In $48^{8-10}$ (already cited, p. 15) the description of the utter ruin of "the kings of the earth and the strong" before the Son-of-Man—"as straw in fire . . . they will burn before the (holy) Saints"—closes with the words "for they *have denied* the Lord of Spirits and His Anointed." This last term has neither sense nor pertinency save as referring to Israel (Elect One, Son-of-Man),—which had indeed been persistently denied by the godless heathen—but surely not to any non-Israelitic "supernatural person," of which the Israelites themselves knew nothing whatever.—Again, in $52^4$, in speaking of "the world-powers" symbolized by mountains of iron, copper, silver, gold, soft metal and lead, which melt "as wax before the fire" "in the presence of the Elect One," the guiding angel says to Enoch "All these things serve the dominion of His Anointed (Messiah, Christ) that he may be potent and mighty on the earth"—which is clear and intelligible when and only when "His Anointed" in v. 4 means the same as "the Elect One" in vv. 6 and 9, i.e., the People Israel.

Once more, as is well-known, Michael is the guardian-angel of Israel (Dan. $12^1$, En. $20^5$ "he that is set over the best part of mankind, over the People"), but that he really symbolizes Israel, the Genius of the People itself, is evident from $40^4$, where he as "the first voice blesses the Lord of Spirits forever and ever"—and this was the special function, in history, of the People Israel. Also as much is manifest in the answer ($40^9$) of "the angel of peace" to Enoch's question "Who are these four presences?" viz. "This first is Michael, the merciful and *long-suffering*." This adjective is singularly appropriate if Michael be understood as the heavenly anti-type or *fravashi,* the *alter ego* or other self, of the People Israel; otherwise its fitness is not naked to the eye (compare Matt. $18^{10}$).

Still further, in $48^4$, it is said of the Son-of-Man "he will be the light of the Gentiles," reproducing Is. $42^6$: "I have called thee in righteousness . . . for a light of the Gentiles, to open the blind eyes, etc.," and Is. $49^6$, "I will also give thee for a light to the Gentiles." Of course, the prophet is speaking of Israel only, Israel idealized, spiritualized, personalized; why then should not Enoch mean the like by the Son-of-Man? As is well-known, Isaiah represents that Israel enlightens the world through his pure Monotheism brought as a blazing torch before the eyes of all men (in the Dispersion), while in *Enoch* the Son-of-Man distinguishes himself mainly by sweeping the Gentiles from the face of the earth. Enoch has taken over the words, without the exalted spirit of Isaiah.

That the *hiding* of the Elect One, the Son-of-Man, for so many ages, alludes (as obviously it must) to the obscure worldly position of the People in History, and his Appearance or Revelation to their coming elevation to the seat of judgment, the throne of glory, comes clearly to light in the corrected reading of En. $38^4$, where instead of "the light of the Lord of Spirits is seen on the face of the holy and righteous and elect," is substituted in Appendix D, "for the Lord of Spirits has caused the light of the face of the holy and righteous and elect to appear."—"The holy (Saints) and righteous and elect" are of course the People Israel, and for "the light of the face . . . to appear" is plainly for Israel to be revealed to the witnessing world in his true character, as "the best of mankind, the People," ordained to "everlasting dominion" over all the earth.

A natural though superficial objection may be made, that in $62^7$ it reads: "For the Son-of-Man was hidden before Him and the Most High preserved him in the presence of His might and revealed him to the elect." Here, then, the Son-of-Man is "revealed to the elect" (Israelites); how then can he be the Elect One, or Israel itself?—The difficulty is one encountered in all such abstractions and personifications, wherever a certain unity reigns and ranges throughout a manifold of diverse particulars. It is present even in our conceptions of our individual selves. The Self is the same and not the same from day to day, from year to year. We speak constantly of Self acting on Self, of changing itself and yet remaining itself.—Self-revealing is indeed familiar enough. A great duty or calamity or even passion may reveal one's self to one's self—and the revelation often well may startle: we say, I did not know nor think that I could do so, feel so, endure so; it was a great revelation.— Naturally, still more is this the case in the history of a race or a world. Prosperity and in still higher measure adversity may reveal a nation to itself, and it may be in astonishing fashion. Such facts are familiar, the slightest reminder should suffice. Witness any great war, as the World War.

Now all this was signally illustrated in the lot of Israel, actually and still more as conceived by an Apocalyptist—whose especial aim it was to waken and quicken the Israel-Consciousness. Ordained to unique distinction and honor among all nations, the Chosen People were none the less doomed to peculiar misfortune, humiliation, and ignominy throughout nearly their whole history, for hundreds of years. During all these centuries of outward abasement the Israel-Spirit (in a select few, despite the long current pessimism) remained marvelously unbroken and unquenched, the same in majesty, grandeur, and favor with God. But it did by no means appear so to the world at large or even to Israel's Actual Self, the afflicted Folk, and many a Psalmist speaking in the person of his suffering People could exclaim in varying tones of anguish, "My God, My God, why hast Thou forsaken me?" (Ps. $22^1$). All this, however, was part and parcel of the deep inscrutable purpose of YHVH, the Lord of Spirits, who was only *hiding* the Son-of-Man, the Elect Ego of Israel, from the world and even from Israel's own consciousness, in the recesses of His own counsel, so that *Ideal Israel* was Unknown in his especial mission and greatness *even to Actual Israel himself*—a literal fact.

Now at length, however—so at least in the Vision of the Seer—this age-long chapter of shame and agony was to be closed, and the true Israel to be revealed in heavenly glory as the Climax of Humanity, "the best of mankind," the Son-of-Man, the Elect of God,—and this denouement is fitly called a *revelation* not merely of the hidden Son-of-Man to the Heathen World but far more and above all to the Actual Israel-Folk itself, "to the elect" themselves, to whom *such* a transcendent exaltation was even in imagination quite unknown, "hidden," and unsuspected, who would be as much astounded by the *revelation* as the Heathen themselves—as if one should suddenly find himself heir to the Crown of England.—So it is plain that this language of the Seer is entirely in accord with the rest of his representation. The whole intent of this *Book of Similitudes*—itself an Apocalypse or Revealing—(as also of *Daniel*) was to arouse the Folk to true Self-consciousness, to *reveal* Israel to Israelites themselves by the Seer's interpretation of their past and his vision of their Empire in the ages to come.—Such is an unforced understanding of the words in question, in no wise jarring with the construction thus far given of the author's language but fitting in smoothly and closely, without any distortion.

It seems worth while to note in passing that the early Faith of Israel found no place for Immortality or any Second Life of the Individual. The blessing of God was felt to be adequately bestowed in a long and happy and earthly life continued only in one's children through following generations. But when the evil days came and the years drew nigh when all Israel must say "I have no pleasure in them," still more as the afflictions of the Chosen People smote harder and harder, and the mountain-load of their miseries was piled higher and higher as the centuries ran on and on, the question of the Justice of God, of His Keeping His sacred Promise, became more and more pressing and importunate, and the later apocalyptic writers could find no answer but in a general Resurrection of all the Elect at the close of this Age and their universal participation in "the Kingdom prepared for them since the foundation of the world." Among many testimonies that might be cited, perhaps this one from iv. Ezra 5[41] may be sufficient: "I said, Ah Lord, but Thy blessing counts only for those that reach the goal; but what shall our forefathers, what shall we ourselves and our descendants do? He spake to me: 'My judgment shall be like a (front) rank (or a "circle," in the 2[d] Arabic translation), wherein the last are not behind and the first not before.' "—A similar expression is found in the Apocalypse of Baruch, 51[13].—We may now see more clearly the force of Enoch's word "preserved" in the verse quoted (p. 23). The Son-of-Man, conceived as (or as representing) the whole race of Israel, is "preserved" by the Most High unto the Consummation at the Day of Judgment, when all Israel will be "revealed" to itself in glory, all generations at once, as the rainbow arch is flashed with instantaneous splendor across the sky.—The one momentous fact in all these matters is this, that the glorification of *Israel—and not of any being distinct from Israel*—is the Alpha and Omega of Jewish thought, that it is "the ultimate goal of the Love of God," iv. Ezra 5⁴⁰ (Gunkel).

No man ever cherished this latter idea more fervidly than the Younger Isaiah, yet he perceived clearly its illusory nature, as commonly held. Hence he did not indeed abandon it, but *transfigured* it into more than earthly splendor by Spiritualizing and Universalizing it into the Concept of the Righteous Servant, who is crushed under incalculable calamities and is immolated as a sacrifice for the sins of the whole world,—but in return is exalted to unique and over-earthly honor, to the spiritual Headship of Humanity as its Redeemer and Savior, the Torch-bearer of Jehovah to the ends of the earth. It is not at all strange that Enoch as well as Daniel proved unequal to the appropriation and mastery of this amazing conception, and that they substituted therefor the figure of Israel as "the People,"—*not* the Beasts—as Humanity, as "Son-of-Man," coming and appearing in splendor on the clouds of heaven, Adopted and Elected by the Most High, the Ancient-of-Days, unto everlasting dominion over all the earth.

Any gleam of common sense (of which such dreamers were by no means devoid) must have shown them that in such a political secular and even military glorification of "the People," not all could figure on exactly equal terms, that differences would assert and display themselves, that some would lead, and the rest must follow. There would be some Chief (like Judas Makkabi) of more or less preeminence, who would head the Elect in their victorious march to universal conquest, and converge on Himself the eyes of all gazers. Such a one would surely be regarded as the *Proxy* of "the People" and *as such* might not unnaturally be very well addressed as Messiah, and might very possibly *pose* as such. But it would be only as such Lieutenant. Another, a successor, possibly a conquering rival, would just as well receive the same title, in the same role. It is the old old story of "the King is dead: Long live the King!" Of course, there might at any time be such a Representative who, like Louis XIV, would declare "L'état c'est moi," or "I am Messiah," and such a one might well find followers and even worshippers, as did Zerubbabel, among the seers themselves. But it would still remain true that in the visions of seer and prophet it is "the People," the Racial Self, that is dominant, that it is the Racial Consciousness, the Genius of Jacob that is figured as robed in divine glory on the Judgment-seat of History, on the throne of universal dominion. Such is the Elect One, the Son-of-Man, the Anointed in the dreams of Daniel and Enoch; such is the "supernatural person,' such and none other.

While commenting on En. 90[37], Prof. Charles (like so many others) refers with much confidence to "the Messiah coming forth from the bosom of the community." But notice: the seer has beheld "a new house greater and loftier than that first," "brought" by the "Lord of the Sheep" and "set up" "in the place of the first which had been folded up." The New Jerusalem! The complete reestablishment and immeasured expansion of the Hebrew State! In this "new house," this awful presence, takes place the "judgment" (31). "And I saw that that house was large and broad and very full (36). And I saw that a white bull was born, with large horns, and all the beasts of the field and all the birds of the air feared him and made petition to him all the time" (37). *Exactly so* in v. 30, "I saw . . . all the beasts on the earth, and all the birds of the heaven, falling down and doing homage to those sheep and making petition to and obeying them in every word." The "sheep" and the "white bull" are treated precisely alike: the "sheep" are admittedly Israel; who then is the "white bull?" "And I saw till all their (different) kinds were transformed, and they all became white oxen; and the first among them became the buffalo, and that buffalo became a great animal, and had great black horns on its head; and the Lord of the Sheep rejoiced over them and over all the oxen (38). And I slept in their midst: then I awoke and saw every thing" (39).

Such (to quote Prof. Charles, p. 258) is "the Messiah coming forth from the bosom of the community. He is a man only, but yet a glorified man, for he is described as a white bull to mark his superiority to the rest of the community of the righteous who are symbolized by sheep. So far as he is a man only, he may be regarded as the prophetic Messiah, as opposed to the apocalyptic of the *Similitudes;* and yet he is not really the prophetic Messiah; for he has absolutely no function to perform, as he does not appear till the world's history is finally closed. Accordingly his presence here must be accounted for through literary reminiscence, and the Messiah-hope must be accounted as practically dead at this period (ca. 62 B.C.). The nation, in fact, felt no need of such a personality so long as they had such a chief as Judas."

A most extraordinary passage, showing what a critic's orthodox prejudice may accomplish. Note that there is no hint of Messiah or Anointed in this text, as for that matter there is none (in this scholar's sense) in the whole Bible, certainly not in the Old Testament. As the "community" were "sheep," we should naturally expect a *ram* to come forth, as in the preceding ch. 89, where Moses, Saul, Samuel, David and such are all pictured as sheep and rams. Why then a *bull?* Is he religiously "superior" to a ram?—But on turning back to ch. 85 we find Adam imaged as a "white bull," Eve as a "heifer" (*lahm* =

both bull and heifer in Ethiopic), Cain and Abel as bulls black and red, Seth as another "white bull" and his descendants as "white oxen." In ch. 86 a star (angel) falls from heaven and amid these white oxen, it corrupts them, and there follow "large and black oxen," also "many stars descend," and the earth is made ready for the deluge, being peopled with "elephants, camels and asses." Ch. 89 opens with "that white bull"—Noah, "he was born a bull but became a man," in order to build the ark, i.e., he was endowed with heavenly wisdom, the unfallen angels being pictured as "like white men" ($87^2$). Shem, Ham, and Japheth are also "three bulls," one white, one red as blood, and one black. These people the earth with all "kinds" of wild beasts and birds, "the enemies of Israel" (Charles), but there is also a "white bull" (Isaac), and this latter "begat a black wild boar and a white sheep" (Esau and Jacob), and "that sheep begat 12 sheep" (tribes of Israel). Herewith the bull disappears from the text, and there follows the piteous history of the twelve sheep guided and controlled by the "Lord of the Sheep" (YHVH). Finally, in $90^{37}$, another "white bull" is born, who does nothing at all but is feared and adored (precisely like the "sheep," Israel—v. 30) by all beasts and birds (Gentiles) till "all their kinds" are "transformed" into "white oxen."

What can all this mean but the restoration (*Apokatastasis,* Acts $3^{21}$) of the early antedeluvian Enochian Age of "white oxen," of pristine innocence before the "star" and "many stars" "fell from heaven," and the race was debauched by "the sons of God" mingling with "the daughters of men," as detailed in Gen. $6^{1-8}$? *If* "the first among them" which "became the buffalo" refers to the "white bull," as Charles thinks, then the sense evaporates. We are at a loss to see in a "buffalo with great black horns" any advance upon the "white bull"; nay, it seems a notable lapse from purity and human perfection back to more or less brutal power. Mark also that the "Lord of the Sheep" does not rejoice over this black-horned buffalo, but "over them and over all the oxen" (proselytes?). Indeed it seems impossible to believe that the Seer would figure the Messiah as first a "white bull," then as developing into a black-horned buffalo or *rhinoceros* ("unicorn," in the Septuagint rendering of the original Hebrew *rem*)! Far better to refer this "buffalo" to the pagan power, which retains a trace of savagery even after "all kinds" (of Gentiles) are "transformed" and "become white oxen." Meantime the Elect (Israel) still retain their preeminence even after the regeneration of Humanity to antedeluvian conditions, they return to the Golden Age of Abraham and the Patriarchs ("white bulls"), as is typified in the statement "a white bull was born, with large horns," whom all the birds and beasts vie in fearing and adoring (exactly as they adore the "sheep"—Israel, v. 30).—The transformation of these latter into "white oxen" is a transparent emblem of the Conversion of the Heathen (into proselytes), the return of Pagandom back to pre-Noachian Monotheism, the worship of the One and Only God. The "white bull" *stands for the renewed Israel-race,* just as the "white bulls" Adam, Seth, Noah, Shem, Abraham, Isaac all "recapitulate" in themselves the generations of their descendants.

Herewith sense and consistency are restored to the queer passage, and the "literary reminiscence" of Charles and Beer, the Buffalo-Bull—Messiah of orthodox fancy, not only becomes entirely functionless (as admitted) but also vanishes like a wraith of mist from the stage forever—a fate not by any means unfit for a purely functionless Messiah, no matter how large and black his horns—But the learned master seems entirely wrong in regarding the "Messiah-hope" "as practically dead at this period." On the contrary, it was very much alive and active, as the whole section (chs. 83–90) amply attests, though it was not an Individual human Messiah, nay, it was rather the *Anointed People* of God.

\*    \*    \*    \*    \*

The Enochian notion of the Son-of-Man was "undoubtedly derived from Daniel vii," where the phrase is "merely symbolical of Israel." *Throughout the* Similitudes of Enoch *the identity of the Saints, the Elect, and the Son-of-Man with each other and with the People Israel is fixed beyond all possible doubt.*

Chapter Three

# The Title Son-of-Man in the New Testament

## I. IN THE SYNOPTIC GOSPELS AND ACTS*
### i. Disputed Meanings

We now come to the New Testament use of the term in debate, "*Son-of-Man*"; but first must present what have been the historic interpretations of the Gospel use of this title.—A theme of endless discussion with seemingly no possibility of any even half-way satisfactory result. As far back as Origen opinions branched out wide asunder. He himself thought it needless (perhaps because hopeless?) to seek any specific reference, as to a particular individual, deeming that "man" in general, humanity at large, was meant† which would seem to be positively fatal to orthodoxy, at least to the conception of an historic Christ, whom it would seem to dissolve as an individual into the broad waters of the species *homo,* all mankind. With plausibility it may be said, "Humanity (human interest or welfare) is Lord of the Sabbath," but it is absurd for any individual to say "I am this Humanity," this human interest or welfare in general. It calls for a deeper metaphysic than is found in the New Testament to unify the concepts of the particular Individual and the Universal, to show that Each is All and the Many identical with the One in the Unconscious. Origen could not, then, popularize his profound insight. Jerome‡ thought "man" or a "human being (*anthropos*) must mean Mary, and this became a common interpretation! Chrisostom,§ Augustine,¶ Cyprian‖ took "man" in a generic sense.

Grotius* fastened on the notion "Man is Lord also of the Sabbath" as the key to the secret, and this view gained currency. Bolten† first appealed to the

* Also (briefly) *Revelation*, for which see Subsection ii. *Editor.*
† Migne, Vol. 13, col. 1537.
‡ Commentary on Ps. 85.
§ Migne, Vol. 59, column 223.
¶ *Contra Arion*, 18.
‖ Commentary on Matt. 12³².
* *Opera Theologica*, "Critica Sacra" 6, p. 445 f. published posthumously, 1679.
† *Der Bericht des Matt.* (1792). Comment on Matt. 9⁶.

Aramaic-Syriac form *Bar-nasa* as a familiar designation of "individual man."
But Paulus,‡ with more fidelity to apparent New Testament sense, went back
to the veiw of Coccejus,§ that it meant "this man, I." Herder¶ elevated the
meaning into that of "Ideal Man," which flattered the Christian consciousness
and won wide acceptance though of course without any critical or logical
justice.

Hofmann in his famous *Schriftbeweis*‖ interpreted it, with the concurrence
of Cremer,* as the Coming Man or Man-to-Come (recalling the Old Testament *Habba,* applied to a "prince-to-come," *nagid habba,* in a very obscure and
probably corrupt passage, Dan. $9^{26}$). Strauss† saw in it a messianic title, and
Ewald‡ pointing wisely to Dan. $7^{13}$ and Enoch 37 to 71, was followed by
Renan,§ Beyschlag¶ and Baldensperger.‖ The great de Wette* thought it referred to the lowliness and human sympathy of Jesus! He was followed incautiously by Baur,† who assigned a meaning as "emphatically low" as Herder's had been "emphatically high." Colani‡ and Hilgenfeld§ were of the few to
follow the great Tuebinger (Baur), though Hilgenfeld still kept an eye on
Dan. $7^{13}$. Ritschl¶ coined the queer conceit that the title was used to conceal
Messianic claims! Holtzmann‖ agreed that there were *two* Messianic meanings kept secret till the Caesarean incident (in Mark $8^{27\text{-}29}$). Keim* thought
that Jesus gradually grew out beyond this early mystifying title. Hase† held it
was used first to conceal, then to reveal (a poor blade that won't cut both
ways)! Charles‡ concluded that this title "adopted by our Lord" involved a
fusion of the two notions, the Isaianic Servant of YHVH and the Danielic
Son-of-Man, but with a deeper, hidden, spiritual significance. Wendt* deemed

‡ Exegetisches Handbuch, 1830.
§ *Schol. in Matt.,* $8^{20}$.
¶ *Christliche Schriften,* Vol. 5, p. 4 (1796).
‖ Vol. 1, Part 2, p. 53 (1853).
* Wörterbuch, p. 846 ff (1866).
† *Leben Jesu* (1835).
‡ *Geschichtl. Christus,* p. 202 (1855).
§ *Vie de Jésus,* p. 131 (1863).
¶ *Christologie* (1866).
‖ *Selbstbewusstsein Jesu,* p. 169 (1892).
* Commentary on Matt. $8^{20}$ (1828?).
† *Z. w. Th.,* 1860, p. 277.
‡ *Jesus Christ et les croyances messianiques,* p. 74 ff. (1864).
§ *Z. w. Th.,* 1863, p. 327.
¶ Theol. Jahrb. 1851, p. 514.
‖ *Z. w. Th.,* 1865, p. 212 ff.
* *Gesch. Jesu* 2, p. 376 (1873).
† *Leben Jesu,* p. 441 (1854).
‡ *Op. cit.,* p. 315–6.
* Lehre Jesu, (1890).

it a riddle used to provoke thought, somewhat like Charles. Holsten§ apparently in despair, took it as merely an equivalent to Messiah; but Dalman¶ could not believe it a Messianic title. Gunkel ‖ regarded it as meaning "man," but as a secret title, of Babylonian origin, used in apocalyptic circles. Fiebig* considered it a familiar designation used ambiguously to mislead(!) the folk, who referred to "man" what Jesus meant for himself! Sanday† and Driver‡ inclined to Charles's view. Others, as Hoekstra,§ Carpenter¶ and James Drummond,‖ looked upon it as the symbol of a coming ideal society—a reminiscence of Herder. Bauer,* Volkmar† and others, catching a faint glimmer of the true state of the case, viewed it as a creation of the Evangelist. More recently, Schulthess‡ thinks "the Son of Man" is a phrase of modesty or humility, a submissive way of saying "I," or "some one" or "one of us," and that the Greek form is framed on Daniel $7^{13}$. This last is a half-way recognition of the patent truth, but he shrinks from applying it, he does not mention Israel, he will have it that Jesus was too humble to say "I," and so hid Himself under the Danielic phrase;—as if Napoleon modestly avoided "I," and merely spoke of the "Conqueror-Monarch of all the world!"

And now to return to Professor Charles§ and his statement:—"This title with its supernatural powers *was adopted by our Lord*," a statement for which we do not today find a single iota of proof. Various New Testament passages are listed, but all these are simply the dicta of entirely unknown writers, and so far as we know without the slightest biographical basis. It is idle today to assert that historicity can be a matter of general consent. Perhaps, indeed, at the date of Charles's work this assumption was admissible, but a sea-change has come over criticism since then. So we repeat, scholarship *today* can find no good reason to ascribe any specified Gospel oracle to an historical Jesus. Professor Charles held that "just as His kingdom in general formed a standing protest against the prevailing Messianic ideas of temporal glory and dominion, so the title 'the Son of Man' assumed a deeper spiritual significance; and this change we shall best apprehend if we introduce into the Enoch conception of the Son of Man the Isaiah conception of the Servant of Jehovah.

§ *Z. w. Th.*, 1891, p. 1, ff.
¶ *Worte Jesu*, p. 191 ff., (1898).
‖ *Z. w. Th.*, 1899, p. 581 ff.
* *Der Menschensohn*, p. 61 ff., (1901).
† Hastings Dict. of Bible, Vol. 2, p. 622 f., (1899).
‡ *Ibid.*, Vol. 4, p. 582, (1902).
§ *De Benaming de Zoon des Menschens*, (1866).
¶ First Three Gospels, p. 383 ff., (1890).
‖ J. Th. St., (1901).
* Kritik der evan. Geschichte, Vol. 3, p. 1 ff., (1842).
† Gustav Volkmar, 1809–1893. The appropriate reference has not come to light. *Editor.*
‡ *Zur Sprache der Evangelien.* 1922.
§ *Op. cit.*, p. 315.

*These two conceptions, though outwardly antithetic, are through the trans-*
*formation of the former reconciled and fulfilled in a deeper unity—in the New*
*Testament Son of Man."*

Such (with his own italics) is the illustrious scholar's conception of the
fusion of these two polar opposites and where in conservative biblical criticism has anything been better said in many a day? He here makes the nearest
approach yet made by orthodoxy to the understanding of the New Testament.
*Nevertheless* he remains far from the goal, even separated from it by an im-
passible chasm. For he neglects entirely the fundamental and indispensable
fact that the "supernatural person," the Son-of-Man, as well as the neither
more nor less supernatural Servant of YHVH is a towering Eponym, a supreme Abstraction, the Human Figure of a National Spirit, a Racial Soul.
Both in *Daniel* and in *Enoch,* as already seen, there can be no shadow of doubt
that such is the only meaning of such technical terms as Son-of-Man and Mine
Elect One. Such also is the meaning, now rarely denied by competent scholarship of the Isaianic Servant of YHVH.

Charles was right in assuming a fusion of these two notions as the basis of
the Christian Doctrine. The fusion was indeed already accomplished or at
least implicit in Isaiah, but it was not then made the point of departure for a
Propaganda, for a religious crusade. Isaiah was half a millennium ahead of
his age, and "he who anticipates is lost." Even in Daniel's and Enoch's times
the religious consciousness had not developed up to a stage ready for the out-
burst of the great Evangel, the world-wide proclamation of the "Eternal Gospel," "Fear God and give *Him* glory" (Rev. 14[7]). The Hellenizing of Western Asia and Judaism had not yet done its work. The wild olive was indeed
grafted on the tame, but was not yet firmly enrooted, not yet ready to bear
fruit.

Another view is set forth by N. Schmidt in a profoundly learned contribution to the *Encyclopaedia Biblica.* Schmidt held that the Aramaic original was
used by Jesus only in its proper sense of "a man," but yet "in such a startling
way," in speaking of natural "rights and privileges," as "to create, contrary to
his intention, the impression among later interpreters that he referred to himself," which then "found its way into the Gospels" "through Greek translations." Thus some general statement, like "man must die but he will rise
again" was misconstrued and exaggerated into a prediction of the Son-of-
Man's (Jesus's) death and resurrection after three days. Into the pros and
cons we cannot enter here.

It is interesting to observe how even such an honest and erudite master as
Schmidt has been entangled and trapped by his own premises. It would be
hard to imagine a better historic and linguistic treatment than that given in
his article. Even so he writes:—"Ibn Ezra interpreted *bar-enas* (of Daniel) as

referring to the People of Israel. In modern times this view has been maintained by many scholars.* Yet a symbolic representation of 'a human regime'
or an 'ideal humanity,' savors more of modern humanitarian ideas than of
the concrete conceptions of Semitic antiquity." Granted, but nothing has been
hinted about "ideal humanity" in treating of Daniel. The sole point was that
the seer, writing from a religious point of view regarded Israel as so far superior to the heathen (and with justice) that, having symbolized the four
pagan powers by beasts, he was logically bound to symbolize Israel by a man-
like being, "like-son-of-man"; not otherwise could he typify the superiority of
Monotheism over Polytheism. There is no question at all of "human regime"
or "ideal humanity" or "modern humanitarianism," but only of Israel's infinite religious preeminence in the eyes of God.†

And so the perfectly correct insight ascribed to the great Rabbi (Ibn Ezra),
who certainly was a most competent judge, is dismissed without further consideration! Now we have seen that beyond any doubt, in *Daniel* and *Enoch,*
Son-of-Man means the People or the Genius of Israel personified and idealized. And what could be more in accord with the "conceptions of Semitic
antiquity"? The old Testament literally swarms with more or less similar
representations. In Amos $5^2$ Israel is portrayed as a maiden: "The virgin of
Israel is fallen, she shall rise no more," and hence it became the habit (says
Driver) to personify thus a city or community. The Second Isaiah is unex-
celled in his fondness for personification (Driver, *Life and Times of Isaiah,*
p. 184). It would insult the reader's intelligence to multiply instances.—We repeat, after figuring the heathen powers as beasts, it was almost unavoidable
for Daniel, and after him Enoch (in *Similitudes,* B.C. 94-64), to introduce
"the People" Israel as a Human Being, a "supernatural person," dwelling in
the presence and especial favor of the Ancient-of-Days, of God Most High.
What else could he consistently, appropriately do?

Such a happy precedent once established, what was there left but to go and
do likewise? The usage of Enoch (*Similitudes*) and of IV Ezra follows as
naturally after that of Daniel as Summer follows after Spring. And Daniel's

---

* Schmidt lists in a footnote the following modern critics who agree that he who is "like-
son-of-man" in Daniel $7^{13}$ symbolizes the Hebrew people:—

Hofmann, Hitzig, Wittichen, Colani, Kuenen, Straton, Keim, Vernes, Smend, Toy, Marti,
Meinhold, Bevan, Réville, Dalman, Schürer, Gunkel, Wellhausen, Leitzmann, Charles, Prince,
Driver, Curtis, Hahn. *Editor.*

† Prof. Schmidt's own view Encyclopaedia Biblica, 1903 is very near related to the view he re-
jects. He regards Daniel's "manlike being as an angel and more particularly Michael, guardian-
angel of Israel." Similar the view of Grill—"a most exalted personal intermediary between God
and the world, and a transcendent prototype of the God-pleasing humanity to be realized in the
People of the Most High." (*Untersuchungen über die Entstehung des vierten Evangeliums.* 1902.)
This last is rather a rhetorical florish, but the Son-of-Man as Israel personified might readily fuse
with Michael, Israel's guardian-angel, *numen, alter Ego, fravashi,* other Self and Representative
before God in heaven. A case of Tweedledum and Tweedledee.

precedent, whether or not savoring of Semitic "concrete conceptions," was certainly and admittedly a *fact*. It does not, then, call for the learning and intuition of Ibn Ezra to see that *bar-nasha* (Son-of-Man) refers and must refer to Israel and Israel only. To suppose a "supernatural person" functioning as does the Son-of-Man, without any peculiar relation to Israel, yet constantly called "Mine Elect One," the well-known peculiar title of Jacob, is to suppose the inconceivable, and is possible only at the bidding of overmastering prejudice.

Well, then, if the title has this reference past all dispute in *Daniel* and *Enoch,* and if the New Testament borrows it from these seers, as even Charles, with so many others, concedes (*"in adopting the title 'Son of Man' from* Enoch, Jesus made at the outset supernatural claims, etc," p. 316), what is the presumption as to the meaning in the New Testament? Could the Evangelists have failed to see the obvious reference of the phrase in *Daniel* and *Enoch*? When Matthew quoted from Hosea 11[1], "Out of Egypt have I called my Son," was it possible for him to overlook the rest of the verse, "When *Israel* was a child, then I loved him and called my Son out of Egypt . . .?"

It seems out of any question that the glorification of Israel was conspicuous in the minds and hearts of the earliest Christians, who were certainly Jews, however hellenized. Not only is the general tenor of the New Testament scriptures unambiguous, not only does the general historic situation appear to compel this assumption, but there is also direct and unequivocal testimony. In Acts 1[6] we read, "They therefore, when they were come together, asked Him, saying, Lord, dost thou at this time restore the kingdom to Israel?" We need not inquire who wrote these words, whether Luke or the Redactor; we need not ask whether the Apostles ever put such a question. It is enough that it was deemed natural, proper and fit to be laid on their lips. Neither does it affect the case that the glorification underwent a complete *transfiguration* in the breasts of the primitive propagandists. This does indeed seem to be the most important single item in the history of Christian Origins, but it does not affect, or at least does not invalidate, the fact under consideration, that Israel and the exaltation of Israel were in *some* form or other dominant in the thoughts of the earliest exponents of the new faith.

So much granted, in their constant use of works (as of *Isaiah, Daniel,* and *Enoch*) that were occupied almost wholly with that same Israel, was it possible for them to overlook or disregard the obvious and repeated allusions of such striking phrases as Mine Elect One and the Son-of-Man? If so, then we may as well close this controversy at once, for in that case we should be dealing with an utterly lawless body of facts, in which it would be impossible to find any general and probable premise as a warrant for any conclusion. We assume, then, unhesitatingly that these primitive propagandists must have known and felt that the seers were thinking and speaking of Israel, idealized and perhaps generalized, in discoursing of the Messiah Mine Elect (as in Luke $9^{35}$, $23^{35}$) and particularly of the Son-of-Man. That these Revivalists should also be Refashioners was natural enough; they may have desired to transform the old profoundly and completely, from top to bottom, to usher in a "new creation"; but if they had any intelligence at all (and their literary remains as well as their historic achievements attest intelligence of high order), they could not have mistaken nor neglected entirely the original sense of the phrases they constantly exploited—a sense, be it repeated, with which they were in lively sympathy, and *the* sense that made the phrases worth quoting. In the absence of positive proof to the contrary, we must hold fast to this assumption as the only working hypothesis.

### ii. An Inductive Analysis

But is it possible to proceed along such lines while interpreting Christian Scriptures? We shall see.—The term Son-of-Man occurs very irregularly in the New Testament: 82 times in the Gospels (30 of these in *Matthew*, 14 in *Mark*, 25 in *Luke*, 13 in *John*) as a *self*-designation of the Jesus, once in *Acts* ($7^{56}$), once in *Hebrews* ($2^6$), twice in *Revelation* ($1^{13}$, $14^{14}$). These latter scattering uses present little difficulty. In the words of the dying Stephen,* "I see . . . the Son-of-Man standing on the right hand of God," we seem to hear an echo of Enoch's conception of the Son-of-Man, the Elect One, "under the wings of the Lord of Spirits" ($39^7$)—as Israel hid in the shadow of YHVH's wings, Pss. $17^8$, $36^7$, $57^1$, $61^4$, $63^7$, $91^4$,—who "standeth before the Lord of Spirits"; at the very least, the words are in full accord with the Enochian idea, and so we need pause no longer upon them.—In *Hebrews* we have only a quotation from Ps. $8^4$, in which son-of-man merely means man the species. Such seems also the case in Rev. $1^{13}$, where "one like son-of-man" means a human-like figure; but in $14^{14}$, "and in the cloud one sitting like unto son-of-man," ready to reap the earth, recalls at once the Danielic vision ($7^{13}$), where one "like Son-of-Man came with the clouds near unto the Ancient-of-Days." The function of this Son-of-Man was to *judge* the world (Dan. $7^{18, 22, 26}$), which is poetically denoted in *Revelation* as reaping the earth (as in Jer. $51^{33}$, "the time of harvest shall come for her"—Babylon, and Joel $3^{13}$, "Put ye in the sickle, for the harvest is ripe"). Thus the later vision corresponds quite well with the earlier, and it is plain that as the Person in the one case represents the People Israel, so must it naturally in the other.

But it is in the Gospels that the phrase in question finds its home, always

---

* Is it an accident that the first to wear the *crown* of martyrdom is named *crown*—Stephanos?

as a *self-designation* of the Jesus. The query that vexes critics, and to which each renders his own answer, always different from all others, is: What did Jesus mean to indicate by this strange usage? or Why choose such a term of self-denotation? It becomes plain enough on reading the foregoing sketch that no satisfactory answer has been extorted by the inquisitions of 1600 years, nor does it seem possible to elicit such an answer.

In scores of cases the reference of Jesus to Himself (in the Gospels) is plain past all debate, and yet in the same breath the most supreme over-earthly and even divine functions and authority are openly claimed. "But *I* say unto you, etc."; "Heaven and earth shall pass away, but my words shall not pass away" (Matt. 24$^{35}$); "When the Son-of-Man shall come in his glory, and all the angels with him, then shall he sit on the throne of his glory" (Matt. 25$^{31}$); "All authority is given unto me in heaven and on the earth" (Matt. 28$^{18}$). Does this sound like modesty or humility? To be sure, if the Jesus were really this "supernatural person," no fault could be found, but what could be more awry than the Judge of all the earth, second only, if at all, to the Most High Himself, proclaiming his world-wide supremacy at every turn, and yet too humble to say "I," veiling all personal reference under the title of the Highest possible Honor, as used by Seer and prophet?!—Much more rational the attempt of Reitzenstein* to find an Iranian (or of Gunkel, a Babylonian) origin for the title, which however looks much like carrying owls to Athens, for the Hebraic sources of explanation seem ample—as soon as one abandons the groundless assumption that the Gospels are biographic and report the actual habit of the Jesus.

On the contrary, the uses are in the main self-explanatory when regarded as free inventions of the Evangelist, in earnest effort to present a "truth severe by fairy fiction dressed." Consider the most impressive of all the eighty-odd passages, the vision of the final judgment (Matt. 25$^{31-46}$): "But when the Son-of-Man shall come in his glory, and all the angels with him, then shall he sit on the throne of his glory; and before him shall be gathered all the nations." The conception is exactly that presented in Dan. 7$^{13}$, but the phrasing seems taken directly from *Enoch,* where "he shall sit on the throne of his glory" is a pet expression. Moreover the separation into sheep and goats also recalls Enoch, who represents the elect (Israel) as sheep in the final judgment: "in the midst of those sheep before the judgment took place," "and the Lord of the Sheep rejoiced over them" (90$^{31, \, 38}$). The designation of the "Gentiles" as goats is a very natural refinement due to the Evangelist, perhaps suggested by Ezek. 34$^{17}$, between sheep and sheep, the *rams* and the he-*goats!* In what follows (Matt. 25$^{34}$), the Genius of Israel (Son-of-Man) calls the sheep to

* See *Poimandres,* p. 81 (1904), where Reitzenstein construes "Son-of-Man" as son of the syncretistic Greek god Anthropos. *Editor.*

"inherit the kingdom prepared for you from the foundation of the world," the burden of the Old Testament and especially of Dan. 7 (as of IV Ezra and other Apocalypses), which tell of His "dominion and glory and a kingdom," "his kingdom that which shall not be destroyed," that "the Saints of the Most High shall receive the kingdom and possess the kingdom forever," "and judgment was given to the Saints of the Most High, and the time came that the Saints possessed* the kingdom," and "the kingdom shall be given to the Saints of the Most High: his kingdom is an everlasting kingdom, all dominions shall serve and obey him." Clearly the vision in *Matthew* is only a poetized intensified version of that in *Daniel*.

But you say, "It is the Son-of-Man that addresses these sheep, hence he must be distinct from them." Yes, as distinct as France, Germany, Britain from the French, the Germans, the British, or as Uncle Sam from Americans. The poetic figure, the Impersonation, *required* this superficial inconsistency, such as pervades all high-wrought emotional literature, from Homer to Bret Harte and Kipling. What reasonable man would take the slightest exception, if in a great national emergency an orator or a poet should represent the *Spirit of his people* as crying aloud and summoning every man to arms? The National Soul is felt as one, as all in the Whole and all in every part.

Hence it is not strange that the Son-of-Man, the Israel-Spirit, declares "I was hungry, and ye gave me to eat," etc., and explains, "Inasmuch as ye did it unto one of these *my brethren* even these least, ye did it unto me." The Communal Self pervades all alike. All Israel (universalized, of course) is one Brotherhood, one Body (the "Body of Christ," "the commonwealth of Israel," so prominent in *Ephesians* $1^{23}$, $4^{12}$ etc. and *Colossians* $1^{18}$, $2^{17}$ etc.): hence there is all propriety in such terms as "my brethren," "my children," applied to all.

This passage is surely one of the most dramatic and poetic in either Testament, and as here interpreted it can give no serious offense. It is only a glowing picture of the glorification of Israel, for which the Racial Soul had been yearning and striving for a thousand years, which it felt had been definitely irrevocably promised by God Himself, whose realization had been at least strangely delayed century after century after century, while the Saints suffered patiently every form of misery and contumely,—hungry and thirsty, dispersed and naked, sick and in prison, the butt and the buffet of ungodly sinners in all the four quarters of earth. The banishment of these persecutors into everlasting torment (Matt. $25^{41,\,46}$) is only a vivid picture of the overthrow of heathen power upon the long-awaited establishment of Israel's "Kingdom of God." As such it certainly expresses a bitter feeling of resentment and even hate, but seems not unnatural under such trying conditions, and of course is not to be taken literally but only as extravagant declamation,

* *N.B.* The same Hebrew verb *yarash* is translated indifferently *inherit* and *possess*.

as high-wrought poetry of passion. Had they possessed the ancients' power of imagination, the opposing peoples in the late world war would have denounced each other in similar terms.

Understood, however, in the accepted orthodox sense, as the words of the Jesus, whether actually spoken by him or imposed upon his lips by disciples, as seeming to fit there, these verses are simply intolerable. Yet it is an essential part of the received tradition, it has shaped and still shapes the belief, the thoughts, the speech and in a measure the lives of myriads of the most earnest Christians; it has even brought into literature and hymnody such lines as these, under the name of Isaac Watts:

> What bliss will fill their ransomed souls,
> When they in glory dwell,
> To see the sinner as he rolls
> In quenchless flames of hell.

Nor is the Matthean passage alone in the New Testament. It has parallels enough. It is the inspiration of nearly the whole book of *Revelation.* Nor can the idea be extruded from the body of the Christian faith as at present taught and defended. Yet it is equally unwarranted and atrocious, the necessary outgrowth of a hopelessly irrational exegesis and understanding of the New Testament.—It is surely one merit of the present treatment, to remove at least one most unsightly blot from the face of Scripture Interpretation.

The obvious explanation here given applies with equal force to many other passages that speak of the Son-of-Man sitting on the throne of his glory, the exact expression so often found in *Enoch.** Thus Matt. $19^{28}$: "Ye that have followed me, in the regeneration when the Son-of-Man shall sit on the throne of his glory, ye also shall sit upon twelve thrones, judging the twelve tribes of Israel." Here the word "regeneration" (palingenesis) not found in classic Greek or Greek versions of scripture or Apocrypha, but only here and in Titus $3^5$, expresses an idea prominent in *Enoch,* as already shown.—After Israel was represented as Son-of-Man enthroned in glory and judging all the earth, it was a natural compliment to the (imaginary) Twelve to seat them on twelve thrones, to judge the twelve tribes of Israel. An inconsistency, indeed, but only such as must pervade all such forms of poetic imagery.

\* \* \* \* \*

In continuing, let us pay attention first of all to the multiple usages in the *Synoptics,* beginning with texts that are found, virtually identical, as many as three times.

First, Matt. $16^{27}$: "The Son-of-Man shall come in the glory of his Father with

---

\* Possibly not taken *directly* from Enoch; it may have been a choice phrase current in the large body of literature in some way associated with that name,—or even in common speech.

his angels; and then shall he render unto every man according to his deeds. Verily I say unto you, There are some of them that stand here, who shall in no wise taste of death, till they see the Son-of-Man coming in his kingdom." Again the words are Enochic; also the idea of the judgment and of the kingdom. There can be no question as to the meaning,—it is the long-delayed glorification of Israel, as now so familiar from Dan. 7.—The passage has been a sore trial, a heavy cross, to commentators; for undeniably the glorification (in any secular sense) has not taken place; only the spiritualized Israel has triumphed in the world-wide proclamation of Monotheism and the Holy Scripture.—Parallel are Mark 13$^{26}$ Luke 9$^{26}$.

Once more (Matt. 26$^{64}$), before the Sanhedrin, "Ye shall see the Son-of-Man sitting at the right hand of Power and coming on the clouds of heaven." Unmistakably the allusion is to Enoch ("sitting, etc.") and to Dan. 7$^{13}$, "came with the clouds of heaven one like Son-of-Man," words certainly written of Israel. In Ps. 110$^{1}$ ("YHVH Saith unto my Lord, Sit thou at my right hand Until I make thy foes thy footstool, etc.") the reference is to Israel as represented by its King or ruler, precisely as the King or the Crown stands for Britain.—Parallels are Matt. 24$^{30}$, Mark 8$^{38}$, 14$^{62}$, Luke 21$^{27}$, 22$^{69}$, also Acts 7$^{56}$—on which we need not dwell.—In John 5$^{27}$ there is another allusion to Daniel (and Enoch?) in "he gave him authority to execute *judgment,* because he is Son-of-Man"—the familiar idea.—These 12 cases from the Gospels* with the other two (in Acts and Rev.) make over 16%, nearly ⅙, of the New Testament usage, where there can be no doubt as to the meaning, the reference to Israel (personified, generalized) being sure and certain. The question arises, Shall we introduce some other more casual sense into the other passages? We cannot reasonably do so, unless it be definitely required,—we must use the meaning already found wherever possible. Let us see.

Very important in the minds of most is the declaration (Matt. 9$^{6}$, Mark 2$^{10}$, Luke 5$^{24}$) "that the Son-of-Man has authority on earth to pardon sins" (of course, against God). Here is truly superhuman power, but what of it? If it be the precise function of Israel, the Son-of-Man, as set forth in *Enoch* and *Daniel,* to judge all the earth and to exercise absolute dominion over the whole world, how could it be otherwise than that he should have power to pardon as well as to punish? The case seems too clear for argument, yet it should be noted that not only is it plain that such a "supernatural person" would naturally have the power in question, but likewise it is exceeding hard to see how any other could have it.

Again (Matt. 12$^{8}$, Mark 2$^{28}$, Luke 6$^{5}$) it is said, "the Son-of-Man is Lord even of the Sabbath." An exalted pretension, but why not? The Danielic-Enochic Son-of-Man may very well have possessed such lordship as part and

* Beginning the count with Matt. 25$^{31}$, on p. 36.

parcel of his universal kingship, nay, of his sole sonship to God (Hosea 11[1], Ex. 4[22], Ps. of Sol. 18[4])—but who else, save God Himself?

Once more (Matt. 17[22], Mark 9[31], Luke 9[44]), "the Son-of-Man is delivered (*not* betrayed) into the hands of men," to be put to death, but to rise again the third day. This surrender into the hands of men had long been executed upon Israel delivered into the hands of Assyrians, Chaldeans, Persians, Greeks, and Romans; nevertheless it was the abiding faith that it was only for a time, two times, and the dividing of a time (Dan. 7[25]), here represented as 3 days* or "on the third day," after which the Resurrection to glory was to follow. It was an achievement of the Christians to represent in detail the humiliation and subsequent exaltation of Israel (personified and idealized) as a physical Death and Resurrection, around which clustered all their hopes and nearly all their speech; but the idea, so elevated into complete dominance, was not new nor original with the Christians; it had already been set forth by *Isaiah* (ch. 53) in very impressive though very inadequate fashion.—The passages seem fully explained by these reflections. *But how can they be explained otherwise?*

In Matt. 20[18], Mark 10[33], Luke 18[31] this delivery is predicted, to be followed by Death and Resurrection. This repetition need not detain us, since the foregoing remarks apply in full force. Also in Matt. 26[23], Mark 14[21], Luke 22[22] we find still another such announcement, which may also be passed by as presenting nothing peculiar or of especial interest. The notion of the surrender of the Son-of-Man into hostile hands, once formulated, other details would be added to enliven the picture and give it plausibility. To be sure, these might not be quite consistent with the original sense of the figure, but that counted little. It is common to press a metaphor, to push it too far, and the prophetic words in Ps. 41[9], "Yea, mine own familiar friend, in whom I trusted, Who did eat of my bread, hath lifted up his heel against me," stood gazing at the Evangelist and demanding fullfillment.

Similarly Matt. 26[45], Mark 14[41], Luke 22[48], the actual surrender of the Son-of-Man, is only a necessary detail in the picture.—Herewith then is closed the list of examples to be found each reported in all the *Synoptics*. About 30 cases have been considered thus far, over ⅓ of all, and in no case have we found any occasion to modify our interpretation: the notion of personified idealized Israel yields consistent sense in every case, nor does any other meaning in any case appear really apposite.

*     *     *     *     *

We pass on now to cases of double or single usage. The first and one of the most striking is in Matt. 8[20], Luke 9[58], the reply of the Jesus: "Foxes have holes and birds have nests, but the Son-of-Man hath not where to lay his head."

* The apocalyptic cryptic number (Geheimzahl)—says Gunkel.

Such a reply to the profession, "I will follow wherever Thou go," does not appear courteous or well-timed in a Teacher seeking to win followers, nor does it seem to fit in well with the facts in the case. Nowhere is any hint that Jesus was destitute in any fashion or degree. The words seem to lack all pertinence to the actual situation, if the Son-of-Man be regarded as an Individual.—But now suppose that Israel be hinted, Israel before glorification. The Nation was deported from its ancestral home in Palestine, scattered through all foreign lands, an outcast, a wanderer on the face of the earth.

> Ay, and a rav'nous hunger the brave earth over ensues him,
> Wand'ring lone, unhonor'd o' mortals alike and Immortals.

With eminent poetic fitness it might be said of this Israel that he "hath not where to lay his head."

A number of sayings refer distinctly to the *Coming* of the Son-of-Man. Thus Matt. 10$^{23}$, "till the Son-of-Man come"; Luke 12$^{40}$, "in an hour that ye think not, the Son-of-Man cometh"; Luke 17$^{24}$, "So (sudden as Lightning) shall be the Son-of-Man in his day"; Luke 17$^{26}$, "as in the days of Noah, so shall it be also in the days of the Son-of-Man"; Luke 17$^{30}$ "so likewise shall it be in the day when the Son-of-Man is revealed"; Matt. 24$^{27}$ "so (sudden as lightning) shall be the coming (parousy, presence) of the Son-of-Man"; Matt. 24$^{37, 39}$ "so (unexpected) shall be the coming of the Son-of-Man"; Matt. 24$^{44}$ "for in what hour ye think not, the Son-of-Man cometh." These nine all present one single idea, that the Coming (presence or Apparition) of the Son-of-Man (in the clouds of heaven) shall be sudden and dazzling as a flash of lightning—a strict literalization of the famous verse in Dan. 7$^{13}$: "I saw in the night-visions and lo! there came with the clouds of heaven one like-Son-of-Man, and he came even to the Ancient-of-Days, and they brought him near before him." With Daniel this visualized the sudden uplift and victory of Israel (by some unspecified Divine assistance) over the heathen world-powers, and the establishment of his supremacy over all the earth. With the Evangelist it can harly have failed to mean something similar, though with what extravagances his fancy, fed on *Enoch,* may have fringed the Daniel-idea, is more than one can say.

Certainly the basic notion of the exaltation of Israel must have been conspicuously present, and there is in these apocalyptic passages, as in 1 Thess. 4$^{15-17}$ and *Revelation,* comparatively little to suggest any notable idealization or spiritualization by the authors. The imagery in Matt. 24$^{1-31}$ and parallels is very sensuous, yet we can hardly be sure that it was meant to describe anything very marvelous. These religious composers were concerned relatively little with facts, their imaginations darted aloft and sailed freely in the airiest heights and flights of fancy. The Psalmist assures us that the mountains skipped like rams, and the little hills like lambs ($114^4$), that YHVH made the cedars "skip like a calf," "Lebanon and Sirion like a young rhinoceros" (Ps. $29^6$), yet we can scarcely believe that he seriously meant to charge the mountains with such highly undignified sophmoric behavior. Of this, however, we may be sure, that the Gospel writers* had pored over Daniel ("which was spoken of through Daniel the prophet," Matt. $24^{15}$), and that they expected a more or less violent elevation of Israel (more or less idealized) to the summits of earthly power and dominion.

If some one object to understanding as the Israel-Folk the high-wrought imagery in these apocalyptic passages, we ask him how then understand it? Does any informed person dream that these forecasts of the immediate future have ever had or will ever have the least symptom of "literal or personal fulfillment?" Well, then, what shall we say of them? Call them "Messianic expectations" and then pass them quietly by, the less said the better? Such is the prevailing method, but is it satisfactory?—True, it cannot be denied that in all ages men have indulged in wildly extravagant hopes and have been incautiously led into all manner of false expectations.

So there *may* have been some in those apostolic times that really and sincerely expected a visible intervention of Divine power in the affairs of men, and someone *may* have written and circulated a *Flugschrift* or fly-leaf in the interest of such views, and parts of it may have been taken up and preserved in our Gospels as we read them today. Naturally enough such compositions would or might have been based on the Danielic-Enochic writings then current and would have represented the Son-of-Man as coming on clouds of heaven to final judgment upon a wicked world. But such a representation would have been made in the Daniel-Enoch Spirit, it would have bodied forth the National Consciousness (perhaps in an exaggerated form), it would have had distinctly in view the Redemption and Elevation of Israel, with vengeance upon heathen oppressors including even Israelites that had been unfaithful to God.

In such a delineation the Son-of-Man or possibly Michael would naturally have been the Spokesman and Plenipotentiary, the *alter Ego,* of Israel. Through Him the Chosen People would normally have spoken and acted, even as God Himself was speaking and acting through them. The writer would have written *as if* this Son-of-Man were an Individual (as did Daniel, Enoch, and the rest),—that would have been a *necessity* of his dramatic stagesetting. But what importance he would actually have assigned such a "supernatural person" would have been another matter dependent upon his own type of thought and feeling. But the genuine Jew could feel little interest in a

---

* More accurately, their unknown *Sources;* no scribe, perhaps, endorsed quite fully every statement that he absorbed into his Collation or Revision.

*Person* that did not depict to his mind the one Supreme datum, object and aim of Creation, the *People* of the Living God. Not to recognize and appreciate this fact would be not to understand the Hebrew nature and therewith to misconstrue and misinterpret both the History of the Jews and the Origin of Christianity.

This intense, amazing National Consciousness of Israel carried with it indeed the defect of its quality, a certain narrowness and Particularism that has branded through all ages the Wandering Jew, as the world has scanned in awe and amazement "the weird senescence of the wondrous man." But still more marvelously there was at least one among them, the Second Isaiah, that rose high over all such limitations and burst all bounds, above, below, and proclaimed a Universalism that knew no barriers of race or tongue, vindicating for his own stock only the tragic preeminence of Vicarious Sufferer for the Sins of All, and of Elect Torch-bearer of God, His light to lighten the Nations of the world. This heavenly seed of doctrine fell upon rich but rather reluctant soil. Slowly it sprouted into Proselytism and spread out wide and wider branches. It grew like a cedar, and the fruit of it rustled like Lebanon. For its fruit was the Christian Propaganda, the doctrine of the Suffering Messiah, the Crucified, Re-risen, and Ascended Christ, the Gospel preached to the Pagans, the Crusade for Monotheism universal.

Thus it is that the Apocalyptic passages in the Gospels as well as elsewhere become understandable and range themselves at peace with even their remotest kinsmen in the long line of Israelitic Literature. But to suppose them the actual utterances concerning *himself* of any individual Son-of-Man, is to make them absurd and impossible. Perhaps there are few sane scholars now who heartily ascribe these predictions to the Jesus, to the Son-of-Man himself, regarding them rather as fugitive Messianic pronouncements encysted in the Gospels. But the method of subtraction will not here avail. Critics have not the right claimed by so many, to accept what sayings they will, as authentic, and reject the rest. Many of these objectionable passages are as well attested as any others; if some be free inventions, why not all? In fact, the logical scale inclines towards this latter possibility so soon as one example is admitted. Besides, everywhere in nature we find the group rather than the sole single individual; a great many such sayings would be far more likely than just one, or even a few. We conclude, then, that thus far there appears no likelihood worth considering that the New Testament "Son-of-Man" sayings form any other species than one belonging to the Daniel-Enoch genus.

* * * * *

There still remain a goodly number of examples yet to examine, scattered and not easy to classify. Thus, Matt. 11[19], we read "The Son-of-Man came eating and drinking, and they say, Behold a man gluttonous and a wine-bibber, a friend of publicans and sinners!" Certainly one of the most puzzling verses in the New Testament and in one of the obscurest contexts. We have no space for any adequate discussion, even if any such be possible, but of one thing we may be sure: the whole passage can lay little claim to authenticity or historicity. The charge stands quite isolate and alone, unsuggested by anything else in the Gospel account, which notably enough has nothing to say about the Jesus as eating, or even drinking (save possibly on the Cross and to fulfill an ancient Scripture). Indeed, it is most remarkable that the Evangelists seem to *avoid* any ascription of eating or drinking to the Jesus. We read of his breaking bread and offering it to others, of his reclining at table, but not of his taking food; the writers seem to have felt quite properly that munching meat would be unbecoming to a God. Even on the cross, though Matthew and Mark tell us they gave him vinegar to drink (as Scripture required, Ps. $69^{21}$, "And in my thirst they gave me vinegar to drink"—which *had* to be fulfilled), and Luke says they "offered" him vinegar, yet none says that he actually drank. Only John, the chief humanizer, might seem to *imply* at least a sipping: "When therefore he received the vinegar, the Jesus said It is finished," and John alone specifies why all this was done, "that the Scripture might be accomplished."

There is, then, nothing in the Gospel to hint even most remotely either gluttony or tippling on the part of Jesus, nay, nothing to suggest such a slander even to his dearest foe; for he does not *appear* to have fed at all, not even on locusts and wild honey, as did the ascetic Baptist. We may be sure, then, that this whole mysterious section is a pure invention, but of whom and with what purpose it might puzzle even the most astute analyst to guess. Certainly no such a passage can bear witness to a human personality of the Son-of-Man.

At Matt. $12^{32}$ it is written, "And whosoever shall speak a word against the Son-of-Man, it shall be forgiven him," but not against the Holy Spirit. This might indeed be understood of a word spoken against the Impersonation of Israel, who, though extremely high in the scale of being, was still a Creation of the Most High and not quite on a level with the Holy Spirit, hard to distinguish from God himself, the "Lord of Spirits." The passage, then, presents little difficulty, rather confirming the present contention.

Again, Matt. $12^{40}$, "So shall the Son-of-Man be three days and three nights in the heart of the earth." A Prediction clearly *ex post facto* but even then distinctly inaccurate and made only to feign a fulfilment of Scripture, to represent Jonah as a prototype of the Son-of-Man (Jonah $1^{17}$). As the incident was originally invented, along with the whole Jonah-story, to enforce the notion of the abounding mercy of God toward all men, not merely toward Israel, and can lay no claim to historic character, so neither can its application in this case. The remark and the event remarked are alike fictions, feigned to "accomplish the Scripture," as so much else in *the Gospel Story.—Parallel Luke 11³⁰.

In the next chapter (Matt. 13³⁷) we read, "He that sows the good seed is the Son-of-Man," and again (13⁴¹), "the Son-of-Man shall send forth his angels, etc." It is the Parable of the Tares—apparently suggested by that of the Sower (1³⁻²³), a pre-christian allegory of the Creation of the world,† as fully set forth in *Der vorchristliche Jesus* (107–135) and since then adopted by Georg Brandes in his *Sagnet om Jesus*. The Parable of the Tares seems clearly to represent a far later stage of Christian experience. The conception of the Son-of-Man is thoroughly Daniel-Enochic, the notion of the good seed appears to come straight from Enoch's description of the revelation of the Son-of-Man, 62⁸: "The congregation of the holy (Saints) and elect will be sown," where the reference is admittedly to Israel.—The "angels sent forth" (also in Matt. 24³¹) "to gather together his elect [Israel] from the four winds," proceed from the same source (62¹¹).—"And the angels of punishment will take them in charge to execute vengeance on them because they have appressed His children and His elect"—that is, the Chosen People Israel. The "furnace of fire" (13⁴²) is also Enochian: "Our souls are satisfied with the mammon of unrighteousness, but this does not prevent us from descending into the flame of the pain of Sheol" (63¹⁰); "Know ye that their souls will be made to descend into Sheol . . . and into darkness and fetters and a burning fire" (103⁷). Once again, Enoch refers often to the *brightness* of the Elect, as 108¹²: "And I will bring forth clad in shining light those who have loved My holy name, and each I will seat on the throne of his honor." Hence Matt. 13⁴³: "Then shall the Righteous shine forth as the sun in the Kingdom of their Father. He that hath ears (to hear), let him hear." And throughout we do hear distinctly the voice of Enoch‡ celebrating the triumph and eternal glory of the "Elect One," of Israel the Son-of-God and the Son-of-Man. It would be greedy to desire a completer confirmation.

Next comes the famous question (Matt. 16¹³), "Who do men say that the Son-of-Man is?" Few will contend that such is the eldest form of the query. Both Mark 8²⁷ and Luke 9¹⁸ put it thus: "Who do men (the multitude) say that I am?" The Matthean reviser has changed "I" (it seems) into "the Son-of-Man," in a certain fondness for this phrase: hence many ancient authorities read "that I the Son-of-Man am." The phrase here can mean nothing but "I," as the following answers clearly show. Its use seems plainly only a concept of the Reviser.

---

* Cf. next Chapter, the Symbolistic Warp and Woof.
† See Appendix, p. 168–9. *Editor.*
‡ And of his kind also; for similar representations abound in Jewish Apocalyptic.

Matt. 17⁹, "And ... coming down from the mountain the Jesus commanded them, saying, Tell no man the vision until the Son-of-Man be risen from the dead." Similarly Mark 9⁹, with the interesting addition, "And they kept the saying, questioning among themselves *what is the rising again from the dead?*" This though only six days before they had been carefully instructed by the Master himself (8³¹)! Luke is content to say only that "they held their peace and told no man" (9³⁶). Each writer appears to have put down what seemed good to him. The Resurrection is of course a fundamental dogma of the New Testament. Of the Son-of-Man merely as figured in *Daniel* and *Enoch* it would be unimaginable nonsense. They conceive (Daniel implicitly, Enoch explicitly) the long agony of Israel as a "hiding" of the Son-of-Man; when he is revealed, brought forth to the Ancient-of-Days and seated on the throne of his glory, the agony is past forever, the endless sway of Israel the Elect of God has begun. But Isaiah, without forming the Concept of the Son-of-Man, content with the idea of Israel as the Elect of the Most High, the Righteous Servant of YHVH, had introduced the notion of this Servant's dying, of his making "his grave with the wicked and with the rich in his deaths," yet rejoicing again in glory and the favor of YHVH. Here then in the New Testament is certainly a *fusion* of the Danielic-Enochic and Isaian conceptions, yet not in the consciousness of any "Son-of-Man" himself, but in very varying measure and manner in the minds of evangelic writers, the primitive propagandists of the new Faith. In one sentence it is Daniel, in another Enoch, in another Isaiah that is heard; the result is a medley,—a mosaic that puzzles the apologists.

The Matthean thought is continued in 17¹²: "So (like Elijah, the Baptist,) shall the Son-of-Man also suffer of them." Of course, this is the Isaian idea and needs no further notice, but just at this point the other Synoptics present interesting variants. Mark 9¹² declares, "He said unto them, Elijah indeed cometh first and restoreth all things: and how is it written of the Son-of-Man, that he should suffer many things and be set at naught?"—a clear allusion to the Righteous Servant Israel (Is. 53). No wonder this proved unacceptable to the later editors and was set aside or changed in form. That the Baptist had restored all things or indeed anything was too plainly false, the question addressed to the disciples and left in the air was too puzzling.* Luke 9⁴⁴ has simplified the situation in his own more literary but not less bewildering way: "He said ... Let these words sink into your ears: for the Son-of-Man shall be delivered up into the hands" etc. Again no wonder that the disciples (45)

---

* Is it not strange that this earliest Evangelist Mark leaves these two basic questions (9⁹, ¹²) in the air? Does this not point to a primitive stage of the Propaganda, before the matter was well thought out, while they were still at a loss to harmonize their ideas in laying the groundwork of the Gospel?

"understood not this saying, and it was concealed from them, that they should not perceive it; and they were afraid to ask him about this saying." This fear seems to be a queer commentary on the alleged gentleness and human sympathy of the Jesus but it is not here the main matter, which is that the solemn warning of v. 44 is entirely unmotivated, quite unconnected with anything in the context either before or after. At this we need not marvel, for it was no easy task to fuse Danielic-Enochian imaginations with the sublime conceptions of Isaiah. On its face it was indeed impossible; in the realm of impersonation, in which our Evangelists moved, it could not be adequately done, for the symbol was imperfect; only when we revert from the Symbol, the Person, to the Symbolized, the reality, the Genius and History of the Israel-Race, do the difficulties dissolve and disappear in the clear light of historical truth.

Already, in Luke $9^{22}$, the like announcement had been made, "saying, the Son-of-Man must suffer many things, and be rejected of the elders and chief priests and scribes, and be killed, and the third day be raised up." The Marcan account ($8^{31}$) is practically in the same words; the Matthean also ($16^{21}$) but with no mention of the Son-of-Man, instead, "from that time began Jesus (Christ) to show unto his disciples, that he must go up to Jerusalem, and suffer, etc. (—These variants demand little attention—save on the false assumption that there was some original strictly correct biographic statement, which has undergone modification. What they, along with those in the preceding paragraph, distinctly show is that there was *one idea* (namely, the introduction of the Isaian conception into the Danielic-Enochic-Apocalyptic mould) animating the general Christian Consciousness, and this expressed itself through various scribes in slightly diverse but in generally equivalent forms. Such was (we might say) the side-by-side latitudinal connectivity; exactly what was the longitudinal one-after-another relation is like the Darwinian question of the Descent of Man, and almost as hard to answer. Fortunately it is comparatively indifferent for the present study.

Another striking example of the shaping power of the individual consciousness upon elements of the common consciousness is to be found in Luke $9^{26}$: "For whosoever shall be ashamed of me and of my words, of him shall the Son-of-Man be ashamed when he comes in the glory of himself and the Father and the holy angels," as compared with Mark $8^{38}$: "For whosoever shall be ashamed of me and of my words in this adulterous (i.e. idolatrous) and sinful generation, the Son-of-Man also shall be ashamed of him, when he cometh in the glory of his Father with the holy angels." We see how Luke has abated the harshness of judgment and heightened the rhetorical effect, without advancing a step beyond the Daniel-Enochic lines. But Matthew thought otherwise. For some reason he seems not to have liked the word "ashamed" (*epaischyn-,* used elsewhere only twice in *Romans,* twice in *Hebrews, thrice* in nine verses of the Pastoral II Tim. $1^{8-16}$!). Accordingly he writes ($10^{33}$): "But whosoever shall deny me before men, him will I also deny before my Father . . . in the heavens." We might consider, why such a preference and such a variance, but might it not be too curious to consider thus? The moral of all such stories is that in these wonderful Scriptures we are not dealing with annals but with doctrine, not with bloodless *behavior* but with edifying thought, with "truth severe by fairy fiction dress'd" now in this fashion now in that, according to the dogmatic prejudice and the literary taste of the evangelic *fashioners* of the common tradition of the primitive preaching.

The next use of the apocalyptic term is found in Luke $19^{10}$, "For the Son-of-Man came to seek and save what was lost," which many authorities, omitting to "seek and," render in agreement with Matt. $18^{11}$ where however it is obviously out of place and in fact omitted from the more careful texts and translations. But the insertion in so many mss. is eloquent and instructive. The preceding verses deal with the "little ones" and their angels in heaven. Entirely independent considerations show clearly that these "little ones" ("that believe on me" $18^6$) are heathen converts, "babes in Christ,"—"little one," *qaton,* being the regular name for such (*Ecce Deus,* p. 117). Likewise the obvious reference in "the lost" is to the heathen world, including apostate or recreant Jews, represented by Zaccheus the publican. The mission of Spiritual Israel was explicitly to such, to find and restore them to knowledge and favor of God—a mission amazingly fulfilled—by the Christian propaganda, but not by any historical Jesus* whose reported preaching can hardly be so described. Now, then, since the speech is about the heathen in verse 11, and also in vv. 1–10, it was natural enough for transcribers who felt the meaning of both passages as referring to the Gentiles, to insert the wandering verse at this point, but certainly very unnatural for anyone who did not thus understand the reference. How utterly unfitting such a position (for v. 11) must have seemed to anyone who thought of the "little ones" as innocent physical babes! We see, then, that the meaning of the symbolism (proselytes as "little ones") had not been quite forgot far down in the centuries, when the manuscripts were transcribed.

The next passage (Matt. $20^{28}$, Mark $10^{45}$), "even as the Son-of-Man came not to be ministered unto, but to minister, and to give his life a ransom for many," need not detain us. It is plainly a case not so much of the fusion of the two fundamental conceptions, of Daniel-Enoch and the Younger Isaiah, as of the phrase of the former applied boldly to the idea of the latter.

---

* Compare the bewildering statement—of an extreme Enochian—in Matt. $15^{24}$: "I was *not* sent but unto the lost sheep of the house of Israel," with *Enoch* $90^{33}$: "the Lord of the sheep rejoiced with great joy because they were all good and had *returned* to His house."

The verse (Matt. 26²), "the Son-of-Man is delivered up to be crucified," belongs to the class already discussed at length (p. 40, discussion of Matt. 17²²) and needs no further comment here than the observation that the parallels (Mark 14¹, Luke 22²), omit any words of the Jesus and merely mention the plotting of chief priests and elders.

\* \* \* \* \*

Passing now to Mark we find no passage not already considered, but in Luke 6²² we read: "Blessed are ye when men shall . . . cast out your name as evil, for the Son-of-Man's sake" (because of the Son-of-Man). To be sure, this might be understood of the Son-of-Man as an historical person ill-esteemed by the "men" in question, but it is also understood with perfect ease of the personified idealized Israel, which soon became an offence to the patriotic Judaists,\* as the symbol of infidelity to the strictly national cause. We need, then, introduce no new reference or meaning for the phrase, either here or in 9²², "The Son-of-Man must suffer many things, etc.," a notion already familiar and fully interpreted as a fusion of Daniel-Enoch with the Second Isaiah.

Similarly of Luke 9⁵⁶ (now omitted from the more critical texts and translations), "For the Son-of-Man is not come to destroy men's lives but to save them": it is the addition of a copyist in whom the Isaianic idea had about crowded out the Daniel-Enochian.

We have already treated the passages about being ashamed of the Son-of-Man or denying him; but Luke presents an addition of his own (12⁸), "Every one who shall confess me before men, him shall the Son-of-Man also confess before the angels of God." This seems to be merely a literary flourish of the Evangelist, marked as such by its want of connection, being introduced quite abruptly. Luke 12¹⁰ has already been discussed along with its parallels, Matt. 12³², Mark 3²⁸.—The evident and abounding want of connection is what impresses one most in the study of many texts, as is strongly witnessed by Luke 17²²: "The days will come, when ye shall desire to see one of the days of the Son-of-Man, and ye shall not see it." The nearest reference seems to be to some general expectancy of the *Parousy,* Presence, Coming, Revelation of the Son-of-Man according to the Daniel-Enochic conception. The loose fit in the context seems to indicate a relatively late insertion.

Luke 18⁸ puts the question, "Nevertheless, when the Son-of-Man cometh, shall he find faith on the earth?" As a mere reference to the Parousy the

* As a protest against Christian doctrine, particularly of the Son-of-Man, we may understand the noted passage in the *Talmud* (of Babylon), Tasnith ii. 1: "Abbahu said: 'If a man says to thee—I am God, he lies; I am the Son-of-Man—he will at least repent it; I ascend to heaven—if he said it, he will not prove it.' "—Here the most notable feature seems to be the moderation in language.

words have no special interest but take their place alongside the many other such allusions already discussed; yet the preceding verses (7, 8ᵃ)—in the Parable of the Widow and the Judge—lend them especial significance: "And shall not God avenge His Elect that cry to Him day and night, and yet he is long-suffering over them (slow to punish Pagans in their behalf)? I say unto you, that He will avenge them speedily." Here, at least, there seems no room for the slightest doubt. "His (God's) elect" are surely the People Israel that for so many generations had been crying aloud to Him (as in the Psalms) for vengeance on their pagan foes; the widow is Zion ("she is become as a widow that was great among the nations," Lam. 1¹), that called unto Jehovah, "Avenge me of mine adversary." Who will not agree? Any reference to later Christians seems quite impossible; their inconsiderable persecutions did not begin so early. Yet this inroad of Divine Power is in the next breath (v. 8) spoken of as the Coming of the Son-of-Man! Here, then, we are solidly planted on Daniel-Enoch ground, and the meaning of the Coming is put beyond dispute. It is given in the oft-cited verse Dan. 7¹³.

Once more, in Luke 18³¹, "Behold, we go up to Jerusalem and all the things that are written through the prophets shall be accomplished unto the Son-of-Man." These "things" are listed in v. 32 as elsewhere, and in v. 34 it is added, "And they (the Twelve) understood none of these things; and this saying was hid from them, and they perceived not the things that were said,"—We note that the Son-of-Man is declared to be the burden of Old Testament prophecy, it is all to be fulfilled through him. This seems mere foolishness, if we suppose him to be any historic individual; every one knows that no individual whatever is the subject of these vaticinations. But it becomes very sound sense when and only when we understand the Son-of-Man as Israel (personified, idealized), for notoriously and incontestably it is the *People of the God YHVH whose tragic history is the Burden of the Old Testament from Genesis to Malachi.*

Nor is it strange that "the Twelve" did not understand. The *Transfiguration* was necessary to make the whole story intelligible, a Transfiguration that idealized, spiritualized, universalized the Elect People—conceived hitherto as the Daniel-Enochic Son-of-Man coming in glorious triumph to judge and rule the earth—into the Isaian Suffering Servant of YHVH, sacrificed for the sins of all men yet glorified as the Head of Humanity, Jehovah's Beacon to the Nations of the World.—Some one may say, But the Transfiguration had already been narrated (9²⁹⁻³⁶). True, a purely symbolic account had been given, but the order of narration counts very little in a story that deals almost exclusively with ideas. In fact, the *Transfiguration* took place solely in the minds of the Disciples (Hellenized Jews) and was the work not of a moment but of many years, if not indeed of many generations.

The verse (Luke 21[27]), "Then shall they see the Son-of-Man coming in cloud with power and great glory," is of course drawn from Daniel's exhaustless wellhead (Dan. 7[13]) and is parallel to Matt. 25[31] already considered (p. 36), but the next verse is notable: "When these things begin to take place, look up and lift your heads; because your redemption is at hand." One naturally asks, What "redemption" (*apolytrosis*)? The only answer is, the political deliverance of Israel from his oppressors. Such alone fits in the preceding framework of "Signs in sun, moon, and stars, and on earth, anguish among the nations" this verse proceeds from a heart still fired with temporal national hopes of the Daniel-Enoch type, that has not yet known nor understood the Transfiguration. Of course there were many such then, everywhere, especially in Palestine, even as there are many such today and yet will be for many ages to come. In all nature-processes the various stages of development do not exclude each other but coexist, from highest to lowest.—The following v. 36, "that ye prevail . . . to stand in the presence of the Son-of-Man," requires no special treatment, belonging plainly to the class just considered. Like may be said of 24[7], "Saying that the Son-of-Man must be delivered up, etc.," a conception already sufficiently discussed.

So then the whole circut of the Synoptic Induction is complete; and at the mouth of so many witnesses the same word, *Son-of-Man = Israel*, is established.

## 2. The Title Son-of-Man in the Fourth Gospel

Herewith we are brought to a very diverse type of usage, the Johannine, as appears in the very first example, 1[51]: "Verily, verily, I tell you, ye shall see heaven wide opened and the angels of God ascending and descending upon the Son-of-Man." With him who reads this as history we have no argument here. Our only inquiry is into the meaning of such words. That they refer in some way to the wide-spread Gnostic notion of Mediation through the *Logos* (Word) between God and Man seems clear enough, but the details can not here be logically and convincingly educed, we can only guess at certain more general features. That Israel was understood as in some ways such a *Daysman* is at least implied in Scripture, in much of it already quoted. As Light for the Gentiles, as the Beacon-Bearer for Jehovah, this mediatorial character he must certainly have possessed. The mere words of John do not imply any such interpretation, but the general historical situation seems to suggest if not in truth to require it. Of course, it would be idealized, spiritualized Israel, for as Clemens Alexandrinus long ago recognized, the Fourth is a "spiritual Gospel." We may note in passing that in verse 34 we should read, according to very high authority, "This is the Elect of God," though the now accepted text is "This is the Son-of-God." The word *Eklektos* at least shows the mind of many scribes at an early date and points directly to the identity of the Jesus with Israel the Elect of God. Compare the two famous passages in Luke: "This is my Son, the Elected" ($9^{35}$) and "This is the Christ of God, the Elect" ($23^{35}$), where the epithet is understandable only of the spiritualized Elect People Israel.

Next we find ($3^{13}$), "And none hath ascended into heaven save he that descended from heaven, the Son-of-Man (who is in heaven)." Here the reference to a thoroughly supernatural being is manifest: in no sense could the like be said of a Nazarene Carpenter,—but of the Ideal People, the Genius of Israel, of true Humanity ("Michael . . . he that is set over the best part of mankind, over the People," Enoch $20^5$)—why not? Indeed, Daniel had long before implied it.—In a following verse $3^{14}$, "so must the Son-of-Man be lifted up" is ordinarily and plausibly referred to the Crucifixion, but such reference is far from necessary. The Greek ("hightened") may just as well refer to the spiritual exaltation (Ascension) of Ideal Israel to the Religious Headship of all Humanity—a far more likely exegesis.

Passing by $5^{27}$, already considered (p. 39), we come to the cryptic $6^{27}$: "Work not for the food that perisheth but for the food that abideth unto eternal life, which the Son-of-Man shall give you; for him hath God the Father sealed." The discussion that follows in John is far from clear or satisfying—else it were not Johannine. But in any case the "Son-of-Man" is represented as *sealed* of God—an idea appropriate to Israel preeminently, but to whom else at all?—and as giving some food or other gift of eternal life, and further on (v. 63) we learn that "the words that I have spoken unto you are spirit and are life." Similarly in $5^{24}$, "He that hears my words and *believes on Him that sent* (*toi pempsanti*) me hath everlasting life and cometh not into judgment, but hath passed from death into life." What can these, especially the italicized, words mean but to restate in a mystical form the Old Testament doctrine of the One God, a dogma that lies at the heart of the New Faith, that is its essence and has all the life-giving and the saving power that can belong to any religious doctrine? The Evangelist seems to have the Gentiles in mind, as appears in the clause "hath passed out of death into life," another expression for conversion from heathendom to Monotheism. Also the words "cometh not into judgment" seem to have a Daniel-Enochic connotation, they suggest the seer's conception of the approaching "judgment set" for all the Pagan powers. We say, then, that the writer is refining and obscuring the familiar idea of Israel as God's Truth-preacher to the World at large, the Herald of his Message of Salvation and life.

Likewise $6^{53}$, "Except ye eat the flesh of the Son-of-Man and drink his blood,* ye have not life in yourselves. He that eats my flesh and drinks my blood hath everlasting life, and I will raise him up at the last day." Such dark and drastic words must refer to the appropriation and assimilation of some truth or doctrine represented by the Son-of-Man—obviously Israel's Monotheism, the dogma of the One God, and His supreme right to the service of man. "Thou shalt love YHVH thy God with all thy heart and with all thy soul and with all thy mind. This is the great and the first commandment." And the sole spokesman of this command in history was Israel, the Son-of-Man. To adopt this essential dogma of the Son-of-Man was to eat his flesh and drink his blood.† Who would ask for a more satisfactory explanation?

They that heard this "saying" seem to have found it "hard," and so they are met by another such (6⁶²): "What then if you should behold the Son of Man ascending where he was before?" No hint of meaning or explanation is vouchsafed. Of course, orthodoxy may point to the traditional Ascension, but the Johannine speaker continues: "It is the spirit that giveth life, the flesh profiteth nothing," which words might seem aimed squarely against such a notion as the Ascension, of which we read *nothing in this Gospel*. Whatever was in the mind of the Gnostic Evangelist, it might probably be interpreted of the Ideal Israel quite as well as of aught else. Remember, this Israel was "Son-of-God," His "First born" (Ex. 4²²).

Once more, in 8²⁸, "When ye have lifted up the Son-of-Man, then shall ye know that I am (he) and of myself do naught, but as the Father taught me, so I speak." Such words may not seem intended to be understood, but, like so much in this Gospel, meant merely to mystify. The uplifting will be referred to the Crucifixion, but any such literalism sounds not only foreign to the whole method of the writer, but also to lend no sense at all to the clause "*then* shall ye know, etc." Far more probable that a spiritual exaltation is intended, viewed as their deed, i.e., as the result of the whole process of history, in which *they* were involved as agents. Such a meaning would be as near fact as the Evangelist ever approaches, and would be in no way inconsistent but

* Heathen may have received such words, as imagery; to the Jews they would have been impossible abomination, for Gen. 9⁴ reads: "But flesh with its soul, its blood, ye shall not eat." Goetz with great learning (*Das Abendmahl*, pp. 68 -1920) would find in this ch. 6 the remains of an original Parable of Jesus, which Paul, Luke, Mark, Matthew have transformed into the story of the Last Supper! Very ingenious apologetic, yet vain,—it sacrifices the text it would save. But Goetz is honest enough to cite the Egyptian magic rite of eating an image of Truth or Wisdom, in order to become wise! Whence, also such words as Jesus Ben Sirach's concerning Wisdom (i.e., Israel's Faith and the Law): "She will feed him with the bread of Insight, And the water of Wisdom will she give him to drink" (15³), and again the Israel-Wisdom says: "*They that eat me shall never hunger again, And they that drink me shall never again thirst*" (24²¹)— Surely the original of the ideas in John 6⁴⁸⁻⁵⁸, as well as 4¹⁴ ("who e'er drinks of the water I give him, shall never thirst").

† The Naassene teaching belongs of course also in this cycle. See p. 165. *Editor.*

rather harmonize with the notion of the Son-of-Man as the Generalized Ideal Israel, Son-of-Man and Son-of-God.*

In $9^{35}$ the received and revised reading is, "Dost thou believe on the Son-of-God?" though many old authorities prefer "the Son-of-Man." The reference is of course the same, and inner grounds for choice seem wanting. "Son-of-God" and "Son-of-Man" designate the same "supernatural being," and are both used of the People, Ideal Israel. Thus, in Hosea $11^1$, "When Israel was a child, then I loved him and called my Son out of Egypt," and elsewhere (Ex. $4^{22}$, Ps. Sol. $18^4$). What other use of the phrase is so justified and well attested?

In $12^{23}$, "the hour is come, that the Son-of-Man should be glorified." The general context shows (as clearly as aught is shown in this Gospel) that the symbolic reference is to a Crucifixion (as in v. 34 and in $13^{31}$), but it throws little light on the question of the multitude: "How sayest thou the Son-of-Man must be lifted up? Who is this Son-of-Man?" All this is left completely and apparently intentionally in the dark.—There is nothing to forbid the notion that here as everywhere in this Gospel the conception is of a Danielic-Enochic Son-of-Man clothed with the Isaianic attributes of the Righteous and Suffering Servant of YHVH,—the Crucifixion being the traditional Symbol of the National Passion.

### 3. COMMENT

So we complete this serial examination of New Testament usage, with the result that it is *nowhere* inconsistent with the interpretation here proposed, which in *many cases* is positively required as alone yielding any acceptable sense. We may then rest assured that at the base of the New Testament use of the expression Son-of-Man is the Danielic-Enochic conception of the Son-of-Man, the Ideal Israel Personified, ordained by the Ancient of Days unto eternal judgeship and dominion over all the earth. Yet it is just as certain that there has been a mingling of the Isaianic idea of the Suffering Righteous Servant of YHVH, the Elect. Centuries before Daniel, the Younger Isaiah† had presented the Elect—Israel—as the Torch-bearer of YHVH, the messenger of His Truth to all the earth, a light to lighten the Gentiles, a sacrifice for the sins of the world. His sufferings, his "deaths" (Isa. $53^9$) were a part of an eternal and infinite purpose of God to reveal the knowledge of Himself to all men, to illumine all dark places of the inhabited world. Israel was indeed the precious Light of Salvation, but only by dispersion, deportation, and

---

* Of course, it is not denied nor excluded that various vague notions, Gnostic, pre-Gnostic, Persian, Hindu—as of *Purusha,* universe, "first-born, *narayana,* man-like," etc.—may have been floating like vapor in the Evangelic mind, but any discussion now and here of such distant kinships would be unprofitable and out of place.

† Author, that is, of roughly chapters 40 to 66 inclusive, of the present Isaiah. *Editor.*

political death could Israel effectively shed abroad the divine spark that dwelt within him.—"I scatter this folk among the nations, that it do the nations good" (Apocalypse of Baruch 1⁴). Israel would certainly be glorified by YHVH, not however as the political but as the Spiritual Head of Humanity, as having borne its iniquities, poured out his soul unto death, and made intercession for the transgressors (Isa. 53¹²).

Now wherever there is a mixture of elements as heterogenious as Isaiah and Daniel, there may always result a varying percentage: in some cases one element, in some cases another, will predominate. In the synoptic apocalyptic passages the Danielic-Enochic vision of the Coming on the clouds of heaven is almost solely to be seen; in the Fourth Gospel all this is mystified into the well-nigh formless form of the Logos, the Only Begotten Son of God, (still identified as Israel, as in Hos. 11¹ etc. See infra, Chap. VI), a Principle of Existence, a Being hovering between heaven and earth. Naturally between these extremes lie many gradations shading insensibly into each other. Yet the fundamental unity remains, for it is the one *Genius of Israel, with all its tragic history,* that is *the one subject of meditation and depiction.*

It must not be supposed, however, that every writer was distinctly conscious of the proper reference of his words. Nothing more natural for the seer than to shape some significant symbol and then to yield to the spell of his own magic, to forget at least half-way that it is symbol at all, and to treat it as the reality itself, overlooking more or less completely the underlying meaning of which it is only the token. Such, indeed, has been the whole course of history.

Chapter Four

# The Symbolistic Warp and Woof *

### 1. Cast in the Mould of Scripture

If the Eternal Mission of Israel for the Redemption of Mankind was to be imagined and reflected in the consciousness of the Gentiles as the earthly life of a Divine Man, why was this particular career chosen rather than some other? What was it that determined the choice and the course of its represented events, its beginning and its end? Must there not have been some human model or pattern at hand, to guide its development, to give it definite size and color? This is a reasonable query, and the answer need not linger: *There was no personal individual prototype or exemplar whatever.* The fancy of the Preacher was free to roam untrammeled by any personal biographic facts in the case. He was at liberty to make whatever representation might please him best† and serve his purpose of edifying his heathen converts. Hence it is that glaring contradictions abound in the Gospels, even in the Synoptics. A few examples may suffice to show the wide license of evangelistic fancy.

Certainly the birth of the Gospel Hero would seem worthy of all attention. Both Luke and Matthew appear to have thought so and accordingly have given minute accounts, but each, alas! in total disregard and in complete contradiction of the other! Moreover their aims were as diverse as could be: Matthew shaped and colored his account so as to make it from point to point a replica of Old Testament dicta—it all happened so and not otherwise, "that it might be fulfilled which was spoken by the Lord through the prophet" ($1^{22}$, $2^{5, 6, 14, 15, 17, 23}$); Luke, on the other hand, is concerned mainly to outdo the Pagan mythologists on their own ground, in their theogonies, to present a birth and youth far more worthy and wondrous than Pagan literature could

---

* This chapter, needed in order to make the argument complete, is kept brief because the topic was treated *in extenso* in *Ecce Deus*, Part II. *Editor.*

† As much seems to be virtually admitted by Prof. F. C. Burkitt ("Luke's Use of Mark," in *The Beginnings of Christianity*, II (1922), p. 106–120), though in extremely cautious terms.

offer, and in pursuit of this he allows his imagination to riot in every form of prodigy and historic incredibility.—Mark, however, and John (whoever they were) apparently took another view of the matter: They disregarded the Birth entirely, as if holding aught of the kind to be quite irrelevant, unworthy of the Savior-God, whom they introduce upon the stage without preliminary, in full-blown manhood and God-hood, heralded indeed by John the Baptist but only in order to fulfil certain ancient Hebrew Scriptures (which, of course, had not the remotest reference to the first century of our era).

Passing by all minor contrarieties, we next note that the general conceptions of the three Synoptics on the one hand and of the Fourth or Johannine Gospel on the other are as unlike as well can be. The unnumbered attempts of nearly two thousand years to "harmonize" the two representations have failed absolutely, and the problem is now generally abandoned as finally insoluble. In the soothing words of Weymouth (Translation, 248), "The Johannine Christ must not be pressed into the Synoptic mould." Not only in broad outlines are the two conceptions ununifiable, but in many specific details they are openly and to all appearances designedly contradictory. Thus the Johannine account makes the Jerusalem Tragedy hinge on the supreme miracle of the resurrection of Lazarus ($12^{9-11}$): but this Lazarus (or any other brother of the sisters Martha and Mary) is totally unknown to the Synoptics, the word (meaning "No-help" Is. $30^5$) appearing only as the symbolic name of the Beggar in the Lucan Parable (which remarkably, is not even put into the mouth of the Jesus! Luke $16^{19-31}$).

Nevertheless in spite of this proven mutual independence of the Evangelists, it still remains that their agreements are much more notable than their disagreements, yea, are indeed so many and so exact that a certain community of origin is universally recognized and appears quite beyond question. It is, of course, impossible to enter here upon the endless wrangling concerning the Prime-Mark (*Ur-Markus*) and the Q-document (the *Quelle* or Source of the *Sayings*), and other such matters.‡ It is enough that there were obviously many slightly varying fragmentary forms of "tradition"; the Life-story came into being very gradually,* during at least two or three generations; it assumed perhaps a hundred or a thousand more or less transient hues and divergent shapes, nearly all of which have been lost in the wreck and dusk of time, only such having been saved as secured (in spite of sharp internal contradictions) in some large measure the general approval of the early Christian Consciousness. Accordingly we may and must regard these Gospels as the image or mirror of the Mind of the Early Christian Church, its way of regarding its

‡ See p. 139. *Editor.*
* Even Klausner is forced to admit, "Thus the story grew from Gospel to Gospel" (*Jesus of Nazareth,* 337).

own self, its origin, its doctrine, its struggles, its hopes, and its fears. More and more the ablest and fairest critics (as Loisy, for example) among historicists themselves are coming to regard the Gospels as the history not so much of the Christ as of the Christian Church.*

But some one may still press the query, Why were such and such incidents chosen and others rejected? What principle determined what should be taken and what should be left? Once again the question is rational, and once again the answer in general is easy: The *Life-story,* being the idealized Story of Israel Personified, was drawn in its main essentials from the *Old Testament;* the incidents were framed to illustrate or *fulfil Old Testament texts.*† Any one of the four Gospels supplies copious examples in point. More than twenty times in Matthew the fulfilment of prophecy is avowed as the reason or explanation of this or that occurrence, and many times the same motive is plainly present though without such avowal. Thus, the vinegar is given to the Jesus on the Cross to fulfil the word of the Psalmist ($69^{21}$), representing Israel, "In my thirst they gave me vinegar to drink." This manifest motive is unmentioned by the Synoptics, but is exposed by John ($19^{28}$), "that the Scripture might be fulfilled."

Sometimes the fixed resolution to cast the Career in the exact moulds of the Old Testament leads to unexpected or even ludicrous results. Thus, Isaiah had proclaimed ($62^{11}$) with great boldness the nigh-approaching redemption of Jerusalem:

> "Lo, YHVH hath proclaimed unto the end of the earth,
> Say ye to the Daughter of Zion, Behold thy salvation cometh;‡
> Behold his reward is with him, And his recompense before him."

* R. Bultmann, a representative of the "formgeschichtliche" method of New Testament study, has provided a masterly work on *The History of the Synoptic Tradition (Die Geschichte der synoptischen Tradition,* 1921). A few of his phrases may be noted,—p. 227,—"The Gospels are cult-legends." They sprang out of a felt want of the converted heathen. "One needed a cult-legend for the Lord of the Christian cult." "The scheme of the Christ-myth needed for its vivid envisagement the conjunction with the tradition about the story of Jesus."—And so it was conjoined in spite of "its lack of the properly biographic." Professor Bultmann's work would not for a moment compromise the historicity of the Nazarene, and yet inescapably it takes a very long stride in that direction. The candid recognition of the Synoptic Gospels as composed in almost exclusive measure of "formative," "secondary," "legendary"—in a word, purely fictive elements, delivers a deadening blow at all theories of the Gospels as historical documents; no feature can be confidently affirmed to be primitive or historic. Bultmann himself is only able to "surmise there was an old report that told altogether briefly of arrest, condemnation and death. This was fitted out at different stages, partly with stories already at hand, partly with new-made formations." (p. 169). The query is inevitably,—Even granted this "old report," was it a record of historic fact, or was it the objectivation of an earlier stage of the nascent Christian consciousness?

† For the principle that events given as fulfilling prophecy are uniformly no more than constructs to accomplish an imaginary fulfilment, see Editor's Orientation (p. xxi) and also *Ecce Deus,* p. 154 ff. *Editor.*

‡ Observe here that the abstract "Salvation" is distinctly personalized.

Zechariah had sought to enliven the verse of his elder into a realistic picture (9⁹):

> "Rejoice greatly, O daughter of Zion; Shout, O Daughter of Jerusalem:
> Lo, thy king cometh unto thee, He that is just and having Salvation;
> Lowly, and riding upon an ass, yea, upon a colt the foal of an ass."

Of course, these dicta of the prophets must furnish the die for the story of the Entry of the Jesus into Jerusalem. The Mark Tradition, followed by Luke and John, was content to observe the sense of the phrases and *identify* the ass with the colt the foal of an ass (strictly, "of a beast of burden"): hence they mention only a colt as found by the two disciples, loosed, and brought to the Jesus, and the garments as spread upon "it" (Mark 11¹⁻¹¹, Luke 19²⁹⁻³⁸, John 12¹⁴⁻¹⁶), and only John notes that it is a fulfillment of prophecy.

Not so, however, the First Evangelist, Matthew; he has read the lines of Zechariah slightly otherwise, and he fulfills them to the letter. He understands the Greek *kai* of the Septuagint, representing the Hebrew *vav*, not as intensive, meaning *yea,* but as additive, meaning *and.* Hence he makes the Jesus say to the two disciples, "Ye shall find an ass tied, *and* a colt with her," and they "brought the ass *and* the colt, and put on *them* their clothes, and he sat upon *them*" (*epano autōn*), 21¹⁻⁷. The absurdity of making the Jesus ride upon the ass *and* the colt, has been a sore trial to translators, who have sought to muffle up the statement of the text in the rendering, "they set him *theron*" or "He sat *thereon*," allowing the reader to refer "thereon" to the clothes, not to the two beasts. Unfortunately, however, the clothes were spread "on *them*," on *both* the beasts, which was senseless, unless he was to mount or ride upon *both*.

To be sure, this was impossible, but not more impossible than many other marvels in which this stately Gospel abounds; the repeated mention of ass and colt—whereas the Marcan Source mentions only the colt—and the insistence upon the plural show clearly that the Evangelist has taken the prophet at his word, which he means to fulfil exactly and at any cost. Could there be plainer proof that the incident is wholly fictive, devised solely in the dogmatic interest of representing the realization of Old Testament ideas (concerning Israel) in a single individual life? The Fourth Evangelist John seems to give his readers a subtle hint that the story was a symbolic fiction feigned by the later imagination of the Disciples. For he says (12¹⁴⁻¹⁶), "And the Jesus having found a young ass sat upon it: just as it is written, Fear not, daughter of Zion; behold thy King cometh, sitting on an ass's colt. *These things his disciples knew not at first:* but when the Jesus was glorified, then they remembered that these things were written of him and these things they did unto Him." Have we not here a confession that a biography of the Jesus was an after-thought, that it was conceived and invented in order to concentrate and accomplish as much Scripture as possible in a single individual life?

But "Scripture" to the evangelist writers must not be equated with "Old Testament" for the modern Christian. That has been well attested by the citations we have already made from Enoch. Other writings also had scriptural authority in their minds. Remarkably, Matthew's description of the sufferings of the Christ is taken directly from the Wisdom of Solomon 2[13-20], which details the malignant reproaches levelled at the Righteous (Israel) by his calumniators: "He vaunteth himself to have the (true) knowledge of God; he nameth himself Servant of God . . . and nameth boastfully God his Father! Let us see whether his words be true! Let us wait on the style of his exit! For if the Righteous be Son-of-God, then will God take him to Himself and deliver him from the hands of his adversaries. With reproaches and ill-treatment let us put him to the test. . . . Let us condemn him to disgraceful death. For according to his words protection will fall to his lot." The reader cannot fail to recall the parallel Gospel passages (Matt. 26[53], 27[39-44], etc.), the resemblances are too close and too many to be accidental. Of course, there were a multitude of sources, all of them "scriptural," used in imaging the suffering of Israel.

Here, then, we seem to touch the nerve of the whole matter. As already stated, it was deemed necessary in the early preaching of the One and Only Savior-God, the Jesus, to the Gentiles, to make a most important concession to the hardness of their heathen heart: they could not readily grasp the great Isaianic conception of an Idealized Israelic leadership, they needed a Personal Objectification of the wondrous thought, and that was supplied to them in a beautiful fiction, the Life-story of the Divine Man, the Jesus, the Savior, the Nazorean.—Not all at once, not by any means!—but very gradually, piece by piece, saying by saying, incident by incident the story was built up by the general Christian Consciousness expressing itself through countless individuals in countless fashions agreeing in the main, though often slightly and sometimes widely discrepant. The fundamental Norm that guided these creative imaginations was the Old Testament; the Life was deftly compounded of Saying and Doing found in the Hebrew Scriptures (generally as already translated into Greek), so as to become in its completion the most consummate and remarkable "mosaic" to be found in all literature.

In estimating the *need* of this "Personal Objectification" of the Isaianic Idea, the reader will hardly fail to think of Saint Nicolas at the present time. Whatever may be this Saint's mythical or legendary origin, for us he symbolizes the spirit of general fellowship, of universal kindliness and cheer, of friendship, remembrance and affection. As "grown-ups" we recognize all this and are quite content to rank "Santa" as he really is, a good-humored imagination, not feeling that he suffers any humiliation or debasement thereby. But for children the case is felt to be different. They are not at home with "spirit" and with far-ranging "universal" concepts, abstractions, and principles. They need the Benefactor as much as the benefaction; they need the sleigh, the reindeer, and tinkling bells, the mystery and the miracle even— So, then we are still facing the ancient problem of meat for men but milk for babes.

## 2. CONVERSIONS, NOT CURES

Along with all this exploitation of the Old Testament there runs throughout, as already indicated, as abounding symbolism, concerned mainly with the casting out of demons, that is, of Heathen Gods, by His word, that is, by the Monotheistic cult. Consider for example, the Demoniac of Gerasa (an apparently symbolic name from the stem G-R-S, meaning "cast-out," as noted by Dr. E. A. Abbott*) the man possessed with a company of Demons, whose name was Legion. Plainly he is *not* an Individual, he is Heathen Humanity (notice Mark's single word, *anthropos, Man,* 5[2]), the multitude of Demons are the Idols, the False Gods, of Heathen worship (the description of the Man is taken from the Old Testament descriptions of idolatrous worship,—compare Mark 5[3-5] with I Kings 18[28], Is. 65[3, 4]); these are cast out by the word of "the Jesus," i.e., by the preaching of the "Eternal Gospel" (Rev. 14[7], "Fear God and give *Him* glory"), and Man is restored to his right mind (Mark 5[15]), Heathen Humanity is Redeemed. As a symbol of the worldwide overthrow of Idolatry by the proclamation of Monotheism, the story is bold, vivid, and almost sublime: as a literal historic incident it would be childish and impossible.

The alternative notion that the Demons stand for all manner of mental and physical ailments is scarcely less inadmissable. No one disputes that such ailments were indeed occasionally ascribed to the presence or indwelling of such foul spirits, though the prevalence of such ideas of disease is strongly exaggerated in the works of scholars who ought to know much better. Allusions to such demoniacal possession are exceedingly scanty in profane literature; it is in Christian literature that they abound. But exactly there they have little or no probative value, for the question at once arises, Is the Christian writer speaking of familiar every-day physical *diseases,* or is he using *religious* phrases and covertly referring to the disease of *Idolatry?*

To be sure, there must have been some cases of supposed demoniacal possession, otherwise the First Christians would not have symbolized Idolatry as such, but that they meant ordinary mental or physical malady by the term in general does not follow by any means. For remember that *exorcism,* or casting out demons, *was the chief duty* and occupation of the Primitive

---

* *I.e.,* the Dr. Abbot who was in controversy with Thomas Huxley about 1890. *Editor.*

Preacher. It is especially stated that the Jesus gave his disciples power to cast out demons and to cure all diseases (Matt. $10^1$, Mark $16^{17}$, Luke $9^1$). When the 70 return exultant they declare, "Lord, even the demons are subject unto us in thy name. And he said unto them, I beheld Satan as lightning fall from heaven" (Luke $10^{17}$). Surely no one questions that this mission of the 70 typifies the general appeal unto Pagandom, and the fall of Satan specifically represents the overthrow of Idolatry. Otherwise one would have not only to think that the Disciples of these 70 were sent forth to heal bodily sickness, but also to suppose that Paul and Barnabas and Apollos haunted the Synagogues, lecture-halls and upper-chambers, in continual word-battle with the Jews over the Scriptures, in pursuit of opportunities to show their medical skill in healing lunatics, paranoiacs and other defectives.

No! a thousand times no! If such had been the original content of the Christian Mission, we should have heard something about it in Acts, in the Epistles, and elsewhere. As it is, there reigns unbroken silence. The apostle never appears as a leech, nor is it ever hinted that Luke the "beloved physician" pursued his own practice after his conversion. All the records show these men and their immediate successors engaged as teachers and not as body-healers; their prime concern is with doctrine, to enlighten the mind, not to cure nor to pamper the flesh.

It is affirmed, then, with confidence that the New Testament healings are spiritual and apparently spiritual only, and especially that the casting-out of demons typifies the overthrow of Idolatry, the rout of the pagan gods. A striking confirmation of this interpretation is found in the observation that in the Gospels we meet with no demoniacs in Judea, although in Galilee they were "thick as autumnal leaves that strew the brooks in Vallombrosa." The reason seems obvious. Galilee was at least half-pagan and is the *emblem* of Pagandom, "Galilee of the Gentiles," where "the people were dwelling in darkness, in the shadow of death" (Matt. $4^{15\ f.}$ from Is. $9^{1,\ 2}$); but Judea was the home of Monotheism, the land of the One God YHVH. Had demons stood merely for the causes of bodily disease, not for the heathen gods, there would have been every reason for finding them in Judea as frequently as in Galilee, and expelling them wholesale.

No less a thinker than T. H. Huxley writes thus of the main Synoptic miracle: "When such a story as that about the Gadarene swine is placed before us, the importance of the decision, whether it be accepted or rejected, cannot be overestimated." Notice that it is with him only a question of accepting or rejecting; the question of the *meaning* of the marvel is not raised.*

---

* Quite so, Martin Luther would throw IV Ezra into the Elbe—because he could not accept its revelations literally!! Certain of the Church Fathers did indeed perceive and even avow the necessity for a spiritual or allegoric interpretation of much New Testament Scripture, but their sound judgments were graciously forgiven by their successors as unhappy vagaries.

But as soon as we recognize the parabolic character of the story, all talk of accepting or rejecting falls out of consideration. We are dealing with ideas, not with biographic facts.—As well talk of accepting or rejecting the Parable of the Prodigal Son.

Still more, if the demons typify heathen gods, then in the Gospel the overthrow of these gods, the redemption of mankind from their sway, is represented as the main activity of the Savior Jesus and the main charge to his Disciples, the main concern of his whole mission—all of which seems precisely as it should be and meets every demand of common sense. But if the demons do not typify false gods but are mere names for supposed spiritual causes of familiar diseases and abnormalities, then is the Gospel free from any allusion to Idolatry, by far the supreme sin of the Age, but to which the mission of the Savior from Sin has no reference whatever! This seems bizarre and wholly absurd. The Gospel of Salvation from Sin *must* have alluded to the principal Sin, i.e., to Idolatry: hence its demons must mean false gods or idols.

Yet another most eloquent witness to the real significance of the demons is found in the Fourth Gospel—which ignores them entirely! They glare through their absence. The explanation is not far to seek. As everyone knows, this Gospel inclines to favor the Gentiles wherever possible. To speak of the heathen gods as demons would be to draw a line of distinction extremely complimentary to the Jew, and this the author (whom we may call John) was indisposed to do. Hence he avoids all reference to demons or exorcism, though these were the burden of the Synoptics! This would be very hard to understand if these demons stood merely for unseen influences causing bodily ills, and if their exorcism meant merely the healing of such maladies, with no allusion to the pagan divinities; whereas it is all self-explained on recognizing the demons as symbols of the gods or idols and their exorcism as the overthrow of Pagan Polytheism.

### 3. SYMBOLIC EVENTS

The like may be said of the other miracles. They are symbols of the Salvation of Pagandom, wrought by the promulgation of the monotheistic Jesus-Cult. As such they are eloquent, impressive, and sometimes beautiful; as facts of a personal Biography, they would be impossible absurdities. The Conversion* of the Gentiles is the burden of the Gospels from first to last, not

---

* Let the reader pause for a moment and consider; What other religious Conversion of the Heathen was possible than from Polytheism to Monotheism? What other was actually accomplished? Undoubtedly moral betterment went along with this conversion, but morality was surely a very secondary consideration; never could it have inspired a universal religious propaganda.

only in the Miracles but also in the Sayings, Parables, and Incidents. Very often we find the Jew and the Gentile opposed, as (Luke 10$^{38-42}$) in the incident of the two sisters, Martha (the Jew), Mary (the Gentile), in the Parable of the Prodigal Son (who is patently Heathendom, the Elder Son being Jewry, as indeed the Fathers perceived and avowed,—Luke 15$^{11-32}$), in the Saying "The First Shall be Last and the Last First" (Mark 10$^{31}$ and parallels), in the Parable of the Rich Man (Israel, the Jew, rich in the favor and gifts of God) and the Beggar (Lazarus, despised Heathendom,—Luke 16$^{19-31}$). Most exquisite of all perhaps is the story (Luke 7$^{36-50}$) of the Sinful Woman with her alabaster box of precious ointment, plainly typifying Repentant Pagandom. (In Old Testament prophecy Idolatry and Adultery are well nigh exchangeable terms.) To accept this account just as it stands is to outrage common sense and to push modern literalism clean over the brink of absurdity. In the Gospel narrative the early and highly poetic Christian imagination has reared a shining and imposing temple of purely Symbolic Truth.

The necessity for this symbolic interpretation of the Gospels was first set forth fully and emphasized in *Ecce Deus* (1911)* though recognized by the writer in *Der vorchristliche Jesus* (1906) and even some years before. It is a chief merit of Loisy's later works to insist upon it strongly. The ancients themselves perceived clearly that an allegorical meaning was present and was the main meaning of the Gospels—as we might prove by abundant citation from the Fathers,—but they did not perceive or at least did not recognize the obvious corollary, that to *admit* the symbolic content was to *reject* the historic content; for it would be quite ridiculous to suppose (e.g.) that a Sinful Woman actually went through all those motions, in order to symbolize Converted Heathendom!! As much may be said of each and every emblematic element in the Gospels. It is the conscious and deliberate creation of a poetic fancy that would present the Glad Tidings, the Eternal Gospel, the Great Message of Primitive Christianity, in a vivid and picturesque guise, impressive and edifying especially to the oriental imagination.

## 4. DOGMA DRAMATIZED

The Gospel, in fact, in its personal-historical form, the whole biographic Gospel, was a concession to the weakness of human and particularly of heathen nature; it was made for the Gentiles because of their hardness of heart, their dullness of understanding for such spiritual Truth; it was excellent "milk for babes in Christ," who could not endure the strong food, the

* The Theologischer Jahresbericht Vol 31, p. 340 in reviewing *Ecce Deus,* says "Above all it is in the demonstration of the original esoteric character of Christianity, and therewith of the necessity for a far more thorough-going symbolic interpretation of the Gospels, that the permanent value of Smith's great work lies." Cf. p. 132.

meat for men, as says the Apostle, after declaring he had "determined not to know anything among you, save Jesus Christ and him crucified" (I Cor. $2^2$, $3^{1, 2}$): "And, I brethren, could not speak to you as to the spiritual, but as to the fleshly, as to babes in Christ. It was milk I fed you, not solid food,"—And in all this, what was there to wonder at? Nothing whatever. The notion of Idealized, Spiritualized, Universalized Israel, of the Individualized Genius of a Race, of the "Righteous Servant of Jehovah," doomed to death and humiliation, ordained to Resurrection and heavenly glory, the Guilt-offering for the sins of the whole world, the Torch-bearer for God Himself, His Light to lighten the Gentiles—all this had been grasped and stamped upon the pages of prophecy by the genius of a Younger Isaiah full five centuries before. Yet it remained withal a superlatively daring and difficult conception, at which the ordinary intelligence of that time and clime must certainly reel and stumble.

Besides, even the purely spiritual Resurrection of Israel and his Glorification as the Religious Head of all Humanity was a doctrine extremely easy to misunderstand and pervert into the conceit of some material and political exaltation of the Jews as the Chiefs of the nations, as the rulers of men,—a conceit abhorrent to the Gentiles and not to be tolerated for a single moment. It was necessary, then, if the wondrous message of Salvation was to be preached successfully to a lost and ruined world, to present it in a simplified, artless, intelligible Form, at which the heathen mind would not balk or rebel, but would eagerly grasp and rejoice. There was one and only one device that could meet the demand of the situation and at the same time lay close at hand: and that was to follow up the precedent of Isaiah, so native and familiar to the Hebrew mind, so appealing to the oriental fancy, and to present the Righteous Servant, the Torch-bearer, the Light for the Gentiles, as a Man, a suffering son of earth, "tempted in all points in our likeness without sin" (Heb. $4^{15}$).

Such (as we trust will be seen more and more convincingly hereafter) appears to be the Origin and such the Object of the Gospel-story, a perfectly natural origin and a worthy religious object, a device that was well-nigh compulsory under the actual conditions. That the missionaries, the Apostles themselves recognized it as merely a handle, a temporary makeshift, is evident from such characterizations as "milk for babes," already quoted, and others of similar import. Now at length, it would seem, the time has come to "put away childish things" (1 Cor. $13^{11}$). Surely the Christian world is not to remain always a babe blinking at the light and borne round helpless in the arms of ignorant priests and princely-vestured ecclesiastical dignitaries.

Furthermore, as the "Righteous Servant" was to be the Torch-bearer of Jehovah, His Light to lighten the Gentiles, to teach them the supreme truths of Monotheism and monotheistic worship and morality, of necessity the Jesus, who impersonates that "true light that lighteth every man that cometh into the world," was pictured as preeminently the great *Teacher,* and on his lips was laid all the higher Wisdom that could be gathered not only from the Law, the Prophets, the Writings, and even the Sayings of the Fathers, but also from the Greek Philosophy, which lined with silver the whole dark cloud of sensual life that hung around the shores of the Mediterranean Sea.

If these miracles and these sayings shall become part of a biography, often an incident must be feigned merely as a setting or framework for the miracle or for the saying—a practice in great favor even today.

### 5. No Other Meanings Needed

When to all the above we add the strong current of Gnostic and Philonic speculation and mysticism that pours through the Fourth Gospel, the whole content of the Great [Gospel] Quaternion is set in order and in its broader outline is explained. There seems to be not one detail of the four Evangels that does not become reasonably clear and intelligible in the light and setting of the foregoing exposition. Conversely, there is not one Gospel incident or saying that is made more understandable by the assumption of a personal historical Jesus.

Is there not, then, an occasion to apply the Principle of Parsimony, the Razor of Occam? It forbids the introduction of unnecessary suppositions or principles of explanation (*Entia non sunt multiplicanda praeter necessitatem*). Now we know for certain that *some* of the Gospel accounts, in fact many, were *invented* to fulfil the Hebrew Scriptures: the incidents are incredible in themselves, and it is expressly declared that they were intended to fulfil some ancient Scripture—whose actual reference is in every case completely and immeasurably another. The accepted principle of Occam, then, commands us to apply this form of interpretation to *as many* Gospel accounts *as possible,* and forbids us to apply any other mode of interpretation (as that the account in question was the overdrawn legend of some actual occurrence) until the impossibility of applying the other—already approved—method is established.

## Chapter Five

# Contributory Testimony

### 1. ISRAEL THE SON OF GOD*

#### i. The Elder Thought

At the portal of Hebrew History (Ex. $4^{22}$) stands this lofty pillar of a people's faith and hope: "Thus saith YHVH, My Son My Firstborn is Israel" (*B'ni B'kori Israel*). Likewise we read in Ps. $89^{27}$, "I will also make him (My) Firstborn," and in the generous chapter of Jeremiah, "I am a Father to Israel, and Ephraim is my Firstborn" ($31^9$). The notion is expressed a hundred times indirectly, though hardly less emphatically. It may be truly said to reign in both the Literature and the Life of Jacob. As the ages rolled by it was echoed from soul to soul and inspired the Hebrew spirit to its highest and widest flights of fancy, to its boldest deeds of heroism and adventure, and most of all to its triumphant patience and fortitude under the persecutions of near 3000 years.

We have already noted and quoted more than once the famous oracle of Hosea, "When Israel was a child, then I loved him, and called My Son out of Egypt" ($11^1$), as well as the striking sentiment in the Psalms of Solomon, "Thy chastening comes upon us as upon a Firstborn Only Son" ($18^4$), where the expression is strengthened by the insertion of Only,—at a certain logical cost, for an Only Son would naturally be the firstborn. It is noteworthy that the same addition, "Thy Firstborn, Thine *Only* Son," is found in IV Ezra— to be discussed later—thus showing how deeper and deeper the conception was burning itself into the heart and mind of the Nation. In fact, we may confidently say that without the continued and active presence of this Idea, the whole history of the Hebrew Race would become a mystery, an insoluble riddle, nay more, it would have been unachievable.

* The reader should hold carefully in mind that the problem of the appellation "Son-of-God" carries back to an entirely different set of biblical and apocryphal antecedents than "Son-of-Man," so that it needs to be studied separately; hence also that conclusions drawn from it have the force of independent evidence. *Editor.*

So much understood, let us ask: Was it possible for the Jews of that day or century, the first of our era, to think and speak habitually of the Son-of-God, the "Son of His love," without thinking at the same time of Israel, God's Only Son, Firstborn? For remember, according to the New Testament and especially according to the Gospel sketch, the Disciples were enthusiastic nationalists and religious patriots. The "Kingdom of Heaven," whatever else it might mean, certainly implied in their minds the restoration (*apokatastasis*) of all things, (Acts 3$^{21}$) and glorification of the national life of the Jews. The claims to be the Messiah (the Christ), and the triumphant Entry into Jerusalem, both imply a splendid Jewish Messianic State—so much at the very least.

Moreover the query in Acts 1$^6$ is explicit and impossible to misunderstand: "Lord, wilt thou at this time restore again the Kingdom to Israel?" Hereby it is not affirmed that any of these alleged incidents are strictly historic. We are concerned only with the indubitable fact that they certainly manifest the mind and temper of the early Disciples, which is the one thing in question at present.—We may instance further the songs and speeches in Luke I and II, as well as large portions of *Revelation*. Thus, in Luke's song of Mary, "He hath given help to Israel his Servant—that he might remember mercy toward Abraham and his seed forever" (1$^{54}$). Similarly the announcing angel: "He shall be called Son of the Highest, and the Lord God shall give him the throne of David his Father; and he shall reign over the house of Jacob forever, and of his kingdom there shall be no end" (1$^{32}$)—all of which is a personalization of the reestablishment of the Israel State. Likewise Zechariah's prophecy, "Blessed be the Lord, the God of Israel, . . . For he hath visited and wrought redemption for his People, . . . And hath raised up a horn of Salvation for us . . . In the house of his Servant David . . . Salvation from our enemies, etc." (1$^{68,\ 71,\ etc.}$).—Once more, the Song of the Angels, "Glory to God in the Highest. And on earth peace among *men\* of good pleasure*" (2$^{14}$). The phrase in italics can hardly mean any other than Israelites; for centuries they alone had been the "men of God's good will."

We ask, then, again: Can these zealous Israelites, burning with passion for "the glory of Thy people Israel" (Luke 2$^{32}$), can they have spoken habitually of the Son-of-God without recalling that "My Son My Firstborn is Israel?"

This is not all, however. The Divine Sonship of Israel, understood in the sense indicated was not only a permissible poetic trope, familiar to the speech and thought of the Chosen People, but in almost any other sense the locution "Son-of-God" could have found little favor with the pious monotheistic Jew, it would have savored too strongly of the hated polytheism around him. As is well-known, the solidarity of the Race, the continuity of one generation with

---

\* It seems not without interest to remark that this invocation, "peace among men," is found exactly so in Plato, *Symposion*, 197 C.

another, was a cherished article of the ancient Hebrew creed. The parents felt themselves as prolongations of far-off ancestry and as passing over without interruption into their distant descendants,—a kind of unconscious cosmic philosophy, which one can hardly read the Old Testament, particularly the Psalms, without sensing. To speak of this endless Racial Unity—in fact, the species *Homo theosebes* (God-revering) in a figure as the "Only Son-of-God" did not seem extravagant and did not suggest any pagan perversities. But to speak of an Individual as God's Only Son, no matter how honored or wondrous he might be, would sound like a profanity, a blasphemy hardly possible to a genuinely religious Hebrew. Certainly we should not attribute such language to a pious Jew, unless under the coercion of irresistible evidence. Is there any such evidence at hand? The answer is direct and unequivocal: There is no trace whatever.

## ii. The Later View (Gospels)

Does someone say that the phrase "begotten son" is used in a double sense? Is not this rather an arbitrary subterfuge?—Or that there is some mystic union of all believers in the one Christ? Granted;—But that can never explain the identity of the believers with any individual *personal* Jesus the Christ; far better however if the Christ is a Collectivity whose constituents are the Believers. Regard this simple syllogism: *Jesus the Christ* was and is the ONLY *begotten Son* (or *Child*) *of God;* but also EVERY *true believer* is a *begotten child of God;* Does not the *Collective Concept* of the Christ relieve this syllogism of its awkward paradox? Exactly this relation is what holds between Israel the Only Son-of-God and the individual Israelites. If then there be any virtue in logic, it appears that the Christ the Only-Begotten of the Father is the same as Israel the Firstborn the Only Son-of-God. The sole difference lies in the minds of Salathiel called Ezra and of the Evangelist John, so-called, *viz.:* the latter has expanded and etherealized the concept of Israel into an Israel of Faith rather than of lineage and of Law.

To be sure, in the biographic symbolism of the New Testament, especially of the Gospel, the Jesus the Christ is presented as an individual and yet as the Son-of-God,—witness the notable confession of Simon Peter at Caesarea Philippi: "Thou art the Christ, the Son of the living God" (Matt. 16[16]; otherwise in *Mark* and *Luke*); but all this (as already so fully set forth) is a mere matter of popular didactic form.

Now let the reader consider how utterly impossible as history the Caesarean incident, at least the words ascribed to Simon (in Matt. only). Think of a Jew fed daily on the *Shema* (Deut. 6[4]), "Hear, Oh Israel! YHVH our God YHVH is *One*"—think of his proclaiming a wandering Rabbi, as the "Son-of-God," yet knowing all the while that "My Son My Firstborn is Israel!" Who can imagine it?

On the other hand, so soon as we face fairly the historical situation of that day, recognizing that Israel alone had been known for a thousand years as God's Son and his Anointed, his Christ, whose holy mission it was to "enlighten the Gentiles," to redeem and to save the world, to suffer the most cruel persecutions even unto death, and yet finally to be exalted spiritually to the Throne of universal judgeship and dominion,—recognizing too that all this was familiar to the First Christians, along with the urgent need of pictorial personification to catch the heathen fancy in teaching—so soon as we fully and clearly envisage this whole plight of the Apostles and Missionaries of Monotheism, lo! everything falls into place in natural order, and we behold a lucid, a rational, a self-consistent, however remarkable, Allegorical Whole.

### iii. The Gnostic Tinge (Colossians and Ephesians)

In conclusion, one single example of the light thus shed even upon such far-lying regions as the Epistle to *Colossians:* "giving thanks unto the Father, who has fitted us (Gentiles) unto partaking of the heritage of the Saints in the light, who delivered us from the power of the darkness, and translated us into the Kingdom of the Son of his love, in whom we have the redemption, the forgiveness of sins, who is the image of God the Invisible, firstborn of all Creation, etc." ($1^{12-15}$).

It is notorious that this amazing Epistle has confounded commentary for 1700 years. Certainly it is Gnostic and mystical, but what is "the mystery the hidden from the ages and the generations, . . . but now it is manifested to his Saints" ($1^{26}$), this mystery about which the writer has so much still more mysterious to say? We can only glance at the enigma, but even a glance may tell us much.—In the parallel *To Ephesians* we read, "ye (the Uncircumcision) were at that time separate from Christ, alienated from the Commonwealth of Israel . . . but now in Christ Jesus ye that once were far off are made nigh. . . ." ($2^{12}$). Observe that *Christ* and *commonwealth of Israel* are here used as equivalents, and now return to the Colossian passage: Here the same *Conversion* of Gentiles is described—"the Father fitted us to *partake* of the inheritance of the Saints in the light." Here the "Saints" are the Chosen Israel-Folk as everywhere in Canonic Scripture, which literally swarms also with "inherit" and its cognates, as in Jer. $12^{14}$: "the inheritance which I have made my People Israel inherit."

By evangelization (or proselytism) the Gentiles are made to *take part* in Israel's heritage; hereby they are brought into "the light," "delivered out of the power of darkness (heathen idolatry) and *transferred* into the Kingdom of the Son of his love," that is, into the "commonwealth of (the new spiritual) Israel," which is here called "the Son of his love." A striking expression, yet now perfectly clear. Israel (as we have seen) is God's Only Son, and as such is the especial object of His unique and eternal love; the Old Testament simply overflows with this idea; says Gunkel (already quoted), "the splendid glorification of Israel, which is the final goal of the love of God."

This locution "Son of his love" will allow no other interpretation. To assume any reference to an imaginary Rabbi of Galilee is psychologically out of the question. Where in the Gospels, even in the Fourth, does God show any surpassing love for the Jesus? Where in truth any love at all? Nay, it is only in the History of Israel (as in so many Pss., 89, 103, 105, 136, etc.), of Israel upheld through centuries of calamity and finally transfigured, glorified as the Beacon-Bearer of YHVH unto the Gentiles, there alone that God reveals his love for his Son, "the Son of his love." Notice further (Col. $1^{15}$) that this Son is the Image of God the Invisible (as also in IV Ezra $8^{44}$), another idea pervading Hebrew literature, which recognizes Israel as the highest if not the only form of humanity proper, and hence as the especial Image of God.

Neither is this yet all. The Son is "the Firstborn of all Creation"—another predicate of Israel, as in Fourth Ezra's "Thy Firstborn, Thine Only Son," "in our behalf Thou hast made this first Eon," "so also is Israel's part: for your sake have I created the Eon" ($6^{58, 55}$, $7^{11}$); witness also the *Apocalypse of Baruch* ($14^{19}$), and especially *Assumption of Moses* ($1^{12}$): "For he has indeed made the world for the sake of his People, but that same (People), the *Firstling* of Creation (*eam inceptionem creaturae*), etc.," where, about the beginning of our era we find almost exactly the Colossian phrase applied to the Israel-Folk.

As time went by, naturally the claims of the Elect People grew larger and higher: at first their "inheritance" included only Canaan with perhaps a margin of safety in neighbor lands; thence it spread in the prophetic and still more in the apocalyptic imagination over all the earth. The "firstling of creation" or "the firstborn of all Creation" is only an uppermost rung in a lofty ladder.

The reader will of course not forget that the Israel so majestically though mystically delineated in these two Gnostic Epistles is by no means the tiny Israel of Judea or Palestine or even the Diaspora. As so often but not too often repeated, it is Ideal Israel, the Israel of religious enthusiasm, personalized and universalized as the Savior Christ, the Son-of-Man, the Son-of-God, "portrayed" as sacrificed on the Roman Cross, not merely to expiate the sins of all mankind, but still more to break down all barriers, such as the Mosaic

Law, between the Races and to unite all Humanity in the one Commonwealth of Israel, in the one Christ the Head but also the Body.

It is seen that the imagination of the Epistolists has indeed run riotously far, but the guiding reins of the traditional thought of the Old Testament have not quite been thrown down hand-free on the necks of the horses. Even such a passage as* Col. 2¹⁵, perhaps the most refractory in the New Testament, may now be found to yield some comprehensible meaning: "Having stripped† off from himself the principalities and powers, he made show of them boldly, triumphing over them in it" (the Cross). The writer would characterize the renunciation ("stripping off from himself") of all the material ambitions and political hopes of Israel, of all pretensions to the physical lordship of the world, its "principalities" and its "powers" (as promised in Ps. 2⁸: "I will give thee the nations for thine inheritance, . . . and the uttermost parts of the earth for thy possession. Thou shalt break them with a rod of iron, Thou shalt dash them in pieces like a potter's vessel"). All such the Christ, the Spiritual Israel, the Son-of-God's-love, renounced openly—such is the thought of the text,— accepting instead the far higher honor of Crucifixion (in the flesh) at Roman hands (the Death of the Israel-State) with the religious Leadership of all mankind—a light to illumine all the dark places of earth.

## 2. Fourth Ezra and the Son-of-God

### i. Introduction

The work known as *Fourth Ezra* (sometimes as *Second Esdras*) is one of the frankest and sanest as well as one of the most poetic productions of the Apocalyptic—one may even say of the Hebraic—mind. It consists of sixteen chapters, of which the first two and the last two may be disregarded as being additions—the first certainly and the last probably at Christian hands. Written in Hebrew, it seems to have been translated into Greek and later into Latin and other half "barbarous" tongues as Syrian, Arabian, Armenian, Aethiopian, etc. Unfortunately both the Hebrew and the Greek versions have disappeared. The Roman wars, especially the disasters of the year 135 A.D., were followed by a very strong reaction in the Synagogue—the sole remaining stay of the Racial Soul—against all Apocalypses (so totally discredited by events), and accordingly the Hebrew original vanished; a reaction not only, however, against Apocalyptic but also against Hellenism as the foe of genuine Hebraism, and so the Greek translation vanished likewise. But the Christian communion received the Apocalypses with open arms and hearts, modifying

---

* For an earlier comment on this passage and its setting, see Appendix, p. 208.

† At this point, apparently in despair, the American Revisers take refuge in a false translation, "despoiled the principalities, etc.," which is senseless and impossible, and even Lightfoot enwraps his own dead-lock in the robes of rhetoric: "the convict's gibbet is the victor's car!"

them here and there to suit its own notions and purposes. Nevertheless the close-following Greek theology became unfriendly, as it sniffed therein not the Hellenic philosophy it loved so much, but rather the oriental mythology it abhorred. Hence the Apocalypses disappeared in a measure from the culture-language of the Greeks, though persisting in the other translations named above (Gunkel).

## ii. Dialogues with Deity

*Fourth Ezra* (so-called) shared the lot of its class, though deserving a kinder fate. The various versions have fastened the attention of the ablest scholars and have provoked not a few ingenious attempts to restore, at least in part, the Greek rendering and even its Hebrew base. With this splendid display of learning we have here little or naught to do. Enough for us now that the book opens (ch. 3) with the author "Salathiel called also Ezra" (which strongly suggests revision or combination) in Babel (Rome), lying on his couch in anguish at the sight (or thought) of Zion in ruins, with Babel's populace reveling in riches; and in his agony he prays earnestly, with vehemence yet without extravagance, to the Most High, posing before Him, with many suggestions of *Job,* the Paradox of History: the Weal of the Wicked, the Suffering of the Saints—these latter of course the Jews. "Has Babel behaved better than Zion? Has any other People than Israel known Thee?" "Weigh Thou our sins and the sins of the others in the scale, that we may see which way the balance turns." "Some few—we might name—Thou'lt find have kept Thy commands; but of Peoples Thou findest none." $6^{31, \ 34, \ 36}$.

Such the pathetic and eloquent complaint of his Reason; the answer comes, of course, from his own religious self, but under the name of an Angel Uriel sent by God from heaven. "But thou a mortal man, that livest in a fleeting world (Eon), how canst thou comprehend the Eternal?" ($4^{11}$). We are reminded of *Faust:* "Thou'rt like the Spirit thou comprehendest—not me." Plainly it is the tale of *Job* again, but in these chapters it is avowedly the *Passion of Israel* that rends the writer's heart, the seeming absurdity of God's choosing a Folk from all eternity as His Own, of making the world for the sake of Israel His Son, of honoring his unique People with the unique knowledge of Himself and His Law,—and then surrendering them all to the godless will and persecution of unholy heathen! No marvel he exclaims, "Wherefore, oh Lord? Wherefore then was I born? . . . Why was not my grave my mother's womb? . . . That I need not see the woe of Jacob . . . Nor distress of Israel's race." ($5^{35}$).—We note in passing and must bear in mind that Ezra is wholly absorbed in his People and speaks for *them.* As in Psalms so often, the "I" is "collective" and stands for Israel. So too, in Uriel's replies, "Thou" means the Race of Jacob.

Again the Angel, who represents the Highest and speaks as God Himself, is at his side to help him, to assure him of God's boundless love for Israel as His own supreme, eternal, and almost exclusive care. Thus the dialectic proceeds, with the gradual unfolding of a theodicy, a high-hearted essay to "justify the ways of God to man." Details may be passed by, especially as the scheme fails to satisfy even the seer himself, but it is to be noted that the End is to be forerun by countless amazing "signs," and yet, with its solution of the riddle of History, is nigh at hand, and also that the pity of the Seer sometimes overflows the borders of Israel and drenches the hosts of heathen (apparently an Isaianic or Christian fringe). "Then shall the heart be changed in the dwellers on earth and transformed to a new spirit . . . Then shall Evil be expelled . . . And Deceit annihilated, . . . Then Faith shall be in bloom . . . And Destruction overcome, . . . And Truth revealed that so long has borne no fruit" ($6^{26-28}$)—which may all well refer to the world-triumph of Monotheism.

But in the "third vision" the Seer resumes complaint: "Thou hast said, Thou madest this first world (Eon) on our behalf; all other tribes that spring from Adam thou hast declared are naught, they are like unto spittle (LXX), Thou hast compared their overswash to a drop on a bucket (Is. $40^{15}$). Yet now, O Lord, even these nations Thou hast held as naught overpower us and tread us to pieces! And we, Thy People whom Thou hast named Thy First born, Thine Only Son, Thy Friend, Thy Nearest, we are given into their hand! *If indeed the world be made on our behalf, why have we not this world in our possession?* How long shall it thus endure?" ($6^{55-59}$).

Herein the Israel-Consciousness is revealed with blinding brightness. And what reply has the Angel? "There is a well-built city lying in a plain and full of all that's good; but the pathway to it is strait and leads along the edge of abysses, where fire threatens on the right, and on the left deep water,—and only a single path between the two, the fire and the water, and this path so narrow that it can hold the footstep of but one single man! If now that city be given to anyone as heritage, how can the heir take possession of his heirship, unless first he has trodden the perilous path thereto? . . . Such, too, is Israel's part. For their sake in truth I made the Eon, but when Adam transgressed my commands, then was the Creation judged: Hence have the ways in this Eon become strait and sad and toilsome, wretched and bad, full of perils and nigh to great needs, but the ways of the Great Eon (the World-to-come) are broad and sure and bear the fruits of life . . . Wherefore, then, takest thou not the future to heart but only the present?" ($7^{6-16}$).

Here, then, the doctrine of the Two Ways, set forth in Matthew ($7^{13}$) and the *Teaching* ($1^{1, 2}$), and long before by Prodikos (*ca.* 480 B.C.) in the Choice of Herakles, but now disguised past recognition! Naturally, the parable is not convincing to Ezra, who is made to answer: "... So may the Righteous well endure the Straitness,—for they hope for the Breadth; but the Godless have suffered the Straitness—and shall never see the Breadth!" ($7^{18}$).— Plainly it is not Ezra that speaks—Ezra of the preceding chapters and quotations, nay rather the Soul of Orthodoxy wrestling as in modern times, and just as vainly—but notice the *turn* in thought: It is no longer the doom of Israel, but of the Godless, the heathen persecutors of Israel, that vexes the soul of Ezra!! Surely a poser! The Angel answers: "*Thou* forsooth art no judge over God, ... No wise one over the Highest!? ... Rather let the multitude of the living go to perdition than God's command and prescript be despised. For God hath solemnly enjoined the living on coming into life, what they should do to obtain life and what they should observe, not to fall under punishment. ... But they disobeyed and gainsaid Him. ... They thought vain thoughts for themselves ... And devised infamous lies (idols), ... Yea, affirmed there is no Highest ... And bethought them not of His ways: ... His law they contemned, ... His covenants they denied; ... His commands they did not believe, ... His works they did not fullfill. ... Therefore, O Ezra, ... Vanity to the Vain, ... Fullness to the Fulfilled ... ($7^{19-25}$).

Is it possible to read such words and not recall the Apostle's in *Romans* ($3^4$), "Let God be true, but every man a liar"? the denunciation that "all are under sin," with the long citation from scripture ($3^{10-18}$)? as well as the heartless unfeeling paradox: "Who hath, unto him shall be given; who hath not, what he hath shall be taken away" (Mark $4^{25}$)?—In this $7^{th}$ chapter are we not breathing another air? Is not the atmosphere of Protochristianity around us? On this, however, we need not insist, but may continue with the Speech of the Angel: "For lo! Days come when the signs I have already told thee shall occur. ... Then will the invisible City appear ... And the Hidden Land disclose itself, ... And everyone that is saved from the plagues I foretold thee shall behold My wonders. [28]For My Son the Christ shall reveal himself along with all beside him and will *give gladness* to the Remnant four hundred years long. [29]After these years shall My Son the Christ die and all that have the breath of men. Then shall the World turn to the silence of primal Time, seven days long, as in the first beginning, so that none shall remain over. But after seven days shall the Eon that now sleepeth awake ... And Perishability shall itself perish (I Cor. $15^{54}$). ... The earth shall give up who rest therein, ... The dust release who sleep within it, ... The chambers restore the souls entrusted to them, ... The Highest appear on Judgment-Throne," etc. ($7^{26-35}$).

Again it is the air of the New Testament, of *Revelation* indeed, that blows about us. Whether or in what measure this seventh chapter, stretched to the inordinate length of 140 verses, be interpolation, we have neither space nor need to discuss, but the Messianic verses (28) demand notice. If this be Ezra speaking, then the interest of the passage is intense, for the question at once starts up, who is this "Christus"? The answer can hardly linger, for he is called "My Son," and already in 6[58] we have read, "But we Thy Folk whom Thou hast named Thy Firstborn, Thine Only Son, Thy Friend and Fellow," —It seems impossible that, after this unequivocal definition of God's Only Son, he should introduce, just 29 verses later, without any forehint or warning, *another* "Son," the Anointed (Messiah), of whom scarce another word is said! Moreover, the only thing this "Son the Christ" does, to reign 400 years, is exactly the longed-for lot of Israel the People. For we read in Gen. 15[13]: "And he (YHVH) said unto Abram, know of a surety that thy seed shall be sojourners in a land that is not theirs, and shall serve them, and they shall *afflict* them 400 years"; and again, in Ps. 90[15], "Make us *glad* according to the days wherein Thou hast *afflicted* us." Hence the notion of Israel's reigning 400 years. "All beside him" are of course the host of heaven, and we have seen that Israel's other self or *fravashi,* or guardian-Angel is spoken-of as Prince Michael the Angel (Dan. 12[1] and especially Dan. 10[18-21], where Greece and Persia have also their princes or spirit-guards). In Slavonic *Enoch* (33[2]), dating from before 50 A.D., we find a special period or world-day of 1,000 years, as also in Rev. 20[2], where the old Devil-Serpent Satan is bound for 1,000 years, during which the souls of those "beheaded for the testimony of Jesus," "reigned with the Christ a 1,000 years" (20[4])—evidently a christianization of the same thought of the kingdom of Israel.—There seems then no reasonable doubt that this remarkable passage—if Ezra's—must confirm the interpretation of the Christ (Messiah) as essentially identical with Israel,—at the furthest remove, only the heavenly Second Self or Prince or Angel-guard of the People.

If the passage be interpolated, it might appear to lose some interest, but the testimony remains unshaken; the interpolator has still the Ezra-sense in mind (of Israel as God's Only Son, 6[58]) and merely gives it a slight Christian tinge, queerly representing the Israel-Christ as dying at the beginning of the New Eon! This may startle as impossible for any Christian of today, but —not to mention pagan analogues—it has close and distinguished kin even in I Cor. 15[28]: "Then shall the Son himself be subjected unto Him that subjected all to him—that God may be all in all." Not strange in the Consummation, the new Eon, "the restoration of all things" (Acts 3[21]), [that] the Israel-Folk should die—be reabsorbed into the Father, Creator of all. To be sure, a most inadequate philosophy or eschatology, yet not without some glimpse of truth.

We must pass over much else of interest in this odd Chapter, merely glancing at the astonishing exclamation of the Seer: "O Earth, what hast thou borne when Reason (*Nus, Mind*) arose from the dust, like every other creature!" These verses seem too notable to omit, though scarcely on our subject. One almost seems to hear the voice of some Holist or Emergentist of old, some Neo-Darwinian before Darwin.

The doctrine of the seven-fold Pain and seven-fold Joy need not detain us, nor the wail of the Seer, "Ah, Adam! What hast thou done!" ($7^{48}$), nor the petition to God—against Damnation—in the name of His own seven Epithets of Mercy ($7^{132-39}$)—a petition that must give the Fundamentalist pause—with the dread response: "The Highest has made this world for many, but the future only for a few: much clay, but little gold; many are made, but few are saved," as compared with "many are called but few chosen" (Matt. $22^{14}$). But we must harken once more and well to the genuine Ezra-voice of protest ($8^{15}$): "Yet will I concede, as concerns men in general, Thou mayst better know; but what concerns . . . Thy People—that gives me pain, . . . Thine Heir, for whom I wail, . . . Israel—for him I moan, . . . The seed of Jacob, for him I complain." There follows the wondrous prayer of Ezra for his people ($8^{20-30}$)—which is hard to omit,—and the stern reply of Uriel comparing Man to seed sown by the Plowman, with Ezra's expostulation to God: "But the child-of-man Thy hands have made, that is called Thine Image, because made like unto Thee, for whose sake Thou hast created all,—hast Thou likened this to the plowman's seed?! Nay, Lord our God! . . . Spare Thy People! . . . Pity Thine Heir! . . . Surely hast Thou mercy on Thy Creature!" ($8^{45}$).

In this matchless pleading, for whom is the petition? The "Child-of-Man,* etc.," sounds like all Humanity, but observe the reiterated claim of the Seer that it was Israel "For whose sake Thou hast created all,"—and the closing lines banish all doubt: "Spare Thy People, . . . Pity Thine Heir!"—these words can apply to Israel and to Israel alone. The Angel (God) replies: "Now for the Now-ones, . . . Once for the Once-ones. . . . For thou art very far from being able to love My creation more than I" ($8^{46}$).—Gunkel magnanimously refers this "wonderful balm" to the "Love and only Love" that God cherishes for the "whole world," but no such notion is in the text. We find almost an exact parallel in $5^{40}$: "So little canst thou comprehend My judgment, or the goal of the Love that I have vouchsafed My People"—and this, Gunkel rightly interprets thus: "That is, the glorious transfiguration of Israel, which is the final goal of the love of God."—Such, then, is the meaning—unless possibly

---

* Menschenkind? The Latin is very odd (*sehr seltsam*), *hic pater et filius homo*—which is meaningless, but the Mazarin Ms. of 11th Century, has *sic pat* (for *patitur*), "So suffers," which would render an earlier Greek *houtos paschei kai huios anthropos*, and this last phrase must render a Hebrew *ben-Adam* (thus far, Gunkel), *Son-of-Man*, and this brings us squarely and flat-footedly to the *barenosh* of Daniel $7^{13}$, the Son-of-Man, the Saints of the Most High, the People-Israel. Stronger corroboration of our position could not reasonably be desired.

a Christian hand has tampered with the text and introduced the term "Creation," to include the Gentile world. The whole spirit of the Ezra-text requires the reference to Israel, but of course it was the whole tendence of the Christian Movement (the Prolongation of Proselytism), to widen the term "God's People," to embrace all heathen converts.

The "Signs of the End" are well-known; they date back at least to Babylon, they need not give us pause ($9^{1-13}$), but it is important to note v. 22 in the Angel-answer at close of the third Vision: "So, then, perish the multitude born unto naught! But saved remain *My Stem My Shoot,* which I with so much pains have prepared." Does this sound like "Love and Love alone . . . for all the world"? The case is clear as noon, that Gunkel (along with interpolators) has unwittingly universalized the Seer.

### iii. Symbolic Visions

For brevity we must move along to the apocalyptic Lion who in Ezra's fifth vision overcomes the many-winged, three-headed Eagle of Rome: "Lo! a lion rushes roaring from the wood and lifts as-it-were a Voice-of-Man against the Eagle: 'Hear thou Eagle as I speak, The Highest speaks to thee: Thou art the last of the four Beasts I had appointed to rule my world and for the End of my Times to come through them, Thou, though, the Fourth that is come, hast surpassed all earlier Beasts. Thou hast lorded the world with great affright, All earth with heavy oppression, . . . Therefore shalt thou, O Eagle, vanish, With all thy frightful wings, etc. . . . So shall the whole world breath easier freed from thy power, to await the judgment and the grace of its Creator' " ($11^{36-46}$).

Thereat the last of the three Heads of the Eagle vanished, etc.

But the *Lion?* "That is the Christ, whom the Highest preserves unto the end of days, who shall arise and come forth from David's seed to speak to them, he will hold their godlessnesses up before them, . . . Punish their iniquities, Display their impieties before their eyes. . . . Then shall he place them before judgment alive; then after he has convicted, them will he annihilate. But the Remnant of My People, who are left over in My Land, he will graciously redeem and grant them gladness till the End, The Day of Judgment comes, whereof I spake to thee at the beginning" ($12^{32-34}$).

Here there is an apparent distinction between the Lion or the Christ and "My People," but it is only apparent, like that in the popular ballad,

> "Uncle Sam is rich enough . . . To give us all a farm,"

where "Uncle Sam" and "us" are the same despite the distinction.* The "Lion that is of the tribe of Judah" (Rev. $5^5$) is the Judah-tribe itself (the

---

* Quite so in $11^7$ the Eagle "Speaks from his own body" to his own head and wings.

Israel-Folk) personified as a Lion. Says Jacob in Gen. 49⁹, "Judah is a lion's whelp." So Israel-sway should be pictured as a Lion with *human* voice, under whom the individual People are redeemed from oppression and blessed with joy. Certainly it is not implied they should *not* have a leader (like Judas Makkabi); to be sure they might, but any such would have significance only as representing the Folk as a whole. This Folk it is (whether on earth or in its Second Self, its *fravashi,* in heaven) that is the Christ, preserved through all the ages, to be revealed in glory at the last, whether of the flesh or the spirit or both. Such is the author's consistent thought throughout. To suppose he is thinking of a "supernatural person" unrelated to Israel (save as a Ruler imposed from without), the Israel that is the pivot of all his thought, is to suppose a sheer impossibility for our author as an intelligent man.

So much for the famous Fifth Vision. The sixth follows at once—another Dream—and lo! a mighty storm at sea, and all its surges aroused. And the Storm bears up from the heart of the sea as-it-were a MAN, and behold he flew with clouds of heaven (quite as in Dan. 7¹³). Everything trembled at his look, yea, all things melted that heard his voice, like wax when it senses fire. "Then I looked, and lo there came from the four winds of heaven a countless host of men together, to contend with MAN that had risen from the sea. I saw how he struck loose a mighty mount and flew upon it. I exerted myself to tell from what region or place the mount had been cut loose, but in vain. Then I looked and lo! a great fright seized on all assembled to war against him, but still they dared the strife. And as he saw the onrush of the host that broke forth against him, lo! he lifted never a hand nor bared a sword or any other weapon, but I saw only how as-it-were from his mouth he let loose as-it-were a fiery stream, from his lips a breath of flame, and from his tongue he let go forth a storm of sparks; but all these commingled together, the fiery stream, the blazing breath, and the mighty storm. And all these fell upon the assaulting host that was ready for the fray, and set them all aflame, so that in the same moment there was naught to see of the countless host save dust of ashes and the vapor of smoke. I saw, and horror fell upon me. Then I beheld how that MAN came down from the mount (Matt. 8¹) and called another peaceful host to his side. Then drew nigh him forms of many men, some rejoicing, others sad, some in bonds, some leading others with them as altar-gifts (proselytes?). Then I awoke, from fearful fright" (13¹⁻¹³).

The Interpretation! "The Man from the heart of the sea," "he it is whom the Highest preserves for long ages, thru whom He will redeem Creation, who will himself establish the new order among the Remnant. As thou hast seen how Storm and Fire and Tempest (literally Weather) went forth from his mouth, how he bore no sword nor any weapon and yet annihilated the onrushing host that took the field against him, that means lo! Days come when the Highest shall redeem the earth's inhabiters. Then shall great commotion seize the earth's inhabiters, so that they plan wars against each other, city against city, place against place, people against people, realm against realm (cp. Is. 19$^2$, II Chr. 15$^5$, Matt. 24$^7$). Then, when this happens and the signs occur that I have foretold thee, then shall My Son appear whom thou hast seen as MAN that arises. Then, when all the peoples hear his voice (Dispersion, Proselytism) will they forsake their lands and their mutual wars; so then shall a countless host, as thou hast seen, assemble at one point (*Harmagedon?* Rev. 16$^{16}$), so that they come on of themselves and assail him. He however himself shall tread upon the summit of Mount Zion; but Zion shall appear and be revealed to all completely builded—as thou hast seen that a mountain was hewed out with no human hands (Dan. 2$^{34,45}$). $^{37}$He however, My Son, shall punish for their sins the peoples that have marched against him —that are like the tempest; he will hold up before them their evil-plottings and their future pangs—which are as the fire, for he will easily destroy them by his breath—which is like the flame.

"But if thou hast seen him call to himself and assemble another peaceful host, these are the Ten Tribes that were deported from their land in the days of King Josiah, whom Salmanassar King of Assyrians hath taken prisoners; he brought them over the River (Euphrates), so they were transplanted into another land. There they themselves took counsel to forsake the multitude of the heathen and withdrew into another land still further away, where never yet the human race had dwelt, that they might there at least observe their statutes, which in their own land they had not kept. So they withdrew themselves—by small fords of the Euphrates River. For the Highest wrought wonders for them and held back the river's floods till they were over (Jsh. 3$^{16}$). But to that land the journey was a year and a half long, but the land is called Arzaret (other-land, Deut. 29$^{28}$). There then they have dwelt till the latest time; but now, since they are to come back once more, the Highest will again restrain the River's wells, that they may come across. Therefore hast thou beheld a host in peace assembled.—$^{48}$At the same time, however, there are also those that have remained over of thine own people—who are found in My holy domain. $^{49}$So then, when he shall annihilate the host of the assembled heathen, he will protect the people Israel, whatever is left thereof. Then will he show them marvels many and mighty.

"Then said I: 'Lord God, show me why I have beheld the MAN arise from the heart of the sea.' He spake to me: 'As none can explore or experience what is in the depth of the sea, so can no inhabitant of earth behold My Son or his company (Angels) until the hour of his day'" (13$^{25-52}$).

So far this famous Dream and its explication! It seems hard for any one to read the foregoing chapters and not perceive the wide chasm in thought and style that separates them from this "interpretation." Critics (as Gunkel) detect the divergence and tell us "these explanations (v. 37) do not fit well" and "this proposition seems to be a subsequent addition" (to v. 48). Other similar observations may be made. It seems to be for the most part a tiresome appendix or perhaps an unhappy overworking of some original that can not now be restored. All this, however, is of relatively slight significance. The all-important point is this: As any careful reader of the foregoing extracts (much more, of the Apocalypse itself) must perceive, the great heart of the author is wholly engrossed with the *problem of Israel,* the "Firstborn the Only Son" of God, for whom the world and all within it were made. Some may smile and call this an amazing conceit of Ezra's—who indeed well represented his race. But that makes little difference. His honesty and sincerity are transparent, and his cosmic scheme is quite as rational as that of his severest critics.—Unless then we are to suppose this deep thinker and eloquent pleader to have lost his senses in this 13th chapter, he must in some way reveal the mental and emotional mood that has swayed him thus far and inspired him to his brilliant dialogues with the Highest. He must preserve his essential ideas and meanings; he must not cast them aside without warning and clothe wholly other notions in their familiar garb.

Now it is certain that for him hitherto Israel has been God's "Firstborn Only Son" ($6^{58}$); he can not then in $13^{32, \ 37}$ mean something entirely different, nay, he *must mean* essentially the *same being,* though of course a rhetorical change in imagery is allowable and natural.—Moreover, the lofty aim, the Redemption of Creation ($13^{26}$), is hardly in harmony with the mind of Ezra. His concern was for the Redemption of Israel from heathen persecutors, as by all odds the main thing. It is true, this latter might be and even was extended and exalted into a spiritual Redemption of the Universe, at least of all mankind, and in the Christian writings this sublimation was actually accomplished in the Great Transfiguration of the Messianic Propaganda. But this was surely not in the thought of Ezra any more than in that of Daniel or Enoch or the authors of Matt. $25^{41}$ and the angel's invitation to birds to attend "the great supper of God" (Rev. $19^{17-21}$). Nay more, it is the grimmest travesty possible of a Redemption of Creation that blasts instantaneously into dust and vapor the whole assemblage of Mankind from all the four winds of heaven ($13^{5, \ 11, \ 37}$).*

It appears, then, plain as day that this "Interpretation" has been re-edited and christianized, to what extent none can say. The MAN from the heart of

---

* The Gentile reader may be reminded that this Ezra-precedent prevailed throughout the Jewish Dark Ages (till 1800); the most pathetic hymns (*Piyyutim*) of the Prayer-book are Dialogues between "Israel complaining of its bitter lot and God assuring it of speedy redemption" (Greenstone, *The Messiah Idea in Jewish History,* p. 300).

the Sea seems obviously parallel to the *Eagle* from the Sea; he figures the
Israel-Folk or Soul, as the Eagle figured the Roman State. As in Daniel, the
Israel-Commonwealth is also figured by the "cut-loose" mountain. These
varying phases of the same Reality are fused with some awkward effort in
the text: the *Man* cuts loose the Mount and *flies to it!*—he also treads the peaks
of Zion. Such inconsistencies in imagery need not surprise us in oriental
poetry; they are far milder than the mixed metaphors that meet us in the
novels, addresses, and even literature of today. From such an amazing Man
one might expect something more than one destroying breath, but there the
story appears to end. Yet no wonder. For almost the sole concern of the
author is the vindication and glorification of the Israel-Folk—and that done,
what more? But that *is done* when the Man arises from the Heart of the Sea
and dissipates all opposition with the burning breath of his mouth. What more
then is left to be done? Only the Return of the Ten Tribes that 500 years before had vanished from history! The want of function for the sea-born Man,
after the extinction of Pagandom, shows clearly that the Seer had only the
Triumph of Israel, the Coronation of Zion, in mind.

### iv. Conclusions from Fourth Ezra

It matters not, then, whether or how far this Ezra-book be interpolated—
at least, not for the argument in hand. If it be not interpolated, then assuredly
we must understand all the references to the Son-of-God in one and the same
sense, as defined in $6^{58}$: Israel the "Firstborn and Only Son" of God; surely
it would require very explicit unequivocal and unanswerable proof to show
that Ezra recognized *two* distinct Beings, each the *only* Son-of-God!!—This
established, the next step is easy, for "My Son" is identified in $13^{32}$ with the
"Man that arises" from the sea, while in $7^{28}$ the same "My Son" is twice
identified with "the Christ" (the Messiah, the Anointed), and lastly in $12^{31}$
"the Christ" is explicitly identified with the *Lion* that springs roaring from
the wood. From beginning to end this symbolic representation or personification appears quite as consistent as such pictorial poetry well can be.

On the other hand, if the chapters be indeed more or less interpolated and
christianized, then the case becomes even stronger still; for then we shall have
not merely a Pharisee picturing the Israel folk as the Christ the Only Son-of-
God, the End and Aim of all Creation, but also some Christian(s) adopting
his general conception and varying his phrases, if at all, not enough to disturb
the foregoing identifications necessarily implied in the text as it now exists.
In other words, we have not only the Jewish view of Israel as the Christ the
"Firstborn and Only Son" of God, but also the practical endorsement of this
view by the Christian Reviser or Revisers.

The Christianization of this Apocalypse of *Fourth Ezra* would then consist almost if not quite solely in the introduction at various points of some humaner sentiments, more sympathetic with the Pagans—in fact, just such a mitigation of Palestinian Particularism as meets us in the Epistle *To Romans,* in parts of *Revelation,* at times in the Gospels, and even in *Isaiah, Jonah, Micah* and others—the mitigation, in truth, that finally converted Jewish Proselytism into Christian Propaganda.

View it then as you will, *the Fourth Book of Ezra is an impregnable bulwark to the central thesis of this volume.*

## 3. REVELATION

A spirit notably kindred to the Fourth Evangelist, yet widely different glimmers through the Apocalypse or *Revelation,* a Jewish document reworked to be completely though very imperfectly Christianized. Of course, no attempt can here be made to penetrate its mysteries, thoroughly, but some outstanding features may be noted. First of all is the entire absence of any historical trace or allusion. "From Jesus Christ, the faithful witness, the firstborn of the dead and the ruler of the kings of the earth. Unto him that loved us and loosed us from our sins in his blood. And he made us a kingdom, priests to God and his Father: to him the glory and the dominion unto the ages. Amen. Lo! he comes with the clouds; and every eye shall see him and they that pierced him; and all the tribes of the earth shall mourn over him. Even so, Amen!" ($1^{5-7}$). Such is the most personal reference, yet it does not advance an inch beyond the bonds of dogma and symbolic faith, it tells nothing of any history or Life. The phrase "comes with the clouds" shows that it is the People Israel, the Danielic Son-of-Man, that swims in the writer's fancy, along with the extremely obscure words of *Zechariah* ($12^{10}$) we find an amazing figure of "the living One; and I was dead, and lo I am alive forever more" (of the revived "Commonwealth of Israel"), a terrifying symbolism without the remotest suggestion of an historic personality.

In the 5th chapter we find "the Lion that is of the tribe of Judah" identified with "the *Lamb* standing as though it had been slain," "the Lamb that hath been slain from the foundation of the world" ($13^8$). This latter mark seems to identify the Lamb (*to arnion*) as the Isaiah "Lamb that is led to the slaughter" ($53^7$), the "Righteous Servant" Israel, of whom it might be justly said, "slain from the foundations of the world," from the beginning of history. That such was the idea of the Apocalyptist may be taken as certain; such and such only is the Lamb of Revelation. There is no hint of any Carpenter of Nazareth. The Lamb here is the same as the Lion and no less formidable and terrifying for being a lamb. What we read in this Apocalypse is manifestly a

(Christianized) glorification of the Chosen People. When the nations of earth call out to the rocks and the mountains, "Fall on us and hide us . . . from the wrath of the Lamb," it seems as plain as any such "revelation" can be that it is the long-delayed vengeance of the afflicted People on its persecutors that is in mind, "the great day of wrath" of YHVH and His Son against the heathen world. If this be not so, then the case of biblical interpretation is lost.

There follows (7th ch.) the sealing of all Israel (12 Tribes) and the countless Proselytes (Christians) "before the Lamb." There is no more inconsistence here than in *Isaiah* and everywhere else. It is the old story of the Many and the One. The Lamb, the Righteous Servant, the Son-of-Man, the Son-of-God, the Christ, all these stand for the People regarded as a Unity, which does not deny the Multiplicity of the same People. We need not pause on the measurement (Preservation) of the temple and altar and the worshippers therein or the two witnesses, but only on the remarkable statement ($11^8$): "the great city, *which spiritually is called Sodom and Egypt, where also their Lord was crucified.*"—An historical reference! But also a patent interpolation. That the author of vv. 1, 2, to whom Jerusalem was "the holy city," who hoped for the preservation of its sacred heart (v. 1), should yet speak of it as "Sodom and Egypt," terms of the vilest designation, seems quite impossible. The italicized words are a Christian gloss on a Jewish original whose spirit sounds clear in v. 15: "the kingdom of the world is become that of our Lord (YHVH) and of His Christ, and he shall reign forever and ever," where His Christ is his Elect One Israel.

We pass by the astrology of ch. 12, noting however that the man-child of v. 5, who is "to rule all nations with a rod of iron" (Ps. $2^9$), is clearly the People Israel or its representative Messiah, and the Danielic note is heard plainly in v. 10: "Now is come the salvation and the power and the kingdom of our God, and the authority of His Christ" (the Chosen Nation). The same note sounds quite as distinct in the Wars of the Saints (Israel) with the Beasts arising from the Sea (Heathendom). Note also that the Lamb "stands on the Mount Zion" ($14^1$), a clear identification with Israel. But most important of all is the Heathen Mission proclaimed in $14^{6-8}$: "And I saw another angel flying in mid heaven having Eternal Gospel to proclaim unto them that dwell on the earth, and unto every nation and tribe and tongue and people; saying with mighty voice, *Fear God and give Him glory,* for the hour of his judgment is come: and worship Him that made the heaven and the earth and the sea and fountains of waters." This sounds as clear as possible, a worldwide call to Monotheism, to the worship of the One God, and correctly proclaimed as the content of the "Gospel Everlasting." Is there anything more luminous or more significant in the New Testament?—Note the utter absence of any biographic allusion.

The "second angel" confirms the message of the first by saying: "Fallen, fallen is Babylon the great that hath drenched all the nations with the wrath-wine of her fornication." Of course, this Babylon is Rome, the seat of Idolatry, the centre of Pagan worship,—both regularly represented as adultery by the Hebrew, both in the Old Testament and in the New. Rome is again denounced in very similar terms in ch. 17, as "drunken with the blood of the Saints" (Israelites),*—to which the Christian interpolator adds "and with the blood of the martyrs of Jesus"—and her doom is foretold. The voice of Daniel is heard again plainly in 14$^{14}$: "and on the cloud one sitting like unto a son-of-man." The "sharp sickle" of this verse and the following is taken from Joel 3$^{13}$: "Put ye in the sickle; for the harvest is ripe," "all the nations being assembled" before YHVH for judgment. "The winepress of the wrath of God" (upon the heathen) is "trodden without the city" (Jerusalem), which indicates with all desirable clearness the strictly Jewish character of these predictions. The ten kings that "war against the Lamb" are evidently the Roman authorities that war with Israel, whom Israel the Lamb is to overcome, "for he is the Lord of Lords and King of kings." Any such reference at such a date to "Jesus the Nazarene" is impossible.

The imagined victory of Israel over Rome is greeted with a Hallelujah chorus in 19$^{1-8}$. The marriage supper of the Lamb (19$^{9}$) is here intercalated in anticipation of the full account in ch. 21. This latter is derived from the prophets, as Is. 54$^{4-8}$: "For thy Maker is thy husband. . . . For YHVH hath called thee as a wife . . . even a wife of youth" . . . 61$^{10}$: "I (Israel) will rejoice in YHVH . . . as a bride adorneth herself with her jewels." 62$^{5}$: ". . . as the bridegroom rejoiceth over the bride, so shall thy God rejoice over thee." Accordingly in this vision of "a new heaven and a new earth," "the holy city, New Jerusalem," descends "out of heaven from God as a bride for her husband." In the prophetic thought the husband is God, and Zion or Jerusalem is only another name for "the commonwealth of Israel"—in Christian phrase, the Church, "the Body of Christ"—in the language of *Revelation,* the Lamb.—But the late Christian Reviser was not satisfied with this representation (21$^{1-8}$), it was not explicit enough in its Christianism. Accordingly he has added vv. 9-27: "And there came one of the seven angels who had the seven bowls, who were laden with the seven last plagues; and he spake with me, saying, Come hither, I will show thee the bride, the wife of the *Lamb.* And he carried me away in the Spirit to a mountain great and high, and showed me the holy city of Jerusalem etc."—Coming after the foregoing verses, this description appears inane and superfluous, a mere show-off on the part of the Recensor. Yet it is interesting that the names at the 12 gates are those "of the 12 tribes of the children of Israel" (v. 12), which would imply that the city is

---

* False and impossible as spoken of Christians,—before any considerable persecution.

the People Israel. The confusion of the author's thought, in his striving to distinguish the City from the Lamb, though both typify Israel, and to picture the City as the bride of the Lamb, though in the saner prophetic thought she is the Bride of YHVH himself, is shown in v. 22: "And I saw no temple therein: for the Lord God the Almighty, and the Lamb, are the temple thereof." The Lamb is the husband of the City, and also her temple! No easy task to dejudaize a thoroughly Judaic document.

Returning to ch. 19, we find (11–21) a particularly warlike and more than Danielic or Enochian vision of the white-horse Rider, Faithful and True, named also The Word of God, and also King of Kings and Lord of Lords (already identified as Israel, $17^{14}$), followed by the armies of heaven, treading the winepress of the fierceness of the wrath of God, and ruling the nations with a rod of iron—or rather slaying them with the sword of his mouth and giving them to the fowls of heaven for prey. It would seem hard to find in this vivid sketch any likeness to the meek and lowly child of Mary; if the author has ever heard of any such child, he has surely forgotten all about it. The "ruling with a rod of iron" leaves no doubt that the Rider is the Chosen People or the Messiah that impersonates them (Ps. $2^9$). The 11 verses are animated by the liveliest consciousness of the divine guidance and mission of the Elect Race, along with the fiercest imaginable resentment against the whole heathen world.

The 20th chapter as is well known, is inspired by the the the Slavonic *Book of Enoch*. The reigning with the Christ a 1,000* years is nothing but the rule of Israel for a millennium over all the earth, the Sabbath of History. The temper of the chapter is quite in key with that of the preceding. It seems amazing that anyone could find any hint of Religion where all is Politics.—The 22nd chapter, with its River of Life harks back to Ezek. 47, but the Christian Recensor has improved on the original phrase "and the leaf thereof for healing" ($47^{12}$) by writing "and the leaves of the tree were for the healing of the nations" (the Gentiles)—quite though in harmony with Ezek. ($47^{22}$). The strict Judaic character is glimpsed in the words of v. 9: "Worship God"— the essential message of the whole *Revelation*. The national character of the speaker Jesus is bared in the "I am the Root and the Offspring of David, the bright, the morning star" (16), which describes the People Israel or its authorized Representative.

It appears, then, that in this Apocalypse, professedly a message from Jesus to the Church(es), there is absolutely nothing to suggest the Galilean Rabbi, but a host of references that all *converge* upon the People Israel or its recognized Symbols and Personifications. The temper of certain chapters is strictly political, and their warlike passages are more than Danielic. *The Chosen*

* In *IV Ezra* only 400 years.

*People and the Messiah that impersonates them are symbolically identical
without the remotest suggestion of an historic personality.*

## 4. STRAY STRAWS
### i. James

Aside from John's Gospel the remaining New Testament books call only
for brief notice. The *Epistle of James* is particularly distinct in its testimony.
Though written to the Jews, to "the 12 Tribes which are of the Dispersion,"
and supposedly by the Brother of the Jesus himself, it contains *not the most
distant allusion* to the Palestinian Life or Death, not any trace of the Gospel
at all; but instead the most satisfying definition of religion to be found in the
Bible ($1^{27}$). How shall we account for the absence of everything distinctively
Christian? Moulton has ventured the hypothesis that the Epistle was not
written to Christians but to non-Christian Jews, whose feelings are spared by
omitting all reference to controversial matters! Certainly a spirit very different from that elsewhere displayed in the New Testament.

### ii. Timothy

A few passages remain in which there are some slight apparent notices of a
Jesus-life; but they all prove to be only apparent or else they are late interpolations. The most noteworthy is in I Tim. $6^{13}$: "I charge thee in the sight of God,
who giveth life to all things, and of Christ Jesus, who before Pontius Pilate
witnessed the good confession, that thou keep etc." This Pastoral Epistle is of
late date, how late none knows, and in no way represents a very early form of
Christianity; the verse in question was hardly written till many years after
the Pilate-legend had established itself in Christian circles; as Bultmann
would say, it is altogether "secondary" and bears no independent witness to
any trial before the Procurator. *Moreover,* the clause itself, "and of Christ
Jesus ... confession," reads much like an interpolation. It is pointless and apparently suggested by "the good confession" in v. 12, where the phrase has full
meaning, while in v. 13 it appears strained and almost senseless. In no case
can the verse bear any testimony to the "Historicity of Jesus."

### iii. "Went about doing good."*

One other passage must be noted. In the speech of Peter (Acts $10^{34-43}$), we
find it said, "... Jesus of Nazareth, how God anointed him with the Holy
Spirit and with power: who went about doing good and healing all that were
overpowered of the devil: for God was with him etc." (38). This is a classic

---

* See Appendix, p. 203; also for dielthe see p. 201. *Editor.*

of apology, and a more unhappy one were hard to discover. The whole speech
is recognized even by the leading historicist, A. Loisy, as a pure invention of
the Redactor, writing full three generations after the incidents in question:
not only so but it is an awkward patchwork of dogmatic phrases and catch-
words; it is hopeless in its Greek syntax, quite impossible to parse. The capi-
tal words "went about doing good" are held to describe the Galilean ministry
exactly. The Greek equivalent is two words, *dielthen euergeton,* literally, "traversed benefiting"—which sounds more technical. The phrase is apparently
Gnostic,† a favorite of Basilides (active at the date of this passage), used to
describe the descent of the heavenly Jesus from the Central Godhead, on
through the encircling Aeons to earth and man on his mission of mercy. He
did not merely *pass through,* said the Gnostic, he "passed through benefiting,"* blessing as he went. A very intelligible expression of an intelligible
Gnosticism (as Gnosticism goes), but very unnatural as a description of a
Galilean ministry—"traversed benefiting!" Consider also the next item, "and
healing all those that were overpowered of the devil." This may be accepted
as a pictorial expression of the Gospel-function (*logon,* 36), delivering all
heathen converts from the power of Satan (idolatry), as in Luke 10[18], "I beheld
Satan fallen as lightning from heaven"; but can any sane man, referring it
literally to exorcisms, regard it as a possible description of the career of any
professed Messianic Individual? Consider also the words "published throughout all Judea," whereas the Gospel account, even that of John, knows nothing
at all of any such publication save in Jerusalem and perhaps on the road to and
from Galilee. *Plainly we are dealing with a perfectly frank fiction, intended
only to formulate a church-theory current in the second century.*

## 5. POST-APOSTOLIC AUTHORS
### i. Didache

When we pass beyond the Canon into the sub-apostolic literature of the
Church, the case becomes if possible more convincing still. Surely if the Gospel was originally biographic, if its content was the Birth, Life, Death (and
Resurrection) of a wholly unparalleled Personality, a Carpenter of Nazareth,
and if the secret of its origin and success lay in the totally unique and overmastering impression of this Personality on his immediate disciples, then we
should expect to find details, anecdotes, and exemplifications of all kinds not
only abounding in the preaching of the First Christians but filtering on down
copiously into the next and the next generation. What, however, is the actual

† Compare with Gnostic hymn reproduced on p. 177. *Editor.*
* The conception of God as this *Savior and Benefactor* is a favorite with Philo (d. abt. A.D. 42),
appearing emphatically many times.

case? *Exactly the reverse,* as complete as can be! We have already seen that the New Testament writings, from Acts to Revelation, are practically destitute of any allusion to or knowledge of a Life of Jesus, being concerned solely (beyond matters of conduct) with the Dogma of the Death and (Spiritual) Resurrection of the Christ (the Genius of Israel), and now we face the further fact that the earliest non-canonical Christian literature is equally void of any such knowledge or allusion.

The general case is presented and discussed at length in *Ecce Deus* but cannot and need not be repeated in this connection; yet there are two highly important documents that demand special emphasis and attention: the so-called *Teaching* (*Didache*) and the *Shepherd* (*Poimen,* Pastor) *of Hermas.* The former is the very earliest extant Manual of Christian practice. It is a composite, the oldest portion dating back perhaps far into the First Century, the latest coming down maybe into the first-quarter of the Second, so that its testimony is very nearly synchronous with that of the Gospels. Nothing more natural, on the historical hypothesis, than that this *Teaching* should overflow with references to the Jesus, with appeals to his authority, with citations of his Sayings, with colorful incidents from his Life, with allusions to his Disciples; in truth, it is hard to see how *all* these could be avoided. Yet what is the fact? *Exactly the reverse!* The work is quite void of any such elements. It knows naught of any Life of Jesus, it makes no appeal to his authority or personality or disciples,—indeed, except in two or three interpolated phrases, it makes no use even of his *name!* How is it possible to explain this perplexing fact in harmony with the hypothesis of historicity?

## ii. Shepherd of Hermas

The case of the *Shepherd* is, if possible, even more impressive. This work (learnedly and ably edited, 1923, by Dibelius as a "Supplement" to the New Testament) appears to date from near the close of the first century,—it may be a generation later,—and so is not far removed from the Apostolic Age, not much later than much of the New Testament itself. It was held in the highest repute, being especially popular in the Ancient Church, particularly at Rome, which even then was beginning to exert a mild directive influence upon other congregations. It was regarded by the greatest Fathers as inspired and narrowly escaped canonization. Still more to the point, it was extremely popular with the second-century Christians, was very widely read as a book of devotion, and was treated almost as a *vade mecum.* What then was its testimony to the Jesus, to his Life and Character and Work? The answer is almost too astounding for belief, too amazing to write down. The testimony is absolutely *Nil!* The *Shepherd* knows nothing at all of the Jesus, never mentions the name, never alludes to any incident in his alleged life! It does speak once of the "Son-of-God" whom it identifies with "the Law of God that is now being preached throughout the world." It seems useless to elaborate such an astonishing fact. Let the reader pause and reflect upon it for a moment, if he would feel its full significance. The author, Hermas, would seem to have taken the Apostle and the writer to *Hebrews* at their word and to have felt that it was high time to "put away childish things," to lay aside the milk for babes and to take the strong meat for men—hence he ignores entirely the temporary "historical" makeshift of the Gospel stories and seeks to strengthen his readers by feeding them solely on spiritual meat.

It is quite irrelevant to our argument, whether this experiment was well-timed and successful. The point is that in Rome, the chief focus of the faith, it was recognized about the close of the first Century that the day of milk for babes had passed, and that the Gospel "history" might be shelved entirely and a purely spiritual doctrine expounded and practiced in its stead. Nor was this merely the wild conceit, the extravagant fancy, of one fanatic or even of a considerable group merely. The unequaled popularity of the *Shepherd* for over a century attests clearly that such was widely recognized as a worthy and legitimate view of the matter. Even Tertullian himself, the most implacable enemy of the *Shepherd,* did not oppose it on any historical grounds, but because of a certain alleged laxity or tolerance with respect to sexual irregularities, wherewith of course we have no concern.

Behold, then, the testimony of two very early and unimpeachable witnesses. In our day the "historical documents" are regarded as the sole foundation and support of the Truth, as the solid base, the irremovable Rock on which the total structure of Christianity rests, without which the whole fabric would fall and crumble into dust, yea, vanish into vapor. But at the beginning of the Second Century, in the principal Church, in the most intelligent circles, these "historical documents" could be and indeed were entirely ignored and the so-called "historical Personality" was passed by without mention even as if never existent! We have seen that all this becomes quite intelligible and quite consistent with New Testament doctrinal precedents—but only on the theory of Christian origins herein set forth and defended. On the traditional hypothesis about the Rabbi of Nazareth, it remains anomalous, a riddle never to be unraveled.

### iii. Ignatius

"At the mouth of two witnesses or three shall every word be established"; and the third is even more important than both the other two. The *Ignatians* are a group of 7 Epistles addressed to Churches of Asia Minor (one of them to a Bishop), ostensibly written by St. Ignatius, second Bishop of the Church at Antioch, while a prisoner *en route* for Rome, about the year 108,* there to be thrown to the wild beasts, as a martyr to his Christian faith. With much-mooted questions concerning the two forms of the text (the Shorter and the Longer Recensions), the details of interpretation, and the authenticity of the whole, we are not now concerned; our opponents, at least, will not dispute the genuineness of the *Letters.* We are interested mainly in the following facts:

The Bishop, standing on the verge of his earthly life, is intensely and almost exclusively engrossed with the *orthodoxy* (both in faith and in practice) of the congregations to which he is bidding a final farewell; above all, he would set them and leave them right in their conviction about the human career and personality of their Divine Savior Jesus the Christ, and especially warn them against *Docetism,* the dangerous doctrine of the *Docetists* (or Seemists), who held that the Body of the Jesus was not substantial, not made of real flesh and blood, but was only a Seeming, an Appearance (something like a rainbow, mirror-reflection or After-image).

This Apparition-heresy meets us in more than one hint of the New Testament. The incident of the doubting Thomas is a commonplace (John 20$^{20,}$ $^{24-29}$): "Reach hither thy finger and see my hands; and reach (hither) thy hand, and put it into my side: and be not faithless but believing." Similarly in Luke 24$^{39}$, "A spirit hath not flesh and bones as ye behold me having." These darts seem surely aimed directly at Docetism. Ignatius (in ch. iii, to the *Smyrneans*) quotes the speech to Peter (referred by St. Jerome to the Gospel of the Nazarenes): "Take, handle me, and see that I am not a demon incorporeal." Jerome himself declares in a well-known passage (*Dial. adv. Lucif.,* 23) that "while the Apostles were still living on earth, while the blood of Christ was still fresh in Judea, the body of the Lord was declared to be a phantasm."† How extremely unlikely that such a "heresy" could have sprung up so very early, in the bosom of the primitive Church, in the open face of countless historic-biographic facts—*if indeed there were any such facts at all!!* And how perfectly natural it all appears from the viewpoint occupied in these pages! The Docetists simply represented an elder (though not the eldest) Christian Consciousness, which refused to mount the wave of Literalism, of

---

* If we accept the recent arguments that the *Epistles of Ignatius* really come from about 150 A.D., (cf. Henri de la Fosse, *Lettres d' Ignace d' Antioche;* 1927, Paris) this still does not remove them from the documentary evidences. Their testimony still shows how unrealistic even the anti-docetists were. Also they show either how long it took for our standard Gospels to become accepted, or else how much freedom of imagination religious writers were claiming to relate events that conflicted with the accepted Gospels. The first alternative makes the standard Gospels so late as to be little dependent on historic fact and greatly dependent on psychological forces and other non-historic influences; the second alternative leaves the implication that early theologians saw in the Gospels not facts but doctrines which could be variously represented, with vastly differing "factual" settings. *Editor.*

† Cf. the teachings of Simon of Samaria, pp. 183-6, and the Docetae, pp. 206-7. *Editor.*

*historization,* on which Ignatius himself was riding, and still clung in some measure to the original figurative sense of the Gospel-story. They were not Progressives, but Reactionists rather; they were passé. One is reminded of familiar "errors" of speech and spelling, which are often only untimely survivals of forms that were once in the best repute and usage.

Ignatius seems to have understood the true state of the case, for in writing to Polycarp, Bishop of Smyrna, he does not (as one would naturally expect) denounce these "errorists" as innovators, but merely exhorts him (ch. 3) not to "let those that seem to be trustworthy and teach other doctrine overthrow thee. Stand firm as an anvil smitten." Their offence was teaching, not a new, but another doctrine—another than the Bishops themselves approved. Moreover, if the Bishop's doctrine was really firm-set in the Christian historic consciousness and bulwarked therein by the unequivocal testimony and tradition of numerous eyewitnesses, what room could there have been for a wild Docetic fancy? How could it have been conceived? how born? how nurtured? how propagated? What need to fear lest such illusionists "overthrow thee"? What occasion to exhort—so grandly—"Stand firm as an anvil smitten"? If Ignatius does not betray the weakness of his cause, his language seems strangely misleading.*

Since the Bishop attaches such supreme significance to the orthodox dogma of a real, not merely apparent (Docetic) body of flesh and blood, might we not rely upon him, being the forceful personality that he was, to put his best foot foremost in its defense, to marshal his facts, to summon his witnesses, to overwhelm the "other-teachers" under a crushing weight of testimony? For was he not barely sub-apostolic, born perhaps before A.D. 40? Dating almost back to the famous Pentecost, as a youth he might, if not must, have known Peter and Paul and Barnabas and Mark, have conversed with James and John, have visited Palestine and Jerusalem (it was only a ten day's journey thither) and learned all that could be learned about the human career of the Saviour. For surely no less would have beseemed a bold and confident leader, a Bishop of the Church that gave the name Christian to the world and sent out its missionaries far and wide. Had he brought forward one single flesh-and-blood fact of the human life, where so many must have abounded on every hand, in the memory of a thousand eyewitnesses, it would have been decisive once for all; a single child of the many that Jesus had "dandled in his arms" would have stopped the mouths of the "Seemists" instantly and forever. Who does not understand this? Is it possible that the Bishop, certainly a man of intelligence, the dominating personality in a principal and primitive Church of Christendom, is it conceivable that he did not understand it?

* For a fuller discussion, see The Open Court (Chicago), Vol. 27, pp. 351–363, 1913. Also see S. Reinach, discussion of Docetism, in *Cultes, Mythes, et Religions,* Vol. 4, pp. 189–206, for an appraisal of Ignatius similar to Smith's. *Editor.*

Nay more, it appears from his own statement (to Philadelphians, 8²) that he had been challenged by Docetists to produce some evidence in support of his faith. And what did he do? Did he produce or pretend to produce it? He did not. Did he make any effort to secure attestation? None whatever. What then did he do? How did he defend the Faith, the Dogma committed to his charge? He reaffirmed it and retired within the citadel of Scripture! He answered, "*Gegraptai!*" "It is written," the well-known formula of appeal to the Old Testament. That was all!

Does the reader ask for still clearer indication of the total inability of this immediate successor of the Apostles to present any historic or documentary refutation of the Docetic heresy? If so, let him read all these Epistles and note how the Saint's own view diverges hopelessly from any data to be found in the New Testament and is plainly a figment of his own fancy. A single citation may here suffice, from chapters 18 and 19 of Ignatius to the *Ephesians:*

"Offscouring my spirit is of the cross, which is an offence to the unbelieving, but to us salvation and life everlasting. Where is a sage? Where a disputer? Where boasting of those called prudent? For our God Jesus the Christ was conceived by Mary according to dispensation (of God) as well of David's seed as of holy spirit, who was born and was baptized, that by the passion He might purify the water. And hid from the Prince of this Aeon was the virginity of Mary and her bringing forth, likewise also the death of the Lord. Three mysteries of shout, which in stillness of God were wrought. How then were they* manifested to the Ages? A star in heaven shone beyond all the stars, and its light was ineffable, and its novelty produced amazement; and the other stars along with sun and moon became chorus for the star, but itself in its light was far surpassing all; and perplexity there was, whence the novelty so unlike them. Whereby was dissolved all magic, and every bond of vileness vanished away, ignorance was annulled, the ancient kingdom was destroyed, God being humanly manifested unto newness of eternal life, and its beginning received what with God had been prepared. Hence were all things commoved by taking death's abolition in hand."

What natural, what inevitable reflections arise on reading these verses thus literally rendered? Surely none can fail to ask, what has Ignatius in mind? Is he stating historic facts? Or even what he himself in heart regards as historic? Is he telling what happened publicly in Judea, known and observed of all men, notorious throughout all Palestine, proclaimed by apostolic witnesses throughout the world? If so, then his language could hardly have been more unfortunately chosen. If so, why does he call these three events, conception, birth and death, "three mysteries of clamor"? Why does he say they "escaped the notice of this age's prince," of Satan, who is commonly considered a keen, ac-

* Or "was He."

curate, and up-to-date observer, especially of such matters, in which he is particularly interested? And what of the heavenly manifestation and of the starry choir? If these be meant as literal history, what would be meant as poetic symbolism? Notice too the results of this manifestation. Are they anything but the overthrow of idolatry, with all that is implied therein? Is not this "cosmic," "eschatologic" revolution, following straight upon this revelation, is it not the conversion of the whole world from heathenness to the worship of the One God, of "our God Jesus the Christ"? . . . About details there may be room for wrangling; concerning the general import there seems to be none. Ignatius seems conscious that he is *not* dealing with matters of earthly experience, with a human life in Palestine, but with imaginery celestial happenings, with spiritual doctrines enveloped in the sensuous robes of figurative speech.—*Truly, Ignatius, "thy speech bewrayeth thee!"*

# Chapter Six

# *The Spirit of the Fourth Gospel*

## THE SPIRIT OF THE FOURTH GOSPEL
### *i. John versus the Synoptics*

At this point, our survey might be ended and our assembled conclusions might be presented, but for the haunting problem of the Fourth Evangelist. There still seems to hang a veil of mystery over his utterances. Of course, the general inquiry into his Gospel is too large to be broached in this connection, but on certain obscurities it may be possible to shed a little light. An unpublished study which I have made appears to demonstrate that a deep Numerical Symbolism reigns in nearly every chapter.* Numbers are never used incautiously, but such as 3, 5, 6, 7, 38, 153 are laden in the Evangelist's mind with esoteric meaning. The probability of this pervading Symbolism amounts to practical certainty.

Moreover, our study will next find beyond reasonable doubt that the Miracles or "Signs" of this Gospel are all Symbols, that there is no biographic actuality to be found or sought in any. Thus, the Resurrection of Lazarus, by all odds the chief miraculous deed in the Gospels, is evidently a visualization of the statement in the Parable of Lazarus (No-Help†) and Dives, Luke 16$^{31}$: "If they hear not Moses and the Prophets, neither will they be persuaded, if one rise from the dead." In this eloquent fable Dives (*Plusios*) is clearly the Jew, "rich" in the favor, the knowledge, the oracles of God, and the *No-Help* Lazarus is the miserable heathen, feeding on crumbs of Jewish proselytism. Yet the heathen is really converted thereby, becomes the Chosen of God, and is carried on high to Abraham's bosom, while the proud race-minded Jew is rejected into flames of Hades. There he looks up and beholds the Helpless in heaven, whom he pleads in vain may be sent to cool his burning tongue, or at

---

* Unfortunately the manuscript referred to has not been found among the papers of W. B. Smith's estate. *Editor.*

† This in no way disputes the customary derivation from Eliezar, "God his help"; compare the rendering of Livorno into English Leghorn. *Editor.*

95

least to his "Father's House" (Palestine), to warn his *five* brothers (Samaritans from Babylon, Cuthah, Avva, Hamath, Sepharvaim, "so these nations feared YHVH," II K. 17$^{24\text{-}41}$)—but nay, "saith Abraham, they have Moses and the Prophets," etc.

It is not strange that this pericope appears quite dislocated in the third Gospel, without any attachment* either this way or that. Luke (or his editor?) would appear to have found it wafted round on the wings of Gentile fancy,† and to have thought it too good to lose, the counterpart of his own far tenderer Parable of the Prodigal Son and the Elder Stay-at-Home (the Gentile and the Jew). Yet it seems he shrank from imputing such anti-Jewish sentiments to the Jesus and accordingly has left it in his Gospel quite unrelated, floating in the air.

But it did not escape the eye of John—as we may call the Fourth Evangelist. He recognized great possibilities in the closing verse and proceeded to develop them—turning prediction into history! *No-Help* becomes the brother of the sisters Martha and Mary (Judaic and Gentile Christianity), he dies and is raised from the dead—to convince the Jews, and lo! *they are not convinced* but proceed straightway to murderous plans against the Resuscitator! "In consequence the Pharisees plot to put Jesus to death" (John 11$^{46\text{-}53}$). Here, then, the Pharisaic counsel and determination against the Jesus are traced directly and unequivocally to this Lazarus-miracle—whereas such a person is unknown to any Synoptic, is absent from the Gospel "tradition"! But surely the Synoptists must have known of the Lazarus-prodigy had it occurred, they must have dropped *some* hint of the one decisive wonder. We must conclude, then, with all confidence that *No-Help's* story is a pure creation of Johannine fancy charmed by the Parable preserved in *Luke*.

What now could be more instructive? The incident is much the most minutely detailed to be found in any Gospel, preempting 57 verses, four pages of Greek text, more than is given in *Mark, Luke* or *John* to the whole story of the Crucifixion! And yet we are sure as can be that it is a deliberate invention from first to last, serving no other purpose whatever than to materialize and vividly objectify a certain conceit of the author, to throw it on the screen! Well, then, if such be the case with respect to *this* narrative, what may we, what must we suppose in case of the others? What right have we to assume an historical basis for a single incident, when the most emphatic and the most vivid one of all turns out to be without any semblance of foundation in fact?

This is not nearly all, however. The Lucan Parable of Lazarus seems deeply

---

* "The connection here is not obvious"—which is Weymouth's modest way of saying it is nonexistent.

† One can hardly repress the query, How many such tropes were there, of which we have never heard even a faint echo? We know only the flotsam and jetsam of a literature wrecked far out at sea.

tinged with unfriendliness toward the Jew, but it implies his former religious preeminence and his unique favor with God. So too the Fourth Gospel, late in origin, and echoing, as we shall see, the bitterness of second century believers against unchristianized Jews, yet in its one and only use of the word "Salvation" ($4^{22}$), it declares, "Ye worship what ye know not; we worship what we know; for Salvation is (comes) from the Jews." Then in verse 23, "For the hour is coming and now is when the true worshipers shall worship the Father in spirit and truth; yea, for the Father seeks such that worship him. God is Spirit, and they that worship him, in spirit and truth must worship." There is perhaps no clearer enunciation in this Gospel. It is the proclamation of a purely spiritual religion and theology, along with the apparent recognition that there are "such" worshipers scattered here and there, whom God now "seeks" (in the Christian Propaganda). The local center of such true worship has disappeared (the hour is coming when neither in this mount nor in Jerusalem shall ye worship the Father $4^{21}$), the true worship is worldwide—yet none the less, "*Salvation comes from the Jews*"!

Such seems to be a statement, as plain as well could be made under the historical conditions, of the permanent religious Headship of Israel—precisely the doctrine we have found encysted everywhere in the deepest vitals of the Primitive Propaganda. And all this from a source pronouncedly unfavorable to the Jews. Seventy times John employs the term "Jews" (or "Jew"), and almost always in a compromising connection, though it is of course admitted that there were some Jews that believed. In all the Synoptics the name is used only 16 times; that is, John uses it about 15 times as often per page as the Synoptics! Similarly he uses Pharisee about 20 times, never in compliment, but Sadducee never once, thus loading all the responsibility on the Jews as a whole and upon the more representative religious part. Now all this consists exactly with the view herein set forth, that the Religious headship of Israel was conceded and even taught once for all, but in this Gospel nothing more. It was Israel whom God had used as the outstretched arm of his Salvation (Is. $53^1$) and revealed to all the heathen world as his atoning Sacrifice for the sins of all mankind—all this unique function, this supremacy, was admitted, yet it carried with it no love for the Jews, and no hint that God loved his own Jew people!

Through this unmistakable Johannine animus is explained the extreme anxiety of the Evangelist to keep the allegory of his Gospel concealed, and to present the Jesus as a Man, as an *Individual,*—which at first may seem strange in view of the deep Gnostic and mystical tinge that colors the whole Gospel. He would in fact obscure and blur what he will not openly deny. He worked over the whole Gospel story in every detail to suit himself, to express his own ideas,—as he had perfect right and title to do, seeing that the Gospel was not biography but Religious Teaching in the first place. He was distinctly conscious of feigning his facts from start to finish of his Gospel. Who could write the Lazarus-story without knowing it was his own invention? And while doing all this, he emphasized at every turn the personal individual aspect of the Jesus, and so would cover up the national-racial character that constitutes his being.

Thus, as already seen, he admits that "Salvation comes from the Jews"; he proclaims of course also the deep foundation-faith of Israel in the One God, but how does he express it? In an extremely daring figure that no one did or could understand without knowing the central fact that the Son-of-Man was Ideal Israel Personified. "Except ye eat the flesh of the Son of Man and drink his blood, ye have not life in yourselves." The flesh and blood of the Son-of-Man was his doctrinal or concept-character as Ideal Universal Israel, the atoning Sacrifice for Sin (Idolatry). To eat his flesh and drink his blood was to accept and assimilate the great all-redeeming truth of Monotheism, which Israel had so long and so vigorously represented.

All the Christian propagandists personalized this over-towering Concept, but John would outdo all the rest in giving it an intensely *human* and *physical* expression, over-shadowing and disguising the National-Racial idea to the utmost. That his efforts have failed to hide the concept which they disguise, is the most striking evidence both of the actual presence of the ground-idea, and of the total absence of any strictly biographic element that could be utilized in his structure. If he had known any actual facts in a life he would so vividly portray, it seems inconceivable that he would not employ them, but would resort instead to such transparent coinage as fills chapter after chapter of his Gospel,—for such is the confession of criticism on every hand.

### ii. Only the Meaning Signifies

Once more, we may now understand another fact that puzzled at least the present writer for many years. Nothing seems plainer than the extreme insistence of the Johannine Jesus upon expounding some doctrine apparently deemed of transcendent significance, of life-and-death importance. Page after page is given to this exposition. Over and over again we are assured that this doctrine is the all-in-all, and beside it there is none other. The reader follows on from chapter to chapter, eager to hear the vital message: *but he hears it not,* at least not in words to be openly understood. In the last verse he is left longing even as in the first. Anyone can test this for himself by a careful unprejudiced reading at a single sitting.—Thus, for such a reading, begin with the first chapter:—

Chapter 1 opens like an oracle concerning the Logos, with bold and imposing words, but it teaches nothing whatever—for who or what was the Logos?

No answer.—It teaches no deep spiritual lesson to see a man under a fig-tree (1[48]).

In chapter 2, the miracle at Cana! In symbol (of the Spiritualization of Judaism by the Jesus, the water of mere rites and ceremonies turned into the wine of the Spirit) it can have meaning, but said literally it is as a teaching a mere nothing. That it has pagan parallels has long been known, and is also without didactic significance.—The cleansing of the Temple is another such symbol, effectively conceived, of the Spiritualization (of Judaism) brought about by Christianity. Others have made it abundantly clear that the actual Temple *was not* so profaned* and required no such cleansing. But even if it were strictly historical the incident would be didactically trifling. The mysterious words, "Destroy this temple, and in three days I will raise it up," could not have been spoken, but were necessarily written after the event.†

We come now (John 3) to the famous conversation with Nicodemus,—a tissue of misunderstandings.‡ The answer in verse 3 has no pertinence whatever but merely states the familiar dogma of Jewish proselytism, that a Gentile must be baptized and born again as an innocent babe before he can enter fully into Israel, "the kingdom of God." The misconception of Nicodemus is quite incredible. But aside from this, what does the discussion teach? Nothing. It merely affirms the necessity of a spiritual birth, but tells naught further. Verse 10 is unintelligible unless "these things" be only familiar Jewish doctrines clothed in mysterious words. The following verses (11–21) are simply assertions on assertions of mystical propositions that could neither be gainsaid nor accepted, and give the hearer no information or instruction whatever. What is said of the Son of God might fit eloquently on the lips of a second century Preacher of the Gospel, but on the lips of the Jesus at the beginning of his ministry it has no perceivable fitness.—Nearly the same may be said of the next incident and discourse (22–36). The Baptist's words may express fitly the reflections of a mystic of a following generation; as uttered by the Baptist they seem scarcely credible, and in any case they were mere asseverations without any attempt at grounding. They appeal only to a faith already formed.

Likewise (John 4) the detailed incident of the Samaritan woman. It represents the Jesus as if talking with a heavy veil before his face, hinting darkly at wonderful truths that are never expressed. Perhaps the clearest statement is (v. 18), "Thou hast had five husbands" (the *five* Assyrian nations that were transported to Samaria and "these feared YHVH," II Kings 17[24-41]). The famous dicta about true spiritual worship are delivered with awe-inspiring

---

* See Gustaf Dalman, 1924, *Orte und Wege Jesu*, pp. 236–237. The words in Jer. 7[11] have no reference to anything of the kind, but with a slight twist in meaning they furnish a good example of a Scripture that "must be fulfilled."

† See Editor's *Orientation*, p. xxi, item 8. *Editor.*

‡ See also Appendix, p. 164, 209. *Editor.*

solemnity, but teach us nothing new.* "God is spirit" had been wide-taught for ages; "Lord of Spirits" is Enoch's favorite phrase. The following verses contain various cryptic utterances, as "the fields . . . are white already unto harvest" (well-said of the expectant condition of the pagan world, its readiness to receive the message of Monotheistic salvation)—all of which may be understood as musings of later years, but have very little propriety on the lips of Jesus at the inception of his ministry and certainly reveal to us no important spiritual truth.

Verse 44 bewilders: "For Jesus himself testified, that a prophet hath no honor in his own country" (Galilee?)—as a reason for going to Galilee! This is inserted between two accounts of *belief,* one by Samaritans (39–43), the other by Galileans (45). No hint of disbelief by any! And what was "his own country"? Again, no hint! This becomes meaningful upon one supposition: That we have here an obscure allusion to the Gentile acceptance of Christianity and to its rejection by the Jews of Palestine (particularly of Judea). Still the implication would seem to be that Judea, and not Galilee, was "his own country"—directly against the Synoptics, and comprehensible only on recognizing the Jesus as an Impersonation of *Israel homed in Judea.*—Note in passing that the Galileans believed (received him) "having seen all the things that he did in Jerusalem at the feast" (45). This merely repeats $2^{23}$, but is strangely silent as to what were the "things" that he did. The Synoptics tell nothing of this "Passover," apparently an invention of John.

The "second sign," healing of the nobleman's son at Capernaum (John $4^{46}$) teaches only the complete efficacy of (monotheistic) faith and notably displays not the least human feeling on the part of the Jesus.—The fifth chapter is concerned solely with the third sign, the healing at the pool of Bethesda, and its consequences, particularly the discourses of the Jesus (19–47). That the cripple (for 38 years) symbolized Humanity powerless for 38 centuries (the Jewish age of the world) seems transparent.—Notice the harsh feeling in "the Jews sought the more to kill him" (18), compared with the recognition of Moses, who "wrote of me" (46). But where and what did Moses write of a Carpenter of Nazareth? Of what did he write? What was his sole interest? *The People Israel.* "Thus saith YHVH: My Son, My Firstborn, is Israel" (Ex. $4^{22}$). Here then the old paradox again: God's Agent of World-Salvation, His Son, is the *Ideal People Israel.* This the Evangelist acknowledges, though he mystifies it to his utmost. But the actual (temporal, transient) People, the Jews, are precisely the ones that reject the Propaganda—

---

* The words of Prof. Goetz of Basel—in his learned book on the Last Supper (*Das Abendmahl,* etc., 1920), with reference to these verses—deserve to be quoted: "*To be sure,* these passages (John $4^{23}$ and Rom. $12^1$) can be derived *perhaps not quite unjustly* from Greek influence" (p. 48). The words we have italicized (in German, *allerdings vielleicht nicht ganz mit Unrecht*) show with what extreme reluctance the honest critic lets the truth escape him.

and it seems that for this cause he condemns them. We need not pause upon the long discourse—a series of mystical affirmations beyond the pale of discussion or comprehension, because of the complete absence of any pretension to explanation or proof.

There follows (John 6$^{1-15}$) the *fourth* sign, the miracle of the loaves and fishes. The fair-minded man can hardly doubt that here again is a pure symbolism, on whose details we need not dwell. The unreality of the whole situation shines forth in verse after verse (as 3, 4, 5, 10, 13, 15). It is very possible that the Evangelist hid mystical meaning in all these strange items, but it is also possible that he inserted some solely for the sake of particularity, to render the account more plausible and picturesque.

Similar remarks apply to the fifth wonder, the walking on the sea (16–21), which seems however hardly more wonderful than the departure of all the 5000 and the disciples, across the sea, leaving the Jesus absolutely alone in the Mountain!! Surely the Evangelist must *mean* something by such a marvelous procedure, but we need not discuss what, nor the walking on the waves, which every open eye must perceive at once as solely symbolical. The following discourse, with its preparatory incidents (22–40), all quite unbelievable, merely affirms the necessity of Faith in Him, without assignment of any reason whatever. All is in the last degree occult and quite incomprehensible as spoken of any Individual. It *may* be understood of Ideal Israel as the Son of God (Hos. 11$^1$ and Pss.), but hardly otherwise. Eating manna and dying in the wilderness (as did the "fathers") may be meant as a contrast between the actual Israel (Jews) and the Ideal Israel, the Eternal Spirit then illuming the World. But on this we need not insist. Plainly, nothing is taught *that the multitude could learn.*

The two following sections (41, 52) give the kaleidoscope another turn. Not strange that the teaching is now admitted by the Evangelist to be sense-confounding (60, 66). We may indeed assimilate it as the musings of a mystic, a century after, who would shadow forth the astounding Paradox of the Actual and the Ideal Israel, but as the veritable teaching of any historical Individual to a throng of listeners out in the fields, it appears wholly impossible.

The 7th chapter would almost deepen a midnight gloom. His "brethren (Actual Israel) did not believe on him," but exhort him to go up to the feast of Tabernacles, into Judea. But he positively refuses, declaring, "I go not up unto this feast" (8). Yet "he also went up, not publicly, but as it were in secret" (10). A manifest contradiction, which shocked the feelings of early readers. Accordingly we find in some manuscripts the word *oupo* (not-yet) inserted in v. 8 after *ouk* (not); but this is pointless and would reduce the whole to triviality. One marvels though, at first sight, that the Evangelist would deliberately impute a falsehood to Jesus—it is incomprehensible, in fact, if by "the Jesus" he really meant a Man, an Individual. Not so, however, if by "the Jesus" he would indicate not so much an historic person as an historic process, the Genius of Israel working throughout the ages, clothed now in this now in that fleshly garb, and only in the latter days clearly recognizable as the Universal and Eternal Sonhood of Man toward God. The rules of individual morality might not apply to such a "supernatural person."

The following sections shed no ray of light upon this "darkness visible." The teaching continues as obscure as words can make it. There seems something like subtle irony in the answer of "the officers the Pharisees sent to take him": "Never man so spake." But it is literal truth and perhaps meant as such. Surely no physically actual man, whatever the circumstances, ever spake in such manner. Of a great Teacher that would bring light into the world it is quite unbelievable. Moreover, the persistent attempts of the Pharisees to lay hands on him, always followed by failure for no intelligible reason, if taken literally, would be simply ludicrous. Nevertheless there flash out a few sparks of suggestion. It is the Mission to the Gentiles that weighs upon the author's mind. Hence the question (v. 35), "Will he go unto the Dispersion among the Greeks, and teach the Greeks?" Here the hidden meaning starts to peep out—of course, still in heavy disguise. Another such allusion in v. 49; the Pharisees ask the officers who have returned empty-handed, "Are ye also led astray? Hath any of the rulers believed on him, or of the Pharisees? But this multitude that knoweth not the law are accursed." How could even Pharisees so denounce a crowd that had come from afar up to Jerusalem, *obeying the Law*, to the Feast of Tents? Is not this multitude unknowing the Law and accursed but a harsh name for the Gentile World—whom yet God so loved as to give for them his only begotten Son (His Israel, His Elect)?

Another section in this darksome chapter bids us pause and consider,—the scene on the great last day of the feast (37–44). "The Jesus" stands and cries aloud: "If any man thirst, let him come unto me and drink. He that believes on (into) me, as said the Scripture, out of his hollow* shall flow rivers of living water." Otherwise, with another punctuation, "and let him drink that believes into me. As the Scripture, etc." The reference of "his" would then be to "the Jesus" himself, as the well of living waters. We cannot discuss the punctuation here; let the reader choose. Of course, the "living waters" symbolize the Spirit, but one would need be more orthodox than Swift and full as foul of mouth to relish the figure, which the later translators swaddle in the phrase "from within him" in lieu of the literal rendering given. The quoted Scripture is nowhere found in just such words.† In Is. 44³ the "Servant Jacob, Jeshurun whom I have chosen" is consoled with the promise, "For I

* Greek *koilia*, hollow of the belly.

† *Vide The Open Court*, vol. 20, p. 640 (1906), A. J. Edmunds, for indications that the Evangelist may here have been influenced at second or third hand by Buddhist symbolism. *Editor.*

will pour water upon the thirsty. . . . I will pour my Spirit on thy seed," which would at least fix the reference to Israel.—Again in $55^1$, "Ho, every one that thirsteth, come to the waters, etc." Duhm assures us the meaning is the same as in $44^3$, the restoration of YHVH's effective favor, "the sure mercies of David"—mark you—"David, i.e., his house and his kingdom," says Duhm, i.e., the Israel-State. A little less vague is $58^{11}$, "And thou (Israel) shalt be like a watered garden, and . . . like a wellspring of water, whose waters fail not." Here at last Israel is become a flowing fount or stream.—So in Ezek. $47^{1\text{-}12}$ we find the vision of the deepening waters of life that gush out from under the Temple, "that all be healed and live," an emblem of Israel (or Israel's Religion) as the Healer of the World.—Quite similarly Zech. $14^8$: "And it shall come to pass in that day that living waters shall go out from Jerusalem," half east and half west over all the earth. Even in the Song of Songs (*understood* of YHVH and Israel), "Thou (Israel) art a fountain of gardens, A well of living waters, And of flowing streams from Lebanon,"$4^{15}$.

This metaphor passed over to the Apocalyptists. Thus IV Ezra $5^{25}$ (in speaking of God's favor to Israel), "Before all deeps of the sea hast thou magnified the *one* brook," and again in Baruch's vision of the Forest, the Vinestem, the Fountain and the Cedar (ch. 36), where Israel is figured doubly as a Vinestem and a Fount, "And from under forth issued a fountain in peace, and that fountain came even to the forest, and was made even unto mighty floods and mightily that fountain prevailed" (3, 4).—So, too, in *Additions to the Book of Esther,* in Mardachai's Dream, $11^{10}$: "And they (Israel) cried to God; and from their tears of grief arose as it were out of a little fount a great stream of much water." The fount has already been interpreted, at the close of $10^6$: "Esther is the stream, she, whom the King made his bride and queen"— but Esther seems to represent the Jewish Folk.—It is plain, then, that the Wellspring and living Waters are only names for the Chosen People. The Evangelist has this in mind but is somewhat puzzled how to introduce it fittingly into his personal picture; yet he must force the idea in some way, even if only by the use of clumsy imagery, which none the less images Israel.

The Feast was that of Tents, commemorating Israel's nomadic life in the wilderness before settlement in Canaan. The 8th day is the 22d of Tisri (Oct. 13), a day of "solemn assembly" (Num. $29^{35}$). On each of the seven preceding days the priest had brought water in a golden bowl, holding over a quart, from Siloam, and had poured it out in libation at the morning sacrifice while the multitude sang Is. $12^3$: "Therefore with joy shall ye draw water out of the wells of Salvation." On the 8th day this rite seems to have been omitted; hence the commentators like Lange tell us the people *felt the need or absence of water!* and that Jesus seized upon the auspicious moment to proclaim himself as the true Fountain!—That the musing mystic, a century after, steeped in Old Testament allusions to Israel as the wellspring of living waters, should take this occasion in his narrative to set forth his own conception of the Jesus-Israel idealized as that Fountain, seems likely enough; but to fancy that the Nazarene Carpenter did so and cried out to the crowd in such imagery (as a method of teaching) seems too grotesque for consideration. Such passages are important mainly as showing how foolish it is to take the Evangelist's words at their face value.

The famous incident of the woman taken in adultery (John $8^{2-11}$) next claims our attention. Doubtless interpolated, it is yet in the Johannine spirit and *ben trovato*. It is a bold but not quite successful attempt to outbid the Old Testament type, to limn a Savior beyond Scriptural Suggestion. The woman is plainly the idolatrous (adulterous) Gentile world; the stealthy departure of her accusers conscience-smitten would denote the frequent lapses of Israel from monotheism. Not strange that Ideal Israel should rebuke Actual Israel; did not the prophets rebuke even the kings, much more the people? The invention did not fully master the mind of the church; in some manuscripts it found place at the end of the Fourth Gospel, in others in Luke, between Chs. 21 and 22, and in most it found no place at all. Though un-Johannine in its diction, we may still regard it as a twig on the tree of "genuine evangelic tradition," a little *outré* in its growth, which is why the majority of the ancient scribes would lop it off. An extremely instructive example.

In the conversation that follows (John $8^{12-39}$) the tone is precisely the same as in so much of this Gospel, ominous denunciation and supreme self-assertion, without ever the least glimmering of evidence of any kind. In verse 30 we read "many believed on (into) him." Does he not rejoice?—for such belief was the one object of his teaching, the requisite for salvation and eternal life. But far from rejoicing, he at once leads these believers into the bogs of incredulity, by the will-o'-the-wisp of misguiding affirmations, such as "the truth shall make you free"(32), and ambiguities about Abraham (37), which pass over soon into unprovoked denunciation of these same believers as children of the devil (44)! What can be the explanation? Surely it can only be the anti-Semitic attitude of the second century Church! While the writer condemns the actual Israel he still recognizes the unique position and mission of the Ideal Israel as God's own Son, "the light of the world" (12), of the Gentiles, as in Isaiah.

This chapter concludes with the averment, "Before Abraham was born, I am. They took up stones therefore to cast at him: but Jesus hid himself (strictly 'was hid') and went out of the temple." Surely it were amazing for any one to write the like as history. A great crowd in the Temple, seizing on stones (lying around loose in the Temple!), to stone him, but he *is hid* and passes out unharmed (as many ancient authorities add, "and going thru the midst of them went his way, and so passed by")! What could be more incredible? And did not the Evangelist know it was so? Why then did he write it? The only rational answer seems to be that he was concerned solely with ideas and did not care for facts, which he shaped like putty to express his thoughts. What, then, was his idea in this connection? It is hard to say, but maybe what hovered in his mystical mind might be the notion of Israel's "hidden" unconscious Self as abandoning the ancient People and Worship and passing out unscathed into the Larger Gentile World which "God so loved" as to sacrifice his own Son (the Israel-Folk) to redeem it.

The 9th chapter brings some relief in the story of the 6th sign, the miracle of healing the man born blind. This we can grasp readily enough, as being a transparent symbol of Gentile enlightenment by the Gospel preached to all, as shines forth in the repeated words, "I am the light of the World" (as was Israel alone, Is. 42$^6$, 49$^6$, 60$^3$, etc.). With the details we are less concerned, as with the word *Siloam* ("sent"), but it must be noted that any *sinfulness* of the blinded is *rejected*: the blindness was only part of the Cosmic Scheme of God for exhibiting His own work in the grand drama of Salvation. A most extraordinary conception,—which must not however divert us from our path.

The following incidents and conversations (John 9$^{13-41}$) are designed to vivify the picture and to enhance the iniquity of the Jews, hostility to whom becomes clearer and clearer as the Gospel unfolds its pleading. Most remarkable is verse 39: "For Judgement came I into this world, that they that see not may see, and that they that see may become blind." This indeed seems clear as noon: it refers and can refer only to the confounding anomaly of history as seen in Christian doctrine, the exchange of places of Jew and Gentile, the Re-incarnation of the Israel-Soul no longer in the sons of Shem but in those of Japheth! Such indeed is the burden of the Apostle's heart in chapters 9 to 11 of *Romans,* where he would gladly be accursed from Christ for his brethren's sake (9$^3$), where he finally cries aloud (11$^{26-36}$), "so all Israel shall be saved," since God will "have mercy upon all," and lifts on high the exultant shout, "O depth of riches both of wisdom and of knowledge of God!" But the Evangelist takes a sterner attitude: "Your sin remaineth" (9$^{41}$).

The tenth chapter opens with the mixed metaphor and the recondite doctrine of the Door, the Sheep, and the Shepherd. It is hard to think of as a unit; how the same being can be at once both Door and Shepherd is puzzling. No wonder "they understood not" (6). "I am the Door of the Sheep. All that came before me are theives and robbers, but the sheep heard them not. I am the Door; by me if any man enter in he shall be saved" (7-9). Again "I am the good Shepherd: the good Shepherd layeth down his life for the sheep" (11, 17). Follows the story of the hireling who flies at the sight of the wolf. All this is recondite past measure, but we are forcibly reminded of Enoch and his long account of the Sheep (Israel) and the Seventy faithless Shepherds, and of the final triumph of the "Lord of the Sheep" ($89^{59}$). Surely this must have been in the writer's mind, and he must have perceived that Enoch was speaking of the Elect People Israel, for he says: "other sheep I have, which are not of this fold . . . they shall become one flock, one Shepherd" (16).* Prof. Charles admits the influence of *Enoch* in at least five other passages of this Gospel ($2^{16}$, $5^{22, 27}$, $12^{36}$, $14^{2}$), so it is not strange for it to be present here also. —As there is nothing else in *Enoch* obscurer than the Seventy Shepherds, so in this Gospel there is naught more confusing than this Door-and-Shepherd pericope. It lies outside our purpose to consider whether it be intercalated.

There follows the incident in "Solomon's Porch." The Jews gather round "the Jesus," and say, "How long dost thou hold us in suspense? If thou art the Christ, tell us plainly" (24). Surely a most relevant and natural request. "The Jesus answered them, I told you and ye believe not" (25). But when and where? The word Christ has indeed been used already 14 times, but never by "the Jesus." Then follow the condemning remarks, "ye believe not, because ye are not of my sheep" whom "none can snatch out of the Father's hand. I and my Father are one" (26–30). It is not easy to imagine discourse more provoking or less satisfying, unless it be vv. 32–38, after "the Jews took up stones again to stone him" (31); whereupon "they sought again to take him; and he went forth out of their hand" (39). In the mind of the author this repeated escape out of their hand, where escape would appear impossible, must have figured as a miracle, though not accounted among the formal *signs*, seven in number.

At last we come (John 11) to the crowning event of this singular ministry, the Resuscitation of Lazarus. Already we have alluded to it, and to evidence showing it to be a pure invention from beginning to end,—his kinship, his illness, death, and resurrection,—in order to fulfil the forecast that he found in Luke's *parable* of Lazarus ($16^{31}$):—"If they hear not Moses and the prophets, they will not believe, not even if some one should rise from the dead." We must note, as we pass, that the Evangelist does not hesitate to lay a second falsehood on the lips of Jesus: "This sickness is not unto death" ($11^{4}$), whereas he afterwards says "plainly, Lazarus is dead" ($11^{14}$). Of course, one may say, "but the Jesus intended all along to revive him." Doubtless, but that cannot modify the misstatement about his not dying. The best explanation is to be sought along the lines already laid down in treating a similar variance from truth in $7^{8}$. Certainly the author did not mean to attribute any moral obliquity to "the Jesus," but rather to exalt him into the regions of super-

---

* Such is the queer Greek, *mia poimne, heis poimen*. Modernizers, as Weymouth, mistranslate it "one flock under one shepherd," where the inserted preposition "under" changes both sense and syntax. Apparently "flock" and "Shepherd" are completely identified, as the allegory would require. (See also Appendix, p. 166 and 177. *Editor*.)

personality and super-morality.—We note also the sharp identification of Mary of Bethany with the woman "who anointed the Lord with ointment and wiped his feet with her hair," as in the next chapter $12^3$. But Luke ($7^{36-50}$) antedates this anointing by many months and attributes it to "a sinner," by no means to Martha's sister. Mark $14^3$ and Matt. $26^6$ both locate the incident in Bethany in the house of Simon the leper, and ascribe it to "a woman," who could scarcely have been the Sister of Martha, in whose house John apparently places the anointing, *not* in the house of Simon the leper ($12^2$)—for it seems hard to think of Martha as "serving" in the house of an unknown leper.

Here, then, is not indeed a falsification of facts, but a perfectly free handling of familiar ideas to suit the whim of the author—to which there is neither moral nor logical objection.—It is notable that the Evangelist seems to have tried hard to make this story pathetic as well as vivid, with what success the reader may be left to judge. One thing at least is certain, that we are taught nothing whatever that is comprehensible concerning any historic person, whether natural or "supernatural."

Of the incidents in chapter 12 we need add little; they have been treated elsewhere and do not bear directly upon our present inquiry—into testimony of the Johannine Jesus concerning himself so far as it appeals to the ordinary understanding.—The incident of the visit of the Greeks and their request is remarkable as illustrating the habitual irrelevance of the Johannine discourses of the Jesus, nearly always talking as it were to himself. No one that heard his words that follow (23-36) could have detected the slightest pertinence to the occasion. The Evangelist is still dreaming along Isaianic lines of the One Great Mystery, the Metempsychosis of the Ideal Israel from Jew to Gentile; he imagines the visit of the Greeks in order to furnish a setting to his own musings upon the wonder, and he puts these musings into the mouth of "the Jesus." The assemblage of index-words is remarkable. "Son-of-Man" heads the list, the Ideal Israel; "the grain of wheat, etc.", reminds us of Enoch's notion of the sowing of Israel ("And the congregation of the holy and the elect will be sown") ($62^8$).—This sowing is here regarded as a burial (of course, the conceit that the grain must *die* in order to sprout and bear fruit is the very reverse of truth, but we cannot require the Evangelist to be a biologist). This burial refers to the national humiliation of Israel, to be followed by his spiritual glorification in a converted Heathendom; "now is the judgment of this world" of course recalls *Daniel* and *Enoch;* "the light among you" re-echoes Isaiah's conception of Israel as "the light of the Gentiles," as does "believe on the light that you may become sons of the light" (true Israelites, 36). That Isaiah is dominating the writer's thought appears in the fact that the prophet is expressly quoted *twice* and named *thrice* in vv. 38-41: "*he saw His glory and he spake of Him.*"

The anhistoricity of the whole crops out in the words, "Jesus spake these things and departed and was hidden from them," followed immediately (for the verses between are the reflections of the Evangelist) by "And Jesus cried and said, He that believeth, etc." (36, 44). This hiding (or rather being hidden) is hard to understand of an Individual Jesus, but it explains itself when referred to the great Paradox, the Mystery of Salvation, the hiding of the Son-of-Man. Also, one asks to whom did he cry? since he had just hidden himself. The "cry" once more calls for Belief and proclaims Jesus as "a light come into the world" ("Israel, light of Gentiles," Isaiah), but there is no didactic pertinence, no proof, no advance in thought.

Chapter 13 opens with the washing of the disciple's feet (3–12), a symbolic act explained in the following vv. 13–20, the whole forming one of the most intelligible passages in the Gospel. But the obvious lesson of service and humility is strangely clouded with obscure references to the approaching surrender (*not* Betrayal). On these we may not dwell, but certain expressions call at least for mention. The scene (21–30) has been immortalized by the brush of the chief of modern geniuses, and the especial feature is the disciple whom the Jesus loved, reclining on the Jesus' bosom (23). Even if one accepts this profound symbolism as mere matter-of-fact, the queries will arise, Who was this disciple? Why did the Jesus love him? Did he not love all (with one possible exception)? All attempts to identify this disciple (unknown to the Synoptics) as an Individual have proved quite futile. To the present writer he seems to typify either the (Gentile) World or more likely that particular phase of Christian faith represented by the Evangelist himself, which favored the Gentiles and antagonized the Jews. The word World (Kosmos) is used sparingly in the Synoptics: 9 times in *Matthew* three times each in *Mark* and *Luke*, with little peculiarity to excite attention. In *John* it is used 75 times, and in 47 of these the sense is "metaphorical," as in "God so loved the world" ($3^{16}$). Again, in 92 verses of the *First Epistle of John* (more Johannine than the Gospel itself) it is used 22 times, 16 times in "metaphoric sense." Can all this be accidental? Surely not. The Johannine teaching must have some special interest in "the world." A closer examination of the texts—for which there is not space here—would show that the Evangelist has nearly always Pagandom in mind, either in its converted or in its unconverted state. This double aspect may somewhat confuse the modern reader, but it was by no means displeasing to the Evangelist, who rejoices no less than Hegel in such antitheses.

### iii. Closing Scenes

Upon the departure of Judas (the Jew), Jesus for the *first* time addresses the disciples as "Little Children" (33). Is this again a mere accident? As is well-known, the expression was regularly used to designate heathen proselytes, "babes in Christ." If Judas stands for Judean (*Iudas* for *Iudaios*), then the case becomes clear: The Jew being gone, the Gentiles are called by a peculiar and appropriate name.—We also notice that Judas is strangely represented as holding "the bag," the contributions for the Feast or perhaps for the poor (29). This recalls vividly the *Acts*, where we read much of contributions to the poor Judeans from the Hellenistic churches. It seems hard to doubt that Judas "the Surrenderer"* stands for the Judeans.

At length, in v. 34, we seem to find something definite and comprehensible: "A new commandment I give unto you, that ye love one another." This appears to be the acme of the Fourth Gospel. No one will question the basic importance of the "commandment," but is it new? Yes indeed, perhaps, to the *Gentile* convert, but not to Israel; for we read in Lev. 19[18]: "Thou shalt not take vengeance nor bear any grudge against the children of thy people; for thou shalt love thy neighbor as thyself: I am YHVH." And the group of neighbors is quite as wide as that of disciples. The claim, then, to give a "new commandment" is valid only if it be understood that by "Little Children" are meant Gentile converts.

The 14th chapter is marked by a still deepening mysticism. "In my Father's house are many mansions" reminds us of Enoch 39[4], "And here I saw another vision, the mansions of the holy (Saints) and the resting-places of the righteous" (of course, Israel), and elsewhere, thus: "And I saw the Lord of the Sheep till he brought a new house greater and loftier than the first" (90[29]), "And I saw that house was large and broad and very full" (90[36]).—The Comforter, the Holy Spirit is promised, but no new truth is proclaimed, nothing upon which a sane intelligence might rest as a basis. Only a gradual revelation of truth is promised for the future (14[26]).

The 15th chapter opens with a notable metaphor: "I am the true Vine, and my Father is the Vineman" (1), and again, "I am the Vine, and ye are the branches" (5), with many variants of the idea and much exhortation. As we know, the figure of *Israel as a Vine* pervades the Old Testament. In Ps. 80[8-16] the trope is set forth at length and in detail: "Thou broughtest a Vine out of Egypt, Thou didst drive out the nations and didst plant it," and it thrived. But now alas! "The boar out of the wood doth ravage it, And the wild beasts of the field feed upon it" (13). Clearly the Evangelist has merely spiritualized the exquisite image. Again, Jer. 2[21]: "Yet I had planted thee a noble Vine, wholly a right seed: how then art thou turned into the degenerate branches of a foreign vine?" Ezekiel also (17[1-10]) speaks "a parable unto the house of Israel" about a "Vine" ... "planted in a good soil by many waters, that it might bring forth branches ... and be a goodly Vine." So also in 19[10-14]. Likewise Hosea declares that "Israel was a luxuriant Vine that put forth

---

* A probable equivalent for Iscariot. See p. xix; also *Ecce Deus*, pp. 303–321. *Editor.*

fruit freely" (10¹).—Similarly Isaiah's "song of my beloved touching his Vineyard.... For the Vineyard of Jehovah of hosts is the house of Israel" (5¹⁻⁷).*— Such passages could not have been absent from the Evangelist's mind as he wrote this chapter. In declaring the Jesus to be the Vine, he identifies him unmistakably with Ideal Israel. So understood, the metaphor is full of truth and beauty; and what other meaning can be assigned it that will appeal to reason? Parenthetically it may be added that no historicist whose opinion is to be quoted believes that any such words were actually spoken by any personal Jesus; they are plainly the musings of a deep-thoughted mystic full two generations after the scene in question.

The next section (15⁹–16²⁴) is well described in 16²⁵: "These things have I spoken unto you in dark sayings (*paroimiais,* side-hints): the hour cometh when I shall no more speak unto you in dark sayings, but shall tell you plainly of the Father." But that hour does not come in this Gospel. What follows is just as deeply shrouded as what went before. The most that seems clear is that a "supernatural person" is speaking; to attribute such language to the Jesus of the "Modernists" would be to speak "as one of the foolish women." By an effort of the imagination it may all be ascribed to the Son of God, the Son-of-Man, the Elect One of the Most High, the Righteous Servant of YHVH, the universalized Israel personified,—and this ascription seems positively required in many important instances. Therefore, by the Law of Parsimony, we are required to adopt it in all.

All this must be said with especial emphasis of the famous Prayer in chapter 17. To whom was "authority" promised in the Old Testament and therefore given along with "eternal life" (2)? Unto Israel, Son-of-Man. Who was entrusted with the knowledge of "the only true God" (3)? It was Israel alone. Who in all the foregoing centuries "manifested Thy name unto men" (6)? Who but Israel only? Who was the Loved of the Father before the foundation of the world (24)? Let Hosea answer (11¹): "When Israel was a child then I loved him, and called my Son out of Egypt"; also, "My Firstborn Israel" (Ex. 4²²), whence Israel as "Firstling of Creation" (*Assumptio Mosis,* 1¹³). Who else than Israel could say, "O Righteous Father, the World hath not known Thee˙ but I have known Thee" (25)? Who but the Chosen People?— Such are "the brand-marks of the Jesus," and they are borne only by the Israel of God.

The 18th chap. naturally contributes little to our inquiry. The story of the Arrest and Trial is given with many minutiae, partly to vivify the narration, partly to suggest various thoughts and shadow forth various ideas, at some

* Compare also IV Ezra 5²³: "I spake, Ah Lord God, out of all earth's forest and all its trees Thou hast chosen thee the one sole Vine."

of which we may with some probability guess. Especially vv. 15-27 seem laden with hints of deep import, which however do not now concern us.

Queer questions arise about Barabbas, which we dare not digress to discuss here. We pass to the 19th chapter, but again must not lose ourselves in the countless queries that start up on every side. The evangelist, caring nought for what any other may have written, has boldly changed the day of the crucifixion from the Passover itself, as the Synoptists give it, to the *eve* of the Passover, the Day of Preparation (John 19³¹)—from the 15th to the 14th of the month Nisan,—thus presenting a patent contradiction which eighteen centuries have striven in vain to abate.

It is important to us to note that the Jesus says unto his Mother* concerning his beloved disciple, "Woman behold thy Son" (19²⁶), and to the Disciple, "Behold thy Mother!" And from that hour the disciple took her into his own. This impressive incident is original with our author. The Synoptics do not mention it, and seem indeed to exclude its possibility. They (Matt. 27⁵⁵, Mark 15⁴⁰, Luke 23⁴⁹) tell us that "many women . . . from Galilee" were "beholding from afar, including two Marys (Magdalene and the mother of James the less and of Joses)"; Luke is rather more generous, saying "And all his acquaintances (*pantes hoi gnōstoi autōi*), and the women that followed him from Galilee stood *afar off,* beholding these things." But only John knows of the Mother and the Disciple as present, nor could they have conversed with him "from far away" (*apo makrothen*). It seems unbelievable that all the Synoptics could have overlooked or ignored such an incident, if historical. Even the ancients recognized that our Evangelist must be speaking "spiritually," and understood that the "Mother" must be the Mother Church at Jerusalem. There seems indeed to be an allusion to the Israel-stock in this term Mother, whereas the Beloved Disciple (as we have seen) appears to stand for that form of Christianity that especially pleased the Evangelist himself, which he regarded as embodying the nerve and core of the new Doctrine. The "Mother" is not unfitly commended to this "Disciple"; in this Isaianic interpretation of the Ways of God to Man, Israel (at least believing Israel) was to find a (sad?) consolation in its tragic fate.

We see how the Evangelist has loaded his story with recondite meaning at every turn. Even to attempt to draw forth all to light would require volumes and would be apart from the purpose of this study. The following verses (28-30, 31-37, 38-42) relate several incidents with just one intent, to fulfil Scripture, as is avowed in 28, 36, 37, and might also have been avowed in 39,

---

* We call her Mary, but we read (v. 25) "his mother and his mother's sister, Mary." Two sisters, both named Mary!! John nowhere recognizes a Mary as the mother of Jesus; nor indeed does the Synoptic Tradition; the "prehistories," the first two chapters of *Matthew* and *Luke* are confessedly free inventions and the other mentions (Matt. 13⁵⁵, Mark 6³, Acts 1¹⁴) are also later insertions.

by a reference to Is. 53⁹,—but notice the exceeding art of the writer: he does not quote as fulfilled the words "with the rich in his tomb"—four such consecutive citations might spoil the triad and become monotonous—but he *implies* as much with all distinctness: not only was Joseph of Arimathea a "rich man" who laid the body in his own new tomb (Matt. 27⁶⁰), but Nicodemus also comes "bringing a mixture of myrrh and aloes, about a hundred pounds" (39). Certainly a goodly portion; we are reminded of the six stone waterpots of two or three firkins each (aggregating about 120 to 150 gallons), all filled to the brim with water, which is then converted into wine—a copious supply for the *close* of a wedding feast (2⁶⁻¹⁰). On both occasions the Evangelist would symbolize the unwasting fulness of the Spirit in its gifts unto men. Here at the tomb he would similarly express the fulfillment of the word of Isaiah, quite regardless of the fact that it reduces to absurdity the datum of the Synoptics, that the women from Galilee, after they "beheld the tomb and how his body was laid . . . returned and prepared spices and ointments" (Luke 23⁵⁶, Mark 16¹).

The attitude of the author is clearly shown in vv. 31–37. These incidents (of not breaking the legs and of piercing the side of Jesus) are quite unknown to the Synoptics, unhinted by any. Certainly they are John's obvious intentions, to *fulfill the Scriptures* cited (Ex. 12⁴⁶, Num. 9¹², Ps. 34²⁰, Zech. 12¹⁰). But he feels that their total omission by the Synoptics must naturally suggest doubts to the reader. What then does he do? He *affirms confidently:* "He that hath borne witness, and his witness is true: and he knoweth that he saith true, that ye also may believe" (35). Now why such intense earnestness? The alleged facts, as facts, have no importance whatever; if exactly reversed, if the legs were broken and the side not pierced, it would affect no man's faith in the least. Why then the purpose, "that ye also may believe"? Plainly it is some dogma, some doctrine that is in mind, and not a mere fact or event.—Again, who is "he," this witness? There is no hint, and no wonder; for it was only in the "mind's eye," that all this was witnessed, and there was no other reason for its being so, but one, which is given in the following vv. 36, 37: "For all these things came to pass that the Scriptures might be fulfilled: 'A bone of him shall not be broken,' and 'They shall look on him whom they pierced.' " The first was first spoken of the Paschal Lamb, and afterwards, in Ps. 34²⁰, of afflicted Israel, the Righteous: "YHVH keepeth all his bones, no one of them is broken"; but for the Evangelist the Lamb was the Jesus (1²⁹, ³⁶), i.e., Ideal Israel, and hence the Scripture *must* be fulfilled in him (in the Spirit if not in the flesh).—The second is found in a very obscure prophecy of Zechariah (12¹⁰), where the text is corrupt, but the better translation is "upon *Me* whom, etc."

To be sure these passages have not the remotest allusion to anything in

Gospel-story, but it fell in with the Evangelist's theory of past history to find there a *type* of the present, and accordingly without any scruple he devises the incident of the pierced side, his only reason being "the Scripture saith, they shall look on whom they pierced."—What can be plainer than that his whole account is made to order, the order of his theory of the Past as a premonitory shadow of the Present? If cross-questioned, he would probably have explained that the Past Shadow was material, the Present Fulfilment purely spiritual, that naught of the kind took place in the Present in any material sense, but only in a spiritual sense, i.e., in the hearts and minds of the spiritually Enlightened, the Believers, the Saved—even as the ancient formula expressed it, that Christ was raised from the dead *"for his disciples"*—not for the world at large. To us, the children of modern science, such an attitude or frame of mind may look bizarre and well-nigh incomprehensible; but unless we recognize its actuality at that day and age of the world, the New Testament Scripture and the Origin of Christianity must remain impossible puzzles.

The 20th chapter tells the story of the Resurrection, or rather of the empty tomb,—of course, in every particular at variance with the Synoptics. These new features are all the author's own inventions, and each has perhaps its own subtle mystical meaning, though what that meaning is it may be too hard to say. Four characters appear in the recital: Mary Magdalene, Simon Peter, the Beloved Disciple, the doubting Thomas. Each of these seems to typify some form of Faith current at the time or distinguished in the early history of the Christian movement—each, of course, as the writer conceived it. If we knew more about the internal features of the early Church, we might perhaps recognize these types readily; as it is, we can only very vaguely guess. The Beloved Disciple almost certainly stands for the deeper universal philosophic mystical demi-Gnostic conception of the Doctrine, as the Evangelist himself understood it. His race with Peter may represent the stages through which the rival factions gradually grew up toward the general Catholic conception of the "supernatural person." Simon first enters the tomb, he beholds the remains of the Resurrection, the outward signs, but it is not said that he believed. It was only the Beloved Disciple, "who came first to the tomb"— but did not first enter in—that "saw and believed." "For as yet they knew not the Scripture,—that he must rise again from the dead" (9).

Fittingly enough, the account closes with the blessing upon pure Faith and the warning against such as demand proof.—"Because thou hast seen me, hast thou believed?" Such belief, founded on fact, is not to be rejected, but it brings no blessing. "Blessed are they that have not seen, and yet have believed."—The writer seems quite conscious that he has no proof to offer for the minute story he has told, he does not profess to have any proof. Indeed he cares little or naught for the story in itself, which is only the outward dress of the inward sense. The one thing is to believe that "Jesus is the Christ, the Son of God, and that believing ye may have life in his name." Of course, this can be understood in a mystical sense only. We must remember that the name Jesus was *understood* to mean Savior and Savior only, and that the Christ, the Son of God, was the Genius of Israel, the Son-of-Man, the Elect of God (Luke $9^{35}$, $23^{35}$), and that it was the recognized Mission of that Chosen People to bring *Salvation* and Eternal Life to the world through Knowledge of the True and Only God.

### iv. Ad Addendum

The following chapter (21) is generally conceded to be an appendix, but is in the general spirit and style of the preceding. It is highly symbolic, as plainly appears. Jesus manifests himself the *third* time to his disciples—*seven* in number, Simon Peter, Thomas the Twin, Nathanael of Cana, the sons of Zebedee, and two others—at the sea of Tiberias, in Galilee. Notice they have *not* tarried in Jerusalem (Luke $24^{49}$); the writer rightly regards the accounts in Luke 24 and Acts 1 and 2 as pure fictions, good enough for Luke's purpose but unsuited for his own. Note also there is no hint of the Twelve or the *Apostles*—this last a term not acknowledged by John, though he employs the verb *apostello* nearly thirty times!—They have apparently given up all thought of propaganda, but not really, for Peter says, "I go a-fishing"—that is, for men? The others agree, but that night they catch nothing—which may symbolize the collapse of Judean or Palestinian preaching. But as "day breaks" (4), Jesus appears (unrecognized) and bids the "children" . . . "cast the net on the right," where it is instantly filled with fishes. Whereupon the Beloved recognizes it is Jesus hath commanded, and on hearing this Peter plunges into the sea, while the others drag the net "full of great fishes, a hundred and fifty and three" (11).

In II Chr. $2^{17}$ we read that the number of sojourners (foreigners) in Israel under Solomon was *a hundred and fifty thousand and three thousand and* six hundred. Remember now the *eleph* (thousand) is also used often in the sense of *tribe* or *people,* and that "sojourners" is also a term chosen to designate heathen converts ("ye are no more strangers and sojourners, but ye are fellow-citizens with the Saints and of the household of God," Eph. $2^{19}$, i.e., are true members of Universalized Israel), and it will seem plain that this coincidence in the number 153 cannot be accidental, that the writer meant something by it, that he meant in fact *all heathendom.* What he has in mind is the evangelization of the world, its union in the one Catholic Church—"and for all there were so many, the net was not rent." If such be not the sense here, then it would seem vain to seek for sense in the New Testament. We notice also that it is Simon Peter that pulls "the net to land" (11), a recognition of the primacy of the name (or what the name stands for) at the time, and of the practical nullity of the rest of the Twelve.

But the Spiritual supremacy of Simon Peter cannot be conceded by the writer. Accordingly he tells the strange story of a dialogue between "the Jesus" and Simon of Joanes, with the closing exhortation or command "Follow me" (19). Hereupon Peter turns round and beholds the Beloved Disciple following,—him that had leaned on Jesus' breast—and asked "Lord, but this man,—what?" "The Jesus" answers, "If I will him to remain till I come, what to thee? Do *thou* follow me."

If any will take this story at its face-value, we have no quarrel,—but hope he may "grow" on the "guileless milk of doctrine." But if any one doubt the literal accuracy of this physical post-resurrectional activity of the Jesus on the shores of Lake Tiberias, such a one will perforce seek for some *meaning* in these words, as already in the emblems of the fishes and the net. Nor will he likely escape the conviction that some kind of rivalry between two leaders or two tendencies in the early church is shadowed forth here in these twilight verses. Surely where the same question is thrice put there must be some doubt that prompts it. Notice also the emphatic and repeated charge to feed, to tend the lambs, the sheep, and no less to "follow Me." No marvel that "Peter was grieved." We cannot specify with confidence, but there can be no reasonable doubt that the writer is protesting gently but firmly against some ruling mode of thought or form of faith in the Early Church, in some wise associated with the name of Simon Peter.

He raises no standard of rebellion against this lordship, he allows its function of feeding and shepherding the flock of the Lord, but he cannot believe that it must permanently endure; the time will come when it shall pass away, grown old and helpless, and shall even glorify God by such an exit. On the other hand, there is a much deeper, a quiet and reticent, conception that nestles as it were in the very bosom of the Jesus himself, the inmost truth of the Gospel, the Wisdom and the Word of God. The dominating Church-tendency beholds this pensive contemplative Christianity following the Jesus of its own accord, without any command or exhortation, and asks with a faint impatience, "But what of this?" And the Jesus guardedly declares that it is this, even this unpretending mystic spiritual conception that alone abides forever, "till I come," not interfering with the practical "business-like" aspect, the faith of the masses and their overseers, but following its own path "the way, the truth, the life."

So understood, this Addendum, the 21st chapter, appears to be one of the sanest as well as profoundest in all the New Testament; in truth, as a parable it is unsurpassed, if indeed anywhere equaled, in human literature. As a literal matter-of-fact history of post-resurrectional flesh and blood, it may still serve some as milk—that has been, if not watered, at least most carefully skimmed.

The closing verses (24, 25) seem to show clearly enough that the writer has all along been speaking quite mystically, in symbols, and would warn the reader against any literal interpretation. "This is the Learner that witnesses of these things and wrote them, and we know that his witness is true. And there are also many other things that the Jesus did, which if they were written one by one, I do not deem the World itself could contain the books so written." The colossal hyperbole says plainly "Beware!" It is impossible to take such words as they stand. Notice also "we know" and "I do not deem." And how could "we" *know* the witness was true, unless "we" ourselves had witnessed? Surely it is a deep internal testimony, of the Soul and not of the eye, that is meant by the author. It is to the inner sense divine that he would make his appeal, an appeal to which all like-minded will hearken.

### *v. Viewed as a Whole*

This Gospel then appears as a plea and a confession. Its author can not and does not deny that another form of Christian faith than his own has taken precedence and is in mastery of the minds of the Many. He passes no unkind or unfriendly judgment upon it, thus displaying a Liberalism that deserves high praise. But it is not the type of belief that appeals to his own spirit, which is far more mystic and less practical. Naturally it is his own type for which he pleads as the true, the unchanging, the eternal.

That his opposition was directed especially against some form of Churchism that appealed to Apostolic authority, seems visible in his utter silence as to the Apostles; only once is the word used ($13^{16}$), and then not in the technical sense but in the general sense of "messenger": "neither is the *one sent* greater than he that sent him." Here, indeed, there seems to be a covert allusion, and one of depreciation. Similarly there is no mention of the choosing and sending of the Twelve; the term itself seems to be avoided: only in $20^{24}$ ("Thomas . . . one of the Twelve") and in a short section, $6^{67\text{-}71}$, is the term used ("Said the Jesus therefore to the Twelve, Would ye also go away?" and again "Have not I chosen you the Twelve, and one of you is a devil? He spoke of the Judas of Simon Iscariot, for he it was should deliver him up, one of the Twelve"). These uses are by no means complimentary.

It has long been the habit to identify this Evangelist with the Beloved Disciple (Learner, *Mathetes*), and this latter with John, son of Zebedee, an Apostle. Now there does seem to be some close relation between this Beloved and the Gospel author: The Learner symbolizes the Religious Idea or theory which the Author holds and would set forth. But to seek for this Learner in the Zebedean is to misunderstand the Gospel totally. Many have sought to explain the minuteness of detail by the assumption that the Zebedean is giving personal reminiscences. But this appears altogether impossible. It supposes that the Gospel is a careful record of biographic facts, a supposition for which there is not a ghost of warrant. "In the beginning was the *Logos,* and the *Logos* was with God, and the *Logos* was God." Does that sound like the opening of a Galilean Diary, or anything of the sort?

We have seen that many extensive portions of the narrative are beyond all doubt pure invention (or parables) of the writer, and full to the brim of dogmatic content or symbolic meaning. The discourses in general, as we have also seen, are philosophic soliloquies, mystical musings, which the author himself describes as "dark sayings," without much or even any relevance or fitness to the occasion, and which would have been quite unintelligible to any Palestinian audience, even as they remain uncomprehended by the theologians of today. The author employs certain familiar ideas and elements of the general Gospel tradition or propaganda, but employs them with perfect independence, making no attempt to conform his narrative to any Synoptic model or even to the Synoptic data. As a result he has produced a representation that is altogether his own, that not only defies any harmonization with all or any Synoptics but also seems equally impossible as the figure of any Individual— whether Man or God or God-man—inaugurating a Religious Revolution in Judea or Galilee or anywhere else. The figure is dim, dark, and shrouded, mysterious and miraculous, every way supernatural and nearly every way enigmatic.

All this seems hopeless to understand of any conceivable Individual but far from impossible to comprehend of a semi-Gnostic Allegorical Being, the Impersonation of Ideal Spiritual Universal Israel, regarded not so much as the Son-of-Man—as conceived by Daniel and Enoch, though this conception is not rejected but only firmly subordinated—as the Righteous Servant of Isaianic prophecy, the Arm of Jehovah outstretched for the judgment but also the Salvation of the World, the Light to lighten the Gentiles, and to exhibit Love as the central Pillar of the Kingdom of Heaven, Love not only of man for man and for God, but above all, of *God* for *Man,* particularly for the *Gentile* World.

This latter idea is by far the most signal contribution of our Evangelist to Religion and its Philosophy. The notion of God's love for His own Elect, for Israel His Son, was indeed in no way new, but not that of the same Deity's Love for the Heathen, the oppressors of His Own People. Our author, who seems to have been a Greek or a completely Hellenized Jew, does not at all deny or abate the religious pre-eminence of Israel or his destiny as the Agent of

God, the far-reaching Arm of His Power. Nay, he is deeply versed in Scripture, and he acknowledges fully the unique position and mission of Jacob. His own explanation of the Paradox of Israel's unhappy History and untoward fate is that the overweening Love of God was *not* for Israel in particular but for the World, the *Gentiles!* The Only Begotten Son is Israel, sacrificed for the world. Such essentially is the idea that reigns in Deutero-Isaiah. Compare also the *Psalms of Solomon* (18⁴): "Thy chastisement falls upon us as on a First-born Only Son."

The idea of Israel's religious leadership and even glorification, while admitted in terms by our Evangelist, was not a favorite with him, and hence he never dwelt upon it, but rather upon the Sufferings of Israel, of the Son of God. He was familiar with the imaginings of Daniel and Enoch, and he accepted them, but only with notable reservations, or rather additions and shiftings of accent.

*　*　*　*　*

The reader may complain that the treasures of mystical thought discovered do not repay for the quest, that the game is not worth the candle. Why dive for pearls in unfathomable depths, when the gems brought forth are only pinheads? The objection seems plausible and would be decisive—if our concern were only for the individual pearls,—but that is far from being the case. It is not they, each for itself, that we are seeking, but the necklace they form, or rather the whole bejeweled robe over which they are sprinkled. This garment of thought is an essential part of the elaborate vesture of the Early Christian Mind. If we would understand the one, we must also understand the other. Not the single minute gem but its connectivity with all the others is of value. Of itself it would signify little that in John 21¹¹ the *number* 153 typifies the whole of Pagandom, that the *net* typifies the Church, and its *unrent* condition the Catholic unity then coming to light, that Simon Peter's pulling in the net points to the prevalence of a certain mode of clerical thought and action, while the Beloved Learner adumbrates a deeper and more spiritual conception of Christianity. It is the entanglement and interlacing of these delicate strands of allusion with the entire drapery of Protochristian Experience that counts so much for our comprehension of the most far-reaching, deep-piercing, all-shaping and enduring single development in the long history of human civilization.

As it appears, then, to the present writer, the work of John is in aim correctly conceived by Clement of Alexandria as a "spiritual Gospel." It is a deep, solemn, intensely earnest but not passionate protest against the *final* triumph and exclusive recognition of the popular Catholic Ecclesiastical Governmental Literalistic and Conventional type of Christianity that was coming to the front more and more in those early days and at last issued in the two colossal organizations, the Roman Catholic and the Greek Orthodox Churches. Over against these he would set—not directly to oppose, but rather to supplement— a far profounder, a mystical, a half-gnostic conception, which he feels must lie at the very heart of Christianism and constitutes its very essence and its life.—It is the bane of the Mystic that his feeling, his sense, his intuition so far outruns his logic, his expression, his ratiocination. The Evangelist pleads earnestly and untiringly, but he never advances in thought, he merely wheels round and round, circling his object again and again, viewing it over and over, but never analyzing, never setting his thoughts into orderly relations. His arguments consist in exclaiming, See there! Behold! If you do not see, he does not show you, but merely deplores your dullness of sense. Hence his discussions are only a loose string of assertions, where the first may well be last, and the last may as well be first.

The Evangelist seems to have been not all unconscious of this lack of logical coherence in his exposition, and so he has sought to relieve it from stage to stage by the introduction of narratives or explanations in narrative form. Of course, all such must be virtual parables. "The deepest can be said in symbols only." And it is precisely such symbolism that is often the clearest and most instructive feature of his impressive pleading. Neither does he lack a certain literary sense and skill. He weaves into his recitals a number of details that serve to enliven the symbolic picture and give it an air of original autoptic testimony, though beneath these seeming trivialities he may have hidden away many a subtle allegoric allusion that might have been detected at the time, but is now covered too deep with the dust of centuries.

Herewith we neither raise nor prejudge any question as to the unity or integrity of the composition and the text, as they have reached us. There appears to be no good reason to suppose that the work has escaped the common fate of redaction and interpolation, but the re-editing seems to have been wrought in the general spirit of the original, with here and there perhaps a perceptible divergence.

The reader may perhaps wonder that the Evangelist should have ever attained such airy or nebular conceptions, and still more that he should ever have given them such studied and elaborate expression. What could he have hoped to achieve by writing such a pamphlet and parading before a select circle such a long procession of shadows in the cloud? But to insist on such questions is to misunderstand the mystic mind, which joys in its own lucubrations and delights to body them forth in words and symbols, and sometimes the darker the better. It was as natural, one may say inevitable, for the Proto-Christian to fall into symbol, parable, and allegory as for the modern after-dinner speaker to arouse his audience with an amusing anecdote, an ancient jest. Consider the long and lengthening list of *Pseudepigrapha,* practically all representing this literary drift and tendence. Consider among Christian or quasi-Christian documents the *Pistis-Sophia* and a host of similars. Consider the so-called *Epistle of Barnabas* and its fellows. Consider the learned and in many ways admirable Epistle *To Hebrews.* Surely it cannot be necessary to load the page down with the names of more such documents of that day. Let the reader glance through the *Book of Enoch* and remember it is only a partial compilation of works that went under his name. Let him read the New Testament Book of *Revelation* and reflect that it also is a mosaic of such compositions, a compilation of such apocalypses. Even the second Century could produce the *Shepherd of Hermas,* exceedingly allegorical and just as popular.

Whether we can comprehend it or no, the fact is indisputable that the Early Christians no less and perhaps even more than their contemporaries were devoted to mysticism both in thought and in expression. In Acts 21[10] we read that a prophet Agabus came to Caesarea and on meeting Paul took the latter's girdle and bound his own feet and arms with it, and said: "Thus saith the Holy Spirit, So will the Jews in Jerusalem bind the owner of this girdle, and will hand him over to the Gentiles." A modern occidental would be content to utter the prophesy, but not so the ancient oriental; he felt that he must enact the process of binding to make the prophesy impressive, and may he not have been partially right? Exactly so Zedekiah made him horns of iron and said. "Thus saith YHVH, with these shalt thou gore the Arameans, until they be consumed" (I Kings 22[11], II Chr. 18[10]). It must have cost some effort to make such horns, however rudely, and to us the symbolism seems puerile and ludicrous, but to Ahab it was vivid and forcible. So too the eating of *one* loaf and drinking of *one* cup was regarded as a sacred and awful emblem of brotherly unity (I Cor. 10[16]) and has partially preserved its meaning even to this day.

Enough. The Proto-Christian soul was fed on "dark sayings" daily (John 16[25]), on signs, on allegory. This dominance of the symbol became absolute in their use of the phrase Son-of-Man in metaphor, in which the urge to personify, to objectify, to mould abstract ideas into individual shapes, attains its fullest bloom, its richest fruition. This concept, which they had adopted from Enochian sources, they had profoundly modified by the Isaianic figure of the Righteous Suffering Servant of YHVH, the Idealized Israel, the Only Son of God, the Fullness of Him that filleth all in all.

Such mystical phrases are mere snapshots of a higher-dimensional Reality —a transcendent conception that might well inspire a Paul, a Barnabas, an Apollos to the boldest rhetoric, the most strenuous evangelization, but was far too ethereal for the masses, and needed to be assimilated to a much humbler order of apprehension, if it was to make any successful appeal to the average heart and mind. This necessary adaptation took the only guise that was possible under all the historical and cultural conditions, the form of a biographical allegory in which the Son-of-Man was presented as a Man moving about among men. Both the outline and the details of the Life were supplied (here in John as in the Synoptics) mainly by the Old Testament, which was essentially the Story of the Life of Israel. The incidents and sayings were at first devised in more or less clear consciousness that they were figments of fancy. But this Symbolization met the common fate of all objectifications; *the Sign is mistaken for the Significate.* Insensibly and yet speedily the *fictions,* the parables and symbols, came to be received more and more as *facts* and their underlying *meaning forgotten;* the guiding forces in the Church (like St. Ignatius) came to accept the situation not merely as a transient stage (depicted in I Cor. $3^2$, Heb. $5^{13}$), but as a permanent condition (I Pet. $2^2$ and the Ignatian *Epistles*). This might well be called the Petrine tendency, long since consummated in the Church of Rome, resulting in the most fixed and perfect organization that cultured man has ever seen.

The merits of this Objectivism—and it had and has many—were recognized by the Fourth Evangelist who still employed it himself, but he could not regard it as a finality or as more than a metaphor, a *likeness* of the deepest, innermost, divinest truth of the Christian doctrine and propaganda. Accordingly he wrote his Gospel—the witness of the Beloved Disciple who lay in the very bosom of the Jesus himself—as a Spiritual Gospel of eternal Truth and eternal Life—the Beloved Learner being none other than himself, or rather his own profounder mystical, more spiritual conception of the Christ, the Son-of-Man. Unfortunately he was himself one of the most mystical of men, and hence his own symbolic representation of the Life and Teaching of the Jesus, while revealing often the keenness and depth of his spiritual intuition, is in general woefully lacking in clearness, persuasiveness and convincing power. By adopting largely its current form of speech, he halfway yields to the tendency he would oppose, and turns the edge of his own argument, his protest against the historic materializations of the Faith. Besides, we have found that he was unhappily antisemitic, and failed to do any manner of justice to the Jews. He transcended completely the Danielic-Enochian conception of the Son-of-Man, abjuring every suggestion of Jewish favoritism, and outstripped even the Second Isaiah in exalting God's Love for the *World.* He strove hard to humanize his picture of the Savior-God,—though with very indifferent success—and to vivify his whole representation, by introducing minute insignificant details. The miracles he narrated are transparent parables throughout, and present his thought much more impressively than do the discourses he laid on the lips of the Jesus.

The writer of the Fourth Gospel is thus seen as presenting its story without

## Chapter Seven

# *The General Picture*

### i. The Great Personification

The exposition thus far sketched seems not only to show the practical certainty of the non-existence *as a man* of the Jesus the Christ, but also to exhibit with fair clarity both the Origin and the Content of the Primitive Propaganda, and so it may be said to make a rift at last in the persistent cloud that has hung for 1800 years about the Cradle of Christianity. But there are various other considerations, of less constructive value, indeed, yet highly important as pointing one and all with converging indications to the impersonal and purely ideal character of the Jesus. A number of these considerations have already been examined at length in the two books, *Der vorchristliche Jesus* and *Ecce Deus,* but some aspects still appear to deserve a survey.

Someone may inquire how, and when, and why, if there never was a human person Jesus, this wonderful Christian movement could take its origin. The answer, expressed in short, is that it was a continuation, prolongation, expansion, and intensification of the Jewish Proselytism, which may be traced back distinctly as far as 139 B.C.* Its key note was the Great Personification, rooted many centuries earlier still in the Hebrew sacred literature. A brief backward look into earlier times will help us.

This Personification of Israel had long existed in Hebrew literature especially under the name of the "Anointed," the Messiah, the Christ. Very naturally and appropriately the title the Elect One, the Chosen, was also frequently used, particularly by Isaiah, and in *Deuteronomy*. Hardly any other idea (except, of course, that of YHVH) so dominates the Old Testament as that of Israel the *Chosen,* and the resulting Personification was as natural and familiar as possible. The Anointing was merely a token and seal of this Election, so that Elect and Messiah (the Anointed Person) mean practically the

* In which year Simon, brother and successor to Judas Makkabi, sent an important embassy to Rome.

123

same. Moreover the controlling presumption is that the term "Mine Elect" is uniform in its reference to Israel and Israel only.

Now every one knows that this Choice of Israel from among all the nations of the earth carried with it the conception and therewith the lively unquenchable hope of the *Glorification* of the Chosen People beyond the power of words to express or even of the mind to conceive. If YHVH, the One Supreme God, the Almighty, the Maker of heaven and earth, had indeed elected Israel from among all the nations as His Only Son and had loved him and reared him (Hos. $11^1$) and revealed His Will and His Law unto Israel and Israel alone, then it would seem impossible to exaggerate the difference or the distance between this People and all other peoples of the earth, and the figurative representation (in Dan. 7) of the kingdoms of the nations as monstrous beasts but of Israel as Human, as One-Like-a-Son-of-Man, would seem not only natural but also necessary. This immense superiority carried with it an altogether superlative and incomparable destiny. It could not be otherwise than that the Eternal and Almighty had decreed his Chosen, His Anointed, His Beloved Son to be the supreme Power on earth and to rule the whole world as the Vicegerant of God Himself. Such was the obvious conclusion, untouched by any exaggeration.

Indeed, the case appeared clear beyond all controversy, and yet it was painfully contradicted in history at every turn by the most persistent experience; —the Chosen People were *not* the rulers of earth, nay, they were subjugated and oppressed, they were outcasts, a hissing and a byword, and their Holy City was trodden under foot of the monstrous heathen. The nearly uniform experience of national history subjected the Faith of Israel to such a test as seems never to have been applied elsewhere in the annals of man, and that the test was heroically and successfully endured appears to be the most remarkable fact of its kind in human annals and to indicate a toughness of racial fibre without parallel in the life of mankind.

As it appears to the present writer, the Old Testament is in the main the reaction of the Hebrew Soul to this Paradox of History. Especially is this true of the Psalms and the Prophets. Through it all, the faith of the prophets (and psalmists) in the *ultimate* forgiveness, restoration, sanctification and glorification of Israel seems hardly to have wavered for a moment. The Deportation to Babylon was an inconceivable trial, but it was bravely borne and triumphantly overcome. Yet it made an indelible mark upon one peculiarly noble spirit. The Later Isaiah* confronted the problem of the Affliction of Israel with a high-hearted resolve to master and comprehend it. His solution of the problem may rank as perhaps the boldest and sublimest flight of poetic

---

* I.e., the author, roughly of Isa. 40–66 inclusive, dating about 400 B.C. A kindred—though by no means a rival—spirit meets us in the Book of *Jonah*—so learnedly discussed in Hans Schmidt's *Jona: Eine Untersuchung zur vergleichenden Religionsgeschichte* (1907).

imagination in human chronicle, well worthy the reverence of all ages to come. He conceived of his People as indeed a Righteous and Suffering Servant, but especially as an Instrument wielded in the hands of the Almighty for the Salvation of the Whole World, as a Light to lighten the gloom of Polytheism that rested over all the globe, as bearing the Torch of Divine Truth far abroad among the Heathen, into the dark and secret places of Idolatry, and so spreading the knowledge of YHVH until it should fill all the earth as the waters cover the sea.

This universal expansion of the Hebrew Monotheism, the conversion of the whole world to Yahvism, could be attained in only one way, by *dispersing* the Hebrews among the heathen, and this *Dispersion* involved the *temporary* overthrow and Death of Israel as a Nation. This confounding calamity was conceived as an act of God, His voluntary surrender and vicarious sacrifice of his own People, His own dear-loved Son, to blot out the sins of the world, and to make all men the children of the Most High, by bringing the Knowledge (the Gnosis) of God unto all. Of course, the Victim has to be figured as a willing Sacrifice, as perfectly submissive to the decrees of Heaven and at least in large measure an innocent sufferer, as bearing the guilt of others and atoning for their sins.

But the majestic conception of the Dying Atoning Sacrifice was not yet enough in itself. A just and loving Father might indeed yield up His own and only Son as a willing sacrifice for the sins of the world, to bring all wandering humanity back to the fold of God, but that could not be the end of the story. The Son whom He Loved could not be surrendered to Death forever; nay, he must be raised from the dead and exalted to glory undreamed-of before. So at least the Prophet seems to have reasoned, for after it pleased YHVH to bruise him, and to make his soul an offering for sin, yet "shall he prolong his days," yet "will I divide him a portion with the great and he shall divide the spoil with the strong" ($53^{12}$).—Such seems to be the *Theodicy* of the Younger Isaiah.

That the Righteous Servant is neither more nor less than Israel Idealized appears to be quite beyond question; in many preceding passages the prophet could hardly be more explicit (Is. $41^{8\,f}$, $44^{1\,f}$, $44^{21}$, $45^{4}$, $48^{20}$, $49^{3}$). Indeed the spirit of the whole twenty seven chapters (40–66, not strictly a unit) shows beyond any dispute the intense patriotism of the seer (or seers) and his glowing faith in the illustrious future of his People.

Yet his brilliant conception of Israel as YHVH's torch-bearer to the Heathen World carried with it of necessity certain modifications in the general theory of Israel's relation to the rest of mankind. The concept of Israel was to be widened so as to include in some sense all the newly-enlightened pagans, to be members of the Elect People, who might in time immensely outnumber the

Hebrews themselves. Now this universalization of the Concept of the People of God was a daring and difficult undertaking. It seemed hardly in the nature of things that complete and perfect equality should be granted, and yet how could it be denied?

The Generalization of the Israel-Idea was conditioned by the development of another process, which may be called the Spiritualization of the same Idea. If the pagan was to be absorbed in Jacob and become a true Son of Abraham, what did it mean? Surely so much at least, that such sonship was not according to the flesh, that it was not a mere matter of physical kinship and communion of blood, but a far deeper affiliation of soul; not a consanguinity but a *conspirituality*. Israel was no longer a continuous series of generations of flesh-and-blood men sprung from a single Abraham-stem, but an exhaustless stream* of spiritual life, the Gnosis of God, welling up from the depths of Deity itself, poured out upon the earth in Palestine, but spreading out thence over every land and watering the whole world into the beauty of holiness, the joy of the worship of Jehovah alone.

Thus it appears that the Idealization, the Universalization, and the Spiritualization of Israel are only three sides of the one triangle, and are all alike implied in the one great Isaianic imagination of the Righteous and Suffering Servant of YHVH. But it must not be supposed that this involved the abandonment of the millennial hope of the Glorification of Israel proper. Had it been so, the notion could never have found a foothold in the Hebrew consciousness, it would have died in its birth, the words of Isaiah could never have won lodgement in the Hebrew canon. The prophet himself is possessed with the vision of the coming aggrandizement of his own People: he beholds Jerusalem arising from the ashes of widowhood and robing herself in the garments of the Bride of YHVH ($49^{18}$).

Precisely how this dignification could be brought about and in what it should consist, was left the future to determine, but meanwhile the individual seer might fancy what he pleased and give his phantasies what literary expression he could.

Very different was the precedure of the prophet Daniel. He is scarcely touched with Isaianism,—intelligible only to a few,—but maintains outright the infinite superiority of Israel, expressing it most vividly by figuring the great Heathen Kingdoms, including the Greek of Alexander and his successors, as 4 Beasts, but Israel as one-like-a-Son-of-Man, *i.e.,* a human being. This latter, who "came with the clouds of heaven," is brought into the presence of the Ancient of Days (the Eternal God), and receives "dominion and glory and a kingdom, that all the peoples, nations, and languages should serve him: his dominion is an everlasting dominion, and his kingdom that which

* Such seems to have been emphatically the notion of Philo, as appears in scores of passages.

shall not be destroyed. . . . And the kingdom and the dominion and the great-ness of the kingdoms under the whole heaven shall be given to the People of the Saints of the most High: his kingdom is an everlasting kingdom, and all dominions shall serve and obey him" ($7^{13, 14, 27}$).

Here the case is perfectly clear: Israel, the People of the Saints of the most High, is the *Son-of-Man*, the higher and only real humanity in its nobler sense, and to him "is given judgement" ($7^{22}$), and he rules all other peoples as God's Vicegerent forever. There is no hint of sharing it with any re-formed Gentiles.

Apparently it was under the inspiration of Daniel that a whole literature sprang up under the name of Enoch of which a considerable block, the *Si-militudes,* is occupied with what might be called the Revelation of the Son-of-Man or of the Elect of God. We found in an earlier chapter that this is a supernatural Being, kept hidden (politically obscured) for ages in the deep counsels of God, but at last revealed, unto judgment, for unto him all judg-ment, "the sum of judgment is committed" (En. $69^{27, 29}$), as he "sits on the throne of his glory."—This Son-of-Man, so named 15 times in Enoch, other-wise called the Elect One, 17 times, the Anointed twice, who acts as the Vicegerent of the Head-of-Days ("Ancient of Days") or Lord of Spirits, is manifestly and by every token a *Personification of the People Israel,* one might say the Israel Ideal, the Chosen of God.

Of course, he may be called the Messiah (Anointed), if by this term be meant the *same Personification.* It cannot be too heavily stressed that in the *Similitudes* of Enoch, the Elect One, the Son-of-Man, designated the People Israel, idealised and personalised, but still all and only Israel, nothing more nothing less, as the sole Agent of "the Head of Days," of "the Lord of Spirits," in the final judgment of the world, though with functions and characteristics somewhat milder and more beneficent towards the nations than appear in the Danielic original. Indeed, the term *Elect,* seems decisive. The Son-of-Man, when equated with "Mine Elect," the Chosen-of-God, must be Israel and Israel only.

Under close and constant touch with the Greek world of thought and feeling, the Hebrew mind and world-view in the Dispersion underwent a profound modification in the direction of the Isaianic idea. Slowly and gradu-ally it came to be realised that the Greek world was *worth saving,* and that Israel was to be God's factotum in the Salvation (*Jeshu-a*) of the Gentiles. It was also seen more and more clearly, at least by some elect spirits, that no other honor could compare with that of being the *Savior* of the world, the spiritual Head of all Humanity. The issue of this development was the *Jewish Proselyt-is,* which we saw traced back nearly to the middle of the second pre-Christian century, whence it spread forward over nearly 300 years. How exceedingly earnest and extensive it was we can never know, we can only judge from scattered allusions here and there.

Now it seems impossible to understand the Early Christian Movement without bearing this Jewish-Hellenistic Crusade for Monotheism constantly in mind. Beyond question it prepared the soil in which the Gospel was sown like a mustard seed, from which it sprouted and sprung and flourished with a rank and overshadowing growth. As is well-known, the Jewish mind itself was far from a unit on this subject of the Conversion of the Heathen. How could it be otherwise with both *Daniel* and *Isaiah* in the Sacred Book? The distant echoes of the strife are still heard in the book of *Acts*. Naturally it was in Palestinian circles that the conservative Danielic view prevailed most strongly: the Jewish patriot longed intensely for the Coming (*Parousy,* presence) of the Son-of-Man, unto judgment, with the clouds of heaven, to behold him seated on the throne of his glory, with all the subject nations of earth assembled around him.

It was solely for the political deliverance of his people that such a patriot yearned; he felt little or no interest in any personal Deliverer; it was the national Redemption, and not the Redeemer, for which he prayed. On the other hand, all history, even of Israel, has one voice in teaching that transcendent national achievements are effected only through transcendent national leaders. It was almost inevitable that such a leader or Deputy should centre on himself the regard not only of apocalyptic writers here and there, but far more, of the crowd at large, to whom the conception of the Nation as a unit was hard, but the conception of a great Commander, easy and ready at hand.

The imagination of some, possibly of many, might clothe such a spokesman with preternatural powers, and might feign marvellous and even miraculous stories about him. But one may feel pretty sure that only a powerful man of action, a doer of daring and desperate deeds, could have spell-bound the general popular fancy and inspired it to its unprecedented freaks of fiction.

Let anyone consider the turmoil that had prevailed in Palestine for over a hundred years, the restless spirit of rebellion against foreign and especially Roman power, which filled the mountains for generations with *sicarii* (knifemen). Let him ponder the increasing ferment that led Mommsen to date the catastrophic war not (as commonly done) from A.D. 66, but from the death of Agrippa A.D. 44; let him reflect on the demonic courage and contempt of death that animated generation after generation of the Jews and urged them on to sacrifices that now appear to have been well-nigh insane, and then let him ask himself where else in history is there shown such a seething cauldron of national feeling?

Doubtless there were many that still retained their poise and reason, but were they of the type to be excited to visions of a fellow-man raised from the dead, ascended to heaven, and throned in glory at the right hand of the Majesty on High? Assuredly not. To the present writer the notion of a dreamer-Messiah at such a focus of ferment, of a gentle Rabbi straying along the shores of the sea of Galilee, preaching repentance in the streets of Capernaum, debating in the synagogues, "dandling infants in his arms" climbing up mountains to preach to his disciples(!), followed everywhere far out into the desert by thronging listeners, the notion of such a man-of-words ever being figured in the minds of the multitude in Palestine as an individual personal Messiah sent to deliver his Chosen People from the thraldom of the Roman yoke,—such a notion seems incredibly out of alignment.

To redeem such an idea for one moment from utter fatuity, we must invest such a Rabbi with inconceivably miraculous powers, such as occupy the whole stage in the Gospels, such as Fundamentalists (but none else) still accord him, —and far more still we must endow him with a *magical* personality, at once charming and overpowering, provoking alike to love and to terror, to awe and to admiration. This obvious necessity was distinctly perceived by the ancients. In *Ep. 65.8 Ad Principiam* Jerome declares, "Unless Jesus had had something starry in his face and eyes, never would the apostles have followed him instantly"; and in commentary on Matt. $9^9$ (calling of Matthew), he speaks of "the radiance itself and majesty of hidden divinity that was shining also in his human countenance"; and again, at the cleansing of the temple (Matt. $21^{12}$), "for something fiery and starlike was flashing from his eyes and the majesty of the godhead was shining in his face."

Herein the learned Father was unquestionably right. Unless there was Deity blazing forth from his visage and echoing in his every word, the literal Jesus of the Gospels is entirely unintelligible in his relations with the people of Palestine; nothing but a perpetual *miracle of personality* could make understandable a single day of his Galilean or Judean ministry. The efforts of liberal criticism to rationalize this story in non-miraculous terms grow daily more and more unsatisfying in spite of all the splendid powers deployed in the attempt. From beginning to end it is Godhead, merely robed in flesh, that walks through the chapters of the New Testament. Withdraw the Divinity, eliminate the miraculous, and where is the superlative personality?—the whole figure collapses in a heap. Again, leave aside the miracles—which in any case were not human, but mere displays of supernatural power, entirely devoid of any moral merit or any suggestion of human personality—and we find not one single distinctly human deed of the great Master, not one single exhibiton of any high order of human virtue, not one single trace of charm or attraction, nothing that could humanly win us to devotion,—in fact we find no personal traits whatever that would mark out a distinct impressive or fascinating character; what is more, *we find no human character at all!*\* It is true that an extremely high moral-religious teaching of a certain type is at times ascribed to this Master; but it might just as well have been ascribed to anyone else; the words might just as well have proceeded from an oracle, or a statue. Not once does he ever exemplify or illustrate his teaching in his own person or conduct. He never gives another his own coat, he never shares his last morsel with another, he never shields another at his own personal risk, he never grieves with another, he never displays a single noble or amiable quality. He talks with wonderful beauty about love (in the Fourth Gospel), but it is all only about a mystical divine love, not a human affection. He washes his disciples' feet (in the same Fourth Gospel), but it is only a symbolic action, and it does not appear that the disciples either needed or desired the washing. In truth, the whole Life, even in the Johannine representation, is singularly devoid of human qualities; it is indeed not a human life at all, but the life of an emotionless God walking up and down the earth, in human guise and vesture. The reader may think of two or three trivial apparent exceptions, which he will find carefully considered in *Ecce Deus;* they do not soften the general verdict. No wonder that Bultmann† regretfully concedes that "the *Character* of Jesus . . . is for us *no longer cognizable.*"

It is, of course, the venerated rule to maintain the exact opposite, to regard the Gospel Life as the one altogether perfect life, the Gospel portrait as the One, the Only One, of perfect beauty and resistless charm. But this is all without any warrant whatever. We have merely *attributed* to the portrait—itself almost a formless and colorless blank—the features and qualities that please us most, and have then exclaimed of our own idealization, "How infinitely beautiful and sublime!" We forget his words allegedly addressed to his mother, "What have I to do with thee, woman?" (literally, "What to me and to thee, woman?"), or inadmissibly accoy it into "Leave it to me." When Peter remonstrates sympathetically against the Crucifixion, "Far be it from thee, Lord," the answer is immediate from the Jesus, "Get thee behind me, Satan!"‡ Such harshness seems quite "unchristian" and unprovoked.

When the Scribes and Pharisees question his claims (entirely unsupported) and trouble him with natural interrogations, he denounces them before the multitude (Matt. 23) in an harangue almost unequaled for savage violence and gross injustice: they are "hypocrites," "blind guides," "blind fools,"

---

\* Extremely significant is the clear perception by R. Bultmann (see page 58, footnote) not only of the "lack of the biographical," but especially of the lack of personal interest, of character-conception, in the Gospels.

† *Die Erforschung der Synoptischen Evangelien,* p. 33, 1925.

‡ The words that follow, "For thou mindest not the things of God but the things of men (Mark 8³³) seem to be almost an exact echo of the words of Herodotos concerning the Lakedaimonians obeying much against the grain a bidding of the Delphic oracle: "For they esteemed the things of heaven more highly than the things of men" (v. 63).

"white-washed sepulchres," "serpents," a "brood of vipers," inevitably doomed to the "damnation of hell." If there is anything in any Gospel that would seem to reveal some human personality in the Jesus, it would seem to be this ferocious tirade in the temple. No wonder the honest and clear-sighted Bultmann† thinks to find here in its merciless malisons, the genuine words of Jesus— "if anywhere (*wenn irgendwo*)." Yet never once, unless by Weidel, is it counted or included as part of the accepted Gospel Portrait!

To be sure, no such words were ever uttered in the Temple by the Jesus or by anyone else; they echo in their allegory the animosities of a later period, after the break between the two religions. But textually we have just as much authority for ascribing *them* to the Jesus as for ascribing the Sermon on the Mount or the final prayer for the Disciples before crossing the Kidron (John 17). It seems plain that the writers have had no historic person in mind but have calmly consulted their own sense of the eternal fitness of things (which is not always *our* sense!), and have laid upon the lips of the Jesus whatever fancies of their own they would clothe with divine authority, regardless of any original or even of any consistency itself.

Another consideration that seems decisive at once and for all time for the unhistorical character of the Gospels, is the open indiputable fact, already argued, that they were in large measure allegories or symbolisms. Of course, every one is familiar with the commonplace that the "Jesus spake in Parables." Their abundance and their frequent exceeding beauty have been a theme of endless comment, an object of amazed admiration to commentators for nearly a score of centuries. But these Parables are only one phase of a general, indeed universal characteristic of the Gospels, the symbolic or allegorical. Such illustrious Fathers of the Church as Clement of Alexandria, Origen, Augustine and others, recognized the symbolic meanings in question without doubt or hesitation and often expressed them clearly and forcibly. Unfortunately they combined this emphatic recognition with fantastic theories of interpretation of the Scriptures as documents of multiple meaning, having sometimes as many as four senses* quite distinct in the same passage, all of which were equally justified! By such means they sought to save the ordinary historic sense (the traditional "milk for babes"), while rendering some show of justice to the undeniable symbolism. Certainly such a method cannot satisfy the prosaic scientific mind of today, which will never believe that a symbolism requires to be cautiously acted out! If it were, in every case the physical marvel would have obliterated completely the deeper sense it was supposed or intended to reveal. Just so the conservative theologian today, when he interprets

---

† In his *Geschichte der Synoptischen Tradition*, 1921.

\* "Literal sense teaches facts; allegoric, what to believe; moral, what to do; anagogic, whither we tend"—so says a noted couplet.

the miracle as literal fact, forgets or even denies the inner meaning; believing it literally, he is shocked and horrified—with justifiable consistency—at the suggestion that the story is an allegory or symbol.

We may conclude, then, confidently that, since the miracles, even according to the most authoritative Fathers of the Church, were undoubtedly symbols of spiritual truth, it is quite impossible they should have physically occurred. What could be more absurd than to imagine the Jesus as wandering round the country, speaking to the people in Parables in order that they might *not* understand him ("that they may look and look but not see, may listen and listen but not understand," Mark 4$^{12}$, Matt. 13$^{14}$, Luke 8$^{10}$) and working all manner of marvels symbolizing spiritual truths that they would be sure never even faintly to suspect! That would be feeding not milk to the babes, but water and water alone!

It seems impossible to stress this point too strongly, for it appears to be as nearly decisive as any single consideration can be. The Gospel content is certainly in large measure purely symbolic. So much is frankly conceded by the highest critical authority. Says the *Theologischer Jahresbericht* in reviewing *Ecce Deus:* "Above all, however, it is in the demonstration of the original esoteric character of Christianity, and therewith of the demand for a far more thoroughgoing symbolic interpretation of the Gospels that the permanent value of Smith's great work lies." Well, then, if the Gospels be to such great extent symbolic, and if so far forth they are not the records of historic physical facts but of religious truths and doctrines, what becomes of the Doer of these marvels, the Hero of these incidents? The only answer seems to be that as a spiritual force and entity He remains unshaken and even strengthened unshakably, but *as a material physical fact He vanishes forever.*

\* \* \* \* \*

In passing we should call attention to one phrase in the foregoing citation: "the demonstration of the original esoteric character of Christianity." This "esoteric character" is given and manifest in the representation of the teaching in parables as intended to enlighten the disciples *without enlightening outsiders,* the folk at large—who could certainly not comprehend such teaching without some help. There are many passages that imply as much. Thus, He spoke in parables, "because it is given unto you to know the mysteries of the kingdom of the heavens, but to them it is not given" (Matt. 13$^{11}$), "what ye hear in the ear, preach ye upon the housetops" (Matt. 10$^{27}$), etc. All this is perfectly comprehensible and in truth quite natural, if the Primitive Preaching was of a refined spiritual doctrine or theory of divine providence, far from easy to understand and requiring to be set forth at first in historic-allegoric form, in order to win the mind and heart of the world at large,—later to be exhibited in more reasoned and difficult terms—"But we speak of

God in mystery, the hidden wisdom" (I Cor. $2^7$), "If our Gospel be hid, it is hid in the lost" (II Cor. $4^3$), "for there is nothing hidden, except to be manifested" (Mark $4^{22}$).—But it would be mere foolishness, if that Preaching were of a set of biographic facts widely and generally known, familiar to the folk, the town-talk of Jerusalem and of every Galilean village. And what possible motive in teaching so quietly and hiddenly the universal principles of a sublime morality, at which the best minds of all the earth had been aiming for so many hundreds of years? It is in the presence of such facts and reflections as these that Modernism and all its pretences are reduced to silence.

The requisition of secrecy becomes particularly self-justifying when we consider two facts: That the Primitive Preaching was aimed directly at Polytheism, and that it was impossible to attack this latter openly without encountering danger and death. The Roman Law protected all forms of religious worship as ministering to the stability of society, so that it was hopeless to assail the Gods openly; most of all, however, the Roman Emperor himself, as representing and embodying the Idea of the Roman State, was held up as the one object of universal worship, as symbolizing a kind of political Monotheism. The intensity of both Jewish and early Christian feeling towards this State-Idolatary is well-shown in *Revelation* (e.g. see Rev. $13^{1-17}$), where the Beast arising from the Sea (the welter of history), which all the earth worships, is the Roman Imperial Power, Embodied in the Emperors.

## ii. Zion versus Antioch

To return from this apparent digression, the Isaianic Jesus-figure of the Gospels, as Teacher and Healer, has hardly any point of contact with the Danielic-Enochian conception of the all-conquering all-judging all-ruling Son-of-Man, the Elect of God, the victorious Messiah or Christ. The conception was nevertheless expressed in them a number of times,—in one passage with particular magnificence (Matt. $25^{31-46}$),—but not duly fitted in with the Jesus-form presented in the Gospels. Indeed militant Danielism is still dominant at least in many hymns. In order to make room for this apocalyptic conception, the Coming (*Parousy*) of the Son-of-Man had to be split in two and all the Daniel-Enochian features of power, glory and judgment were postponed to the Second Coming!! Of course, this was on its face entirely preposterous, quite at variance with the whole body of earlier thought on the subject, but it was none-the-less necessary—if both Isaiah and Daniel were to be retained in honor! For it was in the *contradiction* of these two that the divided fate of Judaism and Christianism lay concealed. And here surely was a contradiction, if any contradiction is possible. Christianity was a labored attempt to harmonize the opposition, with the accent on the Isaianic phase. We might at first suppose that the Isaianists would be men of a far higher type of character than the Enochians: but that would be a very rash supposition. To be sure, the unbiased must admit that the Isaian view far surpasses the other in every dimension, in spiritual height, in breadth of historic vision, in depth of intellectual insight. Yet much remains to be said on the other side. To the normal Judean it could hardly appear more than a splendid dream. The acknowledged realities of history opposed it at every turn. The light of Judaic monotheism might indeed be bright and clear, but the sphere of its illumination seemed hopelessly small. There showed itself but little outlook for any deep penetration of the surrounding polytheistic gloom.

Still more, however, to the honest Jerusalemite the Isaian theory had all the appearance of an unpardonable mockery, a heartless travesty on the thousand-year old faith of Israel. All the good things of life, wealth and power and prosperity, with length of days and unfailing posterity, had been repeatedly, emphatically, and solemnly promised unto Jacob by YHVH himself in the words of his own inspired prophets. And what now was to be the boasted reward of millennial fidelity, the prize of righteousness, the insight of Divine favor and love? Why, to bring "light to the Gentiles," to share with them the prerogative of sonship to God, to make the murderer co-equal with his victim in the eyes of YHVH. To the patriotic Palestinian Yahvist, whose outlook was hemmed within the borders of the Holy Land, all this spiritualization might well show forth as the bitterest of cynical irony. Such a Hebrew must cast in his lot with the Zealots, the Apocalyptists, or else with the Quietists, he must strive to right the crying wrongs of the day, relying upon his own strength upheld by Jehovah,—or he must patiently await the inroad of Divine power from without, a miraculous Coming of the Son-of-Man. The more thoroughly logical and consistent he was both morally and religiously, the more unhesitatingly would he adopt this view and course of conduct, which in all its hues and varieties we may call the *Palestinian*.

Very different was the plight of the Hellenist, the Jew in the Diaspora, who had lived, like his fathers perhaps, all his days in Alexandria or Antioch or Damascus or Ephesus or even in Rome, who had forgotten his mother-tongue and spake only Greek, who read his Holy Scriptures in the Septuagint translation only, who had come to know, however imperfectly, the literature, the science, the art, in a word, the Culture of Hellas, the steady impression of constant intercourse must have revealed the Gentile character as not by any means wholly bad, as comparable at many points with the best that even Israel could boast.

None of this implies that the unquestionable superiority of the Hebrew in religion and in sexual morality was for a moment forgotten; nay, it was rather stressed and enforced by the continual exhibition of these points of Gentile weakness. But the Jew in the Dispersion found many pagans quite open to conviction, many thoroughly dissatisfied with the countless deifications of heroes and nature-powers and human ideas, and eager to welcome a doctrine of One God and Father of all, Creator and Preserver, the Stay and Hope of Mankind. Such was assuredly a keen-felt want of the Early Roman Empire, and, far beyond the reach of Greek philosophy or Asiatic mystery-cult, the Hebrew Monotheism supplied it in large measure and with imposing magnificence of Law and Literature and Life.

True, there was much in Yahvism forever unacceptable to the heathen heart. Among these especially was the persistent delusion that Israel was destined to the lordship of earth, to rule the nations with a rod of iron, to dash them in pieces like a potter's vessel. Certainly the Gentiles could not patiently bear with such an absurd conceit, and the Jew very quickly learned that such a pretension was fitted for private use only, that it was an esoteric doctrine that could be safest left at home.

Yet they were none the less eager to spread the glorious Truth in which they exulted. They became more and more zealous, more and more successful in proselytism. It would be a long story, if we could know and tell the whole of it. The *Fact* of the wide-extended and intensely earnest propaganda in the Dispersion is beyond dispute. All this, however, only in passing. Our present concern is with the *Conception of Israel as it had to shape itself under the demands of proselytism* and of the situation outside of Palestine. If the appeal of the propagandist was to be in any manner or measure adapted to the pagan consciousness, it must leave out entirely the national element, both in its backward and its forward look, and must rest its cause on the rationality and dignity of Monotheism as opposed to the irrational and grovelling Idolatry; and that such was the actual appeal successfully made is amply attested both by what we know of Jewish Proselytism and by the literature of the earliest Christian Propaganda (as in Acts $14^{15\text{-}17}$, $17^{22\text{-}30}$, etc.).

In the Isaianic vision the uplifting and winging thought was that of Salvation, primarily of the distressed Jewish People, but also of the whole Gentile world. The words *save, salvation, savior* abound in the famous 27 chapters. Salvation is used 20 times by the Younger Isaiah* in various forms: *yeshu-ah, yesha,* (where instead of y and sh we may write *j* and *s* and the word transcribes into Greek as *Iesous,* into English as Jesus). Very naturally, the same word is also used frequently in the *Psalms,* 62 times.

In *Isaiah* (and *Psalms*) this Salvation is of course the work of YHVH, but it is often spoken of objectively and might easily be regarded as personified, as a savior sent from God. As is well-known, the habit of personification was universal in Hebrew thinking. Well, then, on the basis of Hebrew usage and in accordance with the regulative Hebrew Scriptures, the name *Jesus* was al-

* Is it a mere accident that the name Isaiah (*Y'sha'yehu*) means *Savior-Yah*?

most of necessity given to a Being conceived as *Jeshu-ah*, Salvation personified.

But why any such Being at all? Why not be content with the abstract, why not preach the simple truth of Monotheism and trust to its intrinsic strength to sway the Gentile mind? There was every reason against such a procedure. The "truth of Monotheism" was very far from simple, and in its bare presentation it was by no means convincingly strong. It might be philosophically sound and yet quite unpersuasive to the average mind, which felt much more at home with a flock of peaceable deities hovering near, ready to render each its appropriate aid.† Besides, the abstract is always hard to grasp: we naturally turn for help to the concrete, we cry aloud for an *example*. Moreover, the pivotal passage in Isaiah ($52^{13}$–$53^{12}$) is the most concrete imaginable. There the Son-of-God, the Son-of-Man, the Chosen People, the Righteous Servant, is set forth and described minutely as a *man,* led as a lamb to the slaughter, even as slain and buried with the rich in his deaths. That the Early Christian Propaganda hinged on this passage is indicated distinctly in the account relating the Conversion of the Ethiopian treasurer (Acts $8^{26-40}$). An angel directs Philip to meet him as he rides in his chariot and ponders vainly the Isaian puzzle; Philip takes it as a text, explains it all, and the official is instantly converted. To be sure, the story is a manifest invention but that matters not. It shows indisputably how the author regarded the famous verses of Isaiah as related to the Proclamation of the Gospel.

Even this is not all, however. There is a still deeper reason. The Apostles or Proselytizers were Jews, hellenized perhaps very strongly, but still Jews, and still convinced that the Hebrews should "divide the spoil with the strong" (Is. $53^{12}$). They were preaching Yahvism, the doctrine of the One God YHVH, God of the whole world, intent on the Salvation of all men, and yet a tribal Jewish God! *They could not possibly lay aside this national tint of their propaganda, and yet they dared not display it,* if they hoped for a Gentile hearing. Once more, we have seen that they could not preach God as an Abstraction, as the Reason of the Universe. Such was not indeed their own notion, nor could it have made any general or powerful appeal to heathen hearers. These latter were used to *biographic* presentations of the Gods, each one of whom had his own local habitation and his name, along with his own individual history. Such could not be claimed for the One God of the Propagandist, and yet could there not be some compromise, some temporary concession to their hardness of heart until they were more grown in grace and better instructed in the divine wisdom?

† During all these centuries the Christian and even the Jewish mind (or heart) has itself been far from satisfied with simple Monotheism, but has girded itself with a protective host of secondary divinities, under the name of Saints or Angels, with whom its relations have been far more homelike and cordial than with the Lone King Jehovah at the vertex of heaven. A like observation might apply to Islam.

Here again it was the Isaian oracle that offered a ready solution, which could not fail to charm the oriental mind. There the Elect People found representation by a single individual, the righteous Servant, the slaughtered Lamb, the atoning sacrifice for the sins of the world. Why not then present this figure to the waiting heathen? Why not tell them the story of Israel, God's well-beloved Son, his Anointed, as the Jesus the Savior of all men, under the form of an earthly life of sorrow, suffering, death, and subsequent resurrection and ascension to glory? What could be more tempting to the Jew? What could be more vivid and impressive to the Gentile? The hallowed example of the Chief of Prophets was not only the complete vindication but even the urgent recommendation of this policy, which thus had everything in its favor and not the least thing against it. Accordingly there is nothing whatever surprising in its employment; it would have been queer, uncanny and calling for explanation, if it had not been adopted.

### iii. Meat? or Milk?*

*The Gospels as we now have them present the final result of the widespread, systematic, gradually growing, and long continued employment of a symbolic exposition to conform the divine Truth of Yahvism to the temper and prejudices of the Heathen mind and heart.* In doing this, the Missionary's role was not without its modicum of candor. He did not disguise the fact that the message he had to deliver was freighted with a heavy burden of spiritual concepts, which it was beyond his power to make clear, understandable and acceptable to the pagan soul untrained to breathing such mountain air. The proselyte was regularly called and considered a new born "babe," the emergence from the baptismal wave was the vivid symbol of this second birth,— hence the universal Christian adoption of this Jewish rite. The very nature of the case seemed to require that the "babes in Christ," in the spiritual "commonwealth of Israel," should be fed on "the guileless doctrinal milk," that they might "grow unto salvation," having tasted that "Chrestos is the Lord" (I Pet. $2^{2\,f}$). This conception of the Gentile convert as a "babe" recurs frequently in the New Testament as Matt. $11^{25}$, $21^{16}$, Luke $10^{21}$, Rom. $2^{20}$, I Cor. $3^1$, Heb. $5^{13}$, I Pet. $2^2$. Sometimes the term "little one" is preferred, as we in affectionate mood often prefer it; thus, in Matt. $10^{42}$, $18^{6,\,14}$, Mark $9^{42}$, Luke $17^2$. So also "Little children," used about 10 times in the Epistles. It is well-known† that *qaton*, "little one" (as in Gen. $44^{20}$) is a regular Talmudic term for "proselyte" (*Ecce Deus* 118). The New Testament usage was completely natural.

* The greater part of the materials in this section and in Chapter VIII were published in Smith's article, "Milk or Meat?", *Hibbert Journal*, vol. 31, pp. 372–383, 1933.

† Lightfoot, *Horae Hebraicae*, III. 265.

The Apostles were indeed using their Personification for the time-being, but on their own statements we behold them waiting none too patiently for the time to come when their converts might hear and comprehend the mystery not as realists "through a glass darkly," but as idealists, "face to face"; as in I Cor. $3^{1\,f}$, "And I, brethren, could not speak unto you as unto spiritual, but as unto carnal, as unto babes in Christ. I fed you with milk, not with meat; for ye were not yet able (to bear it): nay, not even now are ye able." Here the writer is willing to bear with them a while longer. The general spiritual nature of his doctrine, the underlying spiritual truth, had already been darkly hinted in the preceding chapter ($2^{6\text{-}8}$), the "mystery" of God's wisdom, his government of the world, which had the rulers of this world known, "they would not have crucified the Lord of glory" (*i.e.*, they would not have persecuted and slain the Righteous Servant of God, the Ideal Personified Israel).

The author of *To Hebrews* has had a similar experience, but he has far less patience with the dullness of converts (Heb. $5^{12\text{-}14}$): "For when, considering the time, ye ought to be teachers, again ye have need that some one *teach you* the rudiments of the beginning of the oracles of God, and are become such as need milk, not solid food. For every one that partakes of milk has no experience of the word of righteousness: for a babe is he. But solid food is for full-grown men." Only I Pet. $2^2$ seems content for the "Babes in Christ," like the "babes in heaven" to remain "babes" forever, a view of the matter that has prevailed from that hour to this. The order of the day is now the question: Shall this view continue to prevail indefinitely? Shall the "carnal" mind dominate the church to the end of time? Shall the "veil" never be lifted from the face of Christianity? Shall the human race, in religion, always present an example of arrested development? Shall we never dare proclaim the real doctrine of the Apostles, lest the brightness of its beam should blind us, and must we always bow down before a graven image of the Truth rather than the Truth itself? What were this but Paganry, worshipping an Idol instead of God?—Despite the most desperate efforts of conservative and of Fundamentalist, the bondage of ignorance cannot be held permanently fast on the eyes of civilized man. It is long since time-worn, and is fast falling in pieces away.

We maintain, then, that the Gospel-story was a concession to the heathen hardness of heart. The choice that the missionary made was from necessity, expecting soon to set it aside, and it seems to have cost him profound dissatisfaction. But it must not be supposed for a moment that the whole story, or even any large part of it, came into being at any one time or place* or as the

---

* The "Teacher of Righteousness" in the Qumran scrolls is highly suggestive of this same material, derived from Isaiah 53, though it is not used to attract proselytes, but only to edify the initiated. *Editor.*

work of any one man. By no means. The intermediary stages may have disappeared, but their existence at some time and in various forms is a necessary postulate. It is now generally recognized that behind Mark and Q* there lay many far simpler statements of elements of the Gospel story. It may (or may not) be vain to imagine how this or that particular detail or feature was first suggested, or by whom, or under what circumstances. In countless cases we have seen sure indications that the impulse was a desire to fulfil some Old Testament forecast or saying. These scriptural witnesses lent plausibility and vividness to the narrative, and it seems very likely that collections of such *Testimonies* (Rendel Harris†) were very early made, perhaps by many hands. As time went on the incidents grew in number and in detail, and the later extracanonics, no less than the modern romances called "Lives of Jesus," show to what exuberance it was possible to reach.

Though the earliest Missionaries found themselves in a manner constrained to furnish "milk for babes," to present and even adorn the great Personification by Isaiah, yet they seem to have contented themselves with a few central ideas and to have refrained at first from any formal presentation of a *life*. The Apostle appears to have taught almost solely that the Christ *suffered* and *died*, was crucified, and then exalted to glory. Details are well-nigh totally lacking. The preaching filled exactly to the brim the cup of Isaian Prophecy. Not a drop ran over. It was strictly "according to the Scriptures." The Gospel "transmitted to us at first, which I handed on," *begins* with "Christ died for our sins *according to the Scriptures*" (I Cor. 15$^{3, 4}$; the chapter is at best an interpolation). The reference must be to Is. 53$^{7-9}$, which personalized the sufferings and death of the Nation Israel. The epistle tells nothing here about any life, but only about the Death and Resurrection of the Christ, as forecast in the Isaian text.—Someone may cite the account of the Last Supper (I Cor. 11$^{23-26}$); but this again deals solely with a closing scene just before the Death, and is also transparently an interpolation, as appears in v. 23: "For it was from the Lord that I received what I handed on to you." How grotesquely absurd to suppose that the ascended Jesus told Paul about the Last Supper!

The Pauline notion of the Eucharist is given clearly enough in I Cor. 10$^{16 \dagger}$: "The bread that we break, is it not communion of the Body of the Christ? As the bread is one, so we, though many, are one body; for we all partake of the one bread. Consider Israel after the flesh, etc." Plainly it is a rite of communion,‡ of fellowship, symbolizing the unity of the Christian community, "The

---

* The source, now lost, which *Matthew* and *Luke* drew upon for sayings not found in *Mark*. "Q" stands for German *Quelle*, "source." *Editor.*

† This reference is ambiguous; however see J. R. Harris (1919) *Origin of the Doctrine of the Trinity*, p. 13. *Editor.*

‡ See *Ecce Deus*, 150–152, Cp. also the rich-laden volumes of Gillis Pson Wetter on *Altchristliche Liturgien* (1921, 1922).

Body of the Christ" *very* much as in the *Teaching* (*Didache,* Chs. 9, 10, 14). This "one Body" in which all share, "the Body of the Christ," is nothing but the Church or Christian Community, the new and true Israel.

An even more revealing witness is the repeated description, in *Acts,* of the debates of Paul and Apollos with the Jews in the synagogue and elsewhere. All these turn upon the interpretation of the Scriptures, whether they teach the doctrine of a Suffering Messiah. This the Apostles affirmed strenuously and the Jews (in some sense) just as strenuously denied. Thus (Acts $3^{18}$), "But what things God foreshowed by mouth of all the prophets, that his Christ should suffer, He thus fulfilled"; and (Acts $17^{2\,f}$), "And Paul as his custom was . . . reasoned with them from the Scriptures, opening and alleging that it behooved the Christ to suffer and to rise again from the dead, and that this Jesus whom I proclaim unto you is the Christ." Similarly Apollos ($18^{25,\,28}$). So far as we can see, these vehement discussions with the Jews were concerned solely with the interpretation of supposed prophetic Messianic references. There is never anywhere the slightest allusion to any Palestinian pilgrimage of the Jesus,—whose "amazing personality" does not enter into the controversy, not even in the minutest measure.

Indeed it appears impossible that such prolonged *reasonings* "from the Scriptures" should have concerned a Life about which Paul (and still less Apollos) would seem to have known not a single item and about which he seems to have cared nothing at all. And what more could his disputants in Thessalonica and Berea have known? And what could they have found out by examining the Scriptures daily, whether these things were so ($17^{11}$)? Nothing whatever. From beginning to end it was a matter of Old Testament interpretation solely, as to the prophesied nature, character and career of the Messiah: The Missionaries held to the Isaianic, their Jewish opponents to the Danielic view. It was a question of the Cosmic Function and Destiny of Israel. No wonder they could not agree. This seems so natural as to call for no explanation; it was precisely what was to be expected, but it appears forever irreconcilable with the notion that the Apostle was preaching an historic individual Jesus, a Galilean Teacher and Healer.

The story began with the Sufferings and Death, and this account of the Passion has been developed with by far the greatest wealth of detail. Nevertheless even here the varying imaginations have quite failed to produce a consistent and intelligible sketch. The version in Matthew leans very heavily on the account, in *Wisdom of Solomon* ($2^{13\text{-}20}$), of the reproaches levelled against "the Righteous" (Israel) by his calumniators: "He vaunts himself to have the (true) knowledge of God, He names himself Servant of God . . . and nameth boastfully God his Father! Let us see whether his words be true.

Let us wait on the style of his exit! For if the Righteous be Son-of-God, then will God take him to Himself and deliver him from the hands of his adversaries. With reproaches and ill-treatment let us put him to the test. . . . Let us condemn him to disgraceful death. For according to his words protection will fall to his lot." The reader cannot fail to recall the parallel Gospel passages Matt. 26⁵³, 27³⁹⁻⁴⁴ etc.). The resemblances are too close and too many to be accidental. Of course there were other scriptural sources, some used more in one Gospel, some more in another.

The stories of the Galilean life, the Ministry, were added one by one, made, unmade and remade in various forms by various hands, but all in the same general spirit, to express the slowly forming Christian Consciousness as it took shape under the impulse of its original urge and the impress of its mainly heathen environment. The later prehistories of *Matthew* and *Luke,* entirely independent pure inventions, represent the latest canonic attempts to feign a strictly human life for the Personality, that *at the first* was conceived as an Impersonation, without any trace of ancestry, as accomplishing its sublime task of Suffering, Dying, Rising—again into Higher Life without any ordinary incidents of human life, *later* as appearing all at once on the scene of action, as coming "into Galilee preaching," *still later* as born in hellenic fashion of a virgin mother under the overshadowing might of God, and *later still* as disclosing even in childhood his supernatural powers.* With extracanonic extravagances we have no concern, further than to observe how the process once begun goes on and on even to the writers of the present day.

We have figured only the bare skeleton of the process by which the Gospel developed. In life itself skeletons are clothed in flesh and blood. Thus there were many other collateral influences that determined countless more or less important phases of the wonderful Propaganda. There were many varying lines of faith and doctrine, perhaps almost as many theories as there were theorists. Moreover the *stamp* of the pagan milieu was deep and general. The Gospel, as we now have it, was mainly a Hellenistic creation, by Hellenized Jews, and it not only took its *shape* at many points from external pressure, but it actually absorbed no little from its environment. There was endosmosis as well as exosmosis. We need not be startled to find many pagan crumbs in the "pure doctrine" of the Gospel, but to enter into any discussion of such elements is not feasible in this connection.†

The final product, the symbolic quasi-biography which the world knows

---

* Thus it appears that the Gospel story is a *retrostruction,* it is built up backwards, like a dream. In the Fourth Gospel the structure is carried still further back, to the "Beginning"!

† Says the enlightened Dean Inge: "It is useless to deny that St. Paul regarded Christianity as at least on one side a mystery religion." Compare also the deeply significant work of Reitzenstein, *Das iranishe Erlösungsmysterium,* and Gillis Pson Wetter, *Altchristliche Liturgien.*

# Chapter Eight *

# *Summary*

1. The main conclusion from our New Testament studies is that the Gospels have full and appropriate meaning when and only when they are understood as totally allegorical, portraying in symbol the one and only burden of Old Testament prophecy, the marvellous endurance, century after century, of the Israel Folk in their steadfast witness for monotheism,—"Thy Folk, which thou has named Thy Firstborn, Thine Only Begotten Son." Whenever we admit this (or any) symbolic content we are obliged to reject to just the same degree any and all historic content.

2. The nature of the allegorical impersonation was set in the first place in the Isaian prophecies. The Jesus was the "Righteous Servant of Jehovah," the "Ebed YHVH" of the Younger Isaiah, consequently none other than the Hebrew Race itself, the People of God, the Genius of Jacob, the Israel-Folk idealised, spiritualised, universalised, personalised. He is called "Christ" or "Messiah," as God's "Anointed," but more often "Jesus," "the Jesus" as the Saviour, the Salvation, of the Heathen World from the Sin of Idolatry. The stem *y-sh-*, help, save, with which *Iesous* was connected in the mind of that day—Matt. 1²¹, "thou shalt call his name Jesus, for he it is shall save, etc.,— abounds in the verses of the second Isaiah, and could hardly have failed to reign in the thought of the primitive propagandists.

3. Under the term Son-of-Man this identification becomes mandatory. In its various Semitic forms the expression of course signified "human being," but in its prophetic-apocalyptic-religious use it meant just one thing—the People Israel, generally impersonated. Such was the uniform usage ever since Dan. 7¹³.

This Danielic conception prevails crystal clear throughout the Similitudes of the *Book of Enoch*, whose thought and even speech have passed over so often into the New Testament. To be sure, this Son-of-Man, "the Elect" (used

* Much of this chapter, as well as of the last section of the preceding chapter, had advance publication in Smith's article, "Milk or Meat?", *Hibbert Journal*, vol. 31, pp. 372–383, 1933.

constantly as synonyms in *Enoch*), the Chosen People, is personalised and so represented as an individual, often as a Conquering King. But the fact remains that it is the Collective or Communal Consciousness, the National Race-feeling always that objectifies itself in the phrase. "The Son-of-Man sitting on the throne of his glory" (completely Enochian words), so vividly sketched in Matt. 25$^{31\text{-}46}$, is in *Enoch* inescapably the Elect People "Come to judgment," rewarding its friends among the heathen, annihilating all its foes. The echo in Matthew cannot have any different meaning.

4. The Son-of-God means the same thing, an elder conception running through all the literature of the People. The possible illustrations are many. The early prototype is Exod. 4$^{22}$, "Thus saith YHVH, My Son My Firstborn —Israel." But see also Ps. 2$^{7\text{-}9}$, "Thou art my Son, this day have I begotten thee. Ask of Me, and I will give thee the nations for thine inheritance, And the ends of the earth for thy possession. Thou shalt break them with a rod of iron; like a potter's vessel thou shalt dash them in pieces." Such words have sense only as understood of the Israel-Folk—of course, perhaps represented by a King at coronation, or some other dignitary.

These notions of Israel as Son-of-Man, and as Son-of-God, the especial Child of His Love, pervade Hebrew literature, intensifying as the years drag by, often to a superlative degree in the late Apocalyptic, of New Testament times. It seems impossible that a deeply religious individual imbued with the spirit of Jewry in our first century could have used such terms without feeling in himself and arousing in his hearers the National Consciousness they expressed or implied.

5. This National Consciousness appears as a well-nigh unique fact in human annals. And over against it, the Paradox of all time, the paralysing fact of the disastrous Race-career, a tale of suffering and ruin, of political humiliation, of dispersion, deportation, and death! The Danielic theory or forecast, had no explanation to offer, it merely passed by, like priest and Levite, on the other side, and sought forgetfulness in the prospect of a New Eon to come, a New Platonic Year. But a loftier spirit, the Younger Isaiah, did imagine an explanation and set it boldly forth: Israel was the "Servant of YHVH," His torch-bearer, a sacrifice for the Sins of the world. Israel's sufferings, his "deaths" (Isa. 53$^9$) were seen as a part of an eternal and infinite purpose of God to reveal the knowledge of Himself to all men, to illumine all the dark places of the globe. "I scatter this folk among the nations, that it do the nations good" (*Apoc. Bar.* 1$^4$). Israel would certainly be glorified by YHVH, not however as the political but as the Spiritual Head of Humanity. (Isa. 53$^{12}$).

6. Such, in spite of a corrupt text, seems surely to be Isaiah's thought, such at least was fully understood as his meaning (Acts 8$^{35}$; Matt. 12$^{17\text{-}21}$). This

plant budded and bloomed and ripened into fruit in the Dispersion: in Alexandria, Antioch, Cyprus, Cyrene, Damascus, Ephesus—wherever the wandering Jew had settled his foot in the Greek cultured world. Hence the Jewish Proselytism of which the final issue was the primitive Christian Propaganda, —its message the "Eternal Gospel" of Monotheism, "Fear God and give Him glory" (Rev. 14[7]) joined up with the distinctive Isaianic doctrine of the "suffering Servant of YHVH," the Afflicted and Atoning Messiah. This latter doctrine was a spiritual interpretation of the history of Israel, a dazzling Transfiguration of the racial Christ. Very naturally it did not appeal to the Palestinian, who was wedded to the Danielic-Apocalyptic hope of imperial supremacy. No marvel the antagonism was intense, that the matter was debated over and over by Paul and Apollos and a hundred others, daylong, nightlong, in synagogue and public halls and upper chambers, and with no final result! For the common and only arsenal of evidence was the Scripture —"it is written"—and each could prove his case from the Old Testament, for there was Daniel as well as Isaiah! To suppose such a debate was about the Life and Death and Resurrection of a Galilean Rabbi, whom devoted Jewish monotheists like Paul and Barnabas and Apollos were blasphemously calling Son-of-Man and Son-of-God, terms appropriate only to the Chosen People Israel—a Rabbi moreover whom these Apostles had never seen and never heard—but enough! To characterise such a supposition would be unparliamentary.

7. It was natural, it was inevitable, that the Isaianist should "turn to the Gentiles," but in so doing he confronted a formidable problem. He wished to convert Pagans from Polytheism to Monotheism (Acts 14[15-17]; 17[23-30]) and certainly many, with some the very best, were willing and even eager to be converted. But the One and Only God thus proclaimed was not simply the God of the Universe, like related to all men: He was, or at least He had been for many centuries, pre-eminently and peculiarly the God of Israel; It was Israel that had functioned through all the ages and was functioning especially then as His Righteous Servant, His Agent and representative, the Light to lighten the Gentiles, His Anointed (Christ), the Savior of all Mankind. True, this Salvation had been prepared through centuries of humiliation and suffering and sacrificial atoning "deaths," but so much the more it constituted Israel the Spiritual Head of Humanity and transfigured him into unique and everlasting glory.

All this the Apostles might verily believe, and it might inspire them with a missionary zeal that would burst all bounds. But such a doctrine could not possibly as such be made acceptable to the Gentiles, and to preach it to them would have been unpardonable folly. If the Missionaries were to do the heathen any good with their preaching, It was imperative to adapt the teaching to the pupils taught. And this the apostles to the gentiles did on the whole with extraordinary prudence, earnestness, and sagacity, as attested by the rapid and triumphant progress of their propaganda. They were not deceivers, they were not deceived; they were religious zealots fully persuaded of the overtowering importance of their "Eternal Gospel" of Monotheism and their own calling as tools in the hands of the Almighty, for the dissemination of His everlasting world-redeeming truth. But they understood perfectly that any open proclamation of the Gospel, *as they themselves conceived it,* would certainly defeat its own aim, and that they must adjust the Hebraic message to the Hellenic mind.

8. This adjustment is what they named "feeding milk to babes," Paul tells the Corinthians (I Cor. 3¹ ᶠ) that he could not feed them meat, they were not able to receive it; it was milk he was forced to feed them, as being only babes. This metaphor of feeding milk to babes, for adapting instruction to the instructed, seems to have been popular in Jewry; it was a favourite with Philo. And what was this "guileless milk of doctrine"? It was the Gospel-Story—not indeed at first precisely as we have it now. The present accepted form was a very gradual growth, in which it is possible still to recognize a number of earlier stages, like annual rings in a tree, such as the Logian, the Marcan, the Matthean, the Lucan—and far out to one side, like a second stem, the Johannine, little resembling any Synoptic. These are only a few among many, and—to vary the figure—they are knotted together in a tangled skein, which scholarship strives not vainly yet not quite successfully to unravel. Back of these lie or lay many earlier simpler types, less artistic doubtless and less pleasing to the cultured sense and fancy. Others, still later, pass over into rococo and the grotesque. The Gospels represent the best that the literary skill of a century could accomplish in devising the most effective allegory, in supplying a rich, wholesome and palatable milk for babes.

9. The Hero of this "Old, Old Story" is really the People Israel idealised. The incidents are imagined to reflect the history and character of that Folk as found largely in the Old Testament, especially in those outstanding features that seemed to determine and justify the propaganda of the Apostles, yet were impossible to offer the Gentiles as bare historic facts. Such especially are the legends of the Crucifixion and Resurrection of the Jesus. These formed the pivot of the whole preaching, for they symbolised the central thought, the sacrificial suffering, the atoning Death of Israel at the hands of the heathen, the political *Burial* of the Hebrew State to be followed by the spiritual *Resurrection* of the true Ideal Israel and his ascension to Eternal Glory as the Spiritual Lord of the whole earth, as the Captain of Salvation for all Mankind.

10. Along with all this exploitation of the Old Testament there runs throughout an abounding Symbolism, especially in *Luke* and *John,* con-

cerned mainly with the Salvation of the heathen through the Gospel. It is represented under the form of the Healing of the Afflicted by the Savior-God, the Jesus, and especially as the Casting-out of Demons (Heathen gods) by His Word (the Monotheistic teaching). Also, the relation of the Jew and the Gentile is often and repeatedly figured in symbolic miracle and parable. Of necessity, the Jesus who impersonates the bearers of the "true light that lighteneth every man that cometh into the world," was pictured as pre-eminently the great *Teacher,* and on his lips was laid all the higher wisdom that could be gathered not only from the Law, the Prophets, the Writings, and even the Sayings of the Fathers, but even also from the Greek Philosophy.

Lastly we have found that taken as chronicles of actual events, the Gospels themselves are full of contradictions and impossibilities, and that from first to last they are deliberate coinages that became reasonable and meaningful only when understood in symbolic terms, "Truth severe by fairy fiction dressed." This was all so natural as to be inevitable.

11. The writer of the Fourth Gospel ("John") would alter the leading trend of the Synoptic path; he would not renounce it, but turn it deftly to face more toward Mysticism, Gnosticism, and a more spiritualized conception of the whole. The nature of the Jesus here is rarified into the intangible vapor of a difficulty defined *Logos.*

12. So understood, the whole New Testament appears intelligible and marvellously suited for its heathen hearers. We have found witnesses to the correctness of this interpretation abounding on every hand, one might almost say in every chapter of the Gospels. Only a very few simple specimens may be brought back to mind. Thus, everyone must feel that the Fourth Gospel, the most Hellenic of all, breathes condemnation of the Jews from first to last; yet it avows the central thesis of the foregoing, that "Salvation is (proceeds) from the Jews" ($4^{22}$). Also, it identifies the Jesus with Israel unmistakably in using the Old Testament simile of the vine. It seems impossible that the Evangelist did not have the imagery of Isaiah, Ezekial and Hosea in mind, and accordingly, in declaring and repeating "I am the Vine" he affirms unequivocally that the Jesus is Israel—yet in a guarded pictorial way, a "veiled" way (II Cor. $4^{3}$), that would not revolt the Gentile consciousness. What other sense but nonsense?

Again, the *Transfiguration* has meaning—and indeed, overpowering meaning—when and only when it is understood of Israel metamorphosed from an impotently struggling State into the spiritual Leader and Guide of all generations.

Once more, Paul declares he preached to the Corinthians naught "save Jesus Christ and Him crucified" (I Cor. $2^{2}$); but he was then very properly feeding "milk to babes." Among the "fullgrown" he preached "theosophy in mystery," a "hidden wisdom ordained of God before the worlds unto our glory, which none of the rulers of this world hath known; for had they known it, they would not have crucified the Lord of glory" (I Cor. $2^{7\,f}$). This seems to designate as plainly as Paul dared the course of Hebrew History—of *Israel* "having not where to lay his head," crushed, crucified. That such a consciousness should have swayed the Apostle then and there, at that crisis of Jewish history, appears so natural as to be almost necessary.

13. But how did the Apostle discover all these secrets which "the Archons of this Aeon" had not known? Let him speak for himself: "none of the rulers of this world hath known. . . . But unto us God revealed them through the Spirit; for the Spirit searcheth all things, yea, the depths of God" ($2^{10}$). Could he, dared he, make it plainer that it was all a matter of inner rumination, of musing, marvelling, pondering over the dark riddle of Israel's History? The Apostle regarded the explanation he had reached as a revelation of the Spirit. "The Gospel preached by me is not after man. For neither did I receive it from man nor was I taught it save through revelation of Jesus Christ." This can only mean that it was the outcome of his own meditations.

14. The Last Coming of the Son-of-Man as foretold in the Gospel means just what it means in Dan. $7^{13}$, the long-delayed triumph of "the Saints of the Most High"—Israel (Dan. $7^{18,\ 21\ f,\ 25,\ 27}$). The triumph of Isaiah over Daniel was never complete. The hope of a catastrophic and catastatic inroad from the clouds of heaven has lingered on even to this day, and one must not be surprised to find fragments of it strewn here and there throughout the New Testament. Yielding to the exigencies of the situation the Christians split the Coming (*Parousy*) in two—the First in Suffering, the Second in Glory. This did indeed preserve the order of the seers, putting Isaiah in front with Daniel following, but though in a measure a "spontaneous fission" it did no justice to either prophet, for neither had ever dreamed of two "Comings."

15. It is plain to see that the same Danielic conception prevails almost though not quite exclusively in the *Revelation of John*. Thus, "and on the cloud one sitting like Son-of-Man ($14^{14}$)—what is it but an echo of Dan. $7^{13}$? —"The Lion of the tribe of Judah" (Rev. $5^5$) also suggests the conquering nation, while the (little) "Lamb slain from the foundation of the world" ($13^8$) provides an identification with the Righteous Servant Israel (in Isaiah) that is "led as a lamb to the slaughter" ($53^7$). That the Lamb symbolises the Chosen People seems plain from the angelic chant: "Worthy is the Lamb that hath been slain To receive the power and riches And wisdom and might And honour and glory and blessing" (Rev. $5^{12}$). Surely it all has meaning and propriety when understood of Israel however idealised and personalised; but understood of a Galilean Carpenter—who dare say that it has any sense or fitness whatever?

16. The whole story did not come into being at any one time or place or as the work of any one man. The earliest missionaries seem to have contented themselves with a few central ideas and to have refrained from any formal presentation of a *life*. The Apostles taught almost solely that the Christ *suffered* and *died,* was crucified, and then exalted to glory, all *"according to the scriptures."* The Jesus whom Paul was proclaiming was the *Jeshu-ah,* the Salvation by way of Israel, as revealed in the scrolls of Isaiah and the other prophets. This Savior, confessedly the whole Hebrew people, was *depicted* as a humble and suffering individual man.—Thus Israel, *Transfigured* out of the worldly Danielic ambition into the sacrificial Isaianic role of World-*Atonement* (having stripped off from himself the principalities and powers, —Col. $2^{15}$) was dedicated to be *Crucified,* crushed and trodden into dust again and again, dispersed, deported; though politically *Dead* and *Buried* (in homeless exile), yet destined for Spiritual *Victory* (*anastasis*), to *Sit* at last *on the Right Hand of God* (triumphant *parousy*) in *Judgment* for the (Spiritual) *Salvation of the Peoples.*

17. The apostles were using their Personification as a mere transient device, not as ultimate truth. They looked forward confidently to an early period when they might discard these devices—milk for babes—and feed their converts on solid food for men, on "Theosophy in Mystery," pure Spiritual food for the Spiritual-minded, a teaching it would seem, that set aside the Gospel allegory, as in Didache and in the Shepherd of Hermas.

At this point they fed themselves, Alas! on delusion. The Carnal incline to remain carnal, not merely for a few years but for many centuries. The poet prefers his boyish theory of the rainbow to that of the physicist, and boldly declares:—

> I ask not proud Philosophy
> To teach me what thou art.

The sensual pictorial *objective* Gospel, being once sown in the imagination of men, it has struck its roots deeper and deeper into our whole nature, and now it is feared that to tear it up would rock or crumble the whole fabric of our civilization—so inveterately prone is Man to Symbolize, to make Signs, and then to *mistake the Sign for the Signified!* Nevertheless—"and yet it moves." Even the Sequoia does not abide forever, and the colossal mustard-plant of Sensual Christianity, that has sheltered and shadowed Europe and America for so many centuries, now feels blowing through all its branches the breath of the Spirit, which sooner or later must cast its sense-imagery to the ground.

Mightier for the children of men,
Brightlier build it again,
*In thine own bosom build it anew!*
Bid the new career
Commence
With clearer sense,
And let new songs of cheer
Be sung thereto.

William Benjamin Smith.

*Appendix*

# THE CHRONOLOGY OF THE EARLY GNOSTIC SECTS

## A VINDICATION OF HIPPOLYTUS

Based upon

### CHRISTIAN AND GNOSTIC
### TEXTUAL PARALLELS

BY

WILLIAM BENJAMIN SMITH

# Appendix

# The Chronology of the Early Gnostic Sects

## A VINDICATION OF HIPPOLYTUS

### I. EDITOR'S FOREWORD

The Appendix here presented may be thought of as a sort of study-sheet, in which William Benjamin Smith organized the evidence he could gather from Hippolytus, while not yet arriving at his own final conclusions. Internal evidence places it roughly in the period 1903–1904.

Since the time it was written, two highly significant ancient religious libraries have been brought to light, that of the late Gnostic settlement of Nag Hamadi in Egypt, and that of the supposedly Essene monastery at Qumran, by the Dead Sea. It appears that the overlap of subject matter between these and Hippolytus is so minimal that the latter's testimony is not superceded, but is brought into enhanced interest by the new perspectives offered.

Smith's primary interest in Hippolytus was chronological. What sects, he was asking, were early enough to exert a formative influence upon Christianity, and what did they teach? Also what sects dated late enough to be recipients of influence from first and second century Christianity, and what did they receive from this source? Hippolytus is literally the only available source of documentation for every significant pre-Christian sect except the Essenes, and for all these questions he remains to this day exceeded in importance by no other surviving authority.

Unfortunately the work of the nineteenth century critics was very detrimental to the reputation of Hippolytus. Salmon, 1885, indicated that he found peculiarities of diction that made him believe some early swindlers had foisted on Hippolytus a large block of spurious writings, ascribed to Gnostics, but probably composed with no purpose beyond to sell them at a profit to the collector, Hippolytus. In 1890 this idea was upheld vigorously and even expanded by Stähelin, in Germany. The renowned Harnack, in 1893, accepted this hypothesis, and called it "probable that (the account of the Naassenes in the *Refutation*) rests on falsified sources." He retreated just a little from this severe appraisal in a footnote, in 1897, when he said, in his discussion of Valentinus, "In my estimate the question is no longer to be solved; yet there is more evidence than Stähelin believes against such a deception." Harnack's surmises about the dating of the Gnostic sects are limited to deductions from the reports of other ancient authorities, the evidence in Hippolytus being put down as too little trustworthy to employ.

A more recent example of the workings of the orthodox precenceptions may be found in the annotations made by Francis Legge in his English edition of the *Philosophumena* of Hippolytus, 1921. Although he vigorously defended the integrity of his author's sources, he assigned most of them to late phases of their respective sects, in order to allow for their incorporation of such masses of material from "Christian" sources.

If, however, Smith can show by his close textual study that the *Philosophumena* contains a fundamentally sound array of early Gnostic quotations, dating essentially as Hippolytus affirms, we are at once challenged with a multitude of further questions, the answers to which became a major preoccupation for William Benjamin Smith. Herein we find the significance of the theses developed in this Appendix.

Addison Gulick

## II Author's Introduction

It is well known that the earliest heretics, particularly the Gnostics, no less than the later, made frequent use of "Scriptures" and "Sayings" that agree almost or quite exactly with portions of our present Scriptures, Evangelic, Apostolic, or other. Thus far it has been assumed with practical unanimity, and as needing no argument, that in all such cases the Heretics were quoting from our Canonics.* The counter hypothesis, that possibly, at least in some cases the Canonical Scripture may have been a quotation from some heretical writing, has hardly been deemed worthy of consideration. Consistently herewith the Heresies themselves have all been assigned to later sub-apostolic times; or if their germs are admitted to have sprouted in the days of the apostles, yet nothing more—they could not have been sowed at any rate (so it is held) before the Pentecostal miracle, much less in pre-Christian times. Hence, though it seemed to Neander that Euphrates preceded Jesus, yet Bunsen dismisses such a notion summarily, because Hippolytus represents the Peratae as using sayings that are now Canonic (Hippolytus and his Age, vol. 1).

Right or wrong, the prevalent opinions are seen to involve certain assumptions, which may properly be called in question, which we may call on to show their passports. We ask, then, these two questions:

(1) *Do the historical data, so far as in any measure ascertainable, indicate that Heresy, more especially Gnosticism, was an offshoot from the Christianity of the first century, or does it indicate that Gnosticism preceded Christianity, that the latter emerged from the former, rather than that the former diverged from the latter?*

(2) *Do the Gnostic passages point back to the Canonical Scriptures as their ap-*

* This statement is dated as of the period 1903–1904. But even today, the prevalent opinion seems very nearly the same, under the predominant influence of Harnack. *Editor.*

*parent source, or do they point beyond those Scriptures to well-heads now forever sealed, from which they were drawn also by the Canonical scribes themselves?*

These queries are most closely related, yet we shall endeavor as far as possible to keep them apart in our discussion and not to let our judgment as to either be warped by our judgment as to the other. It might be thought most natural to treat the questions in the order of statement, but such was not the order in which we were led to study them. It was the Phenomena presented by the alleged Quotations that started the investigation, and these we shall now consider, banishing as far as may be all preconception as to the dates of the Heresies in question.

In the beginning it may be well to note parenthetically that the critical school, particularly of Tübingen, has been concerned in general to lower to the utmost the antiquity of the Gnostics, in order to break the witness supposedly born by them to the antiquity of the New Testament Scriptures. On the other hand, conservatives have rejoiced at every token of the great age of Gnosticism, which was presumed to force back the Canonics always before it into but never beyond the second half of the first century. Let us try to conduct our inquiry with an eye single to the facts in the case, without any critical prepossession, and without any regard whatever for consequences.

In the course of this study our first and our main authority must be Hippolytus, and more specifically his *Philosophumena*, known also as the Ἔλεγχος κατὰ πασῶν αἱρέσεως, or *Refutatio Omnium Haeresium;* others will be useful principally by way of supplement. We might arrange our quotations in the order of importance, but it is perhaps better to take them just as they come. In this way the reader will observe the formation and growth of the writer's opinion, how it actually arose and developed.

### III. PARALLEL TEXTS COMPARED

#### A. *Brachmanes*

The gleanings from Book I of the *Refutatio* are of course the very scantiest, for Hippolytus is writing of the ancient Philosophers. But on page 46,* discoursing on the Brachmanes, he declares: "They say that God is Light (οὗτοι τὸν Θεὸν φῶς εἶναι), not such as one sees, nor like sun and fire, but for them God is Logos, not the articulate, but that of knowledge (ὁ Θεὸς λόγος, οὐχ ὁ ἔναρθρος, ἀλλὰ ὁ τῆς γνώσεως), through whom the secret mysteries of nature are visible to the wise. And this Light which they call Logos, God, they say themselves alone the Brachmanes, know" etc. In *John* the Logos is repeatedly declared to be Light ( φῶς ); in I John 1[5] the writer declares that the message we have heard from Him and proclaimed to you is ὅτι ὁ Θεὸς φῶς ἐστίν. In I Tim. 6[16] God is said to inhabit Light unapproachable (φῶς οἰκῶν ἀπρόσιτον). In II Cor. 4[6] we read of the "Enlightening of the Gnosis (φωτισμὸν τῆς γνώσεως). It is certainly not likely that the Brachmanes derived their notions from our Scriptures; it is not held that these latter

* Page numbers are those of the Greek edition by the Abbé P. M. Cruice, 1860. These numbers are recorded also in the English translation by Francis Legge, 1921.

derived from the former; but since the ideas and expressions agree so nearly or exactly, it seems that they must have been widely diffused, and little claim to originality can be set up in any quarter.

A few lines further on (p. 47) it appears that they taught the doctrine of the Incarnation or Incorporation of this Logos: "and this Logos which they named God, (they say) he is embodied and clothed with body outside of himself (σωματικὸν εἶναι, περικείμενόν τε σῶμα ἔξωθεν ἑαυτοῦ). Furthermore there is warfare in this enclothing body against passions, desires, and the like, and all men are captives of their own congenital foes (αἰχμαλώτους εἶναι τῶν ἰδίων συγγενῶν πολεμίων).

He alone goes to God who triumphs over these. Here we are forcibly reminded of Romans VII, especially verse 23 (αἰχμαλωτίζοντά με ἐν τῷ νόμῳ), as well as of Is. 61¹, Luke 4¹⁸, and the foregoing remarks apply.

## B. *Aratus*

Book IV is concerned largely with Aratus (*Phaenomena*), a work also cited in *Acts* (17²⁸), and very highly esteemed by the ancients. On page 124, after a quotation from Aratus (*Phaen.* v. 268) there is introduced by φησίν apparently a Jewish allegorizer who declares that if the Adam confessing, and watching the head of the beast (τοῦ θηρίου) according to command of God, shall imitate the Lyre, that is, shall follow after the Logos of God, that is, obeying the Law, he shall receive the Crown placed beside him τουτέστι κατακολουθήσει τῷ λόγῳ τοῦ θεοῦ, τουτέστι πειθόμενος τῷ νόμῳ, παρακείμενον αὐτῷ τὸν στέφανον λήψεται). But if he neglect, he shall be hurled down along with the underlying Beast and have his portion (saith he) with the Beast (τῷ ὑποκειμένῳ θηρίῳ, καὶ τὸ μέρος ἕξει, φησί, μετὰ τοῦ θηρίου).

There is much more about Crown and Lyre and Serpent and Dragon and Beast and Logos and the Engonasis and Adam-in-toils, which we need not quote; and about the first creation according to the Adam-in-toils and the second according to the Christ. It seems impossible to read such overwrought allegories without thinking of the Apocalypse, where all these ideas continually recur, where the Dragon, the Serpent, the Ancient, makes war in Heaven against the Woman with the Crown and her child, and is cast down to earth; especially are we reminded of Rev. 20¹⁰, and 21⁸⁻¹⁰, where the wicked have their lot in the lake of fire and brimstone where also is the Beast. Borrowing here on either hand seems to us unlikely, but it also appears that both have drawn from a common treasury of Phrase and Fable, perhaps Babylonian.

On p. 126 we read: "for few, he says, are they that journey upon the narrow way. But they say that Cynosuris is narrow &c." This we may more properly consider later on (infra, p. 170, on Matt. 7¹³⁻¹⁴). Next (p. 127) it is said that "Cynosuris is the 2d Creation," the small, the narrow way, and that Canis is the Logos, partly guarding and preserving the flock plotted against by wolves, (which recalls John 10⁷⁻⁸) partly generating the Universe (τὰ πάντα), as in the Prologue of *John*. More startling however (p. 128): "This Canis therefore, saith he, being a certain Logos divine, has been appointed judge of Quick and Dead" (οὗτος οὖν, φησίν, ὁ Κύων, λόγος τις ὢν θεῖος, ζώντων καὶ νεκρῶν κριτὴς καθέστηκε). This last remarkable idea is found three times in the New Testament:

Act. 10⁴², ὅτι αὐτός ἐστιν ὁ ὡρισμένος ὑπὸ τοῦ θεοῦ κριτὴς ζώντων καὶ νεκρῶν
I Pet. 4⁵, οἳ ἀποδώσουσιν λόγον τῷ ἑτοίμως ἔχοντι κρῖναι ζῶντας καὶ νεκρούς
II Tim. 4¹, Χριστοῦ Ἰησοῦ τοῦ μέλλοντος κρίνειν ζῶντας καὶ νεκρούς

and these seem quite independent of one another. There is no hint in Hippolytus of any quotation from the New Testament; in fact, this character of Canis is deduced from certain alleged meteorological observations; it is highly unlikely then that there has been any borrowing from Holy Scriptures; so that the noteworthy turn of expression must have been a wide-spread usage and by no means peculiar to Christians or even of Christian origin. On page 129 the plotting Beast ( τὸ ἐπίβουλον θηρίον ) re-appears to be slain by Perseus, the Logos, who frees the woman Andromeda,—all of which winks at the ancient (Babylonian) mythical basis of Rev. 12.

Further on (page 134) we find that the last member of Simon's Hebdomad is "He that stood, stands, will stand (ὁ ἐστώς, στάς, στησόμενος )," which is quite parallel with the Apocalyptic Was and Is and Will be (1⁸). Since Simon appears to have died long before the earliest possible date for *Revelation* either the idea and form of speech were familiar or else in *Revelation* they were derived from some Simonian source. (See below.)

## C. *Naassenes*

We now enter a region prolific of parallels. Book V opens with a discussion of the Naassene or Ophitic Heresy. These Hippolytus regards as the very earliest, who in fact antedated Gnosticism, and were only subsequently called Gnostics, claiming alone (p. 139) to know the depths (φάσκοντες μόνοι τὰ βάθη γινώσκειν ). Here we instantly recall the Apocalyptic Thyatirans (Rev. 2²⁴) who "knew not the depths of Satan, *as they say*" (οἵτινες οὐκ ἔγνωσαν τὰ βαθέα τοῦ Σατανᾶ, ὡς λέγουσιν). Unless all signs fail, the Apocalyptist has here quoted the high pretension of these Gnostics, perhaps adding "of Satan" of his own accord.

Of these Naasseni the central trait is the worship of Humanity: they honor the father of all things else, the Logos, as Man and Son of Man (οὗτοι τῶν ἄλλων ἁπάντων παρὰ τὸν αὐτῶν λόγον τιμῶσιν ἄνθρωπον καὶ υἱὸν ἀνθρώπου).

This Man is Arsenothene and is called Adam; and hymns arise to him many and various, after this type: "From Thee (springs) Father and through thee Mother, the two immortal names, parents of Aeons, thou Citizen of Heaven, illustrious Man." Aside from the famous locution "Son of Man," we meet here with the doctrine of the Heavenly Adam, elsewhere hinted at (I Cor. 15⁴⁵ ᶠ). It seems very unlikely that these doctrines are quite independent of each other; nor can we believe that the Naassene is derived from the Pauline. For this latter is introduced in a way that presupposes it as already known, a familiar dogma that needs merely to be hinted in order to be applied. Surely no one will contend that the doctrine of the Adams as given in Corinthians is in and of itself intelligible; the explanation must be sought elsewhere. On the other hand, we do not assert that the Epistolist has derived from the Naassene; all that appears is that there was a more or less familiar doctrine of Adam, the Type Human, with which both he and they were acquainted and which both adopted in somewhat varying forms, the one as central and regulative, the other as peripheral and occasional.

All the characteristics of this Naassene Man re-appear in Paulinism, though merely as *disjecta membra,* not in collected consistent shape. Thus in Gal. 3²⁸ it is declared there is not male and female (οὐκ ἔνι ἄρσεν καὶ θῆλυ), not to mention II Clement and the Gospel of the Egyptians. The citizenship in Heaven (πολῖτα οὐρανοῦ, on p. 140) recurs in Phil. 3²⁰ (ἡμῶν γὰρ τὸ πολίτευμα ἐν οὐρανοῖς ὑπάρχει), of which see below—and in I Cor. 15⁴⁷. This Human Nature was tripartite in Naassene theory; rational, animal (psychic), earthy (τὸ μὲν νοερόν, τὸ δὲ ψυχικόν, τὸ δὲ χοϊκόν). This is repeated in I Thes. (5²³) (Spirit and Soul and Body), but not in I Cor. 15⁴⁵ᶠ, where a strict dualism reigns, though all the ideas are present: τὸ πνευματικὸν, τὸ ψυχικόν, ὁ χοϊκός. The presence of the same elements, in such striking diversity of collocation, testifies that there has been no direct borrowing, but the free use of common property.

It must not be supposed that these Naassenes identified Man and God; they distinguished sharply and inserted this Ideal Humanity as an intermediate link between actual humanity and Divinity, as is evident from their deep thoughted aphorism (p. 140): "Beginning of Perfection is Gnosis of Man, but Gnosis of God is Perfection consummated (ἀρχὴ τελειώσεως γνῶσις ἀνθρώπου, θεοῦ δὲ γνῶσις ἀπηρτισμένη τελείωσις). These words are enough to show that these Heretics were by no means to be despised but were earnest and acute speculators, however grotesque may have been some of their tenets.

All these three elements were united, he says (φησί), in one man Jesus the begotten of Mary, and these three men, saith he (φησίν) used to speak at the same time each of his own to his own. For according to them there are three kinds of all things: angelic, psychic, earthy; whose names are Elect, Called, Captive." Here we revert at once to the Gospel of *John,* where the notion of "Own" (ἴδιος) is so prominent, as in "He came to his own and his own received him not" (1¹¹), "when he speaks the lie he speaks of his own" (8⁴⁴, also 13¹, 15¹⁹). But we observe that John uses this phrase casually as something familiar and needing no explanation, whereas in the Naassene speech it is articulated closely with their general doctrine. It would be very strange then if the Naassene had seized upon such an idea and mortised it so cunningly into the structure of his own thought.—The notion of the three churches does not appear in our Scriptures, but the distinction of Elect and Called is conspicuous as, Matt. 20¹⁶, 22¹⁴. Here must be added *Barnabas,* cited in Hom. Cl. 8, 4. Since in neither place in *Matthew* is the passage demanded by the context, and since its use in *Barnabas* is not apparently derived from

*Matthew,* and since its form is plainly proverbial, it seems unavoidable that here we are dealing with a current saying, not without classical parallel: πολλοί τοι γὰρ θηκοφόροι, βάκχοι δὲ τε παῦροι.

With respect to the Naassene doctrine of Jesus, we cannot speak with confidence; Hippolytus gives us only the faintest glimpse. Whether the phrase τὸν ἐκ τῆς Μαρίας γεγενημένον be not his own addition is indeterminable. The doctrine of the Jesus seems to have been a very old one and may well have found place in the Naassene system; especially, as Jesus is continually spoken of as Son of Man in the Gospel, and the Naassenes worshipped the Logos as Man and Son of Man. Their doctrines and writings seemed to have been very extensive (πολλῶν πάνυ λόγων); that they were "handed down to Mariamne by James the Lord's brother" is of course a fiction, but of what date is not clearly seen. It may have been a very old or only a very late pretension—Hippolytus denies it, and with justice, all historicity and proceeds to discover the proximate source of this doctrine in the mysteries (τελετάς) barbaric and Hellenic whence the myth arose (ὅθεν αὐτοῖς οὗτος ὁ μῦθος). With this aspect of the matter we are not now concerned.

Passing on we meet on page 144 with an extraordinary passage: "Therefore that finally may be over-powered the mighty Man from above, *from whom,* as they say, *all paternity named on earth and in the heavens is constituted,* there was given him also a soul, that through the soul he may suffer &c." Here the ἀφ' οὗ πᾶσα πατριὰ ὀνομαζομένη ἐπὶ γῆς καὶ ἐν τοῖς οὐρανοῖς suggests instantly the ἐξ οὗ πᾶσα πατριὰ ἐν οὐρανοῖς καὶ ἐπὶ γῆς ὀνομάζεται. No one will pretend that the phrases originated altogether independently; it seems equally clear that the phrase in Eph. 3¹⁵ is not original. For it is quite alien to its context, unsuggested by anything before and suggesting nothing after. Hence our translators have been quite at a loss how to render it. "Every (or the whole) family" has held its own, though manifestly incorrect and meaningless; the last revisers have put "Fatherhood" in the margin. The commentators can make nothing out of it. On the other hand, it is quite in place in the Naassene doctrine of the Primal Man, the Great, the Illustrious, the Citizen of Heaven. We cannot then hesitate to pronounce the Naassene the more original, and here is one instance where certainly *an ancient Gnostic expression has found lodgement in our Scriptures.*

A few lines further on (in p. 145) we find: "Accordingly every nature of things celestial (saith he) and terrestrial and subterrene yearns for soul" (πᾶσα οὖν φύσις ἐπουρανίων, φησί, καὶ ἐπιγείων καὶ καταχθονίων ψυχῆς ὀρέγεται). The phrase ἐπιγείων καὶ καταχθονίων meets us again in Phil. 2¹⁰. Independent origin is again unlikely, still more so the supposition that the original is in *Philippians.* For the preceding observations apply. In *Philippians* the phrase, though not forbidden, is not invited by the context, it falls away naturally, and leaves the sense and the structure improved (every knee shall bow and every tongue confess); whereas it is entirely in place in the Naassene context, almost essential. The phrase every nature yearns for soul (ψυχῆς γὰρ, φασί, πᾶσα φύσις, ἄλλη δὲ ἄλλως ὀρέγεται) has just occurred in a well-reasoned scientific* connection. We must allow then that the triple epithet belongs by preference to the Naassene, though both he and the Epistolist may have drawn from a common source.

On page 146 we are told the the emasculation of Attis typifies this transit from the earthy part of the lower creature below to the everlasting substance above where (saith he) is neither female nor male but new creation, new man, who is arsenothele (ὅπου, φησίν, οὐκ ἔστιν οὔτε θῆλυ οὔτε ἄρσεν, ἀλλὰ καινὴ κτίσις, καινὸς ἄνθρωπος ὅς ἐστιν ἀρσενόθηλυς). When we compare this with Clem. Hom. p. 2, 12, where the "Lord himself" replies to one asking when the Kingdom should come, "When two shall be one, and the without as the within, and the male with the female, neither male nor female," it becomes clear that we are dealing with a wide-spread mode of thought and speech; that it is by no means original in Gal. 3[28], (οὐκ ἔνι ἄρσεν καὶ θῆλυ etc.) but is there a quotation from some uncanonic source.

The next passage, a very long one (p. 147), the most important to be found in Gnostic remains, has already been mentioned in the writer's "Did Paul write Romans?" (*Hibbert Journal,* January 1903, p. 322).

Naas. Τὰ γὰρ ἀόρατα αὐτοῦ ἀπὸ τῆς κτίσεως τοῦ κόσμου τοῖς ποιήμασιν αὐτοῦ νοούμενα
Rom. " " " " " __ " __ " " " __ "

Naas. καθορᾶται, ἥ τε ἀΐδιος αὐτοῦ δύναμις καὶ θειότης, πρὸς τὸ εἶναι
Rom. " " " " " " " " εἰς " "

Naas. αὐτοὺς ἀναπολογήτους. Διότι γνόντες τὸν Θεὸν, οὐχ ὡς Θεὸν ἐδόξασαν
Rom. " " " " " " " " " "

Naas. ἢ ηὐχαρίστησαν, ἀλλ' ἐματαιώθη
Rom. " " " ἐματαιώθησαν ἐν τοῖς διαλογισμοῖς αὐτῶν, καὶ

Naas. ἡ ἀσύνετος αὐτῶν καρδία· φάσκοντες γὰρ εἶναι σοφοὶ
Rom. ἐσκοτίσθη " " " " " __ " "

Naas. ἐμωράνθησαν, καὶ ἤλλαξαν τὴν δόξαν τοῦ ἀφθάρτου Θεοῦ ἐν
Rom. " " " " " " " " "

Naas. ὁμοιώμασιν εἰκόνος φθαρτοῦ ἀνθρώπου καὶ πετεινῶν καὶ τετραπόδων καὶ
Rom. ὁμοιώματι " " " " " " " "

Naas. ἑρπετῶν. Διὸ καὶ παρέδωκεν αὐτοὺς ὁ Θεὸς
Rom. " " __ " " " " ἐν ταῖς ἐπιθυμίαις

Rom. τῶν καρδιῶν αὐτῶν εἰς ἀκαθαρσίαν τοῦ ἀτιμάζεσθαι τὰ σώματα
Rom. αὐτῶν ἐν αὐτοῖς· οἵτινες μετήλλαξαν τὴν ἀλήθειαν τοῦ
Rom. Θεοῦ ἐν τῷ ψεύδει, καὶ ἐσεβάσθησαν καὶ ἐλάτρευσαν τῇ
Rom. κτίσει παρὰ τὸν κτίσαντα, ὅς ἐστιν εὐλογητὸς εἰς τοὺς
Rom. αἰῶνας. Ἀμήν. Διὰ τοῦτο παρέδωκεν αὐτοὺς ὁ Θεὸς
Naas. εἰς πάθη ἀτιμίας· αἵ τε γὰρ θήλειαι αὐτῶν μετήλλαξαν τὴν
Rom. " " " " " " " " " "

---

* I.e. *wissenschaftlich.* Smith at times makes the English "scientific" serve as equivalent to this untranslatable German expression. *Editor.*

*Naas.* φυσικὴν χρῆσιν εἰς τὴν παρὰ φύσιν.
*Rom.*    "    "    "    "    "    "

*Naas.* Ὁμοίως δὲ καὶ οἱ ἄρρενες    ἀφέντες τὴν φυσικὴν χρῆσιν τῆς

*Rom.*\*   "    τε   "   " $\left\{ \begin{array}{c} " \\ ἄρσενες \end{array} \right\}$   "   "   "   "   "

*Naas.* θηλείας ἐξεκαύθησαν ἐν τῇ ὀρέξει αὐτῶν εἰς ἀλλήλους,
*Rom.*   "    "   "   "   "   "   "   "

*Naas.* ἄρρενες ἐν ἄρρεσι τὴν ἀσχημοσύνην κατεργαζόμενοι, καὶ τὴν

*Rom.* $\left\{ \begin{array}{ccc} " & " & ἄρρεσιν \\ ἄρσενες & " & ἄρσεσιν \end{array} \right\}$  "    "    "    "    "

*Naas.* ἀντιμισθίαν ἣν ἔδει τῆς πλάνης αὐτῶν ἐν ἑαυτοῖς ἀπολαμβάνοντες.
*Rom.*   "    "   "   "   "   "   " αὐτοῖς ἀπολαμβάνοντες.

The Naassene agrees with Rom. 1[20-27] but inserts τοῦ before κόσμου, αὐτοῦ before νοούμενα, puts πρὸς for εἰς before τὸ εἶναι, omits -σαν ἐν τοῖς διαλογισμενοῖς αὐτῶν καὶ ἐσκοτίσθη, inserts γὰρ after φάσκοντες, puts ὁμοιώμασιν for ὁμοιώματι, inserts καί after διὸ, omits ἐν ταῖς–ὁ θεὸς vv. 24–25, puts δὲ for τε † None of these changes worsen the text, the most better it decidedly; especially the omission of 24, 25 which are manifest repetitions of 26, 27. On the face of it the Naassene form seems older and preferable, and it seems hardly possibly a quotation from *Romans.* This judgment is corroborated by the fact that according to Hippolytus the Naassene did not quote this as from Paul or Romans but as "spoken by the Logos" (τὸ λεγόμενον ὑπὸ τοῦ λόγου). It seems plain then that it was a fragment of the extensive Wisdom—or Logos—Literature, which has been encysted in the *Epistle to Romans.* We observe at this point that none of the sayings thus far discussed are mentioned by Hippolytus *as quoted* from the Scriptures. Had they been so quoted, it seems highly probably that Hippolytus would have said so. This observation applies to all the passages hereafter discussed, except in case of special mention to the contrary.

We merely note in passing the phrase "living water"‡ (ζῶντι ὕδατι, p. 148) used of τὸν λουόμενον (the baptized?).

At the turn of the page (bottom p. 148) we find an alleged citation from the Gospel "according to Thomas," found however in the edition neither of Fabricius nor of Thilo.

Just preceding is found a deep and just thought: "the happy nature which in

---

\* Lower line Wescott and Hort, upper line Tischendorf.

† In agreement at this point with the text favored by Woide and Cowper. *Editor.*

‡ The notion seems to be extremely ancient: in the Descent of Ishtar we read. "Sprinkle Ishtar with the waters of life (*mi balati*) and take her from before me." "Water of death" (*mi mu-ti*) is also conspicuous in the Gilgamesh-Epos, as at x 1, 2, 25: And deep the waters of death that before him encamp.

fact (quoth he) is the sought-for Kingdom of heavens within man" ( μακαρία↑ κρυβομένην ὁμοῦ καὶ φανερουμένην, φύσιν, ἥνπερ, φησί, τὴν ἐντὸς ἀνθρώπον βασίλειαι οὐρανῶν ζητουμένην ). In Luke 17²¹ we find the similar ἰδοὺ γὰρ ἡ βασιλεία τοῦ Θεοῦ ἐντὸς ὑμῶν ἐστίν.But here the ἐντὸς means "among" (viz. *inter*). If then the Naassenes have taken this idea and that of seeking the Kingdom from the Gospels, they have greatly refined it.

Concerning the Eternal, the "I Am what I Am," "moving all things, himself unmoved," the Naassene says he alone is good (p. 150) and concerning him was said what was said by the Savior (τὸ ὑπὸ τοῦ σωτῆρος λεγόμενον) "Why declarest thou me good? One is good, my Father that is in the heavens, who makes rise his sun upon just and unjust and rains upon saints and sinners." It is well known that with respect to this famous saying about the Good, our Canonics are not agreed, Mark and Luke differing very slightly,* Matthew diverging widely.

| | | | | |
|---|---|---|---|---|
| Naas. | Τί με λέγεις | ἀγαθόν; | εἷς ἐστὶν ἀγαθὸς | |
| Matt. 19¹⁷† | Τί με ἐρωτᾷς περὶ τοῦ ἀγαθοῦ; | | εἷς ἐστιν ὁ ἀγαθὸς | |

| | | | | |
|---|---|---|---|---|
| Mark 10¹⁸ | Τί με λέγεις | ἀγαθόν; οὐδεὶς | ἀγαθὸς εἰ μὴ εἷς | |
| Luke 18¹⁹ | Τί με λέγεις | ἀγαθόν; οὐδεὶς | ἀγαθὸς εἰ μὴ εἷς | |

| | |
|---|---|
| Naas. | ὁ πατήρ μου |
| Matt. | |
| Mark | ὁ Θεός |
| Luke | ὁ Θεός |

| | | | |
|---|---|---|---|
| Matt. 5⁴⁵ | ὅπως γένησθε υἱοὶ | τοῦ πατρὸς ὑμῶν | |
| Luke 6³⁵ | καὶ ἔσται ὁ μισθὸς | ὑμῶν πολύς | |

| | | | |
|---|---|---|---|
| Naas. | ὁ ἐν τοῖς οὐρανοῖς | ὃς | |
| Matt. | τοῦ ἐν οὐρανοῖς | ὅτι | |
| Luke | καὶ ἔσεσθε υἱοὶ ὑψίστου ὅτι αὐτὸς χρηστός ἐστιν | | |

| | | | |
|---|---|---|---|
| Naas. | ἀνατέλλει τὸν ἥλιον αὐτοῦ | ἐπὶ | δικαιους |
| Matt. | τὸν ἥλιον αὐτοῦ ἀνατέλλει | ἐπὶ | πονηροὺς |
| Luke | | ἐπὶ | τοὺς ἀχαρίστους |

| | |
|---|---|
| Naas. | καὶ ἀδίκους, καὶ βρέχει ἐπὶ ὁσίους καὶ ἁμαρτωλούς |
| Matt. | καὶ ἀγαθοὺς, καὶ βρέχει ἐπὶ δικαίους καὶ ἀδίκους |
| Luke | καὶ πονηρούς. |

Here we have a third text, broadly divergent, and yet every way quite as good and completely confirmed by Justin *Contra Trypho Iud.* 101, who gives it precisely as the Naassenes! True, in the Apol. 1¹⁶ we read: None is good but God alone who made the Universe (οὐδεὶς ἀγαθὸς εἰ μὴ μόνος ὁ θεὸς ὁ ποιήσας τὰ πάντα ) a varia-

---

* In fact identical in most editions. *Editor.*

† Matt. 19¹⁷ here is given according to the texts of Tischendorf and of Westcott and Hort. Woide and Cowper, editors of Codex Alexandrinus, make Matt. 19¹⁷ the same as in Mark 10¹⁸.

tion with respect to which it is needless to hazard conjecture. The Apol. is very strongly interpolated. Similarly in the Clem. Hom. 18, St. Peter quotes it thus: Do not call me good, for the God is one, the Father, that is in the Heavens (μή με λέγε ἀγαθόν· ὁ γὰρ εἷς ἐστὶν ὁ πατὴρ ὁ ἐν τῶς οὐρανοῖς), and so Simon at 18¹, 3⁵⁷, 17⁴. Likewise Irenaeus I, XIII, 2: Τί με λέγεις ἀγαθόν, εἷς ἐστὶν ἀγαθὸς ὁ Πατὴρ ἐν τοὺς οὐρανοῖς where it is uncertain and indifferent whether Irenaeus quotes the Catholic or the Marcosian version. So too Valentinus in his epistle quoted Cl. Str. 2, 488: εἷς δὲ, and others of less significance.

Here all talk of lapse of memory and carelessness (Harvey) is out of order. The attestation both catholic and heretic of the Gnostic text is much the oldest, so that there can be no reasonable question that it is not borrowed, or corrupted from either of the two irreducible Evangelic forms, but is a genuine independent form, apparently more ancient than either. It is also plain that the idea, "Only one is Good, the Heavenly Father," was a favorite in Gnostic circles (witness Valentine, the Naassenes, the Marcosians, and Simon), and it seems also clear that the Matthaean text (Matt. 19¹⁷ with its intentional ambiguity (ἀγαθός = good person, ἀγαθον = good thing, ἀγαθοῦ = of good thing or of good person) was an after-thought. Here then we are sure of one Gnostic parallel not taken from our Canonics, apparently the relation is the inverse.

Passing now to the second half of the pericope, and its parallel in Matt. 5:45, we note first that the ὅs for ὅτι is very strongly attested by the versions and the Church Fathers (as Irenaeus, Tertullian and Eusebius (ὅστις) ); secondly, that Justin (*Apol.* 1, 15) gives ἁμαρτωλούς καὶ δικαίους καὶ πονηρούς and again (*Tr.* 96) ἀγαρίστους καὶ δικαίους, καὶ βρέχοντα ἐπὶ ὁσίους καὶ πονηρούς; still other fathers quote frequently ἀγαθούς while the *Codex Sinaiticus* omits the whole clause καὶ βρέχει ἐπὶ δικαίους καὶ ἀδίκους! Plainly then the idea was floating in the religious atmosphere, now taking this form, now that, nor is there the least reason for supposing it borrowed by the Naassenes from Matthew. Thirdly, *in Matthew the whole verse 45 is apparently an interpolation,* for the connection is close between 44 and 46, but very loose between 44 and 45 and 45 and 46.

We proceed to page 154. According to Hippolytus the Naassenes identified the Logos with the Kyllenian Hermes of the Golden wand, who enchants the eyes of the dead and rouses from sleep the slumberer. "Concerning these, he says, the Scripture speaks: Awake, thou that sleepest, and arise and the Christ shall shine on thee" (περὶ τούτων, φησίν, ἡ γραφὴ λέγει· ἔγειραι ὁ καθεύδων καὶ ἐξεγέρθητι καὶ ἐπιφαύσει σοι ὁ Χριστός). "This is the Christ, he says, the (in all the begotten) Son of Man portrayed from the unportrayable Logos." Here the case is unmistakably clear. From the phrase "The Scripture speaks," we might think there was a reference to Eph. 5¹⁴, but *there it is also a quotation:* διὸ λέγει, ἔγειρε ὁ καθεύδων καὶ ἀνάστα ἐκ τῶν νεκρῶν, καὶ ἐπιφαύσει σοι ὁ Χριστός. The Christian fathers, in particular Jerome, sought in vain through their Scriptures for this saying; and no wonder. It is Gnostic, most probably a fragment of one of those numerous hymns for which the Heretics were noted. The Naassene idea that the Christ in every man (ἐν πᾶσι τοῖς γενητοῖς) is the Son of Man (Humanity, *bar nasha*) portrayed from the unportrayable Logos is remarkable and worthy of high Christian philosophy.

The phrase "to him all has been subjected" (αὐτῷ πάντα ὑποτέτακται) reminds one of I Cor. 15²⁷, but allows no conclusion since even there the writer is quoting from Ps. 8⁷ (πάντα ὑπέταξεν). Neither does the next concerning "the Stone, the chief Corner Stone, become head of the corner," but the following parenthetic phrase (p. 155), "from which (brain) all fatherhood is fashioned" (ἐξ οὗ πᾶσα πατριὰ χαρακτηρίζεται) is interesting as showing that this "all fatherhood" was a favorite Gnostic notion and as increasing the likelihood, already so great, that Eph. 3:15 is a Gnostic intercalation.

Immediately after this we meet with the locution "the inner man" (ὁ ἔσω ἄνθρωπος), "thither (within the 'hedge of the teeth') fallen from the Primal Man above, Adam" (ὁ ἔσω ἄνθρωπος ἐκεῖσε ἀποπεπτωκὼς ἀπὸ τοῦ ἀρχανθρώπου ἄνωθεν Ἀδάμαντος). Here this idea is defined and fitted into a system of thought and Scriptural interpretation. Far more probable then that it is original here than in the Pauline Epistles (Rom. 7²², II Cor. 4¹⁶, Eph. 3¹⁶) where it is introduced abruptly, without hint of explanation, as something perfectly familiar. Not that the Epistolist has taken from our Naassene, but that the notion was a common one in Gnostic circles.

Further on, of flight from Egypt across the Erythraean into the desert (p. 156), "that is, from intercourse below to the Jerusalem above, which is mother of the living" (τουτέστιν ἀπὸ τῆς κάτω μίξεως ἐπὶ τὴν ἄνω Ἰερουσαλήμ, ἥτις ἐστὶ μήτηρ ζώντων). At once our thought reverts to Gal. 4²⁶: ἡ δὲ ἄνω Ἰερουσαλήμ, ἐλευθέρα ἐστίν, ἥτις ἐστὶν μήτηρ [πάντων] ἡμῶν. Perhaps no one will maintain that the Galatian passage is quite intelligible; but the Gnostic is, and perfectly accordant with Philo (De Agricul. 1.); also the word ζώντων is altogether in place and could not have come from the Epistle. The probable inference is that the Epistolist and the Naassene have drunk from the same well.

Immediately (p. 157) we find a clear distinction between the two births: "For mortal, saith he, is all generation below, but immortal that generated above. For (he) is generated from water alone and spirit, spiritual not carnal; but he (generated) below is carnal; this is, saith he, what is written: the begotten of the flesh is flesh, and the begotten of the spirit is spirit.* This is the spiritual generation according to them." It goes far back apparently to the Homeric γένεσίς τε θεῶν γένεσίς τ'ἀνθρώπων the Oceanus with its circling flow, now up now down ποτὲ ἄνω ποτὲ κάτω). It seems as intelligible as such a speculation might be expected to be. At any rate, the thoughts, such as they are, are related and closely connected. Now compare John 3¹⁻⁶. Here the doctrine of generation from above (ἄνωθεν) is suddenly enounced without the slightest hint or preparation. When the astounded Nicodemus asks about this birth, no answer whatever is given, but the doctrine of the birth from water and spirit is enounced. Then follows "that which is written." What follows does not in the least clear up what goes before. No wonder

---

* In this connection compare page 209 of this Appendix.

Nicodemus finally exclaimed, "How can these things be?" There is no concatenation of thought, no explanation of any kind. Moreover, that the passage is patchwork peeps out in this fact: "Marvel not that I say unto *thee, ye* must be born again." This seems unnatural despite the generality of τις. Verse 6, is to all appearances a quotation. It sits loosely in its context. Remove it, and the connection is no worse, if not indeed better than before. It is therefore in high degree unlikely that we have here any citation from the Fourth Gospel, but just such a use of proverbial material as we have met with often before.

Again, page 159, we find spoken of the all-pervasive asexual humanity (ὁ ἐν πᾶσιν ἀρσενόθηλυς ἄνθρωπος) the famous πάντα γάρ (φησί) δι' αὐτοῦ ἐγένετο καὶ χωρὶς αὐτοῦ ἐγένετο οὐδὲ ἕν. Ὃ δὲ γέγονεν ἐν αὐτῷ ζωή ἐστίν with which John 1³, ⁴ agrees exactly omitting the δέ. The Naassene explains straightway that "This life is the ineffable generation of the perfect men, which to the earlier generations was not known. But the Nothing (τὸ δὲ οὐδέν) which without him came into being, is the formal world" (ὁ κόσμος ἰδικός). We note that the Naassene text, by its δέ, decides positively against the accepted punctuation of Tischendorf and for that of Westcott-Hort, which is most strongly supported by the versions and the Fathers. Furthermore, the passage is articulated in the Naassene system, whereas in the Gospel it is at best very loosely set in its context. That it is original in that context, there is not the least probability. The Naassene does not cite it even as a "Scripture" and has apparently drawn upon the general Gnostic consciousness.

On page 160 we find reference to the miracle at Cana: "and this is the water, in those fair nuptials, which the Jesus turning made into wine. This, saith he, the Great and True beginning of the signs, which the Jesus wrought in Cana of Galilee, and manifested the kingdom of the Heavens. This, saith he, is the kingdom of the heavens within us deposited as a treasure, as leaven hid away in three measures of meal." Here are notable contacts with John 2¹⁻¹¹, Luke 17²¹, Matt. 13³³, ⁴⁴. But the divergencies are equally notable "Kingdom of the heavens" is unknown to John, "Kingdom of God" appears but twice (3 ³, ⁵). The profound conception of the kingdom hid away "within us" is lost in Luke, where the kingdom is "among" the Pharisees. The notion of the likeness of the kingdom to the hidden leaven is entirely different in Matthew and less subtle. There seems then to be no evidence here that the Gnostic is using the Gospels; these rather seem to be as it were popularizing the deep symbolisms of the *Speculator spiritalis.*

On page 161 we meet with this remarkable passage: "This is, saith he, what is spoken (τὸ εἰρημένον) by the Savior: unless ye drink my blood and eat my flesh, not at all may ye enter into the kingdom of the Heavens: but even if ye drink, he says, the cup that I drink, where I go there ye cannot enter." This recalls vividly John 6⁵³, Matt. 20²², Mark 10³⁸, John 8²¹, 13³³, but how unaccountable the divergencies! Do they indicate that the Naassene has derived from the Gospel? Far from it! The saying remains undoubtedly very hard even in the Naassene form; but the ancient phrase "kingdom of the heavens" indicates that this form is older than the Johannine; it can hardly be an intentional variation, for the Gnostic gloried no less than the Evangelist in the notion of Life; on the other hand, this latter has studiously eliminated everywhere the phrase "Kingdom of the heavens." On the face of it, then, the Naassene is the elder if not the better; as to the rest of the passage we can only say that there is nothing to show clearly which form is the nearer original.

On page 162 we find, "This is, saith he, the saying (τὸ εἰρημένον) His voice we have heard, but his form we have not seen" (φωνὴν μὲν αὐτοῦ ἠκούσαμεν, εἶδος δὲ αὐτοῦ οὐχ ἑωράκαμεν). Is it likely that this comes from "thou hearest the voice thereof" (τὴν φωνὴν αὐτοῦ ἀκούεις) (John 3⁸) or from (John 5³⁷), "Ye have *neither* heard his voice at any time *nor* seen his form"? Certainly not!

On page 164, "therefore, says he, speaks the Jesus: I am the gate, the true one" (ἐγώ εἰμι ἡ πύλη ἡ ἀληθινή) Cl. Hom. has it: "Therefore himself being a true prophet spake: I am the gate of Life; who enters through me enters into Life." These are much nearer to each other than is either to John 10⁹—"I am the door; through me if any enter he shall be saved and shall pass in and pass out and find pasture." Some distant common origin seems altogether the most probable.

Immediately following thereupon we find the notion of the Perfect Man (τέλειος ἄνθρωπος) as he that is portrayed above from the Unportrayable (ὁ ἀπὸ τοῦ ἀχαρακτηρίστου, φησίν, ἄνωθεν κεχαρακτηρισμένος τέλειος ἄνθρωπος). This notion recurs often in the New Testament but always as familiar though technical, needing no explanation: as "we speak wisdom among the perfect" (I Cor. 2⁶); "let us therefore, as many as be perfect" (Phil. 3⁶⁻¹⁵); "but solid food is for Perfect Man" (Heb. 5¹⁴); "if any stumble not in word the same is a Perfect Man (Jas. 3²). The perfect seem thus to be a distinct class, of whom Clement of Alexandria never tires of speaking and calling distinctly Gnostic. Confidently then we may say the notion is Gnostic.

On page 165 we find again the Philippian phrase (Phil. 2¹⁰) τῶν ἐπουρανίων καὶ ἐπιγείων καὶ καταχθονίων λεγόντων; this then was a favorite with the Naassene, and it seems incredible that he took it from the Epistles.

Immediately after we find the mandate of the *Papa*: παῦε, παῦε, τὴν ἀσυμφωνίαν τοῦ κόσμου καὶ ποίησον εἰρήνην τοῖς μακράν, τουτέστι τοῖς ὑλικοῖς καὶ χοϊκοῖς, καὶ εἰρήνην τοῖς ἐγγύς, τουτέστι τοῖς πνευματικοῖς καὶ νοεροῖς τελείοις ἀνθρώποις. Here the phrases "peace to those near" and "peace to those far" remind us of Eph. 2¹⁷, but in wholly different, almost opposed senses, namely, of Gentiles and Jews. Here again the ideas of far and nigh are dealt with as familiar, but yet are explained elaborately. To us the Epistle seems to be forcing new wine into old bottles; but at any rate there is here no sign that the Gnostic has borrowed from Ephesians. The phrases are taken from the Septu. Is. 57¹⁹, εἰρήνην ἐπ' εἰρήνῃ τοῖς μακρὰν καὶ τοῖς ἐγγὺς οὖσι.

Immediately following, and the Phrygians call the same also *corpse* (νέκυν), as it were in a mausoleum and tomb, buried in the body. This, saith he, is the saying. Tombs are ye, whited, full (saith he) within of bones of the dead, because there is not in you the living man; and again, he says, they shall leap forth from the graves the dead, that is, from the bodies of earthly, regenerated pneumatics, not carnal (τὸ εἰρημένον· τάφοι ἐστὲ κεκονιαμένοι, γέμοντες, φησίν, ἔσωθεν ὀστέων νεκρῶν, [parenthesis by Hippolytus] ἐξαλοῦνται ἐκ τῶν μνημείων οἱ νεκροί). The suggestion is of Matt. 23[27], but the Gnostic has not drawn from this latter. For Justin twice (*Tr.* 17, 112) quotes this "saying" using the exact words of our Naassene: τάφοι κεκονιαμένοι, ἔξωθεν φαινόμενοι ὡραῖοι (καὶ* ) ἔσωθεν (δὲ† ) ὀστέων νεκρῶν. This can hardly be accidental and attests the Gnostic as most probably the earlier as it is the bolder and more natural form.‡ The saying "the dead shall leap from their tombs" is not in the New Testament, though echoes may perhaps be heard in Matt. 11[5], Luke 7[22], Matt. 27[52, 53], John 5[28].

Next we find (p. 166): "This gate (of Resurrection into Heaven) he says, Paul the Apostle knew, having opened it in a mystery and said he had been rapt by an angel and borne as far as the 2d and 3d heaven into Paradise itself and had beheld what he beheld and heard words unutterable which it is not allowed for man to speak." These, he says, are the unutterable by all called mysteries which (also we speak) not in words taught in human wisdom, but in (words) taught of spirit, comparing spiritual with spiritual, but the psychic man receives not the things of the spirit of God, for to him they are folly."

Here for the first time we find an apparent quotation from our New Testament. But we cannot be quite sure that the Naassene referred to in φησί actually refers to Paul the Apostle, though he may well have done so, for his date is quite uncertain. The Naassene work (or books) quoted may have been written in the 2d century but yet have used materials two centuries older. Granting, then, it is the Gnostic, not merely Hippolytus who refers to Paul, we note that the phraseology departs widely from II Cor. 12[2-4] and can hardly be a quotation: (Naassene) ἡρπάσθαι ὑπὸ ἀγγέλου, καὶ γεγονέναι ἕως δευτέρου καὶ τρίτου οὐρανοῦ εἰς τὸν παράδεισον αὐτόν, καὶ ἑωρακέναι ἃ ἑώρακε, καὶ ἀκηκοέναι ῥήματα ἄρρητα ἃ οὐκ ἐξὸν ἀνθρώπῳ εἰπεῖν. Compare II Cor. 12[2-4]: ἁρπαγέντα τὸν τοιοῦτον ἕως τρίτου οὐρανοῦ. καὶ οἶδα τὸν τοιοῦτον ἄνθρωπον, — εἴτε ἐν σώματι εἴτε χωρὶς τοῦ σώματος [οὐκ οἶδα,] ὁ Θεὸς οἶδεν, — ὅτι ἡρπάγη εἰς τὸν παράδεισον καὶ ἤκουσεν ἄρρητα ῥήματα ἃ οὐκ ἐξὸν ἀνθρώπῳ λαλῆσαι.

Even here then another form of the account is indicated. The same can not be said of the 2d passage which gives the received text of I Cor. 2[13, 14] exactly. Is the Naassene then quoting from our Canonic Epistle? Very possible, for his date is unknown; but by no means certainly. For *the Corinthian passage and all its context seem* to us at least *to be imported.* Has even the genius of Holsten been able to interpret this series of paragraphs, 1[17]–3[2], in relation either to each other or to the preceding and following? Certainly not! We have spent many hours over them in vain, and have written many pages in the effort to reconstruct the *Gedankengang,* all of which

---

* In Tr. 17.

† In Tr. 112.

‡ Both in Matthew and in Justin the clause "that indeed appear fair without" (appearing fair without) seems a later addendum, to adapt the saying to the Pharisees.

are fit only for the fire. A very slight hint of the original detachment of our paragraph is given by manuscripts F. and G. in the omission of ἃ before καὶ λαλοῦμεν (verse 13). This gives we suspect an older text. The ἃ has been deftly inserted to attach the paragraph to the preceding χαρισθέντα. On this however we do not insist. To this important passage and its context we hope to return in a paper "Mysteries in the New Testament."

Straightway we read: Concerning these (the Pneumatics), he says, the Savior has spoken: No one can come to me, except my Father the heavenly draw some one. Can this be corrupted from John 6[44]? Surely not! Such a departure from the

Naassene:

οὐδεὶς δύναται ἐλθεῖν πρός με, ἐὰν μή τινα ἑλκύσῃ ὁ πατήρ μου ὁ οὐράνιος.

John 6[44]:

οὐδεὶς δύναται ἐλθεῖν πρὸς ἐμὲ ἐὰν μὴ ὁ πατὴρ ὁ πέμψας με ἑλκύσῃ αὐτόν.

sacred text seems wilful and unaccountable. Besides the Naassene form, the "celestial Father," seems much more likely original than the ὁ πέμψας με. Moreover, the sentence is introduced abruptly in the Gospel and is best accounted for as a quotation or apophthegm. Omit it, and the thought does not suffer.

On page 167: "And again, he says, spoke the Savior: Not every one &c." precisely the received text of Matt. 7[21]. Is it then a quotation from our Gospel? Why so? Here in Matthew the saying is embedded in a concretion of such sayings. Why suppose it original in this connection rather than v. 19, which is plainly a proverb, already used in Matt. 3[8]? The supposition is plainly gratuitous.

Continuing on this page: "And again, he says, he spoke: 'The publicans and the harlots precede you into the kingdom of the heavens'." Comparing this with Matt. 21[31], we note that the Gnostic form τῶν οὐρανῶν is apparently older than the Matthean τοῦ θεοῦ. Again, there is little reason to think this saying original in its Gospel context. It could scarcely be introduced more abruptly, without any relevance to the foregoing, where again the text wavers forever between πρῶτος and ἔσχατος. There is no ground then for assuming any derivation of the Naassene passage from our Gospel.

The interpretation of τελῶναι (publicans) as from τέλη (ends) seems extremely fanciful and even ludicrous, but not more so than many that meet us in the pages of the Fathers. "But, he says, we are οἱ τελῶναι εἰς οὓς τὰ τέλη τῶν αἰώνων κατήντηκε· For τέλη he says, are the seeds sown down into the world from the Unportrayable, through which the whole world συντελεῖται; for through them also it began to be. The coincidence with I Cor. 10[11] is perfect but proves nothing; for the clause there, though very well in place, sounds strangely like an apt quotation, and such we believe it is, a belief which can neither be proved nor disproved. The astonishing interpretation of τέλη seems unlikely to have originated in early Christian days, when the τέλος was eagerly anticipated. — Coming now to the famous parable: "Went forth the sower for to sow, and some fell by the way and were trodden down; and some upon the stony places, and sprang up, (saith he), and through not having depth it withered and died; and some fell, he says, upon the earth the fair and good and brought forth fruit, some a hundred, some sixty some thirty. Who hath, saith he, ears to hear, let him hear."

Naassene:

Ἐξῆλθεν ὁ σπείρων τοῦ σπεῖραι· καὶ τὰ μὲν ἔπεσε παρὰ τὴν ὁδὸν καὶ κατεπατήθη, τὰ δὲ ἐπὶ τὰ πετρώδη· καὶ ἐξανέτειλε, [φησί] καὶ διὰ τὸ μὴ ἔχειν βάθος ἐξηράνθη καὶ ἀπέθανε· τὰ δὲ ἔπεσε [φησίν,] ἐπὶ τὴν γῆν τὴν καλὴν καὶ ἀγαθήν, καὶ ἐποίει καρπόν, ὁ μὲν ἑκατόν, ὁ δὲ ἑξήκοντα, ὁ δὲ τριάκοντα. Ὁ ἔχων, [φησίν,] ὦτα ἀκούειν ἀκουέτω.

We find the three Gospel forms very diverse. It will hardly be contended that all three of the widely diverging Evangelic forms are the original; or any two; why then any one? It is in fact quite impossible to derive any two from the other. They must then have had some common ancestry, and rather remote, since they are so far apart. Looking at the Naassene form, we see it is still farther divergent but much simpler than any of the three, leaning rather to the *Matthew-Mark* type (Matt. $13^{3-9}$, Mark $4^{3-9}$), but agreeing with *Luke* ($8^{5-8}$) in the important κατεπατήθη. It omits entirely the thorns, but calls the earth both fair and good, whereas *Matthew-Mark* call it *fair* and *Luke* calls it *good*. Examined carefully this Gnostic form seems underivable from any or all the Canonics, but to have every appearance of greater age and comparative originality. These three on the contrary seem unmistakably to be diverse elaborations of a much simpler primitive.

We find on page 168: "This, saith he, is the saying (τὸ εἰρημένον): Every tree that bringeth not forth good fruit is hewn down and cast into the fire." As this recurs exactly in Matt. $3^{10}$ and $7^{19}$, it is plain that it is neither more nor less than a current "saying," probably of very great antiquity. But "fruit" (καρποί) is immediately explained as only the rational (οἱ λογκιοί) the living man, [men] who have entered through the third gate. Where it is well to bear in mind Rom. $1^{13}$, Phil. $4^{17}$. Further on, "This is what he says," saith he: "Cast not the holy to the dogs nor the pearls to the swine" (μὴ βάλητε τὸ ἅγιον τοῖς κυσὶ μηδὲ τοὺς μαργαρίτας τοῖς χοίροις). Compared with this, Matt. $7^6$ is apparently a later and expanded form. It also stands quite isolated, without any contextual attachment. Moreover, at least the first half was a well known injunction—*Sanctitates non redimuntur ut canibus projiciantur in cibum.* Schebuos F. 11, 2. It is palpable then that the Naassene has not drawn from Matthew but that Matthew has taken up an adage.

On page 170 we find "the Jerusalem below" (τὴν κάτω Ἰερουσαλήμ) defined as "not the city in Phoenicia but the generation below, the mortal." This is the necessary complement of the Jerusalem above (ἄνω), but does not appear as such in Gal. $4^{25, 26}$. This makes it probable, though not certain, that the Naassene idea was earlier than the Pauline.

We need not dwell on the "perfect man the regenerate of water and spirit, not carnal," see supra, p. 164. At this point is repeated the splendid apophthegm of the "Beginning of Perfection."*

---

* Above, p. 158.

After a good deal that is hard to understand we come, on page 173, to a passage of extreme significance. This (doctrine of Higher Humanity), he says, is what they say that have been initiated into the Eleusinian mysteries. It is statutory ($\theta\acute{\epsilon}\sigma\mu\iota\sigma\nu$) for those initiated into the less to be again initiated into the greater. For greater dooms do greater doles obtain ($\mu\acute{\sigma}\rho\sigma\iota\ \gamma\grave{\alpha}\rho\ \mu\epsilon\acute{\iota}\zeta\sigma\nu\epsilon s\ \mu\epsilon\acute{\iota}\zeta\sigma\nu\alpha s\ \mu\sigma\acute{\iota}\rho\alpha s\ \lambda\alpha\gamma\chi\acute{\alpha}\nu\sigma\nu\sigma\iota$). And small, he says, are the mysteries those of Persephone below, concerning which mysteries and the way that leads thither, which is wide and broad and conducts the perishing to Persephone . . . and the poet too says:

> But under her is a pathway rough,
> Hollow, miry; but 'tis best to lead
> To lovely grove of high-honoured Aphrodite.

These are, he says, the lesser mysteries, those of the carnal generation, initiated into which lesser (mysteries) men should pause and be initiated into the greater, the heavenly. For they who have got the dooms there receive greater doles. For this, he saith, is the gate of the heaven and this the house of God, where the good God dwells alone, into which shall not enter, he says, any one unclean nor psychic nor carnal, but it is kept for pneumatics alone, where need they that have come to cast ($\beta\alpha\lambda\epsilon\hat{\iota}\nu$), or receive ($\lambda\alpha\beta\epsilon\hat{\iota}\nu$) their garments and all to become bride-grooms emasculated through the the virginal spirit. For this is the virgin that bears in womb and conceives and brings forth a son not psychic, not somatic, but a blessed aeon of aeons. Concerning these, saith he, distinctly spake the Savior, that narrow and contracted is the way that leads into life, and few are they that fare into it, but broad and spacious the way that leads into perdition and many are they that thoroughfare through it.

Here there is much that is obscure, grotesque, ill-jointed, the last might be expected in such a mass of extracts. But some things are palpable and unmistakable. The Naassene distinguishes between the lesser and the greater Eleusinian mysteries. The former he takes to represent the inferior carnal birth, the latter the far superior birth spiritual. The former he also finds symbolized in the broad spacious way which all men tread, which leads to death and to the "dark walled home of Persephone"; the latter is symbolized in the narrow way that leads to God and Heaven, to eternal, spiritual, pure human, asexual life. And this, he says, is the reference of the famous words which "distinctly spake the Savior." The temptation is great to say at once, "of course, he is quoting from the Sermon on the Mount," but in turning to Matt. 7[13, 14] we find a wide difference. The text is very uncertain, but as the great editors put it:

Naassene $\sigma\tau\epsilon\nu\grave{\eta}\ \kappa\alpha\grave{\iota}\ \tau\epsilon\theta\lambda\iota\mu\mu\acute{\epsilon}\nu\eta\ \grave{\epsilon}\sigma\tau\grave{\iota}\nu\ \acute{\eta}\ \acute{\sigma}\delta\grave{\sigma}s\ \acute{\eta}\ \grave{\alpha}\pi\acute{\alpha}\gamma\sigma\upsilon\sigma\alpha\ \epsilon\grave{\iota}s\ \tau\grave{\eta}\nu\ \zeta\omega\acute{\eta}\nu,\ \kappa\alpha\grave{\iota}\ \grave{\sigma}\lambda\acute{\iota}\gamma\sigma\iota$ $\epsilon\grave{\iota}\sigma\grave{\iota}\nu\ \sigma\acute{\iota}\ \epsilon\grave{\iota}\sigma\epsilon\rho\chi\acute{\sigma}\mu\epsilon\nu\sigma\iota\ \epsilon\grave{\iota}s\ \alpha\grave{\upsilon}\tau\acute{\eta}\nu,\ \pi\lambda\alpha\tau\epsilon\hat{\iota}\alpha\ \delta\grave{\epsilon}\ \kappa\alpha\grave{\iota}\ \epsilon\grave{\upsilon}\rho\acute{\upsilon}\chi\omega\rho\sigma s\ \acute{\eta}\ \acute{\sigma}\delta\grave{\sigma}s\ \acute{\eta}\ \grave{\alpha}\pi\acute{\alpha}\gamma\sigma\upsilon\sigma\alpha\ \epsilon\grave{\iota}s$ $\tau\grave{\eta}\nu\ \grave{\alpha}\pi\acute{\omega}\lambda\epsilon\iota\alpha\nu,\ \kappa\alpha\grave{\iota}\ \pi\sigma\lambda\lambda\sigma\acute{\iota}\ \epsilon\grave{\iota}\sigma\iota\nu\ \sigma\acute{\iota}\ \delta\iota\epsilon\rho\chi\acute{\sigma}\mu\epsilon\nu\sigma\iota\ \delta\iota'\ \alpha\grave{\upsilon}\tau\hat{\eta}s.$

Matthew 7[13-14] $\epsilon\grave{\iota}\sigma\acute{\epsilon}\lambda\theta\alpha\tau\epsilon\ \delta\iota\grave{\alpha}\ \tau\hat{\eta}s\ \sigma\tau\epsilon\nu\hat{\eta}s\ \pi\acute{\upsilon}\lambda\eta s\cdot\ \acute{\sigma}\tau\iota\ \pi\lambda\alpha\tau\epsilon\hat{\iota}\alpha\ \acute{\eta}\ \pi\acute{\upsilon}\lambda\eta\ \kappa\alpha\grave{\iota}\ \epsilon\grave{\upsilon}\rho\acute{\upsilon}\chi\omega\rho\sigma s$ $\acute{\eta}\ \acute{\sigma}\delta\grave{\sigma}s\ \acute{\eta}\ \grave{\alpha}\pi\acute{\alpha}\gamma\sigma\upsilon\sigma\alpha\ \epsilon\grave{\iota}s\ \tau\grave{\eta}\nu\ \grave{\alpha}\pi\acute{\omega}\lambda\epsilon\iota\alpha\nu,\ \kappa\alpha\grave{\iota}\ \pi\sigma\lambda\lambda\sigma\acute{\iota}\ \epsilon\grave{\iota}\sigma\iota\nu\ \sigma\acute{\iota}\ \epsilon\grave{\iota}\sigma\epsilon\rho\chi\acute{\sigma}\mu\epsilon\nu\sigma\iota\ \delta\iota'\ \alpha\grave{\upsilon}\tau\hat{\eta}s\cdot$

ὅτι στενὴ ἡ πύλη καὶ τεθλιμμένη ἡ ὁδὸς ἡ ἀπάγουσα εἰς τὴν ζωήν, καὶ ὀλίγοι εἰσὶν
οἱ εὑρίσκοντες αὐτήν.

We notice that the clauses are reversed in order, that the Naassene contains no
"gate," that Matthew has εἰσερχόμενοι δι᾽ αὐτῆς and εὑρίσκοντες αὐτήν but the
Naassene the much superior εἰσερχόμενοι εἰς αὐτήν and διερχόμενοι δι᾽ αὐτῆς. Not
one of these variations is easy to account for if the Naassene be quoting from
Matthew. Again, the repetition of ὅτι in Matthew is very strange and unnatural
and extremely hard to believe original. On the whole, the Naassene version seems
decidedly preferable and much nearer the polished form of an epigram. Matthew's
looks like an elaboration akin to that which has overtaken the Parable of the
Sower.

Furthermore, the saying is *absolutely isolated* in the Gospel text, wholly unrelated to anything before or after. It seems impossible then that it should be primitive in this connection. Still more, however, it is impossible to suppose that the
Jesus or any man would utter such mysterious words without a syllable of
preparation or explanation. If the ideas were not already familiar to the hearers,
these could not have understood them without interpretation. We hold then with
confidence that these verses in Matthew are not there in primal form or connection, but they belong in some now indeterminable fashion to the doctrine then
current of the Two Ways, of Life and of Death, and that there is no semblance of
reason for supposing them quoted from the Gospel by the Naassene. Whether this
latter's relation of them to the Eleusinian mysteries and to the Ways of Carnal and
Spiritual generation have any element of correctness we need not discuss, but no
one can deny the dignity and elevation of his thoughts.

It may be as well to remark right here that the Naassene statement as quoted
by Hippolytus, that "the Savior spake" thus, cannot be understood to constate
any historic fact. Such expressions stand on a par with "God said," "Jehovah
Spake," "Oracle of Elohuin," "The Logos spake," "the Christ declared," "the
Jesus says" (in the recent papyri), and was simply a formula of authoritative
prophetic or dogmatic deliverance. The prophets regularly opened their discourses
with a "word of the Lord." Besides, "the Savior" was a notion distinctly Gnostic,
as we shall see. This however merely in passing.

"So," he says, (p. 174) "the Phrygians call (the Father) 'The Amygdalus'
(from ἀμύξαι = to rend), from whom proceeded and was born the Invisible,
through whom the Universe was made and without him was made Nothing. And
Syrictas, say the Phrygians, is what is generated thence, because spirit harmoni-
ous is what is generated. For spirit he saith, is God: wherefore, he saith, neither
do worship in this mountain nor in Jerusalem the true worshippers, but in spirit.
For spiritual, he says, is the worship of the perfect, not carnal. But the spirit, he
saith, is there where also the Father is named and the Son from this Father
(there) begotten." The coincidence with John 1[8] has already been discussed. Another famous Johannine (4[21-24]) is also recalled, but the diversities are quite as remarkable as the agreements. The fact that the Naassene says "in this mountain,"

for which we know of no reference, might seem to point to the Gospel as the original, since there we find "this mountain" mentioned. But we know nothing of the Naassene context from which Hippolytus quotes, it may very well have contained the "mountain" referred to. Again, the reference to "mountain" in John 4[19] may very well have been introduced to prepare us for the "mountain" of v. 21, much in the manner of the Evangelist. However, let the circumstance have its due weight. On comparing the two texts, it seems impossible to doubt that the Naassene is the simpler, the older, and every way the superior. The thought is absolutely unadorned, but the nakedness of the statue is the beauty of a god. The same cannot be said of the other. Naturally, the text is very uncertain. Verse 22 is plainly an additament extremely harsh and out of place. Unhappy too is the repetition of "comes an hour" ($\check{\epsilon}\rho\chi\epsilon\tau\alpha\iota$ $\omega\rho\alpha$ verses 21 and 23); unhappier the addition and repetition of "and the truth," and not logically justified; most unhappy the disorder and repetition of "those worshipping in spirit and truth"—in fact, the whole v. 23 is palpably superfluous and misplaced;* the worst of all is the throwing forward of all into the future—as if true worship had not always been in spirit. Notice too the unintelligible final clause of v. 23. On the whole, the Johannine passage is a jumble, and there appears not the slightest reason for thinking it the original of the Naassene—*au contraire.*

Continuing with the next page, "this, he saith, is the many-named, myriad-eyed Incomprehensible, for which every nature, but each in its own wise, yearns.†
This, he saith, is the Word of God, which, he saith, is Word of Announcement of the Mighty Power ($\dot{\rho}\eta\mu\alpha$ $\dot{\alpha}\pi o\phi\dot{\alpha}\sigma\epsilon\omega\varsigma$ $\tau\eta\varsigma$ $\mu\epsilon\gamma\dot{\alpha}\lambda\eta\varsigma$ $\delta\upsilon\nu\dot{\alpha}\mu\epsilon\omega\varsigma$). Wherefore it will be sealed and hidden and concealed, lying in the habitation where the Root of the Universe has been founded, of Aeons, Powers, Intelligencies, gods, Angels, Spirits delegated, Entities, non-Entities, Generables, Ingenerables, Incomprehensibles, Comprehensibles, Years, Months, Days, Hours, Point indivisible (Instant?) from which the Least begins to increase gradually—the Point, he saith, being naught and consisting of naught, being indivisible will become by self-intelligence ($\dot{\epsilon}\alpha\upsilon\tau\eta$ $\dot{\epsilon}\pi\dot{\iota}\nu o\iota\alpha\nu$) a certain magnitude incomprehensible. This, he saith, is the Kingdom of the Heavens, the grain of mustard (seed), the Point subsisting Indivisible in the body, which none, he saith, hath seen save the Pneumatics alone." This extraordinary passage seems worth quoting for its prodigious conception, which almost out-Hegels Hegel himself, of the Evolution of the Universe from the focal point of Being by an act of self-intelligence. The good Bishop of Portus was evidently impotent in the presence of such amazing metaphysics, and he merely says: "These things thus they feign, . . . affirming all things are spiritual" ($\tau\alpha\hat{\upsilon}\theta$' $o\hat{\upsilon}\tau\omega\varsigma$ $\sigma\chi\epsilon\delta\iota\dot{\alpha}$-$\zeta o\upsilon\sigma\iota$ $\tau\dot{\alpha}$ $\dot{\upsilon}\pi\dot{o}$ $\pi\dot{\alpha}\nu\tau\omega\nu$ $\dot{\alpha}\nu\theta\rho\dot{\omega}\pi\omega\nu$ $^\vert\lambda\epsilon\gamma\dot{o}\mu\epsilon\nu\dot{\alpha}$ $\tau\epsilon$ $\kappa\alpha\dot{\iota}$ $\gamma\iota\nu\dot{o}\mu\epsilon\nu\alpha$, $\pi\rho\dot{o}\varsigma$ $\check{\iota}\delta\iota o\nu$ $\nu o\hat{\upsilon}\nu$, $\pi\nu\epsilon\upsilon\mu\dot{\alpha}\tau\iota\kappa\alpha$ $\phi\dot{\alpha}\sigma\kappa o\nu\tau\epsilon\varsigma$ $\pi\dot{\alpha}\nu\tau\alpha$ $\gamma\dot{\iota}\nu\epsilon\sigma\theta\alpha\iota$). But it is plain, even in the confused presentment of Hippolytus, that the Naassene is thinking connectedly and systematically. It is interesting then to note here certain turns of speech elsewhere recurring.

---

* As Blass now recognizes for entirely different reasons.
† Cf. Rom. 8[22]. *Editor.*

Thus the "Announcement of the Mighty Power" meets us again as a title of Simon's book; compare also Acts 8[10], also Eph. 3[20], Col. 1[11].

Again (p. 180) we read: "This, he saith, is the water that is above the firmament, concerning which, he saith, the Savior spake: If thou knewest who it is that asks, thou would'st have asked of him and he would have given thee to drink living water that leaps" ($\epsilon i$ $\H{\eta}\delta\epsilon\iota s$ $\tau i s$ $\dot{\epsilon}\sigma\tau\iota\nu$ $\dot{o}$ $a i\tau\hat{\omega}\nu$ $\sigma\dot{v}$ $\dot{a}\nu$ $\H{\eta}\tau\eta\sigma a s$ $\pi a\rho'$ $a\dot{v}\tau o\hat{v}$, $\kappa a i$ $\H{\epsilon}\delta\omega\kappa\epsilon\nu$ $\dot{a}\nu$ $\sigma o\iota$ $\pi\iota\epsilon\hat{\iota}\nu$ $\zeta\hat{\omega}\nu$ $\H{\upsilon}\delta\omega\rho$ $\dot{a}\lambda\lambda\dot{o}\mu\epsilon\nu o\nu$). On comparing this with John 4[10, 14], we find that remarks similar to those already made apply. The Naassene form has every sign of comparative originality, the Johannine seems worked over and elaborated but by no means improved.

Lastly, "but if any one, he saith, is blind from birth ($\tau\upsilon\phi\lambda\dot{o}s$ $\dot{\epsilon}\kappa$ $\gamma\epsilon\nu\epsilon\tau\hat{\eta}s$) and has not beheld the true light that lights every man coming into the world, . . ." Here then are exact coincidences with John 9[1] and 1[9]; but on which side is the priority? In the text there is nothing to determine. Our decision will depend upon our critical tenets. If we regard the incident in John 9 as historical, we shall naturally think the Naassene has taken thence his phrase; but if we regard it as unhistorical, as invented merely as a frame work for the discussions of the chapter, then we shall see no reason for believing the Naassene has borrowed thence; on the contrary.

Herewith then we close this list of Naassene agreements with the sacred text. It is seen that they are very numerous, and often very exact. But we have failed to find any indication worth mentioning that the sacred text has actually been quoted. On the contrary, in the great majority of instances, the probability lay heavily against such a proposition, and in not a few cases it seemed downright impossible. In only one case was the use of the Scripture suggested as at all probable (II Cor. 12[2-4]), but there the relations remained obscure and doubtful. The overpowering impression of the whole body of facts is that the Naassene writer has at least in the main derived his material from *sources much older* than any of our Canonic Scriptures; he may have done so in every instance, though it is possible that in one or two cases a reviser has drawn from Canonic sources.

Such then is our provisional conclusion; and we now ask, is this conclusion confirmed or refuted by the history of Naassenism so far as known to us? And first we observe that the statement of Hippolytus is clear, positive, and unambiguous, that the Naassenes were the oldest of the Errorists, that from their "dogma" many, detaching parts, have constructed with many subdivisions the heresy which is one, inasmuch as they deliver the same things in various dogmas. Against this testimony, very awkwardly worded but unequivocal in its import, it is of no significance that Irenaeus mentions the "Sethians, whom some call Ophians or Ophites," in the penultimate place. The account of Hippolytus is broad daylight compared with the pitchy dark of Irenaeus, who besides has followed an inverted order, going back from the last (Valentinians) to the first. His testimony then is not really opposed to that of Hippolytus, but rather confirms it. Epiphanius mentions the Ophites as the thirty-seventh heresy, but his order is not chronologic, and his testimony not independent. Theodoret seems hardly to deserve mention.

Hippolytus alone has attempted to follow the order of time and to let the heretics speak in some measure, though disconnectedly, for themselves.

Now the Simonians occupy the fifth place in our author's list. They must then have followed the Naassenes at some considerable distance. But the Simonians were at least as old as the Pentacost. For in *Acts,* at the beginning of the preaching of Peter, we find Simon already well known in Samaria, worshipped as that so-called Mighty Power of God, where he had been long time a wonder (Acts 8⁹⁻¹¹). Moreover all Christian tradition represents him as an elder contemporary of Peter (Clem. Hom. and Recog.). We can see no motive for antedating him. Unless then the record in *Acts,* and all tradition, be unaccountably at fault. Simon must date at the latest slightly before the earliest proclamation of Christianity. Hence Naassenism, which must be still earlier cannot be brought down later than the birth of Christ—a result of extreme importance.

Of course, it may be said that the doctrine was gradual in its development, which is very true. Hippolytus bears witness that it ramified into many schisms (πολυσχιδὴς ), but we are not concerned with remote developments, our business is with the central dogma and its immediate corollaries. This was the dogma of the Spiritual Humanity, the All-Father, the Citizen of Heaven, the Logos, the Christ, the Jesus. If we may put any trust at all in the statements of the learned and diligent Bishop, fortified at every point with profuse quotations from the Naassene authority, this doctrine was the very heart of the whole system, from which all else was offshoot. It is well to note that certain of these terms are well known elsewhere as foci of Jewish-Hellenic speculation. Philo never wearies of the Logos, nor does even the most ancient sage of Ephesus, Heraclitus. The Rabbis have much to tell of the First and the Second Adam. It is not strange, then, that such ideas should be central in such an early heresy.

We note further that Hippolytus is careful not to claim that the Naassenes derived their ideas from apostolic preaching which they corrupted—a chronologic absurdity that he carefully avoids. He declares (p. 141) that they have collected the secret and ineffable mysteries of all the nations and slandering the Christ deceived the ignorant. (ἴδωμεν ὡς τὰ κρυπτὰ καὶ ἀπόρρητα πάντων ὁμοῦ συνάγοντες οὗτοι μυστήρια τῶν ἐθνῶν καταψευδόμενοι τοῦ Χριστοῦ ἐξαπατῶσι τοὺς ταῦτα οὐκ εἰδότας τὰ τῶν ἐθνῶν ὄργια).

Now let us ask whether the Naassene doctrine as given by Hippolytus points to an early or to a late heresy. The answer cannot linger for a moment. It is plain on its face that this doctrine is not only old but *very old,* in fact, the oldest that we meet with anywhere in studying the Origins of Christianity. This fact shines out most clearly through the absence of so many ideas conspicuous in latter heresy. We hear nothing of the Cross, nothing of the Death, nothing of the Resurrection, nothing of the Aeons and their Procession, nothing of the infinite brood of Simon and Basilides and Valentinus, nothing of the strife of Law and Gospel. The whole theory revolves in a high but narrow sphere round a pivotal idea of the Spiritual Man as the beginning and the end of History. The interpretation of Scripture is quite parallel with the allegorizing of Philo, and had been familiar for generations. The dependence is very great upon Gentile myth and literature, the affinity very close with the ancient mysteries and the current philosophical-religious cults. The constant reference to the Phrygians and even to the Samothracians, the frequent quotations from the Greek writers, and the whole atmosphere of thought direct us to Northern or central Asia Minor as the birth place or seat of this speculation. The reverential use made of the Old Testament guarantees the Jewish element, but for which we might take the whole heresy to be purely Pagan. We must suppose it developed in the Jewish Diaspora; whether the author quoted be Hellenized Hebrew or Hebraized Hellene, we cannot say. With only two merely apparent exceptions already discussed we find not a single hint of a date later than the beginning of our era. In its many outlines the doctrine seems to be much older still.

The most fitting designation of this school would be the *Pneumatics*. So they seem to have called themselves at first, but later Gnostics. The names Naassenes and Ophites were perhaps given them by their enemies. Though their defamers continually reproached them with serpent worship, it is plain that this is a mere slander. The serpent was for them the mere symbol of water, the liquid substance of the world, like the modern solid ether, (an idea taken from the illustrious Milesian, Thales); the derivation of all temple worship from the serpent (*Naos* from *Nachash*) is neither better nor worse than many other etymologies current then or even now. However, it is very far from indicating that these Pneumatics worshipped the Serpent, quite the contrary. They were merely explaining (fantastically enough) the prevailing temple service as at best a merely half-conscious worship of the principle of the Material Universe; but they themselves had transcended all such ceremonies as merely of the formal world. They boasted that they alone had sounded the depths, they alone worshipped in spirit a God who was spirit. The unfriendly Bishop of Portus himself brings against them no charge of immorality or unseemly deportment of any kind. Neither does he lay at their door any corruption or perversion of Scripture, nor in fact any citation of canonic Scripture. The sum of their offending seems to have been that they attempted a comprehensive spiritual interpretation of ancient myths, rites, and doctrines, thereby "slandering the Christ."

Have we any historical evidence of the existence at or before the beginning of our era of any such Pneumatics? The presumption is very strong in favor of their existence. In all ages there have lived men much better, or at least more liberal than their creeds. Of old it was declared, that to obey is better than sacrifice, and to hearken than fat of lambs. And later "I hate, I despise your feasts and will not delight in your assemblies. . . . But rather let justice roll down as waters and righteousness as an ever-flowing stream." "Thou delightest not in sacrifice, thou hast no pleasure in burnt offering. The sacrifices of God are a broken spirit. A broken and contrite heart, O God, thou wilt not despise." Such examples might be multiplied. But neither is the historical evidence wanting. In his story of Izates (Ant. 20, 2, 4) Josephus tells how both he and his mother were brought over to Judaism by a certain Jewish merchant Ananias, who nevertheless dissuaded his royal convert from circumcision as quite unnecessary, since he could "without the circumcision worship the divine, for this is more important than to be circumcised." Josephus himself had no sympathy with such liberalism, for he proceeds to tell with manifest approval how Eleazor persuaded the young king to submit to the rite; hence his testimony seems unimpeachable. Strabo, too (certainly devoid of Jewish prejudices), (760, 761) tells of Jews who professed to go back to a purer spiritual worship, the original Mosaic, free from all ceremonial circumcision, excisions, and other such enactments. There exists abundant rabbinical evidence to like effect.

We may then regard the *Pneumatics* as historically assured.

Let us now consider into what difficulties the accepted theory leads us. Since these Naassenes (as it is said) quote copiously from the Fourth Gospel, and since no one places its composition earlier than about A.D. 96, it follows that the Naassene heresy was active, and if not at the very beginning, at least in the bloom of its youth as late as A.D. 100! And yet it foreran Simonianism which was at its height not later than 60 years before! And yet it foreran Basilides and Valentinus and Sethianism and Justinism, all of which saw the days of their strength in the first quarter then of the second century! The anachronism is patent. Does any one really believe that these more than half-pagan heretics were quoting abundantly from the Gospel of John almost immediately after its composition and fully half a century before it obtained notable recognition in orthodox circles? How utterly ridiculous! The impossibility of such chronology comes out clearly in Bunsen's scheme. He recognizes that the Naassenes must take the first place in the Hierarchy of heresy, that they must precede the Simonians, and that they must be allowed a chance to use the Johannine writings. Hence he put them down between A.D. 70 and 99, giving them a scanty lustrum in which to learn and adopt the Fourth Gospel! But how about Simon? He must come earlier, although he is later! Hence Bunsen writes him down between 27 and 65! In other words he is half a century older than his elders! The whole attempt to make room for these Naassenes *after* the preaching of Christianity and the composition of the New Testament Scriptures must forever issue in failure.*

A further evidence, and a very striking one, of the great antiquity of Naassenism is found in the fact that, altho it was certainly of first class importance, as appears from its extensive literature, its numerous ramifications, the nobility of its teachings, and the preeminence assigned it by Hippolytus, yet we hear of it in the 2d century practically not at all. No other historian of heresy has anything to tell of it that is worth a moment's notice. It seems plain then that its force was spent long before the end of the first century, that it passed over into other schools and lost its identity in the lap of its first and second century successors. The debt that we owe to Hippolytus for exploring its literature and handing down to us even a garbled and inadequate statement of its doctrine is great beyond all computation.

We must not close this discussion without noticing the extraordinary hymn quoted by Hippolytus. According to Duncker the text is indeed hopelessly corrupt

* For additional on the dating of Simon the Samaritan, see the discussion of him later, p. 183 ff.

(*citra spem salutis corruptum*). Never-the-less we find the general idea, spirit, and intentions unmistakable.

> A law generative of the Universe was the First Mind.
> And the Second was of the First born the outpoured chaos.
> And Soul in third place received operative law.
> Therefore with nimble form enveloped
> It succumbs to death with care overpowered.
> Now kingdom-holding it beholds the light,
> And now into misery whirled it weeps,
> And now it bewails, rejoices,
> And now it wails, is judged,
> And now it is judged, dies,
> And now becomes an exile, the hapless, of ills
> A labyrinth has entered straying (wandering).
> But Jesus said: Behold, Father,
> A strife of ills upon earth
> From thy breath wanders in.
> (He) strives to flee the bitter chaos
> And knows not how he will fare therethrough.
> On this account send me, Father,
> Bearing seals, I shall descend.
> Ages whole shall make way through,
> Mysteries all shall lay open,
> And forms of Gods shall show
> And the secrets of the holy way,
> Having called it Gnosis, I shall deliver.

This we think is the first recorded appearance of the concept "Jesus" in religious history. This supernal Being, "in the bosom of the Father," beholds with compassion the strife and misery of the Soul upon earth and its inability to free itself from the whirlpool of Time and Change in which it is caught, and he asks the Father for permission to be sent down to earth to *traverse the ages,* to clear up all mysteries, to reveal God to Man, and to teach the secrets of the holy path of the lordly-named Gnosis.

In the presence of this most ancient hymn the prevailing liberal theory that the Man Jesus was at first the Carpenter's son, then a distinguished Rabbi, a Mighty Teacher, then a crucified Messiah, then a spiritually or otherwise re-risen Lord, then by degrees an exalted Saviour, Redeemer, Son of God, and second person in the Trinity,—all this theory of the gradual deification of a remarkable human personality, collapses instantly in the presence of this Hymn.

### D. *Peratae*

We pass now to the Peratae. These "Transcendentals," we are told, maintain the doctrine of the "Triad" "called Perfect Good and Paternal Magnitude." The text of Hippolytus is here corrupt and obscure, it seems clear only that he did not understand what he would describe, but any way it is said "they maintain" that "in the times of Herod," "for reasons we shall later state," there descended from unorigination and the first world-segment a certain three-natured and three-bodied and three-powered man called Christ (τριφυῆ τινὰ καὶ τρισώματον καὶ τριδύναμον ἄνθρωπον καλούμενον Χριστόν)having in himself all the concretions and powers (proceeding) from the three parts of the world. "And this he says is the saying (p. 187): all the Fullness pleased to dwell in him bodily and in him is all the Godhead of the Triad thus divided" (Πᾶν τὸ πλήρωμα εὐδόκησε κατοικῆσαι ἐν αὐτῷ σωματικῶς, καὶ πᾶσά ἐστιν ἐν αὐτῷ ἡ θεότης τῆς οὕτω διῃρημένης τριάδος). The parallel is of course Col. 2⁹—Because in him dwells all the Fullness of the Godhead bodily, and Col. 1¹⁹—Because in him pleased all the Fullness to dwell. Here we are met by this same constantly recurring phenomenon, namely: the Gnostic passage fits well enough in its context, however grotesque that context may be; whereas the canonic passages are scarcely intelligible in their context and have every appearance of being foreign importations. Thus 1¹⁹ is so clearly parenthetic and unconnected with either 18 or 20 that our translators have felt compelled to throw in the phrase "of the Father" which however does not relieve the difficulty. Similarly 2⁹ seems plainly out of place, and the ὅτι assigns only the vaguest of reasons. Moreover, the repetition of the πᾶν τὸ πλήρωμα (Col. 1¹⁹ and here) with no hint of explanation, marks it as a familiar and technical phrase. From all of which it seems indubitable that there is no reason for supposing that the Peratae took their saying from Colossians, but excellent reason for holding that both verses have been imported into the latter.

Pursuing his thought, the Transcendental makes precise the mission of the descending Christ, namely: to *save* the Triply Divided. "This, he says, is the saying: for the Son of Man came not into the world to destroy the world, but that the world might be saved through him." In the Johannine parallel (3¹⁷) we find "For God sent not his son into the world that he might judge the world, but that the world might be saved through him." By world the Transcendental here understands the upper two-thirds of the Triad, the unbegotten and the self-begotten. "But when it (the Scripture) says, he saith, that we may not be condemned with the world, it speaks of the third part of the world, of the formal. For this third part must perish, but the two upper-lying parts must be rescued from corruption."

Once more we observe that the connection in John is better decidedly with v. 17 omitted. Moreover, the notion of the world is here introduced strangely in a discourse accenting individual faith and salvation. Elsewhere (9³⁹) it is said, "unto condemnation (i.e. to condemn) came I into this world." And again, "now is the judgment of this world" (12³¹). But it is vain to seek for consistency in the Johannine use of the notion "world." The Peratic version seems markedly the older also in its use of the phrases "the Son of the Man" and "Destroy." Certainty is here not attainable, but the probability is high that the Peratic has not taken from the Gospel, but both from a common fount. The second phrase ("not be condemned with the world") which "the Scripture says," is also unintelligible in its Corinthian context (I Cor. 11³²). It seems most likely that there too it is a quotation, from what "Scripture" we know not.

A long leap brings us now, on page 201, to the expression "the God of this world" and "The Master (δεσπότης) of this world." The former is found in II Cor. 4⁴ (with αἰών for κόσμος), the latter is of common occurrence in both John and Paul, with ἄρχων instead of δεσπότης. The idea seems to be everywhere the same. It is distinctly Gnostic, and was elevated into extraordinary prominence by Marcion. Everywhere in the New Testament it is used as perfectly familiar, with no hint of explanation. It seems impossible then that it should be original in its New Testament context; it must have been drawn from a circle of thought where it was native and naturally in place and either self-explanatory or explained; that is, it is taken from some Gnostic source.

Close upon this comes (in speaking of the Serpent set up by Moses, page 202): "this is, he says, the saying: and what wise Moses lifted up the Serpent in the desert, so must be lifted up the Son of the Man." Here again we observe that "the saying" is certainly better placed in the Peratic discourse on serpents than in the Gospel, where it is unconnected with its context as it can be. Apparently this saying is flotsam and jetsam of some long-wrecked treatise (or Gospel?) on the "Son of Man," and has been taken up into the Fourth Gospel (John 3¹⁴) as something too good to lose.

Almost immediately (pp. 202–3) follows the famous Johannine prologue from ἐν ἀρχῇ to ζωή ἐστιν; it is cited by the word εἴρηται (has been spoken). Is the Gospel quoted here? We have no reason to believe it. For even there the passage is apparently a quotation, and we have yet found no ground for supposing the Gospel older than the Heresy.

The next parallel has already been discussed (p. 159, 166); here it appears in the negative form καὶ γνώσεται ὅτι χωρὶς αὐτοῦ [οὐδὲν] οὔτε τῶν οὐρανίων οὔτε τῶν ἐπιγείων οὔτε τῶν καταχθονίων συνέστηκεν whence it would seem that the triple group was a current one and very improbably primitive in Philippians (2¹⁰).

The first phrase of Section 17 (p. 204), Αὔτη ἡ παμποίκιλος σοφία τῆς Περατικῆς αἱρέσως "this the manifold wisdom of the Peratic Heresy," suggests instantly the Ephesian locution "the manifold wisdom of God," (Eph. 3¹⁰), but many possibilities lie open. Since Hippolytus is evidently writing sarcastically, he may be playing upon the canonic expression, but this seems not quite consistent with his reverence for the holy text; more likely that he is quoting a boastful expression of the Peratics themselves, to which an edifying turn has been given, as so often, in Ephesians.

From the quotations from "the Savior" (p. 206), "your Father which is in the Heavens" and "your Father is a murderer from the beginning" (John 8⁴⁴), no conclusions it would seem can be drawn, nor from the next (p. 207), "I am the door."

## E. *Sethians*

We pass to the Sethians. These also profess the dogma of the Triad, namely: Light and Darkness, and the Spirit midway between; this latter conceived as an all-penetrative power, a celestial fragrance, which bears the Light from above into the fearful waters of Darkness below. The points of contact in Scripture are here extremely few. We note (p. 214) that "Perfect God, who from unbegotten Light above and Spirit is borne down into human nature as into a temple . . . born of water commingled and commixed with bodies, as it were a salt of existents (or created things, γενομένων) and light of darkness. . . ." The noble thought that human nature is the Temple of the Divine is also found in Corinthians (I 3[16, 17]; 6[19]; II 6[16]) and elsewhere; in the first passage the οὐκ οἴδατε shows that the writer is citing a familiar doctrine. With the Sethians it is an integral part of their system. Also the comparison of this "Light sown down from above with the Spirit's fragrance" (τὸ κατεσπαρμένον φῶς ἄνωθεν μετὰ τῆς τοῦ πνεύματος εὐωδίας) to the salt and the light of Darkness is perfectly natural and exactly in place. Will any man say as much of the splendid verses in Matt. 5[13, 14]? Can any one fail to perceive their inappositeness? Are they not visibly transplanted flowers? Again, "every thought therefore and concern of the Light from above is how and what way it may be absolved (ἀπολυθείη) from the death of the evil and darkened body from the Father that is below. . . ." Here we find suggested the strange language of Romans 7[24]: "who shall deliver me from the body of this death?" We strongly suspect the existence of a common original, in neither case quite understood.

Further on (p. 216), discussing the descent of the "Perfect Logos" into the sensible world, the Sethian declares; "a Beast's is this the form of the servant Θηρίου αὕτη, φησίν, ἐστὶν ἡ τοῦ δούλου μορφή) and this the necessity of the descent of the Logos of God into a virgin's womb." There is here an unmistakable agreement with the famous Christologic passage Phil. 2[7], but not apparently any appropriation. We have already seen that the tenth verse contains a triple epithet twice used by the Gnostics in connection more natural than the Philippian. Surely no one can have failed to wonder that a passage of such immense technical import should be found encysted in a body of very homely practical exhortations. That the Apostolic mind made of its own accord such a short and sudden flight from the earth into the highest regions of speculation and as suddenly dropped down to earth again, is hard to believe. It is much more natural to look upon these verses as a choice bit of Gnostic theory considered too good to be lost and so quoted by the writer in a form modified to his own wishes.

The second clause expresses merely the familiar thought of the virginal birth as a philosophic necessity. Two views are here possible. Did the historic fact call for some theoretic explanation? Or did the theoretic necessity call for a traditional fact? We are not yet in position to decide. Plainly, however, in any case there is no reason to suppose here any reference to *Luke* or *Matthew*.

In the same paragraph we find "he drank the cup of living water that leaps" and "to invest himself with heavenly vestment" (ἐπενδύσασθαι ἔνδυμα οὐράνιον) assonant to John 4⁷⁻¹⁴ and II Cor. 5¹⁻⁴, but allowing no inference.

After some quotations from the Old Testament we find (p. 217): "But a primitive law it is that says: Thou shalt not commit adultery, thou shalt not murder, thou shalt not steal." Here the order of the μοιχεύσεις and φονεύσεις, as compared with Ex. 20¹³, ¹⁵ and Deut. 5¹⁷, is reversed; likewise also in Rom. 13⁹. But in the latter οὐκ ἐπιθυμήσεις is added. We see no clear reason for supposing that either has borrowed from the other; most likely, both from some common source.

We note in passing (p. 221) that "storax and myrrh and frankincense" suggest Matthew's "gold and frankincense and myrrh." (Matt. 2¹¹)

Further on, apropos of the Sethian doctrine of the composition and dissolution of all things: "This, he says, is the saying: 'I came not to cast peace on the earth but a sword,' that is, the dividing and separating the commingled. For separate and distinguished is each of the commingled on reaching its own proper place. For as there is one place of commingling for all animals, so also has been established one of separation, which no one knows, he says, but we alone, the regenerated Pneumatics not Sarkics, whose is the citizenship in the heavens above." Here we are reminded of the famous Synoptic saying, Matt. 10³⁴. Has the Sethian quoted it? or is it quoted in Matthew? We answer that it is very hard to believe such words were really uttered by the Prince of Peace. What then becomes of the glorious Doxology, Luke 2¹⁴? The saying in Matthew is introduced most abruptly, and the following explanation seems inadequate. In v. 38 we find the anachronism, "He that does not take his cross &c.," which shows clearly that the saying has been put into the mouth of the Savior, it did not proceed thence. But if this v. 38, then why not v. 34? The probability then is that both the Evangelist and the Sethian have quoted and interpreted each in his own way a dark saying from the philosophic-religious treasury of the day.

The like may be said of the renowned sentiment concerning citizenship (p. 222). Both here and in Phil. 3²⁰ it seems clearly a quotation of a familiar sentiment; thus Philo (*De Confusione Linguarum* § 17) says of the souls of the wise "their fatherland the heavenly region, in which they are citizens (ἐν ᾧ πολιτεύονται)." The idea was certainly then not primitive with the Epistolist, but adopted.

Hippolytus refers us for these doctrines of the Sethians to a book Παράφρασις Σήθ. Of its date we know nothing, but there is no reason yet given for fixing it later than any New Testament Scripture. We note that Hippolytus does not charge them with perverting Scripture but only (p. 222) "Speeches" and "sayings" (ἀποχρώμενοι ῥητοῖς, εἰς ὃ θέλουσι συνάγοντες κακῶς τὰ καλῶς εἰρημένα). Why does he not accuse them, if they were really guilty?

## F. *Justinus the Gnostic*

Passing now to Justinus, known only from Hippolytus, we find (p. 225) that he administers an oath to his followers: "Swear now" (δέ) says Justinus, "if thou wilt know what eye hath not seen and ear not heard nor into heart of man has ascended, him God above all, the Superior, to guard ineffable the secrets (σιγώμενα) of the discipline"; and so he leads to the Good (καὶ οὕτως ἐπὶ τὸν ἀγαθὸν ἄγει).— Here we are cast back in mind to the Corinthian passage (I Cor. 2⁹), which however is there professedly *quoted*. Whence? No one has ever been able to say. Hippolytus seems quoting from Justinus' *Book of Baruch*. We know of no reason why the expression may not have been original in that work, certainly it fits perfectly in its context. However, it may be that Justinus is quoting or adopting some still more ancient saw. In any case we here have a clear and indisputable example of a Gnostic saying quoted in our Canonic Scripture. We note further the prominence of the notion of the Good Being (p. 226), afterwards so powerful in the hands of Marcion.

Hippolytus charges that Justinianism is Paganism and derived from a legend in Herodotus. There is commixed, however, a large element of allegorical interpretation of the Hebrew Scriptures. Justinus seems to have set himself the task of constructing a Philosophy of History in terms of Eastern and Western myths spiritually understood. Of course, little success could attend any such attempt. That he inserts (pp. 236–7) an account of Baruch's being dispatched by Elohim, in the days of Herod the King, to Jesus the 12 year-old Son of Joseph and Mary at Nazareth feeding sheep, would at first seem to place the date of this book far down in the first or 2nd century. But this whole paragraph may be a later addition to much older work, or at least the words, "in the days of Herod the King," which are perhaps due to Hippolytus himself. The statement of the 12 years contradicts the New Testament account, according to which Herod the King died in the infancy of Jesus. But this account is extremely interesting by virtue of the suggestion of the Temptation in the fruitless effort of Naas to seduce Jesus from allegiance to Baruch and the Good, also in the distinct statement that Naas in revenge caused Jesus to be crucified, as is hinted very vaguely in Luke 4¹³; but far more in the following: "He (Jesus) then having left the body of Edem on the tree ascended to the Good. And having said to Edem: Woman, thou hast thy son (Γύναι, ἀπέχεις σου τὸν υἱόν) that is, the psychic man and the earthy, but himself having commended the spirit into the hands of the Father, ascended to the Good." To us it seems every way impossible for John 19²⁶ to be historical. More likely that the Evangelist has seized upon some Gnostic phrase and given it pictorial setting.

Hippolytus seems particularly horrified by the profanities of this pseudognostic Justinus, "though meeting with many heresies, beloved, not a man worse than this have I met"; but this wickedness seems to have consisted solely in doctrinal syncretism, no other dereliction is alleged. In conclusion the purpose is distinctly declared (p. 241) to set forth in the following books (ἐν ταῖς ἑξῆς βίβλοις) the opinions of the heresies that followed Justinus (τὰς τῶν ἀκολούθων αἱρέσεων). There can be no question whatever, then, that according to the information at the command of Hippolytus apparently a student of the sources, the Justinian and still more the preceding three heresies sensibly antedated the Simonian and all the others that follow. Moreover the view of Hippolytus on the spot is fully confirmed by every feature thus far observed in these heresies; for they all appear crude and undeveloped by the side of the more refined and elaborate systems now to be examined. The one and only fact that might incline us to post-date these heresies is their copious employment of sayings now read in our New Testament. But in a number of cases it is absolutely certain that these "sayings" are taken in the New Testament from some older sources; in very many more it is most highly probable that they were derived similarly; and in not one single case is such derivation excluded or unlikely. Every logical consideration conspires therefore to recommend the view that we have really been dealing with prechristian Gnostics, and that our Canonics have drawn measurably from prechristian sources.

## G. *Simon of Gitta*

Hippolytus, weary of insisting on the superior antiquity of the foregoing Ophites, once more repeats that he will now deal with their successors and he begins with the great arch-heretic Simon the Samaritan, of Gitta, already familiar to us from Acts 8⁹⁻²⁴ and from Justin the Martyr, who says, speaking of men inspired by demons and greatly honored: "A certain Simon, a Samaritan from the village called Gitta (Γιττῶν) who, under Claudius Caesar, through the craft of in-working demons, having exerted magic powers in this city of yours, Imperial Rome, was deemed a God and was honoured by you as a God with a statue, which statue was set up on the Tiber River between the two bridges, bearing this Roman inscription: *Simoni Deo sancto;* and almost all Samaritans and a few also among other nations confessing him (to be) the first god, also worship him." Now the statue pedestal dug up in 1574 does indeed bear the inscription *Semoni Sancto Deo. Fidio Sacrum Sex Pompeius S. P. F . . . Donum Dedit,* but this Semo was a Sabine god of contracts (Ovid, Fast. VI²¹³ ᶠ). Granting that Justin erred as to the statue, there seems yet no reason to doubt his other statement as to the date of Simon and his presence in Rome under Claudius, hence before A.D. 54, with which agrees the account in Acts 8⁹⁻²⁴. As the Fathers and Apologists were particularly concerned to idealize the early days of Christianity and to represent all heresy as a much later device of Satan, it seems incredible that they should appreciably antedate the arch-heretic Simon. Be this as it may, we pass to the New Testament Parallels.

The first is found (pp. 245-6) where Hippolytus proposes "teach the parrots of Simon that Christ was not Simon, who stood, stands, will stand but was a man, from seed, offspring of woman from bloods ( αἱμάτων ) and carnal desire ( ἐπιθυμίας σαρκικῆς), just as also the rest are generated." We think at once of the Apocalyptic "Was and Is and Will be" (Rev. 4⁸ etc.); the ideas are evidently equivalent and seem to mean the Eternal, but neither seems derived directly from the other. We quote this remarkable passage as showing that the Simonians *identified* or were thought to *identify Simon with the Christ regarded as a supernal Being,* against which sublimation Hippolytus protests energetically, affirming the complete humanity in the most unequivocal terms with almost unnecessary bluntness. Can it be then that the whole earthly history of the Christ was a dogmatic reaction from an all-too spiritual and supra-mundane theory of the Messiah?*

We note the beginning (apparently) of Simon's work; "this the writing (γράμμα) of announcement of voice and name from intelligence of the great Power, the Infinite. Wherefore it will be sealed, secreted, hidden, laid in the habitation where the root of the Whole ( τῶν ὅλων) has been founded." Of this we have already spoken. It is seemingly a quotation from an earlier Naassene work. These hard words Simon proceeds to interpret. He divides the Universe (pages 247-8) into the sensible and the intelligible (after Plato and Aristotle). The former he likens to the stem, branches, leaves, bark of a great Nebuchadnezzar-tree (*Ygdrasil?*); the latter, apparently to the *fruit,* an extremely important concept in Gnosticism. Those are flung into the flames of all-devouring fire, this is gathered into garner. Here we are reminded of Matt. $3^{10-12}$. But it can hardly be that Simon is quoting therefrom. Aside from the fact that his date is many years too early, the Matthean passage could scarcely suggest such an elaborate philosophy, in which this image belongs naturally, and moreover it is itself apparently quotation or redaction, as seen in v. 10. Does any one really think these verses have any fitness as applied to Jesus?

It is interesting (p. 248) to compare Simon's citation of Is. $40^6$ with I Pet. $1^{24, 25}$ and Jas. $1^{10}$. Peter has πᾶσα δόξα αὐτῆς, with the Hebrew, but Simon πᾶσα δόξα σαρκός, both against Septuagint ἀνθρώπου; also both Simon and Jas. insert αὐτοῦ (its) before ἐξέπεσε. Both Simon and Peter put "Lord" for the "Our God" of the Hebrew and the Septuagint. The indication, then, is of independent quotation from slightly varying versions.

Since Hippolytus says (p. 249) that Simon "denominates a perfect intelligible in the Great Announcement" (ἐν τῇ ἀποφάσει τῇ μεγάλῃ καλεῖ τέλειον νοερόν), this latter, (ἡ 'Απόφασις ἡ Μεγάλη) would seem to have been the title of his book. In this work he finds the root of all being in the Unbegotten Fire. Whence six roots in pairs: Mind and Intelligence (Νοῦν καὶ 'Επίνοιαν), Voice and Name (Φωνὴν καὶ "Ονομα), Reasoning and Thought (Λογισμὸν καὶ 'Ενθύμησιν). In these six roots dwells together all the Infinite power (who Stood, Stands, Will Stand) potentially, not actually. Without going further into this Heraclitean-Platonic-Aristotelian Mosaism, it seems clear that any genesis of the same from the New Testament at any early period, or indeed at any period at all, is entirely out of the question; that it is far less elaborate than Valentinianism, of which it forms the natural predecessor; that it is far more elaborate than Naassenism et al, of which it might easily be the successor.†

Of the phrase "that we be not condemned with the world" (page 253) we have

---

* Here Smith follows Macmahon's rendering, which sees Hippolytus agreeing at this point with Carpocrates, *infra,* p. 206, that Jesus was son of Joseph. Francis Legge interprets otherwise, that Hippolytus was aiming at Simon, in refutation of his supposed supernatural claims. *Editor.*

† These six roots are elsewhere seen to be spiritualization of the six elements of creation: Heaven and Earth; Sun and Moon; Air and Water—Gen. $1^1$, $7,16$.

already spoken.\* Simon refines upon the phrase, perhaps a very old one. He has also the notion of generation from the Indivisible Point which would seem to show him affected by Naassenism,—or perhaps both borrowed the notion from the Pythagorean Monad, the one Jot or Tittle. Simon taught that in every one there was a blessed and incorruptible element hid away, potential not actual, namely, who Stood, Stands, Will Stand. Only through instruction (discipline) is it actualized, "is there perfect fruit, full-formed, equal and like to the Unbegotten and Infinite Power. But if a tree abides alone ('Εὰν δὲ μείνῃ δένδρον μόνον), not bearing *fruit,* not full-imaged, it is annihilated. For, nigh somewhere, he says, is the ax by the roots of the tree; every tree, he says, not bearing good fruit is cut down and cast into the fire." Here (p. 258) we are astonished to find the Johannine phrase "abides alone" (John 12²⁴) but spoken of a tree and in entirely different connection. Moreover the Simonian thought is quite intelligible and suited to its context and consistent with the system. The same can not be said of the Johannine. The notion that a seed must die is of course false (in spite of Hegel). The whole verse in John lacks all proper connection with its context. That it furnished the original for Simon seems every way incredible. Far more likely that the Evangelist has Christianized a Simonian original. The adage (p. 258) "every tree &c." appears thrice in the Scripture: Matt. 3¹⁰, 7¹⁹, Luke 3⁹. In the second, Matt. 7¹⁹, it is plainly out of place, inserted because it spoke of trees. That it is primitive in either of the other verses has not the least likelihood. The connection in Simon's use of it is better; but it is improbably primitive even there; more probably a very ancient adage.

Simon's interpretation of "Who Stood, Stands, will Stand" seems to show clearly that he is in no wise dependent on the Apocalyptist: Stood-above in the Unbegotten Power, Stands-in the flowing of the waters (*Lebensfluthen*—Tides of Life?) begotten in image, Will Stand-above in the blessed Infinite power, if he be effigiated.

In the same section (17) we find it declared (page 259) that the desire of mutable generation is named therefore to burn (πυροῦσθαι), which explains this term used strangely in I Cor. 7⁹ (better to marry than to burn) as well understood without hint of explanation.

What follows offers few points of attachment to Scripture, and much of it is ascribed not to Simon but to his imitators and disciples. It is declared (p. 265) they "do whatso they will, as freemen; for they allege they are saved according to his grace," which suggests Eph. 2⁷ (by grace ye have been saved). Palpably and admittedly, however, the Ephesian phrase is at best a parenthesis, without aim or fitness in its context, on its face intercalated; whereas the passage fits perfectly in its Simonian milieu. This latter, then, is much more probably original.

The story of Helen is apparently a mere fiction, perhaps a malicious historization of Simon's allegorical interpretation of the Homeric myth. That some Simonians perverted the doctrine of "Salvation by grace" into licence seems likely enough; but that Simon himself was a sorcerer or magician or charlatan seems

\* See Peratae, p. 178.

nothing but a slander. On the contrary, he seems to have been a religious philosopher, as philosophy went in those days, by no means feeble in power, certainly noble in purpose and exalted in conception. Unclear he may very well have been, without being at all worse than his contemporaries. Very interesting but extremely difficult are the questions, How did he stand related on the one hand to Jesus Christ, on the other to Simon the Apostle? To which we shall here attempt no answer.

## H. *Valentinus*

We now approach the realm of definable history. The system of Valentinus is next treated by Hippolytus, who therein departs slightly from chronologic order, for the evident reason that he regards it, and on good grounds, as merely a further development of Simonianism. The six roots of Simon are confessedly, he says, the six Aeons of Valentinus, but under the new names of Mind, Truth, Logos, Life, Man, Church. He might also have added that Silence (Σιγή), the contemporary of Bythus, is the Valentinian mother of Nous and Aletheia, and that this same *"Sige invisible, incomprehensible"* is the Simonian "one root" whence the male and female offshoots, *Nous* and *Epinoia*. That Simon then was a philosophic father of Valentinus, seems certain. But Hippolytus finds other elements, Pythagorean and Platonic, in this great heresy. The imaginings of Valentinus were set in a stiff numerical frame-work, and this was supplied by the great master of numbers. This latter asserted that Unbegotten Monad was the originating principle, the Father; thence the Begotten Duad, Mother of all things begotten; thence the Triad and the rest, up to Ten. In geometry this Monad becomes the Point, which flowing out generates the Line and the Line the Surface, and the Surface the Solid—these Four. Hence the Pythagorean oath:

> By him that to our head Quaternion gives,
> Fount that has roots of nature everlasting.

This Quaternion is the Principle (ἀρχή) of all Sensibles, as the Monad of all Intelligibles. The Quaternion generates the Perfect number, the Ten, thus: $1 + 2 + 3 + 4 = 10$. Now the symbol for this Ten was iota ($\iota$); "and there is according to the Pythagorean the $\iota$ the one tittle (τὸ ι, ἡ μία κεραία), first and lordliest of the Intelligibles, substance intellectually and sensually perceived." It is certainly startling to meet here (page 271) the familiar Matthean phrase (Matt. 5[18]), one jot ($\iota$) or one tittle (ἰῶτα ἓν ἢ μία κεραία), where the form $\eta$ is the same, though the meanings (or and the) are so different. Have the two expressions originated independently? We do not think so. The Rabbis have much to say of the complaints of Jod and of the divine assurances given it of eternal stability. Strongest perhaps, at least nearest to the Gospel expression, is this (Jalkut Rubeni F. 167. 2.3 and Schemoth R. 6. Thauchuma p. 681): Said God, "Solomon and a (100) thousand like him shall perish from the world, and *one apicle of the letter Jod shall not perish.*" Again, the immense importance of the tittles in the Hebrew letters is often celebrated, as in Vajikra R. XIX: "If any one should change Daleth in Deut. 6⁴ into Resh (*one* into *second*), he would concuss the whole world." But nowhere do we find such an idea as "one jot or one tittle of the Law." We must add certain other considerations. It seems extremely hard to believe such words are properly attributed to Jesus at any time, much less at the very beginning of his ministry. In Luke they appear much later (16¹⁷) and then in no intelligible connection. Moreover, the text is uncertain. Clement (Hom. 3⁵¹), Origen, Irenaeus, *et al* add "and the prophets" (καὶ τῶν προφητῶν); Luke has only (ἢ τοῦ νόμου μίαν κεραίαν πεσεῖν) and the recently discovered most ancient Syriac has in Matthew only "not one jot shall perish from the Law." It seems plain then that we are dealing with a saying that appeared in many slightly varying forms, very probably influenced by the Pythagorean expression and most improbably an original utterance of Jesus.

Again, speaking of the Pythagoreans, Hippolytus continues (p. 272) "Nought, he says, of the Intelligibles can become known to us through perception (δι' αἰσ—θήσεως), for that (thing) neither eye has seen nor ear hath heard nor has known, says he, of the other senses any whatsoever." (See Isa. 64⁴; I Cor. 2⁹.)

Here the connection of this famous saying with its context is perfect, and we seem to be plainly in the presence of a most ancient saw whose primary reference was rather philosophic than religious. The same idea has been otherwise expressed by the Pythagorian Epicharmus: Νοῦς ὁρῆ καὶ νοῦς ἀκούει· τ'ἄλλα κωφὰ καὶ τυφλά. Reason sees and Reason hears, all things else are deaf and blind. The same thought is expressed by Empedocles.

It is interesting to note in passing (page 275) that Hippolytus accredits distinctly to Pythagorus the notion of Resurrection (ἀνάστασις): "And (he says) that these (souls) are indeed mortal when they are in the body just as if buried as in a tomb, but that they arise (ἀνίστασθαι) and become immortal when we are loosed from our bodies. Whence Plato having been asked by some one, What is philosophy? Said: 'Separation of soul from body.' "

In studying the Gnostic fragments it is impossible not to be struck by the exceeding frequency and prominence of the notion of "Father." Hence we are not surprised that the "Monad Unbegotten, Incorruptible, Incomprehensible, Inconceivable, Generating and the cause of the generation of all generated, is called by them Father" (p. 280). Next we find the aloneness of this Father strongly accentuated: πατὴρ δὲ ἦν μόνος...ἀλλὰ ἦν μόνος...αὐτὸς ἐν ἑαυτῷ μόνος...ὥσπερ ἦν μόνος. It is noteworthy how sparingly this idea is used in the New Testament. Only in John 5⁴⁴ (The glory that cometh from the only God ye seek not), where the text is uncertain; John 17³ (that they may know thee the only true God), which is not quite to the point; and the Doxologies, Rom. 16²⁷ (μόνῳ σοφῷ Θεῷ), I Tim. 1¹⁷ (μόνῳ Θεῷ), Jude 25 (μονῷ Θεῷ), all Gnostic in their leaning.

Again, (p. 281) "for Love, he says, he was wholly" (ἀγάπη γὰρ, φησίν, ἦν ὅλος); we turn to I John 4⁸, ¹⁶, God is Love" (ὁ Θεὸς ἀγάπη ἐστίν). The context seems perfectly fitting both in the Gnostic and in I John 4⁸, though not in v. 16, where it reads strangely: "And we know and have believed the love which God has in us." There is at least nothing to indicate that the Gnostic has borrowed from I John.

It is well known that the vestibule to the Valentinian temple has eight pillars, the Ogdoad. Father and Silence, Mind and Truth, Logos and Life, Man and Church (p. 282). Most remarkably, at least five of these re-appear in John $1^{1-18}$; Father, Logos, Life, Man, Truth; Silence is absent, Nous seems represented by Light, and Church by "as many as receive him" (ὅσοι ἔλαβον αὐτόν); John has also the Pleroma, and Grace, likewise a Gnostic notion (See p. 185). It is easy to surmise that Valentinus has borrowed from the prologue, but Hippolytus does not say so, does not think so, for he refers the Valentinian Aeons to the Simonian roots (p. 184), with obvious justice, as the important common element Sige shows. Now it will hardly be contended that Simon borrowed from the Johannine prologue. Is the latter then under obligation to Valentinus? Chronologically it is not forbidden, but it seems more likely that the Prologue has merely worked up freely the general idea of these abstractions as emanating from God, an idea widely diffused and doubtless popular. Of the numerous other Valentinians only Monogenes (p. 282 and 285); Faith, Hope, Love (p. 283); and especially Paraclete (p. 283) are interesting. The great trio reappear in I Cor. $13^{13}$, very abruptly, in a way that long ago forced us to pronounce the verse intercalated. It would at least be hard to make it likely that the Valentinians have here copied from Corinthians, though these secondary Aeons are perhaps later grafts on the Valentinian trunk. The Paraclete appears five times in the New Testament, only in the Johannines; obviously used as a familiar term, but interpreted as the Spirit of Truth. It cannot be made out on which side is the dependence; perhaps it is on neither.

The last and for the Valentinian heresy most important of the Aeons, Sophia, is most conspicuous in the New Testament, appearing 49 times, as already in the later Hebrew writings as Chokmah the instrument of creation, and Valentinus retains her in essentially this capacity. Most remarkable, however, is the technical term (page 285) for the projection by this rash and presumptuous Aeon, of "Substance unformed and unprepared," namely, ἔκτρωμα, "for so they call it." This word is found only once in the New Testament, I Cor. $15^8$, though repeatedly in the Septuagint, but severely condemned by Phrynichus. A very similar passage is found in the Ignatian Romans $9^2$, where Ignatius declares "I am ashamed to be called one of them; for neither am I, being last of them and ἔκτρωμα." The false modesty renders this very suspicious. Moreover the verse sits too loosely in its context. The use of both ἔκτρωμα and ἔσχατος points to the Corinthian passage, and the whole verse is best taken as an interpolation in this much redacted Epistle. But the Corinthian passage remains unexplained. There the phrase is, "Last of all, as if to *the* ἔκτρωμα, he appeared also to me." There is good authority for omiting τῷ (Irenius, Origen, Eusebius, Epiphanius *et al.*); but the omission seems so natural and almost necessary, whereas the insertion seems utterly unintelligible. In any case the article τῷ appears to point to a well known idea and specific; *we know of none but this Valentinian.* Not that the Corinthian writer took it from Valentinus directly, but that the notion was already present and was adopted by both writers. The Valentinian use is every way the preferable; the Pauline is exceedingly forced and unnatural.

Next we note, passing over much, the *"Joint Fruit* of the Pleroma, the Jesus, the High Priest the Great" (pages 287 and 298). This Fruit reminds one of the Pauline fruit in Rom. $1^{13}$, while the Great High Priest suggests Heb. $4^{14}$. But we can draw no conclusions. To our mind the whole treatment in Hebrews of this Melchizedekean High priesthood harks back to a prechristian and little known "Heresy," which attached itself to the mysterious High Priest and King of Righteousness of Gen. $14^{18}$ (M. Friedländer), and with which the *Author ad Hebraeos* was in more or less remote sympathy.

It is worth while to note, as showing clearly that Valentinus or the Valentinians operated with Rabbinic, and not solely by any means with Christian, conceptions, that they called "the psychic substance" *Topos* (p. 290), as well as Hebdomad and Ancient of Days. Now topos reappears in Philo ($\tau\rho\iota\chi\hat{\omega}s$ $\delta\grave{\epsilon}$ $\grave{\epsilon}\pi\iota\nu\text{o}\epsilon\hat{\iota}\tau\alpha\iota$ $\tau\acute{\text{o}}\pi\text{o}s$—*De Somniis,* Maugey, I, 630) and is frequent in the Rabbis as *Maqom,* Place, in Jalkut 117, on Gen. $28^{11}$, it is declared that God is so named because he is the *Place* of the world, not the world his place. Hence too the notion of Pleroma, the Fullness of Place (Space), i.e., of God.

At this point also the Valentinian writer identifies the Ogdoad, as the goal (of the Soul?) fashioned like those above, with the "Heavenly Jerusalem." This idea is here plainly imported, but whence? Seemingly not from the New Testament but from some common much older source.

Thus too the following notion (p. 291) of the "Ruler of this World" ($\acute{\text{o}}$ $\mathring{\alpha}\rho\chi\omega\nu$ $\tau\text{o}\hat{\text{u}}$ $\kappa\acute{\text{o}}\sigma\mu\text{o}\text{u}$ $\tau\text{o}\acute{\text{u}}\tau\text{o}\text{u}$) which in the New Testament appears as a known magnitude requiring no definition or description. Here the text presents a lacuna, which estops any further affirmation than that there is apparently no borrowing from the New Testament.

Peculiar is the Valentinian notion (p. 290) of the "Day formed" ($\mathring{\eta}\mu\acute{\epsilon}\rho\alpha$ $\mu\epsilon\mu\text{o}\rho-\varphi\text{o}\mu\acute{\epsilon}\nu\eta$) underneath the Ogdoad, where Sophia is, and the Joint Fruit of the Pleroma, but over above the Matter, of which (it) is Demiurge. This day reappears in Barnabas XV, as the New World begun by the Resurrection and Ascension of Jesus. "I will make Beginning of Eight Day, which is, Beginning of another world. Wherefore also we keep the Day the Eighth for rejoicing in which also the Jesus uprose from the Dead and having been manifested ascended into heavens." Observe the phrases $\mathring{\eta}\mu\acute{\epsilon}\rho\alpha$ $\acute{\text{o}}\gamma\delta\acute{\text{o}}\eta s$ and $\tau\mathring{\eta}\nu$ $\mathring{\eta}\mu\acute{\epsilon}\rho\alpha\nu$ $\tau\mathring{\eta}\nu$ $\acute{\text{o}}\gamma\delta\acute{\text{o}}\eta\nu$, how close to the Valentinian $\acute{\text{o}}\gamma\delta\text{o}\acute{\alpha}s$! Here is some obscure *genetic* relation, we can not say what. Observe too that Jesus arises and ascends on the *same* day, the Ogdoad, clearly an older notion than that in Acts, where Arising and Ascending are separated by 40 days! Again, in Ign. ad Mag. $9^1$ we find an extremely obscure perhaps adulterated passage concerning certain persons who "came into newness of hope no longer sabbatizing but living Lord's (day)-wise ($\kappa\alpha\tau\grave{\alpha}$ $\kappa\upsilon\rho\iota\alpha\kappa\mathring{\eta}\nu$) in which ($\grave{\epsilon}\nu$ $\mathring{\eta}$) also our life arose through him and his death which some deny." Here the *Day* (understood) seems also to figure as a new Age, and strangely the Resurrection and Ascension are not mentioned, but only our life uprose (ἀνέτειλεν)—But in that chaotic era, what need surprise us?

The phrase "Beelzebub Prince of Demons" (p. 291) occurs twice, in Matt. 12²⁴, Luke 11¹⁵, in the palpable proverb about casting out one demon by another (See Eus. Contra Hieroclem ch. 30, δαίμονας γὰρ ἀπελαύνει, ἄλλῳ ἄλλον, ἦ φασι, δαίμονι). The Rabbis speak of various princes of Demons as Asmodaeus, Samael, but not apparently of Beelzebub. The notion appears in the synoptics as familiar and needing no explanation. Here in Valentinus as one of the Quaternion "fount of everlasting nature, having roots"; "Sophia, called spirit; the Demiurge, called Soul; the Devil (called) the Ruler of the World; Beelzebub (called the Ruler) of the Demons." To us it seems absurd to suppose that such a system finds its roots in the New Testament, where these notions, if mentioned at all, are mentioned merely casually as part of the domestic stock of ideas. The Valentinian sources lie aside from the Scriptures.

Next (p. 292) we find this Sophia defined as "Mother of all the Living," and of "angels heavenly, citizenized in Jerusalem that is above, that is in heavens. For she is Jerusalem that is without (the Pleroma), Sophia, and her spouse the Joint Fruit of the Pleroma." Here again the often recurring Gnostic notion of the Heavenly Jerusalem, which is visibly not original in Gal. 4²⁵, ²⁶; along with it the notion of the "mother of all the living," which likewise reaches far behind the Gal. Epistle. What then of this Joint Fruit of the Pleroma (the Jesus) as Bridegroom of this Sophia-Jerusalem-Mother? Does it come from Rev. 21²? There we find no implication of Bridegroom, the holy city Jerusalem descending new out from the Heaven, from God is merely "adorned like a bride adorned for her husband," but the suggestion might be enough to start fancy a-working. This very passage then *might* be the point of development for the Valentinian scheme, but *no one knows how old the passage is*. It has been taken up into Revelation, but even after over-working has remained pure Jewish, as appears from v. 12, 24, 27. It is plain from the repetition of v. 1, 2 in 9, 10 that there has been over-working; the later writer has taken out the *simile* of v. 2 and developed it into a *fact*. Most probable would seem the supposition that both Valentinus and the Apocalyptist have drawn on a common stock of ideas.

At the heels of the quotation of Gen. 2⁷ we find (p. 293): "This is according to them the inner man, the psychic, dwelling in the material body, which is the material, corruptible, imperfect (man), moulded from the devilish substance." Here the notion of the "inner man" is precisely defined. Still it is certainly not original here, but taken from elsewhere. Yet it can hardly be taken from Rom. 7²² or II Cor. 4¹⁶. There the notion is used as well-known, and needing no definition, and does not agree with this of Valentinus. The idea itself was very old and well-established in Greek Literature. Plato (Rep. IX, 589 B.) says of the triple composite ὅθεν τοῦ ἀνθρώπου ὁ ἐντὸς ἄνθρωπος ἔσται ἐγκρατέστατος (Whence the inner may most be master of the man) Plotinus too (En. 1¹⁰) says ἦ αἱ μὲν τούτου, αἱ δὲ τοῦ ἔνδον ἀνθρώπου, and V. 1¹⁰ οἷον λέγει Πλάτων τὸν εἴσω ἄνθρωπον. Though Plotinus be writing A.D. 250, it will hardly be said that he is following Scripture, but Plato. So also Jalkut Ruben F. 10, 3 declares: "Flesh is man's inner vestment, but spirit is inner man, whose vestment is body." The thought is by no means far-lying. Notice in proof of its familiarity the varying forms: ὁ ἐντὸς ἄνθρωπος, τὸν εἰώσω ἄνθρωπον, ὁ ἔσωθεν ἄνθρωπος, τὸν ἔνδον ἄνθρωπον.

But now (page 294) follows a most important phrase. Apropos of the Valentinian notion of the body as a habitation into which are *sown down* the Logoi from above, Hippolytus says: "This is, he says, that which is written in the Scripture: Τούτου χάριν κάμπτω τὰ γόνατά μου πρὸς τὸν Θεὸν καὶ πατέρα καὶ κύριον τοῦ κυρίου ἡμῶν Ἰησοῦ Χριστοῦ, ἵνα δῴη ὑμῖν ὁ Θεὸς κατοικῆσαι τὸν Χριστὸν εἰς τὸν ἔσω ἄνθρωπον (τουτέστι τὸν ψυχικόν, οὐ τὸν σωματικόν), ἵνα ἐξισχύσητε νοῆσαι, τί τὸ βάθος (ὅπερ ἐστὶν ὁ πατὴρ τῶν ὅλων), καὶ τί τὸ πλάτος, (ὅπερ ἐστὶν ὁ σταυρός ὁ ὅρος τοῦ πληρώματος), ἢ τί τὸ μῆκος, (τουτέστι τὸ πλήρωμα τῶν αἰώνων)."

Compare Eph. 3¹⁴, ¹⁶, ¹⁷, ¹⁸.*

14. τούτου χάριν κάμπτω τὰ γόνατά μου πρὸς τὸν πατέρα, (τοῦ Κυρίου ἡμῶν Ἰησοῦ Χριστοῦ,)

16. ἵνα {δῴη / δῷ} ὑμῖν κατὰ {τὸν πλούτου / τὸ πλοῦτος} τῆς δόξης αὐτοῦ, δυνάμει κραταιωθῆναι διὰ τοῦ

17. πνεύματος αὐτοῦ εἰς τὸν ἔσω ἄνθρωπον, κατοικῆσαι τὸν Χριστὸν διὰ τῆς πίστεως

18. ἐν ταῖς καρδίαις ὑμῶν ἐν ἀγάπῃ ἐρριζωμένοι καὶ τεθεμελιωμένοι, ἵνα ἐξισχύσητε καταλαβέσθαι σὺν {πᾶσι / πᾶσιν} τοῖς ἁγίοις, τί τὸ πλάτος καὶ μῆκος καὶ βάθος καὶ ὕψος,

Evidently the Valentinian text is related to Eph. 3¹⁴, ¹⁶⁻¹⁸, but how? As a quotation? We might think so from the phrase τὸ γεγραμμένον ἐν τῇ γραφῇ but we have no right to assume that this comes from Valentinus, it may just as well be from Hippolytus. But even if Valentinus did use the words, is it our Ephesians that he cites as Scripture? There is no evidence; for elsewhere, as we have repeatedly seen, citations are made as Scripture that are not in our Scriptures. We are left then to the internal evidence. On comparing *Ephesians* we find that the Gnostic form is much shorter and in many ways preferable. "For this cause I bow my knees unto the God and Father and Lord of our Lord Jesus Christ that to you God grant for the Christ to settle down into the inner man, that ye be full strengthened to understand what the depth and what the breadth or what the length." We submit that it is every way impossible to derive this sentence from the *Ephesians;* the subtractions and the additions equally forbid. Common sense perceives at once that the Gnostic idea is clear-cut, direct, comprehensible; whereas the Ephesians is over-loaded, padded, dropsical, confused, inconsequential, and incomprehensible. We

---

* The main line is from the K. G. Woide and B. H. Cowper edition of *Codex Alexandr.* Written above the main line is from the Scholz text. The comma after τεθεμελειωμένοι is from Scholz. The last phrase of verse 14 (in parenthesis), is not found in Woide and Cowper. *Editor.*

have already seen that v. 15 is simply high-sounding words; "strengthened with power" is pleonastic; 17 simply repeats 16; "in love rooted and grounded," is irrelevant and harsh in construction (the nominatives are in the air); "with all the saints" is mere padding; and so on. The whole passage is plainly a very awkward elaboration of some original which was also the basis of Col. 1⁹⁻¹¹ and was very near the Gnostic form. This comes out clearly in the impossible (so called pregnant) construction (Eph. 3¹⁶) of εἰς in the clause κραταιωθῆναι διὰ τοῦ πνεύματος αὐτοῦ εἰς τὸν ἔσω ἄνθρωπον. The Gnostic phrase is perfectly clear κατοικῆσαι τὸν Χριστὸν εἰς τὸν ἔσω ἄνθρωπον "for the Christ to settle down into the inner man," the reference being to the descent of the pneumatic powers into the psychic nature, to redeem it. Moreover that this whole *Ephesians* chapter is a piece of over-working is tangible in the repetition of τούτου χάριν (verses 1 and 14). The sentence begun in v. 1 is never completed; v. 2 wheels off the thought at right angles into a discussion absolutely impossible for Paul writing to Ephesians, and without any obvious pertinence to the context. The thought is resumed after a parenthesis of 12 verses! But for what cause? No one can find out from verse 1, but even if we had known the cause at v. 1, we should have forgotten it before reaching v. 14. It seems hard to imagine a much clearer case. Every consideration agrees in the indication that the Gnostic text is incomparably nearer the primitive than the Ephesian. (Add extreme text-uncertainty).

"Therefore he says: A psychic man receives not the things of the spirit of God; for they are foolishness to him." This agrees exactly (save as to δὲ) with I Cor. 2¹⁴, which is embedded in a discourse (apparently of a Pneumatic) on The Spirit. The whole of it seems to us an intercalation, unintelligible not in itself but as addressed to the Corinthians, Christians of two or three years, and without any divinable relation to the preceding 1¹⁰⁻¹⁷. But this we cannot argue here. It is enough that there is no apparent reason for referring the sentence to *Corinthians* rather than to extra-canonic Gnostic literature which did certainly so abound.

In connection with the ignorance of the demiurge (p. 294), "Therefore, he says, the Savior speaks: All that before me came are thieves and robbers, (πάντες οἱ πρὸ ἐμοῦ ἐληλυθότες κλέπται καὶ λῃσταί εἰσί) and the Apostle: the mystery which to the former generation was not made known." The Johannine phrase (10⁸), πάντες ὅσοι ἦλθον πρὸ ἐμοῦ κλέπται εἰσὶν καὶ λῃσταί, exactly the same in sense, is markedly different in form and could hardly have been quoted in the Valentinian form. On close scrutiny it becomes plain as day that the v. 8 is intercalated. Could any man in his senses originally say or write "I am the *door* of the sheep, all that come before me are thieves and robbers; but the sheep did not hear them, I am the *door*"? What is the meaning of "all that came before the door"? In v. 11 is only a partial explanation, "I am the good shepherd &c." Put *good shepherd* for *door,* and the image is saved, but not the sense. For why should and how could a good shepherd come last, after thieves and robbers had done their worst? It seems plain that here is a patch-work of ill-matched colors. We do by no means ever vouch for the Valentinian interpretation, but certainly there is here no borrowing from John, who has certainly borrowed from elsewhere.

τὸ μυστήριον ὃ ταῖς προτέραις γενεαῖς οὐκ ἐγνωρίσθη. This second sentence brings up various memories of Pauline passages as Rom. 16²⁵; Eph. 3³, ⁵, ⁹, ¹⁰; I Cor. 2⁷; Col. 1²⁶, 4³. The closest is Eph. 3⁵ ὃ (μυστήριον) ἑτέραις γενεαῖς οὐκ ἐγνωρίσθη τοῖς υἱοῖς τῶν ἀνθρώπων. Now we have just seen that this whole pericope is an over-working and interpolation. In this phrase the cramped hand of the reviser shows clear in the double dative "to other generations" "to the sons of men," where the rendering "in other generations" remains at best unnatural and contradicted by the Gnostic form.

Next, on page 295:—"When accordingly the creation attained end, and there needed finally to be made the revelation of the sons of (the) God, that is, of the Demiurge, the (revelations hitherto) inveiled, which, he says the psychic man veiled himself in and had a veil upon the heart,—when accordingly needed to be lifted the veil and be seen these mysteries" . . .

Here again confronts us the ever recurring phenomenon (like Banquo's ghost), namely, a Scripture phrase found in connection almost entirely new, and yet more natural in that connection than in the Scripture itself! The revelation of the sons of God meets us in Romans 8¹⁹, but is not there intelligible by utmost effort of critical faculty. It is plainly a technical phrase, familiar enough in the circles for which the passage was primarily intended, but we can only guess at its meaning now. The like must be said of the doctrine of the "veil," II Cor. 3¹⁴⁻¹⁸, of which no satisfactory exegesis seems possible, especially v. 17 seems certainly interpolated. Of course, we are as far as possible from affirming that the Valentinian reference is the original one. But that the Valentinians have not here taken from Corinthians seems plain in two facts: the absence in Hippolytus of any hint to that effect, and the utterly different applications of both phrases. Especially, it seems impossible that a Valentinian, accepting II Cor. 3¹⁴⁻¹⁸ as an authority to be quoted, should put such glaringly foreign sense upon the words.

Not quite the same holds of the next quotation, as of "the saying" (τὸ εἰρημένον): "Holy Spirit shall come upon thee (but Spirit is the Sophia), and Power of (the) Highest overshadow thee (Highest is the Demiurge), wherefore that which is born from thee, holy shall be called." (cf. Luke 1³⁵) In omitting καὶ and inserting

| Gnos. | πνεῦμα | ἅγιον | ἐπελεύσεται | ἐπὶ | σέ, | καὶ | δύναμις | ὑψίστου | ἐπισκιάσει |
|-------|--------|-------|-------------|-----|-----|-----|---------|----------|------------|
| Luke  | "      | "     | "           | " " | "   | "   | "       | "        |            |

| Gnos. | σοι· | διὸ |     | τὸ | γεννώμενον | ἐκ | σοῦ | ἅγιον | κληθήσεται. |
|-------|------|-----|-----|----|-----------|-----|-----|-------|-------------|
| Luke  | "    | "   | καὶ | "  | "         | — — | "   | "     | υἱὸς Θεοῦ.  |

ἐκ σοῦ the Valentinian is strongly supported by very old authorities. It also seems older in the omission of υἱὸς Θεοῦ. Since it will hardly be denied that these two chaps. (Luke 1 and 2) are a late addition to the Lucan Gospel, there seems no reason for supposing that Valentinus is here quoting from Luke, but rather again that both are quoting from an older.

Immediately after (on page 296), in stating the doctrine of the occidental Valentinians, Heraclean & Ptolomaeus, that the body of the Jesus was psychic, Hippolytus quotes as their proof-text "the saying" (τὸ εἰρημένον): "He that raised Christ from (the) dead shall make alive also your mortal bodies." Here the Valentinian omission of 'Ιησοῦν has the very strongest support, while the following clause in Rom. 8[11], "through his indwelling spirit in you," is condemned as unintelligible and by the existence of the equally well supported reading διὰ τὸ ἐνοικοῦν αὐτοῦ πνεῦμα. Once more the indication is that both Valentinus and Romans quoted from an ancient source, but Valentinus more closely.

## I. *Marcus the Gnostic*

Passing over Secundus we come to Marcus, who seems to have been an important heretic, if we judge from the space accorded him by Hippolytus and Irenaeus. He is represented as a juggler, a mere imposter, and this representation is accepted even by Harnack (Marcus war wohl ein Schwindler), and it may be correct, we cannot disprove it. But neither is it proved. For Irenaeus is such a partisan and heretic-hater that it is impossible to take his statements without salt. Hippolytus is far more temperate, but even his statements must be received with much caution. The only jugglery that Hippolytus charges, seems to have been performed over the Eucharistic cup, and to have involved some pretended transformation of the liquid. It looks like discretion to hold judgment in reserve. The sentence of consecration contains no more trace of jugglery than some much more modern and in high repute. The doctrine of the second Baptism (of Redemption) presents no clear evidence of charlatanry. The vision of truth is evidently to be understood metaphorically. It is noteworthy that the severe charges of Irenaeus are not repeated by Hippolytus after close examination; on the contrary, it seems clearly implied by the comparatives that Hippolytus did not approve of the "roughness" of "the blessed Presbyter Irenaeus," as well as that the Marcosians themselves repudiated them. The language of Hippolytus is very obscure, but the interpretation of Bunsen seems correct. Harnack (U. u. B., p. 180) indeed says that "Hippolytus examined all exactly and found it confirmed," but Hippolytus says no such thing, his words are (pages 308–9): "for also the blessed presbyter Irenaeus having approached the refutation too confidently (παρρησιαίτερον) set forth such washings and redemptions. Stating too roughly (ἀδρομερέστερον) what they do, which (statements) some of them having happened on, deny that so they have received, learning always to deny. Wherefore it has been our anxiety to inquire more accurately and discover minutely what they deliver in the first bath so-called (τὸ τοιοῦτο καλοῦντες) and on the second which they call Redemption. But neither has their ineffable (τὸ ἄρρητον αὐτῶν) escaped us. But these things be forgiven (συνκεχωρήσθω) to Valentinus and his school."

The main counts in the Irenaean indictment Hippolytus has not repeated, nor has he said he found them confirmed; but rather the contrary, and this is true, even if we put "more" in place of "too."—The Marcosian numeral symbolism is neither more nor less fantastic than much similar current in those days of "Gematria."

*The gleaning in Hippolytus concerning Marcus is very scanty. More than once, however, the Heretic is said to refer to the guardian angels, e.g., on page 311: "These are the forms which the Lord called angels, (forms) that perpetually ($\delta\iota\eta\nu\epsilon\kappa\hat{\omega}s$) behold the face of the Father." The passage in Matt. 18$^{10}$ is manifestly out of place, and is omitted by the Anglo-Saxon translation. Apparently then it was a floating saying, and not taken from *Matthew,* but inserted therein.

Irenaeus has given a section† (I, 13, 2) to alleged Marcosian perversions of the Gospel. The first nearly agrees with L. 2$^{49}$, but has $o\mathring{\iota}\delta\alpha\tau\epsilon$ for $\mathring{\eta}\delta\epsilon\iota\tau\epsilon$ and $\mu\epsilon$ $\epsilon\mathring{\iota}\nu\alpha\iota$ for $\epsilon\mathring{\iota}\nu\alpha\iota$ $\mu\epsilon$. Inasmuch as this whole Prehistory is plainly a prefix to an earlier form of the Lucan Gospel, it remains of course an open question whether the Marcosians took from Luke or from Luke's source.—The second example "why callest thou me good?" &c. we have already discussed (p. 162)—The third, "By what *power* doest thou *this?*" substitutes $\delta\upsilon\nu\acute{\alpha}\mu\epsilon\iota$ $\tau o\hat{\upsilon}\tau o$ for $\mathring{\epsilon}\xi o\upsilon\sigma\acute{\iota}\alpha$ $\tau\alpha\hat{\upsilon}\tau\alpha$ whence it certainly cannot be concluded that Matt. 21$^{23}$ is quoted. The 4th instance is remarkable: "But also in his saying, Often I desired to hear one of these words and had not any to say it ($\tau\grave{o}\nu$ $\mathring{\epsilon}\rho o\hat{\upsilon}\nu\tau\alpha$)." Irenaeus seems to cherish no doubt of the authenticity of this "saying"; he puts it among "those lying in the Gospels" ($\tau\hat{\omega}\nu$ $\mathring{\epsilon}\nu$ $\tau\hat{\omega}$ $E\mathring{\upsilon}\alpha\gamma\gamma\epsilon\lambda\acute{\iota}\omega$ $\kappa\epsilon\iota\mu\acute{\epsilon}\nu\omega\nu$), but it is not found in *our* Gospels. Certainly then the Marcosians were here quoting from some other Gospel, and since in *this* case, then probably so in *every* case. The nearest Canonic parallel is in Luke 17$^{22}$—"Days will come when ye shall desire to see one of the days of the Son of Man and shall not see (it)." The two passages are hardly unrelated.—The 5th parallel, "If thou hadst known today the things of peace! But now they are hidden," compares thus with Luke 19$^{42}$:

| | | |
|---|---|---|
| Gnos. | $\epsilon\mathring{\iota}$ $\mathring{\epsilon}\gamma\nu\omega s$ $\kappa\alpha\grave{\iota}$ $\sigma\grave{\upsilon}$ | $\sigma\acute{\eta}\mu\epsilon\rho o\nu$ $\tau\grave{\alpha}$ $\pi\rho\grave{o}s$ $\epsilon\mathring{\iota}\rho\acute{\eta}\nu\eta\nu$ |
| Luke | " " " " $\kappa\alpha\acute{\iota}\gamma\epsilon$ $\mathring{\epsilon}\nu$ $\tau\hat{\eta}$ $\mathring{\eta}\mu\acute{\epsilon}\rho\alpha$ $\sigma o\upsilon$ $\tau\alpha\acute{\upsilon}\tau\eta$ " " " $\sigma o\upsilon\cdot$ $\nu\hat{\upsilon}\nu$ $\delta\grave{\epsilon}$ |
| Gnos. | $\mathring{\epsilon}\kappa\rho\acute{\upsilon}\beta\eta$ $\delta\grave{\epsilon}$ $\mathring{\alpha}\pi\grave{o}$ $\sigma o\upsilon.$ | |
| Luke | " – " $\mathring{o}\phi\theta\alpha\lambda\mu\hat{\omega}\nu$ " | |

Here the divergence is considerable, and the Marcosian form is simpler and apparently earlier.—The sixth is this: "Hither to me all that labor and are burdened (and I will give you rest) and learn of me." Here the Greek agrees exactly with Matt. 11$^{28, 29}$ but omits "take my yoke upon you." The Latin translation of Irenaeus also omits "and I will give you rest," and, we suspect, correctly. There is no reason to suppose a quotation from Matthew. For the Matthean text has evidently been over-worked. This is seen in the loose connection of its parts, and especially in the double reason: "because &c." and "for &c."; also in the play on the word $\chi\rho\eta\sigma\tau\acute{o}s$ (Christ), a very unnatural word to use of "yoke," the sense "easy" is not known. The Marcosian form seems simpler and earlier.

---

* From here on, the account of Marcus given by Hippolytus is a word-for-word transcript from the Greek of Irenaeus *Adversus Haereses. Editor.*

† Smith's remaining Marcosian parallels are from Irenaeus, including paragraphs which Hippolytus omitted from his transcript. *Editor.*

But as the very "crown of their hypothesis," Irenaeus tells us they adduce the famous passage: "I will thank (confess to) thee, Father, Lord of the Heavens and the earth, because thou didst conceal from (the) wise and prudent and reveal them to babes; yea, my Father, because in thy sight good pleasure it was. All (things) are delivered me by my Father; and none has known the Father, but the Son, and the Son but the Father, and to whom the Son may reveal." Here the resemblance is very close to the Matthaean—Lucan text (Matt. 11[25-27], Luke 10[21-22]), but the variations are noteworthy:

>    ἐξομολογήσομαι for ἐξομολογοῦμαι
>    τῶν οὐρανῶν for τοῦ οὐρανοῦ
>    ἀπέκρυψας (with Luke) for ἔκρυψας (in Matthew)
>    ταῦτα omitted (but inserted in the Latin)
>    οὐά for ναί
>    μου after ὁ πατήρ.

in fact, the whole sentence

Gnos.   Ἐξομολογήσομαί σοι, πάτερ κύριε τῶν οὐρανῶν καὶ τῆς
Matt. 11[25-27]  Ἐξομολογοῦμαί   " ,    "    "   τοῦ οὐρανοῦ "  "
Luke 10[21-22]        "        "    "    "   "   "   "   "   "
                               ,

Gnos.   γῆς, ὅτι ἀπέκρυψας —— ἀπὸ σοφῶν καὶ συνετῶν, καὶ
Matt.   " ,  "  ἔκρυψας ταῦτα "    "    "    "    ,    "
Luke    " ,  "  ἀπέκρυψας  "    "    "    "    "    ,    "

Gnos.   ἀπεκάλυψας αὐτὰ νηπίοις· οὐά, ὁ πατήρ μου, ὅτι ἔμπροσθέν
Matt.       "        "    "   · ναί, "   "   —,  " οὕτως
Luke        "        "    "   . "  "   "   —    "   "
                              ,         ,

Gnos.   σου εὐδοκία ἐγένετο ——   —. Πάντα μοι παρεδόθη
Matt.   —   "     "  ἔμπροσθέν σου.  "   "   "
Luke    —   "     "     "       "    .  "   "   "

Gnos.   ὑπὸ τοῦ πατρός μου, καὶ οὐδεὶς  ἔγνω   —  —  τὸν πατέρα
Matt.   "   "   "    "  ,  "   "   ἐπιγινώσκει —  —  " υἱὸν
Luke    "   "   "    "  ,  "   "   γινώσκει  τίς ἐστιν ὁ υἱὸς

Gnos.   εἰ μὴ ὁ υἱός,  καὶ  —  —  τὸν υἱὸν       εἰ μὴ
Matt.   "  " "  πατήρ, οὐδὲ  —  —  "  πατέρα τις ἐπιγιώσκαι " "
Luke    "  " "   "  ,  καὶ  τίς ἐστιν ὁ πατὴρ  —   —   " "

Gnos.   ὁ πατήρ καὶ ᾧ ἂν   —   ὁ υἱὸς ἀποκαλύψῃ.
Matt.   " υἱὸς " " ἐὰν βούληται " " ἀποκαλύψαι.
Luke    "   "   "  " ἂν   "   "   "   "        .

diverges widely from both *Luke* and *Matthew*, which diverge notably from each other. It seems most improbable, almost impossible, that either *Luke* or *Matthew* should be the original of the Marcosian quotation, which differs so strangely from both, while agreeing now with one, now with the other. Moreover, it is plainly simpler than either, and so apparently more primitive, though itself showing signs of overworking. The untranslatable Syrian exclamation of joy, οὐά, seems distinctively original as against ναί; moreover it is remarkably reflected in the Lucan ἠγαλλιάσατο (rejoiced, beginning of v. 21). Every consideration then points here to the Marcosian as presenting an earlier type of this signal passage. This latter has long been a crux to commentators. Notoriously it is out of place in its context, and even unintelligible. That it really belongs elsewhere is clearly hinted in the absence of ταῦτα in the Marcosian version, where αὐτά is object of both ἀπέκρυψας and ἀπεκάλυψας. The lost preface to the prayer doubtless contained the proper antecedent to αὐτά; the framers of our text, like the Latin translator of Irenaeus, endeavored to supply the defect with ταῦτα, but the question at once recurs, What is the antecedent of ταῦτα? "These things"—but what things? *Neither Matthew nor Luke gives any answer.* Now add finally that "that season" in *Matthew* is wholly different from that "same hour," and that the two halves of the pericope, "I thank thee" and "Come unto me," in Luke are quite unrelated (cf. Luke 18$^{16}$.) and it must become superfluously clear that the whole pericope in both Matthew and Luke, and in the Marcosian version has been borrowed from a much older source and elaborated by each writer, but much less by the Marcosian.

If we are to be absolutely honest we cannot repress the question, Is there any element of correctness in the Marcosian interpretation of this passage: "that the Father of Truth was known to no one at any time before his (the Son's) Parousy"? and we must answer, there seems to be; *apparently the Marcosians were right.* It is noteworthy that Irenaeus evidently felt the force of their pleading, for he makes no answer either here or elsewhere. The passage would seem to be most genuinely a Gnostic one, but one which both Evangelists very properly thought too good to lose.

These "heretics" seem to have laid great stress on the doctrine of Redemption (ἀπολύτρωσις) symbolized in a baptism instituted by Jesus (Christ) for the sake of Perfection. "And this it is concerning which he says: And another baptism I have to be baptized (with), and eagerly I hasten to it." This reminds us of one of the most obscure passages, Luke 12$^{49, 50}$: "Fire (it is) I came to cast upon the earth; and what will I it were already kindled. But (and?) a baptism have I to be baptized (with), and how am I straitened till it be accomplished!" The Lucan words are plainly an importation, whence we know not. Can any one seriously imagine they were really spoken by Jesus? That the Marcosian could have taken from Luke, and corrupted, is unbelievable. For what object could they have in such corruption? Moreover Epiphanius (784) represents his Ἀρειομανῖται as saying "that a cup I have to drink, and how hasten I until (ἕως οὖ) I drink it; and a baptism I have to be baptized, and how I wish that already I were baptized." Whence it seems that this obscure idea of the Saviour's mission to cast fire on earth, to establish "another baptism" (of fire? Matt. 3$^{11}$) had obtained great currency and expression in many forms, the most primitive of which have not reached us.

## J. Basilides and Lesser Gnostics

We pass now from this "mere imposter," Marcus to one of the most imposing figures in the history of Heresy. It is indeed charged that Hippolytus has violated his professed chronological order in treating of Valentinus before Basilides, but this charge is hardly just. Hippolytus expressly declares Valentinianism to be a mere continuation or offshoot of Simonianism, even as Marcus and Colarbasus budded off from Valentinus; and hence he naturally and properly follows up his Simon Magus immediately with Valentinus and the latter with Marcus and Colarbasus. It would have been absurd to thrust Basilides before Valentinus and then return to the Simonian-Valentinian-Marcosian school. Besides, the time-relations are here by no means certainly determined. Basilides may have been 15 years the senior of Valentinus but they were practically contemporaries, along with the third, with Marcion, whom Harnack dates thus 85–165(?). He too was then at the acme of his power, side by side with Basilides and Valentinus (125–150). Of these three Heresiarchs, Marcion appears to have been the most vigorous of affairs, the greatest organizer of that century, but with the least turn for speculation; Valentinus would seem to have had the most artistic temperament, the liveliest fancy, the richest eloquence, perhaps the keenest spiritual insight; but Basilides strikes us as the profoundest philosopher, the acutest metaphysician, the most comprehensive and scientific* world-thinker. Indeed, he is in many respects an earlier Hegel (we say this, who are no disciple or admirer of Hegel), by no means an unworthy anticipation of the great Berliner. In reading of his doctrine of the Absolute, the Non Ens (Οὐκ "Ο ν , it is impossible not to be reminded of the Hegelian Paradox, *Das Sein ist das Nichts.* This was not a mere imagination with Basilides, but was deduced from the Aristotelian doctrine of the Categories, from the nature of Predication itself. We can not here enter into the subject of Basilidianism, though an attractive one, further than to remark that, speaking broadly, Hippolytus seems to be right in his derivation of the system from Aristotle, and that to imagine it started from *Romans* or any other New Testament writings is just as preposterous as to suppose that Hegelism started not from Kant, Fichte, and Schelling, but from the Gospel of St. John.

The first parallel that Hippolytus affords us in his "Basilides" is a famous and important one (page 348): "Was born (γέγονε), he says, from non-existents the Seed of the World, the Logos the Spoken (λεχθείς), 'let there be light,' and this, he says, is the saying in the Gospel: Was the light the true, which lightens every man coming into the world." He takes the principles (ἀρχάς) from that Seed and is lightened. "This is the Seed, which has in itself all the total seed-potency (omni-semination, πανσπερμίαν), which, says Aristotle, is genus divided into infinite species (ἰδέας), as from the Animal we divide ox, horse, man—which (animal) is non-existent." Here, it is said, Basilides quotes from John 1⁹. But why so? It is not claimed by Hippolytus that Basilides used any Canonic, but that both he and his son Isidor footed on sayings reported by Matthias: "Basilides therefore and Isidor,

---

* In the sense, evidently, of the untranslatable German word *wissenschaftlich. Editor.*

the true son and disciple of Basilides, say Matthias spoke to them sayings ( λόγους) secret, which he heard from the Saviour, (having been) specially instructed." And again: "Which (Aristotelic doctrine) these affirm as their own and something new and some of the secret discourses (λόγων) of Matthias." Of course, Hippolytus must regard such claims as a calumny on Matthias and on Christ. Furthermore we know that Basilides wrote twenty-four books of commentary (ἐξηγητικά) to the Gospel, presumably this Matthian. Origen charges him, doubtless falsely, with daring to write a "Gospel according to Basilides." We are concerned only with the fact that Basilides planted himself, not on the Johannine, but on another Gospel. The fact that the sentence agrees exactly with *John* signifies nothing, unless a far more ancient common source. The use of the plural "Gospels" weighs naught. We cannot tell whether it is Hippolytus or the Basilidian that uses the word. In any case no inference that Basilides has quoted from *John* is for a moment allowable.

After mention of Basilides' doctrine of the Spirit as an uplifting "wing" πτερόν), apparently taken from Plato's Phaedrus, echoed also in the Hymn of Clement, "Wing of unwandering birds" and "heavenly Wing of the all-holy flocks." Hippolytus goes on to say (page 351): "but as contra-natural and destructive to the fishes air pure and dry, so to the holy Spirit was contra-natural that place at once of the non-existent God and the Sonship, place more unspeakable than unspeakables and higher than all names." This notion of the name (or here place), surpassing all names we encounter at least three times in the New Testament: "and made him to sit at his right hand in the heavenly (places), far above all rule and authority and power and dominion and every name that is named" (Eph. $1^{21}$), "Wherefore also God highly exalted him, and gave unto him the name which is above every name" (Phil. $2^9$); "Having become by so much better than the angels, as he hath inherited a more excellent name than they" (Heb. $1^4$). Not one of these seems to be derived directly from the other; nor the Basilidian from any. All seem diverse expressions of the same general idea of exalted being.* The Basilidian is apparently the oldest, the Ephesian the youngest.

The phrase "wise master-builder" ( σοφὸς ἀρχιτέκτων) (p. 354) is used admirably by Basilides of the Great Archon, the World-artificer. In I Cor. $3^{10}$ Paul is made to say "I indeed as wise master-builder laid foundation"; the image is also here in place, though the time elapsed since the foundation of the Corinthian church, not three years at most, would hardly seem to justify or suggest it. In any case there is no reason to suppose any borrowing from *Corinthians*.

In the next chapter the (second) archon Arrhetus *seems* called Topos (Place) and *is* called Hebdomad (p. 356). This Topos (Heb. *maqum*) is a preferred Rabbinic name of God, a fact mentioned here as pointing towards certain sources of this system.

"And it was necessary for the (third) Sonship left behind to be revealed and reinstated (p. 357). Speaking of the Revelation and reinstatement above there, above the conterminous Spirit, near the Sonship, the refined and imitative, and the non-existent, as is written (he says): and the creation itself groans together and

* This is not the place to discuss the significance of *Name*. (However, see p. 14–15. *Editor*.)

travails together, awaiting the Revelation of the Sons of God, and Sons (he says) are we the Pneumatics, left down here to dispose and mould and rectify and perfect the souls below with nature to remain in this region. Therefore until Moses from Adam reigned the Sin, as has been written. For the Great Archon reigned that has his limit ($\tau\acute{\epsilon}\lambda os$) as far as the firmament, deeming himself to be God alone, and beyond him to be nothing, for all things were guarded by unrevealed silence ($\sigma\iota\omega\pi\hat{\eta}$). This (he says) is the mystery, which to the former generations was not made known." We note first that the notion of the (ruler) Archon of this world, the Hebdomad, as contrasted with the Great Archon, the Ogdoad, is here developed and defined with as much precision as might be expected in such elemental thinking, whereas in the New Testament the notion is assumed as well-known and familiar—an already oft-repeated phenomenon. The first "Scripture" quoted (p. 357) reminds us of Rom. 8[19-22]: "For the earnest expectation of the creation awaits the Revelation of the Sons of God. For the creation was subjected to vanity, unwilling, but on account of the subjector, in hope. Wherefore also the creation itself shall be freed from the bondage of (the) corruption into the freedom of the Glory of the Children of God. For we know that all the creation groans together and travails together until now ($\tau o\hat{v}$ $\nu\hat{v}\nu$). And not only, but also ourselves having the first fruits of the Spirit, we also ourselves in ourselves groan expecting adoption, the redemption of our body."

Gnos.   $\kappa\alpha\grave{\iota}$ $\mathring{\eta}$ $\kappa\tau\acute{\iota}\sigma\iota s$ $\alpha\mathring{v}\tau\grave{\eta}$ $\sigma\upsilon\sigma\tau\epsilon\nu\acute{\alpha}\zeta\epsilon\iota$ $\kappa\alpha\grave{\iota}$ $\sigma\upsilon\nu\omega\delta\acute{\iota}\nu\epsilon\iota$
Rom. 8[22] — "    "    — $\sigma\upsilon\nu\sigma\tau\epsilon\nu\acute{\alpha}\zeta\epsilon\iota$ "    "
Gnos.   $\tau\grave{\eta}\nu$ $\mathring{\alpha}\pi o\kappa\acute{\alpha}\lambda\upsilon\psi\iota\nu$ $\tau\hat{\omega}\nu$ $\upsilon\mathring{\iota}\hat{\omega}\nu$ $\tau o\hat{v}$ $\theta\epsilon o\hat{v}$ $\mathring{\epsilon}\kappa\delta\epsilon\chi o\mu\acute{\epsilon}\nu\eta$.
Rom. 8[19] "    "    "    "    "    " $\mathring{\alpha}\pi\epsilon\kappa\delta\acute{\epsilon}\chi\epsilon\tau\alpha\iota$
Gnos.   $\upsilon\mathring{\iota}o\grave{\iota}$ $\delta\grave{\epsilon}$ $\mathring{\epsilon}\sigma\tau\grave{\epsilon}\nu$ $\mathring{\eta}\mu\epsilon\hat{\iota}s$ $o\mathring{\iota}$ $\pi\nu\epsilon\upsilon\mu\alpha\tau\iota\kappa o\acute{\iota}$

Here it seems that the case is particularly clear. As a piece of original writing by Paul to Romans the foregoing is impossible, if anything can be impossible. It is incomprehensible even to the utmost efforts of the human intellect. There is no consecution whatever of parts; the fors and wherefore are without any meaning. That the writer is stating or trying to state some well known doctrine is perfectly clear in the word $o\mathring{\iota}\delta\alpha\mu\epsilon\nu$ (we know). Compared with this the Basilidean teaching is lucidity itself. Moreover the Scripture of Basilides is perfectly natural in its construction and could not have been taken from *Romans,* except by suffixing the last half of v. 19 to the mid-half of v. 22, an extremely improbable procedure. And how simple and transparent is the Basilidean "But sons are we the Pneumatics," in comparison with the unintelligible v. 23 with its $\kappa\alpha\grave{\iota}$ $\alpha\upsilon\tau o\grave{\iota}\ldots\kappa\alpha\grave{\iota}$ $\alpha\upsilon\tau o\grave{\iota}$ $\ldots\mathring{\epsilon}\alpha\upsilon\tau o\hat{\iota}s$ It seems to glare upon us that in these verses we find an old Gnostic text, incomparably more original in Basilides, here overworked in extraordinary sense-defying fashion.

Passing now to the next parallel, we find this conclusion strongly corroborated. The diversity is great between Basilides:—$\mu\acute{\epsilon}\chi\rho\iota$ $\mu\grave{\epsilon}\nu$ $o\mathring{v}\nu$ $M\omega\sigma\acute{\epsilon}\omega s$ $\mathring{\alpha}\pi\grave{o}$ $\mathring{A}\delta\grave{\alpha}\mu$ $\mathring{\epsilon}\beta\alpha\sigma\acute{\iota}\lambda\epsilon\upsilon\sigma\epsilon\nu$ $\mathring{\eta}$ $\mathring{\alpha}\mu\alpha\rho\tau\acute{\iota}\alpha$ and Romans $\mathring{\alpha}\lambda\lambda\grave{\alpha}$ $\mathring{\epsilon}\beta\alpha\sigma\acute{\iota}\lambda\epsilon\upsilon\sigma\epsilon\nu$ $\mathring{o}$ $\theta\acute{\alpha}\nu\alpha\tau os$ $\mathring{\alpha}\pi\grave{o}$ $\mathring{A}\delta\grave{\alpha}\mu$ $\mu\acute{\epsilon}\chi\rho\iota$

Μωσέως. How derive that from this? Furthermore, it is plain as can be that these verses, Rom. 5¹²⁻¹⁴, have undergone repeated redaction: v. 12 has no connection with v. 11, v. 13 no connection with v. 12; v. 14 no connection with v. 13! The reigning of Sin lies much nearer at hand than that of Death, in v. 14. Every way the Basilidian text is to be preferred. We strongly suspect that the original read not unlike this: "Therefore through one (man) Sin came into the world; consequently on the one hand (μέν) even from Adam unto Moses Sin reigned." There followed doubtless a clause δὲ —"But on the other hand"; this however has been lost. Once more, then, the indication seems plain that Basilides has quoted from an earlier version than appears in our *Romans*.

Very remarkable is the Basilidean conception (pp. 358–9) of the entrance of the Gospel into the world: "When accordingly, he says, we the children of God needed to be revealed, concerning whom, he says, the creation groaned and travailed awaiting the revelation, there came the Gospel into the Cosmos, and traversed every rule ( ἀρχῆς ) and authority and dominion and every name (that is) named. But it came really (ὀντῶς) even though nothing fared down from above, nor departed the blessed Sonship of (from) that inconceivable and non-existent God. Nay, for just as Indian Naphtha, seen merely from far enough remove, attracts fires, so from below, from the formlessness of the heap attain the powers even up to the Sonship." Here we remark everything seems perfectly in place: however fantastic the notion of Basilides, yet his statement of it is natural and to be expected. Now compare with Eph. 1²⁰⁻²¹:

| Gnos. | καὶ διῆλθε διὰ | πάσης ἀρχῆς | καὶ ἐξουσίας |
| Eph. | ἐν τοῖς ἐπουρανίοις ὑπεράνω | " " | " " |

| Gnos. | | καὶ κυριότητος, καὶ παντὸς | ὀνόματος ὀνομαζομένου. |
| Eph. | καὶ δυνάμεως | " " " " | " " |

Here in Ephesians is a single sentence, or rather a concrete of sentences of nine verses of seventeen lines, inflated and dropsical, ungrammatical ("*erläutert wird dies v. 18 durch ein asyndetisch angefügtes und darum parallel zweites Object zu δώη*"—Weiss; also at v. 22, "The previous participial construction passes over into the finite verb"—Weiss.) unclear to the last degree. That this paragraph has been overworked and intolerably padded seems palpable. Only consider such a phrase as "unto us those believing according to the energy of the power of the might of him which he energized in the Christ." Where there is so much padding it seems reasonable to think that the words καὶ δυνάμεως are also intercalated and that the Basilidian form is nearer the original than this Ephesian.*

At the top of page 360: "This is the wisdom spoken in mystery, concerning which, he says, the scripture says: Not in words taught of human wisdom, but in (words) taught of Spirit." This parallel to I Cor. 2¹³ has already been discussed.†

* Matt. 12³² provides a parallel to the last clause of Eph. 1²¹.
† Page 167.

We have seen there is no reason to suppose it endotic to the Corinthian text. That it is cited as Scripture would signify nothing, even if we were sure that it is not Hippolytus that is responsible for γραφή, but Basilides or a Basilidean. For why might not these cite a Gnostic original as Scripture?

The word ἐπέλαμψεν, used of the Son of the Great Archon, reminds us of ἔλαμψεν in II Cor. 4⁶, but no conclusion is allowed, as does the general notion of the illumination of the Hebdomad through the Gospel: Ἐπεὶ οὖν καὶ τὰ ἐν τῇ ἑβδομάδι πάντα πεφώτιστο καὶ διήγγελτο τὸ εὐαγγέλιον αὐτοῖς· κτίσεις γάρ εἰσι κατ’ αὐτὰ τὰ διαστήματα κατ’ αὐτοὺς ἄπειροι, καὶ ἀρχαὶ καὶ δυνάμεις καὶ ἐξουσίαι. Here we must think of "principalities and powers" in Eph. 3¹⁰, part of the long interpolation between the two "τούτου χάριν"’s. Hippolytus tells us in a parenthesis of a long and prolix Basilidean treatise on these matters, partly astrological. The point in the comparison with Ephesians is that the latter passage is plainly interpolated, and that it assumes this amazing notion of making known to the principalities and the powers in the heavenly regions, through the Church, the manifold wisdom of God, as a notion familiar enough to the readers not to startle them. In the Basilidian system this idea is very properly in place and is read without special wonder: the Gospel started from above and traversed all these regions on its way to Earth; but in Ephesians it is "through the church" on earth that this notification is now to be made to these same super-terrestrial existences. This is an extravagance, and apparently a new turn given to the ancient Gnostic thought.

Similarly must we judge of the next parallel (p. 361): "But when, he says, these things happened thus (Illumination and Gospel Announcement) it needed also for the formlessness *chez nous* to be enlightened and for there to be revealed to the Sonship, which was left behind in the Formlessness, as it were ἔκτρωμα, the mystery which to the former generations was not made known, as is written, he says, *According to Revelation was made known to me the mystery,* and *I heard ineffable words which it is not allowed man to speak.*" It is impossible to deny that this Basilidian doctrine of the cosmical range of the Gospel is clearly thought out link by link, that it is at least a colossal doctrine and worthy to be named a "mystery." But in the parallel Eph. 3³⁻⁵ we find this "mystery" explained as the mere fact that "the Gentiles are co-heirs and co-members and co-partakers of the promise." Once more, then, it would seem that the Epistolist has merely turned the edge of an ancient Gnostic saying, and by blunting has made it harmless.

The next parallel, ἤκουσα ἄρρητα ῥήματα ἃ οὐκ ἐξὸν ἀνθρώπῳ εἰπεῖν, agrees with II Cor. 12⁴ except in ἤκουσα for ἤκουσεν and εἰπεῖν instead of λαλῆσαι. No confident conclusion seems warranted. So far as they indicate anything at all, these differences indicate some other source than *Corinthians*. If any one believes that the Apostle was really rapt into Paradise, whether in the body or out of the body, and heard unutterable things, then such a one will naturally think the Corinthian passage the original of any such parallel, though such a conclusion would not even then be necessary, since Paul might have elsewhere stated the same in writing or orally. But if any one takes the expression as he would take it in dealing with ordinary Apocalyptics, whose name is Legion, as a mere *façon de parler*, then he will probably regard ἤκουσα as the earliest form and will think that both *Corinthians* and Basilides have taken from some lost Apocalyptic. It seems at least strange, if Basilides is quoting from Paul, that he does not say so.

"Descended (therefore) from the Hebdomad, the light that descended from the Ogdoad above to the Son of the Hebdomad upon the Jesus the Son of Mary, and he was enlightened, co-kindled by the light that shone into him. This is, he says, the saying: *Spirit holy will come upon thee,* that from the Sonship through the conterminous Spirit upon the Ogdoad and the Hebdomad came through unto the Mary, *and power of Highest shall overshadow thee,* the power of the annointing (χρίσεως for κρίσεως)" (p. 362).

Here is an exact agreement with Luke 1³⁵,* but not the least reason for supposing any borrowing therefrom. For it is late in the day to observe that the Lucan Prehistory is a later addendum and purely fanciful; there is no reason to suppose the phrases in question native to the Lucan context.

A few lines further on we find an idea frequent and central with Basilides, of "all the Sonship, that left behind to benefit the souls in Formlessness and to be benefited" (εἰς τὸ εὐεργετεῖν τὰς ψυχὰς ἐν ἀμορφία καὶ εὐεργετεῖσθαι). Here is suggested a remarkable phrase standing quite isolated in Acts 10³⁸, "who went through benefiting" (ὃς διῆλθεν εὐεργετῶν). It is well known that this whole passage, verses 35–39, is an inextricable tangle. Verses 34–35 are not continued either in thought or in structure by verse 36; τὸν λόγον is without any governing word or relation; "He is Lord of all" is clearly an interpolated parenthesis; verse 37 has no grammatical connection with verse 36; the participle ἀρξάμενος hangs in the air without any possible attachment; in verse 38 Ἰησοῦν τὸν ἀπὸ Ναζαρὲτ is also asyntactic, nothing governs it in the accusative and it is a *pis alter* to refer it to ῥῆμα (word) by apposition. The theme announced in verses 34–35 is never heard or hinted again in the speech! That any one could have thought or spoken or written so originally is incredible. The text is at best very uncertain: βλασκήρυγμα for βάπτισμα etc. The paragraph is intelligible only and easily as rather rough patchwork, in which edifying phrases are tacked together with little respect for grammar or logic. Such a phrase seems to be this "who traversed benefiting." We note it follows immediately upon the phrase "how God annointed him with Holy Spirit and power." Here then we find a whole group of Basilidian ideas, and the resemblance can hardly be accidental. In Basilides these ideas are all in place and naturally connected; in Acts we have just seen that they are part of a patchwork. The conclusion seems hard to resist that Acts has borrowed from some ancient source also represented in Basilides. Wendt declares ἀρξάμενος "*grammatisch unmöglich*" and adopts ἀρξάμενον, evidently a later correction to restore syntax. Weiss recognizes redactor's additions in 39a, 41b, 43b; Spitta and Jüngst in 36–43. Patchwork, then, certainly. Note furthermore the word διῆλθεν; This *may* of course be rendered "went about," but "went through" is the more natural, frequent, near-

* Compare p. 193.

lying meaning, and it is repeatedly used in Basilides of the progress through the Cosmos. In the sense "went about" it is not used in profane Greek, though used of a *report* (λόγος) by Thucydides and Xenophon; nor indeed without any limitation is it used even by Luke of a single person. In Acts 8⁴ it is used of the numerous disciples that διῆλθον, some this way, some that; in Acts 20²⁵ ἐν οἷς limits διῆλθον, so that the bare phrase διῆλθεν εὐεργετῶν is highly improbable.

We now come to one of the most noteworthy Basilidean thoughts (pp. 362-3): "When therefore, he says, all sonship shall have come and shall be above the Conterminous, the Spirit, then shall suffer mercy (ἐλεηθήσεται) the creation, for it groans until (the) now and is tormented and awaits the revelation of the Sons of God, that all may ascend thence the men of the Sonship. When (thus) this takes place, he says, God will bring on the whole Cosmos the Great Ignorance, that all (things) may remain according to nature and naught desire aught of the things contrary to nature." The process of history is thus conceived as an Evolution of the Higher (the Sons or Sonship) through the midlying (Spirit) from the lower lying Cosmos (world of sense). When this process is complete, when the throes of Creation at birth of this Sonship are over, God in mercy upon the residuum, which is thus left behind as the dross of the Universe, will bring the Great Ignorance, will release it from all desire for the unattainable. Thenceforword it will not be as a fish would feed with Sheep on the mountains, but while all things abide within their proper bounds all sorrow and grief and groaning will depart. "And so the restitution will take place (ἀποκατάστασις ἔσται) of all things that by nature have indeed ( μέν) been founded in the seed of the Unniverse in (the) beginning, but (each) are to be restored at proper times" (p. 364). Here the philosophic idea of Basilides is reasonably clear and is astonishingly sublime. We see precisely what is meant by the travailing of Creation and the Revelation of the Sons of God. The parallel passage, Rom. 8¹⁹⁻²⁵ has been discussed on page 193. All the Basilidian ideas are found there, but in a form unintelligible. It is the old, old story.

How ancient is the idea that sorrow, grief, and groaning all proceed from striving beyond nature may be seen in myths of Genesis and in the exclamation of the Psalmist: "O Lord I have not striven for things too high for me" etc.

The important notion of the restoration of all things (ἀποκατάστασις πάντων pages 364 and 366) occurs again in Acts 3²¹, a remarkably instructive passage: "Repent therefore and turn (again?) that your sins may be blotted out, in order that there come times of refreshing from presence of the Lord and that he send (you) the (for you) predestined Christ Jesus, whom must heaven receive (retain) till times of restoration of all things which God spake by mouth of his holy prophets from eternity (*Aeon*)." We notice that this extraordinary idea of the "restoration of all things" is made senseless by this appended relative clause "which God spoke by mouth of his prophets from aye." "Restoration of the Universe" has meaning; but "restoration of the prophecies" has none. This clause must then be rejected as addendum. We note again that the purpose of this repentance that God may send them the predestined Christ Jesus, seems to show clearly that as originally preached this sermon looked forward to a Messiah to come, not backward upon one already come. It is almost exactly the note struck by the Baptist, "Repent for the Kingdom of Heaven is at hand." With this the phrase "whom heaven must receive" is in perfect accord. Since nothing has been said of any ascension of Christ Jesus to heaven, the phrase cannot naturally have any other meaning. Any reference in "may send" to a "second coming" seems extremely artificial. Whereas the notion that Christ Jesus could not come at all "till the times of restoration of the Universe,"* is most natural and thoroughly in accord with notions then generally prevalent. We believe then that the Basilidean notion has been here taken up and worked in by the original writer of this sermon, which latter has been revised and interpolated by the author of Acts. "And that, he says, each thing has its proper times, sufficient (witness) is the Saviour's saying (page 364): Not yet is mine hour come," "and the Magi gazing at the star; for himself was at the genesis of the stars and of the restoration of the hours preconceived (of reason) ($\pi\rho o\lambda\epsilon\lambda o\gamma\iota\sigma\mu\acute\epsilon$-$\nu os$) in the mighty heap." We may not approve the Basilidian interpretation of the aphorism, but it is certainly better than the Johannine. In John 2⁴ no meaning at all attaches to the words; they are instantly contradicted by the miracle wrought. We must regard them therefore as a mystical saying attributed to "the Jesus," which each used and interpreted after his own fashion.

We note in passing the Basilidean definition of the inner man: "This one is according to them the mentally conceived inner man pneumatic in the psychic (man)—which is Sonship (that) there has left behind the soul, not mortal but abiding there by nature, even as the first Sonship left above the holy Spirit the conterminous—(that) has then thrown about it its own soul." This may be unclear, especially Hippolytus' parenthetical explanation, but it shows that these "heretics" dealt with this notion as with something definite and definable.

Another more interesting definition is this (page 365): "Gospel is according to them the *Gnosis of the hypercosmical* (things) as has been elucidated, which (Gnosis) the Great Archon did not understand." The word Gospel is now in our Canonics about 75 times, mainly in the Epistles—4 times in *Matthew*, (7) 8 times in *Mark*, twice in *Acts*, once in *Revelation*—once in *I Peter*—never in any Johannine Gospel or Epistles, or *James*, or *Hebrews*, or *Luke*. This seems very extraordinary, and demands closer investigation than we can here give it. In general the notion is assumed as perfectly well understood. Only once is there any approach to a definition, in I Cor. 15¹⁻¹¹, a passage long ago strongly suspected as interpolation (Straatman). As here defined Gospel means "body of facts respecting Jesus Christ," that he died for our sins according to the Scripture, that he was buried, and that he rose on the third day according to the Scriptures, and that he appeared to Kephas and others, lastly to the writer as the Ektroma. That such is not the meaning of Gospel in *Matthew* (as 9³⁵, preaching the Gospel of the Kingdom) and in *Mark* (as 1¹⁵, repent and believe in the Gospel) is plain beyond argument; neither has it any relation whatever to the Eternal Gospel of Rev. 14⁶⁻⁷, "Fear God and give him glory; for the hour of his judgement is come: and worship him that made the

---

* The completion of the *great* or *Platonic year*, the completed revolution of the Equinoxes; whence the fundamental Equation of Eschatology: End = Beginning.

heaven and the Earth and sea and fountains of waters"; neither can it be (since the writer of *First Corinthians* received it by tradition—ὃ καὶ παρέλαβον) the Gospel preached to Galatians (Gal. 1[11, 12]) which was "not according to man, for neither did I receive it from man nor was I taught it (οὐδὲ γὰρ ἐγὼ παρὰ ἀνθρώπου παρέλαβον αὐτὸ) but by Revelation of Jesus Christ." Elsewhere (II Cor. 11[4], Gal. 1[6]) we read of "Another Gospel" than the Pauline. It seems vain then to seek in the Scriptures for any definite sense of this term. Certain it is that Basilides could not have gotten *his* notion from the New Testament. The word was probably first used in Gnostic circles,—there seem to have been many Gnostic Gospels—, and its content was most probably some Gnosis, some philosophico-religious doctrine. John, Luke, and the *Autor ad Hebraeos* seem to have avoided the term, aware perhaps of its origin.

Passing by Saturnilus and Marcion, of whom the discussion by Hippolytus is strangely deficient, we note that the Christology of Carpocrates (p. 385) is strikingly like that of the modern advanced critic: "(the) Jesus was generated from Joseph and born like unto men, was juster than the rest, and his soul born strenuous and pure remembered the things seen by it in its converse with the unbegotten God, and therefore by that God was sent down upon it power, so that it might be able to escape the world-makers (Cosmic powers); which power (or soul) having passed through all, made free in all, reascended unto (God) Himself, and likewise the soul that embraces like things with it." It seems hard to believe we are not reading from some English Unitarian or from some German biographer of Jesus. But the important point, one that meets us repeatedly and cannot be stressed too strongly, is this: We have in the Carpocratic a comparatively *late* form of heresy (if we may trust Hippolytus, or Ir. 1[24], Ter. *De An.* 23–25, Praescr, 48, Eus. IV[7], Epiph. Haer, 27[2], Theod. Haer. Fab. 1[15], St. Aug. Haer, VII). It approaches very close to the Catholic faith, especially in its accenting the earthly life of Jesus and slurring his over-earthly metaphysical being. Compared with the earlier heresies already discussed, Carpocrates is orthodoxy itself.

### K. *The Docetae*

Passing over Cerinthus and a number of minor heresies and heretics, which contribute only insignificant material for our consideration, we come to the Docetae (p. 396), evidently another grand division for Hippolytus. As to the date of this elaborate heresy there is no clear indication. Clement of Alexandria (Str. iii[13]) refers to Julius Cassianus (a pupil of Valentinus?) as princeps sectae Docetarum (ὁ τῆς δοκήσεως ἐξάρχων), quoting from his work *De Continentia vel De Castitate*—But we are not sure that ἐξάρχων means "originator," perhaps only leader, nor can we determine the date of Cassianus. The heresy resembles those of Valentinus and Basilides, and was perhaps nearly contemporary, probably a little later. Clement quotes Julius Cassianus as quoting from the Gospel according to Egyptians the passage about male and female. The all-important passage in Hippolytus's account of Docetism is this (p. 406): "Was born the (generated) from her as is written. And that same generated he put on that came from above, and all things he did so as in the gospels is written, bathed himself in (to) the Jordan, but bathed himself having received, type and seal, in the water of the body born from the virgin, in order that when the Archon condemned his own figment (τὸ ἴδιον πλάσμα) to death, to the cross, that soul (that had been) nourished in the body, having put off the body, and having nailed (it) to the wood, and having triumphed through it over the principalities and the authorities might be not found naked, but put on instead of that flesh, the body (that had been) detypified in the water. This is, he says, what the Savior says. Except a man be born of water and spirit, he shall not enter into the kingdom of the heavens, because what is born of the flesh is flesh." (Cf. John 3⁵,⁶.) We are not concerned here with the unreal and fantastic in this Dokesis. The point is that the doctrine is consistently thought out and intelligibly expressed. If any one accepted at face-value the accounts "in the Gospels," Canonic or Apocryphal, and at the same time held to the metaphysical concept of Jesus, we do not see why he should not think and write this way. The representations seem to follow naturally, the one upon the other, nothing seems out of place or dragged in by force. Now compare this with the following from Col. 2⁸⁻¹⁵. "See lest there be any that spoils you through (the) philosophy and vain deceit, after the tradition of men, after the elements of the world and not after Christ; because in him dwells all the fullness of the God-head bodily, and in him ye are made full, who is the head of all principality and authority, in whom ye were also circumcized with circumcision not made with hands, in the putting off of the body of the flesh, in the circumcision of the Christ, having been buried with him in the baptism, in which (whom?) also ye were raised together (with him) through the faith of the energy of God, who raised him from (the) dead. And you being dead (in) the trespasses and the uncircumcision of your flesh, he co-quickened you with him, having forgiven us all our (the) trespasses, having blotted out the handwriting against us (in) the ordinances which was contrary to us, and he took it out from the middle, having nailed it to the cross, having put off from himself the principalities and the authorities* he made show in confidence, having triumphed over them in it."

It is not too much to say that this passage is hopelessly unintelligible; human understanding has never understood it and never will. Speaking of v. 15 Holtzmann (*Eph. u. Kol. Briefe,* 156) well says *"welcher rein exegetisch betrachtet, unauflösliche Schwierigkeiten bietet,"* it stands, as Nitzsch remarks, "out of all connection" with the foregoing, and Ritschl, Hofmann, Schmidt, have exploded all attempts at elucidation. This is not nearly all, however; on its face the pericope is a concretion of philosophenes and edifying phrases, without any internal coherence or evolution one from another. Thus, v. 9 does not follow from v. 8; v. 11 does not cohere with v. 10 and is made up of three appositives that are quite incongruent: the Colossians had not put off the body of the flesh, they were still in it, and who could call such a putting off the circumcision of the Christ?—in fact

* See also comment, of later date, on pp. 72 and 149.

every clause in the paragraph detains our reason and at times defies. That we are dealing with a compaction, shines out in a number of details, as in the abrupt change from 2d person to 1st in v. 13, and the repetition of "against us" in "contrary to us," and the impossible αὐτοὺς of v. 15, which has *no antecedent,* even Reuss has not hesitated to mistranslate ἡμῖν (us) by "vous," and say nothing about it!

This is not nearly all, however. On comparing the Canonic (especially v. 14, 15) with the Docetic passage we observe that the ideas and phrases are far too closely allied for any work of accident; the difference is that everything is in place in the one and out of place in the other: thus, (Doc.) "that soul, having stripped off from itself the body and nailed it to the tree," *but* (Col.) "having nailed it (the handwriting) to the cross and having stripped off from himself the principalities and authorities, having triumphed through it (tree or body?) over the principalities and authorities," *but* "having triumphed over them (whom? apparently the principalities and authorities, but these are fem. whereas αὐτοὺς is masc.) in it" (the cross? or *in himself?*).

Notice again the "lest it (the soul) be found naked," introduced here perfectly rationally and naturally. Compare now II Cor. 5[1 ff]. Here the "we know" (οἴδαμεν) tells us that we are dealing with a well-understood doctrine, of the eternal unhandmade home (of the Spirit) in the heavens. "Yea, for in this (τούτῳ cannot refer to οἰκία, to what then? to σκήνους before, or to οἰκητήριον after? Both seem unnatural. A compilation? Weiss would translate *on this account,* which seems quite inept) we groan (στενάζομεν suggests this Basilidean notion of the groaning, travailing Creation) yearning to put on over besides our habitation that is from heaven." Now comes the perplexing εἴ γε (or εἴπερ?) καὶ ἐνδυσάμενοι, οὐ γυμνοὶ εὑρηθησόμεθα where εἴπερ is quite as strongly attested as εἴ γε "if so be that having put it on we shall not be found naked." Here the tangle of ideas is inextricable. If it were merely a question of putting on and putting off, we might think the writer referred to death, when the soul (or spirit?) might be said to put off its temporal garment of flesh and put on an eternal body (of what?). But he distinctly says this is not what he means: it is not putting on but putting on over (ἐπενδύσασθαι), he does not wish to put off but to put on *additional,* the immortal over the mortal and swallowing it up. With this the simple "having put on" (ἐνδυσάμενοι) of v. 3 is at hopeless variance. The idea of being "naked" is here dragged in visibly, and the clause seems to be an unfortunate comment on the preceding. V. 4 then takes up the thought, repeats and attempts to explain v. 2, quite disregarding v. 3! Can any unbiased mind think this is original thinking? Have then the Epistolists borrowed directly from the Docetist? Perhaps not, but the docetic notions and phrases were in all likelihood very old, belonging at least to the 1st Century (even tradition puts Cerinthus somewhere near A.D. 90), and the Epistolists have sought here as elsewhere to give them a new turn, to put new wine into old bottles. That the Docetist has not despoiled the Epistolists seems doubly sure. For the latter can make no pretence either to originality or to intelligibility, and even if they could, no genius was equal to the task of extricating the clear-cut docetic notions from the jungle of Canonic phrases.

The next parallel,* and a close one, is found in John $3^{5-6}$. It must be confessed

Doc.　ἐὰν μή τις γεννηθῇ ἐξ ὕδατος καὶ πνεύματος,
John $3^5$　"　"　"　"　"　"　"　"

Doc.　οὐκ　εἰσελεύσεται εἰς τὴν βασιλείαν τῶν οὐρανῶν·
John $3^5$　οὐ δύναται εἰσελθεῖν　"　"　"　τοῦ θεοῦ.

Doc.　ὅτι τὸ γεγεννημένον ἐκ τῆς σαρκὸς σάρξ ἐστιν.
John $3^6$　—　"　"　"　"　"　"　"　,
Naassene　—　"　"　"　"　"　"　ἐστι,

Naassene　καὶ τὸ γεγεννημένον ἐκ τοῦ πνεύματος πνεῦμα ἐστίν.
John $3^6$　"　"　"　"　"　"　"　"

that the Docetic form is superior at both points of divergence: "shall not enter" against "is not able to enter," and the "because" (ὅτι), not found in John, while the form "Kingdom of the heavens" seems older than "Kingdom of God." But the main point is that the Evangelic passage shows itself every way to be an over-work-ing of older turns of speech. It seems inconceivable that a ruler of the Jews should pay such a visit by night, should declare so early, as the general belief of Pharisees, that Jesus was a teacher sent from God; still more, that Jesus should make such an answer so utterly irrelevant; yet more, that Nicodemus should make so absurd a reply, displaying such gross ignorance; even stranger still, that Jesus should at once wheel off from birth from above to birth from water and Spirit, should re-turn to birth from above in verse 7, and instantly fly away to birth from Spirit in v. 8,—we may say these births are the same, but it is not said in the text, no rela-tion is indicated; lastly, that Jesus should charge unfaith (vv. 11–12) precisely where faith had been affirmed in v. 2! How can these things be? Surely every open eye must see that this is compilation of a particularly patent variety. The conclu-sion then must be that both Docetist and Evangelist have drunk at the public fount.

In a very remarkable paragraph (p. 408) Hippolytus closes his discussion of the Docetae, making no attempt whatever at refutation, but merely asserting (per-haps correctly in a measure) that the Greek Sophists of old had at many points anticipated this docetic dogma, as his readers might find out if they would.

### L. *Monoimus*

Hippolytus now proceeds to Monoimus, apparently an important heretic, but elsewhere not mentioned save by Theodoret. His was the doctrine of the Iota (pages 410–411): "(the) one Jot, the one tittle," whence by Pythagorean or Cabbalistic jugglery he derived the Universe. He seems to have been no inconsiderable thinker. From his letter to Theophrastus we gather that his system was markedly

* Compare p. 99 and 164.

Fichtean (his Iota or tittle seems to have been the ultimate irresoluble Ego), a kind of early subjective Idealism. "Having abandoned seeking God and creation and things like these, seek him from thyself and learn who is he that expropriates all things absolutely (ἀπαξαπλῶς) within thee and says: My God, my mind, my understanding, my soul, my body (notice the anti-climax, the movement from God to matter), and learn whence the grieving and the rejoicing and the living and the hating and the waking unwilling (μὴ θέλοντα) and the nodding unwilling and the being angry unwilling and the being unwilling, and if these things, he says, thou researchest accurately, thou shalt find them in thyself, one and many, after that tittle, from Himself the issue (διέξοδον) that found." His Iota centres in itself all possibility of existence in pairs of contradictions.

Concerning the date of Monoimus we know nothing. Everything indicates that he was very early. His allegorizing Moses seems parallel to Philo's, but may have been before or after. His aphorism, "This (tittle is) mother, this father, two immortal names," seems to relate him to the Naassenes, as well as his doctrine of the "perfect invisible Man and of the Son of Man." The suggestion of the Scripture (New Testament) is the rarest in this heretic, who seems to have trod his lofty path alone. But we find (p. 409): "And this is, he says, the saying (εἰρημένον) in the Scriptures, Was and Became (ἦν καὶ ἐγένετο), which is, Man was and his Son became, as one should say, Fire was and Light became, timelessly and indeliberately, unordainedly along with the being (of) the fire." Here *"alludere videtur ad initium Ev. Joh."*—Duncker. Why so? To say that such a thinker evolved such a system from this Prologue seems preposterous. The most that can be imagined is deduction from a common source. Again, "For these, he says, are the multipartible (πολυσχιδεῖς, pp. 410, 411), numbers residing in that, the simple and uncompounded one tittle of the Iota. And this is the saying (εἰρημένον), Because (or that) all the Pleroma pleased to settle down upon the Son of (the) Man bodily. For such compositions of numbers out of the simple and uncompounded one tittle of the Iota become, he says, somatic substances." There are 2 verses in *Colossians* ($1^{17}$, $2^9$) (See Bernay's *Ep. Crit.*) that present a parallel, but there it is the Christ in whom all the Fullness (of the Godhead) dwells (bodily). The repetition which is needless, occurring in a passage already shown to be highly suspicious, shows that here we are dealing with an important apothegm, and the varying form countenances only the supposition that Monoimus was quoting not from *Colossians* but from the source of *Colossians*.

## M. *Later Heretics*

From this point on our gleaning is very slight. Strange to say, the later heretics seem to make not nearly so much use of "Scripture" as the elder! We must note however the quotation made by Hippolytus himself (p. 419) against the Quartodecimans as to that which is spoken by the Apostle, in comparison with our present text: ὅτι διαμαρτύρομαι παντὶ περιτεμνομένῳ ὅτι ὀφειλέτης ἐστὶ τοῦ πάντα τὸν νόμον ποιῆσαι. Compare Gal. $5^3$ μαρτύρομαι δὲ πάλιν παντὶ ἀνθρώπῳ περιτε_ μνομένῳ, ὅτι ὀφειλέτης ἐστίν ὅλον τόν νόμον ποιῆσαι. Here the divergencies are certainly considerable, but we might ascribe them to imperfect memory were it not that a long line of authority agrees with Hippolytus in omitting πάλιν, very many put πληρῶσαι for ποιῆσαι, while Marcion* gives the more natural form οὐδὲ γὰρ οἱ περιτεμνόμενοι αὐτοὶ νόμον φυλάσσουσι, "that a man circumcised is debtor to do the whole law." All this seems to indicate that the Hippolitan text of Gal. 5³ most probably differed from ours.

This conclusion is strengthened by another quotation made by Hippolytus (page 422) against the Encratites, from I Tim. 4¹⁻⁵. This agrees exactly with our text except at the beginning where it omits ὅτι and puts ὑγιαινούσης διδασκαλίας for πίστεως. This too might be thought mere lapse of memory, but that Origen also inserts ὑγιοῦς and Ath. inserts four times ὑγιαινούσης and Epiphanius has once (1034) ὑγιαινούσης διδασκαλίας and once (1053) ὑγιοῦς διδασκαλίας whence it would appear that Hippolytus presents really an early reading. We must also note that the words, "But the Spirit expressly (ῥητῶς) says" introduces this in I Timothy as itself a *quotation,* whence we know not.

In deriving the tenets of Noetus (p. 425 ff) from Heraclitus, Hippolytus presents us the important saying of this obscure Ephesian (page 428): "Aeon is a child, sporting, playing at draughts; of a child is the Kingdom" (παιδὸς ἡ βασιλῆίη ). So that the idea and almost the expression of Matt. 19¹⁴ appears of immense antiquity (also cited by Lucian, *Vit. Auct.* 1, p. 554 Hemstech.)

Once more, Hippolytus attributes with great confidence the doctrine of the resurrection of the flesh to Heraclitus (p. 431): "And he affirms even of flesh a resurrection, of this palpable (flesh) in which we have been born, and God he knows as this resurrection's cause, thus speaking: Then needs it that (God) raise them up and that they become guardians of the living and the dead." The text is unfortunately corrupt but seems to support fairly well the contention of Hippolytus.

In the description of the Esseni, which seems taken most probably from the source of Josephus, we find many reminders of the New Testament, but we cannot here enter into the Essene question. It seems worth mention, however, that in summing up the teaching of the Pharisees (pp. 467–8) Hippolytus says: "They acknowledge a resurrection of flesh and soul (as) immortal and judgement to come and deflagration (ἐκπύρωσις), and (the) just will be imperishable but the unjust punished in fire unquenchable." All this sounds very Christian, and especially the last words agree hardly accidentally with Matt. 3¹².

## IV. Final Comment on Appendix

As has already been observed, the later heretics seem to make not nearly so much use of "Scripture" as the elder! Not less amazing is the phenomenon that the earlier heresies depart incomparably farther from the Catholic Faith than the later! How could such a thing be? If these heresies be really divergencies from the

---

* Cited by Epiphanius, *Panarium*, Ch. 42, the last citation in defense of *Galatians.*

central primitive doctrine, like branches from the trunk of a tree, we should certainly expect to find the first forms least radical, the alienation more or less gradual. Especially, if the earthly life, the historic personality of Jesus was the focal point of emanation for all this doctrine, then we should certainly expect to find the heresies laying gradually less and less emphasis on this history and moving off from it into the region of speculation. In fact, any other development of heresy on the basis of the scripture tradition seems positively inconceivable. The earlier heresies have practically or absolutely nothing to do with the earthly historic Jesus, they move in a realm of super-terrestrial entities, but the later heresies adopt more and more the historical element and descend from the regions of speculation! We hold that this phenomenon is forever irreconcilable with the current idea of the genesis of heresy, whereas it is precisely what we should expect if the relations be reversed, if we suppose the old Catholic Faith with its gradual deposit of quasi-historical tradition to have emerged and settled down upon earth from an elder region of hyper-physical speculation.

## V. Editor's Summary of Appendix, with Postscript

We assemble from Smith's article the following principal conclusions:—

1. The extant portions of the "Refutation" by Hippolytus state very carefully the temporal sequence of Gnostic groups ("sects") as follows:—Naassenes, Peratae, Sethians, Justinus the Gnostic, Simon of Gitta; after which was Valentinus, succeeded by the Valentinian pupils Heraclean, Ptolomaeus, Marcus (head of the Marcosans), Colarbasus, etc.

2. Less clearly dated by Hippolytus are Basilides and Marcion (both of them placed from other sources as approximately contemporary with Valentinus), also the later Gnostic Carpocrates and the Christian Docetic heresies. Monoimus, apparently an early Gnostic, is not distinctly dated; neither are the Encratites, whom Hippolytus treats only briefly.

3. Internal evidence powerfully corroborates the early date assigned to the Naassene writings by Hippolytus. Their authors knew nothing of the cross, nothing of a dying Savior, or a resurrection, or of a strife between Law and Gospel; equally nothing of Simon's Nebuchadnezzar Tree, or his six roots of all being, or his (or Paul's) doctrine of Salvation by Grace; again nothing of the later Gnostic speculations upon the Aeons and their procession, or the numerological fantasies and the infinite other "brood of Valentinus and Basilides," characterizing the Gnostics of the second century. Had the sources used by Hippolytus been written (or forged) much later than Hippolytus represents, *some* echo of *some* of these concepts must have crept in. Accordingly Smith credits the testimony of Hippolytus on the early Gnostic chronology and the Gnostic sayings.

4. Second century authors knew little or nothing of Naassenism, hence by that time it was either extinct or nearly so, or had lost identity, merging into other schools.

5. Internal evidence shows the writings of the Peratae and Sethians quoted by

Hippolytus to be a development out of Naassenism antecedent both to Paul and to Simon of Gitta.

6. Simon of Gitta is revealed as no mountebanc but a religious thinker of merit, his thought-pattern pre-Pauline in agreement with his date as known from other sources. His most important contribution was the concept of Divine Grace, but this did not include the Pauline pattern for salvation. Though hardly the "Father of All Heresies," he sowed the seed from which second century Valentinianism sprouted.

7. No sure and precise cases have been detected of direct quotation of Christian canonical writings by recorded Gnostics, or vice versa.

I Tim. $4^{1-5}$ is a quote from somewhere, and *may* be from the Encratitic source found in Hippolytus. (p. 211)

Eph. $3^{15}$, "from whom all paternity" etc. *seems* to be from an original Naassene phrase, here quoted. (p. 159, 164)

Eph. $5^{14}$ is beyond doubt a quotation from an unknown Gnostic source. Both Paul and the Naassene author indicate that they are citing "scripture." (See p. 163)

I Cor. $2^9$ is almost certainly a Gnostic quotation, but its source is in doubt;—possibly the Book of Baruch? (See p. 182)

I Cor. $2^{13-14}$ superficially *appears* to be an original for a Naassene citation, but is itself probably an insert. (p. 167)

Rom. $8^{22}$, "the whole creation groaneth," etc., indicated by Paul to be a citation, is Gnostic on strong circumstantial evidence. Whether Paul and Basilides borrowed from the Naassenes, or all three from some unknown earlier source, is not clear.

8. There are innumerable Pauline, Johannine and Synoptic passages that conspicuously parallel the Naassene texts. Paul and the Fourth Gospel contain parallels to the Peratae and Sethians. New Testament counterparts too close for accident are observed in almost all the Gnostic schools. All but a very few of them are best interpreted as coming independently from common sources earlier than any now preserved.

9. A very high proportion of parallels show grammatical or literary symptoms of being out of place in their New Testament setting. Usually the corresponding passages appear to be in place in the Gnostic setting, and many of them are essential elements of the Gnostic reasoning. Accordingly they are most probably from sources belonging to the Gnostic sequence, pre-Christian fore-shadowings of the recorded Gnostics.

10. The writings of the early Gnostics are richest in parallel passages; with the late sects they become sparce.

11. In the progressive growth from early to late sects, we see not a divergence away from Christianity, but a convergence, starting rather remote from canonical Christianity and moving ever nearer to Christian norms of belief. Christianity, it seems, is not a parent religion from which they break away, through a process of losing contact with its founder, but a sister movement, which step by step they come to resemble more and more intimately.

12. Pre-Christian Gnostic schools, and among them especially the Naassenes,

had an extensive lore about "the Jesus," a supernatural being coming from highest heaven, yet described as "Man," and "Son of Man," who descended as a heavenly redeemer. "His voice we have heard," says a Nassene text, "but his form we have not seen."

* * * * *

By way of postscript the point should be brought up that Smith's later writings considerably minimized the ties between early Gnosticism and primitive Christianity. The textual parallels have value to the investigator, he still insisted, as an important part of the evidence as to their relative dates, and as indicating in which direction their common concepts had been transmitted. But when broadly viewed the differences between Gnostic writings and the Synoptic Gospels impressed him as more important than the similarities. The early Gnostics were so much influenced by exotic mystery cults and Greek schools of philosophy that it is hard to tell whether they arose among Hellenized Jews or perhaps in communities that were largely Judaized Greeks. In contrast, Smith found the pattern of the Christian canonized writings and most particularly of the Gospels, to be determined by the way in which their writers extracted symbolic elements not from Gentile but from Jewish source materials,—materials which were derived in overwhelming proportion from sources that Jewish opinion honored as scripture. He felt that this emphatically Jewish character of the primitive Christian movement refutes its derivation in any fundamental sense from the semi-pagan early Gnostics.

## VI. List of the New Testament-Gnostic Parallels Here Considered*

| *Brachmanes* | Hippolytus page |
|---|---|
| I John 1[5] ("light") (I Tim. 6[16]; II Cor. 4[6]) | 46 |
| Rom. 7[23] ("captives") (Luke 4[18]) | 47 |

| *Aratus* (directly quoted, Acts 17[28]) | |
|---|---|
| Matt. 7[13-14] | 126 |
| John 1[3] | 127 |
| John 10[7-8] | 127 |
| Acts 10[42] (II Tim. 4[1]; I Pet. 4[5]) | 128 |
| Rev. 12[4] | 129 |
| Rev. 20[10] etc. ("beast") | 124 |

| *Naassenes* | |
|---|---|
| Matt. 3[10] (7[19]; Luke 3[9]; John 15[6]) | 168 |
| Matt. 5[45] (Luke 6[35]) | 150 |
| Matt. 7[6] | 169 |
| Matt. 7[13-14] | 173 |

* Including a very few patent parallels which were not discussed.

| | |
|---|---|
| Acts $15^{11}$ (Eph. $2^8$) | 265 |
| I Cor. $7^9$ | 259 |
| I Cor. $11^{32}$ | 253 |
| Jas. $1^{10}$ (I Pet. $1^{24}$) | 248 |
| Rev. $1^4$ ($4^8$) | 250, 258, 261 |

## Valentinus

| | |
|---|---|
| Matt. $1^{19}$ (Luke $1^{35}$) | 295 |
| Matt. $3^{16}$ (Mark $1^{10}$; Luke $3^{22}$; John $1^{32}$) | 296 |
| Matt $5^3$ | 283–4 |
| Matt. $5^{18}$ (Luke $16^{17}$) | 271 |
| Matt. $10^{25}$ ($12^{27}$; Mark $3^{22}$; Luke $11^{15,\,19}$) | 291–2 |
| Matt. $11^{19}$ (etc. etc., "Sophia") | 284 |
| Matt. $13^{13}$ (Mark $4^{11\text{-}12}$) | 299 |
| John $1^{1\text{-}18}$ | 282 |
| John $1^{14}$ | 285 |
| John $1^{16}$ (Eph. $3^{19}$; $4^{13}$; Col. $1^{9,\,19}$; $2^9$) | 281, 284, 286 |
| John $5^{44}$ ($17^3$; Rom. $16^{27}$; I Tim. $1^{17}$; Jude 25) | 280 |
| John $10^8$ | 294 |
| John $12^{31}$ ($14^{30}$; $16^{11}$; I Cor. $2^6$; II Cor. $4^4$; Eph. $2^2$; $6^{12}$) | 292 |
| John $14^{16}$ ($14^{26}$; $15^{26}$; $16^7$; I John $2^1$) | 283 |
| Acts $4^2$ ($17^{32}$; $23^6$) | 275 |
| Rom. $1^{13}$ | 287, 298 |
| Rom. $7^{22}$ (II Cor. $4^{16}$) | 293 |
| Rom. $8^{11}$ | 296 |
| Rom. $8^{19}$ | 295 |
| Rom. $16^{25}$ (I Cor. $2^7$; Eph. $3^{3,\,5}$; Col. $1^{26}$; $4^3$) | 294 |
| I Cor. $2^9$ (Cf. Isa. $64^4$) | 272 |
| I Cor. $2^{14}$ | 294 |
| I Cor. $13^{13}$ | 283 |
| I Cor. $15^8$ | 285 |
| II Cor. $3^{16}$ | 295 |
| II Cor. $13^{11}$; I John $4^{8,\,16}$) | 281 |
| Gal. $4^{25\text{-}26}$ (Rev. $21^2$) | 290, 292 |
| Eph. $3^{14}$ (Col. $1^{9\text{-}11}$) | 293 |
| Eph. $3^{16\text{-}18}$ | 294 |
| Heb. $4^{14}$ | 287 |

## Marcus the Gnostic

| | |
|---|---|
| Matt. $3^{11}$ (Luke $12^{49}$) Iren. Adv. Her. $20^2$ | |
| Matt. $3^{16}$ (Mark $1^{10}$; Luke $3^{22}$; John $1^{32}$ | 318 |
| Matt. $11^{25\text{-}27}$ (Luke $10^{21\text{-}22}$) Iren. Adv. Her. (MASS) $20^3$ | |
| Matt. $11^{28\text{-}29}$  "  "  "  (MASS) $20^2$ | |

Matt. 18$^{10}$

Matt. 19$^{17}$ Iren. Adv. Her. (MASS) 20$^2$

Matt. 21$^{23}$   "   "   "   "   "

Mark 10$^{38}$ (Luke 12$^{50}$)

Luke 2$^{49}$   "   "   "   "   "

Luke 12$^{49-50}$ "   "   "   "   "

Luke 17$^{22}$   "   "   "   "   "

Luke 19$^{42}$   "   "   "   "   "

### Basilides

| | |
|---|---|
| Matt. 13$^{31}$ (Mark 4$^{31}$; Luke 13$^{19}$) | 346 |
| Luke 1$^{35}$ | 362 |
| John 1$^9$ | 348–9 |
| John 2$^4$ | 364 |
| Acts 3$^{21}$ | 364, 366 |
| Acts 10$^{38}$ | 362 |
| Rom. 5$^{13-14}$ | 357 |
| Rom. 8$^{19-25}$ | 362–3 |
| Rom. 8$^{22}$ | 357 |
| I Cor. 2$^{13}$ | 360 |
| I Cor. 3$^{10}$ | 354 |
| I Cor. 15$^{1-10}$ (Matt. 9$^{35}$; Mark 1$^{15}$; II Cor. 11$^4$; Gal. 1$^{6, 11}$; Rev. 14$^6$) (the "Evangel") | 365 |
| I Cor. 15$^8$ | 361 |
| II Cor. 4$^6$ | 360 |
| Eph. 1$^{20-21}$ | 358–9 |
| Eph. 1$^{22}$ (Phil. 2$^9$; Heb. 1$^4$) | 351 |
| Eph. 3$^{3-5}$ (II Cor. 12$^4$) | 361 |
| Eph. 3$^{10}$ | 361–2 |

*Saturnilius* Smith omits comment on parallels found here.

*Marcion* Smith omits comment on parallels found here.

However see Gal. 5$^3$ and citation of Marcion in Panarium of Epiphanius.

*Carpocrates* Smith omits comments on parallels found here.

(Some of these were already discussed à propos of other sects)

### Docetae

| | |
|---|---|
| John 3$^{5-6}$ | 406 |
| II Cor. 5$^3$ | 406 |
| Col. 2$^{8-15}$ | 406 |

*Monoimus*

|  |  |
|---|---|
| Matt. 5[18] | 411–2 |
| Col. 1[19] (2[9]) | 411 |

*Quartodecimans*

|  |  |
|---|---|
| Gal. 5[3] | 419 |

*Encratites*

|  |  |
|---|---|
| I Tim. 4[1-5] | 422 |

*Heraclitus of Ephesus* and *Noetus*

|  |  |
|---|---|
| Matt. 3[12] (13[42]; 25[41]; Mark 9[43]) | 432 |
| Matt. 19[14] | 428 |
| I Cor. 15[35] (etc.) (bodily resurrection) | 431 |

*Essenes*   Smith omits comment.

*Pharisees*

|  |  |
|---|---|
| Matt. 3[12] (etc.) (unquenchable fires) | 468 |
| I Cor. 15[35] (Resurrection of the flesh) | 467 |

# Index

221

* Each Hippolytan citation that Smith appraises is recorded here once and only once.